TECHNICAL EDITING

CAROLYN D. RUDE
Texas Tech University

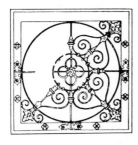

WADSWORTH PUBLISHING COMPANY
Belmont, California
A Division of Wadsworth, Inc.

TO DON AND JONATHAN

English Editor: Angela M. Gantner
Assistant Editor: Julie Johnson
Editorial Assistant: Lisa Ensign
Production Editor: Sandra Craig
Text and Cover Designer: Andrew H. Ogus
Print Buyer: Karen Hunt
Permissions Editor: Jeanne Bosschart
Copy Editor: Thomas L. Briggs
Compositor: T·H Typecast, Inc.
Signing Representative: Linda Tiley

Printed in the United States of America

1 2 3 4 5 6 7 8 9 10–95 94 93 92 91

Library of Congress Cataloging-in-Publication Data

Rude, Carolyn D.
    Technical editing / Carolyn D. Rude.
        p.   cm.
    Includes index.
    ISBN 0-534-15000-4
    1. Technical editing.   I. Title.
    T11.4.R83 1991
    808'.02 – dc20
                                                                    90–49997

BRIEF CONTENTS

CONTENTS

CHAPTER 7   PUNCTUATION   125

PREFACE

Technical Editing presumes that the full range of editing, including substantive editing, can and should be taught. It expands on previous publications on editing that explain copyediting and sentence-level editing for style but do not address the substantive issues of content, organization, and format. These whole-document issues affect the usefulness of the document more than do sentences. Sentence-level editing is ultimately meaningful only in the context of the whole.

A guiding thesis is that editors collaborate with writers in the design of documents. This thesis purposely conflicts with the definition of editors as fixers of errors. As document designers, technical communicators are like architects and engineers, who plan buildings and bridges for use as well as for visual pleasure. Technical documents are used by readers to provide information and to enable actions such as making a decision or completing a task. Document design encompasses all the features of a document that facilitate those uses, including its content, organization, format, style, visuals, and grammar. Even when editors begin work on a project after planning is complete, they make choices about these features to accommodate specific readers and purposes—that is, to achieve the design goals.

This book is written for students who have completed at least one college course in technical communication and for practicing editors with some experience in technical genres. It presumes that readers have been introduced previously to such terms as *style, noun, line graph,* and *instruction manual,* and it presumes some competence in technical writing. Chapters on spelling, grammar, and punctuation review concepts readers have learned before and do not substitute for a handbook. One important purpose of those chapters is to refresh students' vocabularies so that they can talk about their editorial choices and can choose on the basis of knowledge, not just preference. The glossary reinforces the premise that professional technical communicators master the vocabulary of their discipline.

Specific instructions for editing are rooted in theories of how readers comprehend and use documents. The book emphasizes reasons for making editorial decisions, assuming that editing requires high-level thinking and judgment. The suggestions for further reading point students to sources that will expand their knowledge of how and why documents function and thus develop their bases for making editorial decisions. The discussion and application exercises aim to develop concepts and sound thinking as well as skills.

The book is arranged to parallel the typical career path of editors and the typical instructional sequence in an editing course. Just as editors generally must master copyediting before they are given responsibility for substantive editing, so here do copyediting functions precede substantive editing and managerial functions. Courses for advanced students may review the early chapters quickly and concentrate on substantive editing. The arrangement from copyediting to substantive editing also facilitates use of the book in sequential semesters or quarters, with the basic course focusing on copyediting skills and the advanced course focusing on editing that requires more judgment.

Part I, Definition of Editing, includes two chapters of background material, Editing: The Big Picture, and Readers and Documents. Although some chapters in Part IV, Management and Production, could be suitable foundations for learning about line and substantive editing, both students and teachers are probably eager for some hands-on experience. Thus the seven chapters in Part II, Copyediting, immerse students in the concepts and details of line editing and proofreading, including copymarking; spelling, capitalization, and abbreviations; grammar and usage; and punctuation. Chapter 8 offers specific guidelines for quantitative and technical material. Part III, Substantive Editing, focuses on the process of substantive editing and such topics as style, organization, format, and visuals.

This arrangement means that students will have considerable practical experience in both types of editing and will be able to better appreciate the material in Part IV. Chapter 15, Collaborating with Writers, and Chapter 16, Computers as Editorial Assistants, both argue that the first step is to master editing. However, neither chapter presumes knowledge from earlier chapters, and they may be interspersed with material in Parts II and III. The remaining chapters, Type and Production (Chapter 17) and Management (Chapter 18), take students beyond issues of content to the appearance of the final document and the complete print production process.

Technical Editing welcomes the use of computers in editing. Most of the chapters include suggestions for using the computer, and Chapter 16 summarizes the ways in which computers can assist editors. The book asserts throughout, however, the necessity of human judgments for making editorial decisions and for using electronic assistants.

I would like to acknowledge the assistance of many people. The following reviewed the manuscript: Lynn Beene, University of New Mexico; David K. Farkas, University of Washington; M. Jimmie Killingsworth, Texas A&M University; Jere Mitchum, Tennessee Technological University; Mark Rollins, Ohio University; Doug B. Smith, California Polytechnic State University, San Luis Obispo; Herb Smith, Southern College of Technology; Katherine E. Staples, Austin Community College; Tom Williams, University of Washington; and Kristin Woolever, Northeastern University. David Farkas, Jere Mitchum, and Tom Williams also class tested portions of the book. Steven Auerbach, Elizabeth Bilbro, Debra Clifford, Fred Kemp, and Ernest Mazzatenta read all or parts of the manuscript and offered thoughtful suggestions for revision. The editors at Wadsworth confirmed through their assistance the merits of writer-editor collaboration and proved that the reality of editing can match the ideal. Gerard Bensberg, Kae Hentges, Ken Morgan, Lane Mayon, Carlos Orozco-Castillo, Ellen Peffley, Tony Santangelo, William Stolgitis, and Charles Veazy helped to locate examples. And special thanks to my students and to students in the test classes, who read critically and took seriously their editorial task of helping me shape a book that would be useful and pleasing as well.

Carolyn D. Rude

PART I DEFINITION OF EDITING

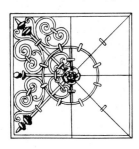

1 EDITING:
THE BIG PICTURE

If you are coming to the study of editing without prior experience as an editor, you may be bringing along a stereotype something like this one: editors resemble certain English teachers we all once had – prim, strict, pedantic, and inflexible. Editors never kick their shoes off and never laugh. They sit hunched over at their desks growing nearsighted while they pounce on misused commas. Editing basically entails correcting errors in spelling and punctuation.

This stereotype probably reflects our own fears about making mistakes rather than the realities of technical editing. You will discover through study and experience that technical editing is a fast-paced, demanding job that requires good judgment, the ability to manage long-term projects, a capacity to collaborate with others yet maintain independence – and mastery of punctuation.

In this chapter, you will see specific editing responsibilities in the context of the whole process of conceiving, writing, reviewing, and publishing documents – the "big picture" of editing. Let us begin with some definitions – specifically, with answers to these questions: What does an editor do and why? How does a *technical* editor differ from any other editor?

To help answer these questions, we will review the history of one printed document, a 55-page manual for users of Waterloo SCRIPT, a word processing program on a mainframe computer. The editor's roles in this project were comprehensive: defining a need, purpose, and scope for the manual and appointing a writer to the task; formatting the pages; reviewing the text when it was written; and negotiating with the printer to have the manual published in quantity. In addition to serving as a language expert, the editor was supervisor, graphic designer, and production manager. Her responsibilities were comprehensive in part because the organization and project were small. In a larger organization and for a major project, several editors would have shared these responsibilities.

EDITORIAL RESPONSIBILITIES IN PRODUCING THE SCRIPT MANUAL

Elizabeth Bilbro served as documentation editor for Academic Computing Services (ACS), the office responsible for providing computer facilities and services to administrators, faculty, and students at Texas Tech University. One of her responsibilities was training people to use the programs and equipment. Printed manuals and classes provided much of the training, but Elizabeth also consulted with users who had specific questions.

Project Definition

The idea for the SCRIPT manual arose from the need to solve a specific problem: an increasing number of requests from users for individual help on SCRIPT. Users like to work one to one with tutors, but usually it is impractical for tutors to provide the primary instruction for equipment and procedures. Not only are printed manuals cheaper, they are readily available as a reference tool. The demands on Elizabeth's time from the requests for help on SCRIPT were so great that she could not complete her other responsibilities. To solve the problem, she decided to develop a manual.

Two manuals existed for SCRIPT—a user's guide and a reference manual—but both were lengthy (around 300 pages long) and complex, and neither was written specifically for the users at Texas Tech University. Beginning users had trouble getting started with the program using the existing manuals. The most useful manual, therefore, would introduce the program by explaining basic functions and procedures.

Employee Supervision and Training

Elizabeth assigned a staff writer, Debra Clifford, to the task of writing the manual. Because Debra was a new employee and unfamiliar with SCRIPT, Elizabeth expected to spend a good bit of time training her, both in the program itself and in the basics of manual development. The supervision and training were part of her management responsibilities.

They met for an initial discussion of the task. Elizabeth explained the need for the manual and her thinking about its readers, purpose, and scope. She showed Debra the user's guide and reference manual for SCRIPT. They discussed SCRIPT functions that a new user would be most likely to need, which gave Debra a sense of the contents of the manual. Through their discussion of the proposed manual and the program, they were able to refine some of Elizabeth's original ideas for the manual.

In addition to discussing the users, purpose, and content of the proposed manual, Elizabeth and Debra considered its graphic design and printing plans. They determined that, in keeping with other manuals produced at ACS (part of the **document set** to which the SCRIPT manual would belong), Debra would produce **camera ready** copy using SCRIPT and a laser printer. That is, they would bypass the professional typesetting part of printing and produce pages that could be photocopied. The pages would be 8½ × 11 and stapled. (The manual would look like the other ACS manuals and would fit on the shelves where these manuals were displayed for sale.) These design criteria helped to determine content by establishing length restrictions.

Elizabeth pointed out special features of the other ACS manuals for beginning users, such as the prose overviews and the practice exercises. She also noted other parts of the manuals, such as tables of contents and indexes. This information, too, helped Debra to conceptualize her task.

The schedule for various stages in the development of the manual was also discussed. As editor, Elizabeth needed a schedule in order to coordinate this project with her other concurrent or upcoming projects. As writer, Debra needed a schedule in order to manage her own time. The most important dates for both were the deadlines for a rough draft and for the final printed copy. They also scheduled two other drafts and reviews plus field testing.

This initial discussion thus identified document users and established purpose, scope, format, and schedules. The initial discussion also established a collaborative working relationship between writer and editor. The editor defined herself as a helper rather than a critic. The writer could begin with a clear sense of her editor's expectations. Because she was invited to discuss possibilities for the manual rather than simply assigned an outline, Debra also saw her importance in helping to shape the expectations.

Because Debra was unfamiliar with SCRIPT, her first task was to learn the program. Both she and Elizabeth saw her novice status as a plus because she could have the same learning experience as the readers who would eventually use the manual. As she studied the program, Debra kept notes of her procedures and their sequence so that she could use them in the manual. As an experienced computer user, Debra learned quickly, but she occasionally had to consult with Elizabeth for help with the formatting commands.

Editorial Review: First Draft

Debra produced a first review draft for Elizabeth according to the schedule they had agreed on. Actually, her initial draft did not represent the first words she had put down on paper but rather a draft that incorporated a number of her own revisions. She didn't want to waste Elizabeth's time by asking her to write content or to fix problems she could fix herself. On the other hand, she didn't want to spend too much time polishing a draft if she had misconceived her task. So the early review draft enabled Elizabeth to refine her concept of the manual as needed before too much time had been invested in it. Because Debra was working with a word processing program that included a spelling checker and a proofreader, she was able to correct surface errors herself and to present Elizabeth with a copy that was nearly free of spelling, punctuation, and grammar errors.

As she reviewed this draft, Elizabeth was mostly concerned about content, including the selection of procedures, the organization, and teaching strategies. If she saw typos and errors in grammar or punctuation, she marked them, but she mainly reviewed the draft to determine whether someone at Texas Tech could begin to use the SCRIPT program and print a simple document without calling her up with questions. So Elizabeth reviewed in particular the steps in the process to determine whether there were errors or omissions or steps that could be deleted for these readers. She also evaluated the teaching strategies.

Elizabeth met with Debra to discuss her responses to the document. They debated in particular whether to include an exercise that required users to perform a task incorrectly. Elizabeth suggested adding such an exercise and explained that other ACS manuals used this strategy in order to show users the consequences of common errors. Debra questioned the merit of directing new users to practice an incorrect procedure lest the practice reinforce the error. Both points of view had some merit. Elizabeth, as the senior staff person, could simply have insisted on the exercise without discussion, but she trusted Debra's judgment. They mutually agreed that the exercises should all direct users to practice the right procedures, but should describe common errors and their consequences as well.

Management:
Contracting for Printing

Confident that the manual would be completed on schedule and that she could estimate its actual length, Elizabeth arranged for printing. Some decisions, such as choice of paper, ink colors, size, and binding, were easy because they had been made before with other ACS manuals. Because she knew the name and weight of the paper as well as the size and number of pages and the binding style, she sought bids for printing by phone, contacting three printers who had done jobs before for ACS. She investigated costs as well as schedules to determine which printer to hire for this job. She contracted with the printer who offered the best rates and schedule. She promised to deliver the completed typescript by a certain date and in turn received a promise for delivery of the printed manual by a certain date.

Editorial Review: Second Draft
:

Debra revised her draft again, working in particular on making the steps accurate and complete. When Elizabeth reviewed this draft, she checked first for content. Because the primary content decisions had already been made, however, she focused on other text characteristics, especially the visual aspects, that were important at the final-draft stage.

Considering the document visually, Elizabeth looked at pages as a whole to ensure effective page design, including meaningful page breaks. One goal was to enable users to complete steps without turning pages. She also evaluated the examples to determine whether examples and instructional text could be clearly distinguished visually. Within the examples themselves, she considered the distinction of text from commands to be sure that a reader could determine when to type something and when to follow a command.

Elizabeth also evaluated headings for consistency and clarity. She verified a consistent use of capitalization, spacing, and boldfacing to establish various levels of headings and to guarantee sufficient distinction between level-one and level-two headings. Although the headings and other format patterns had been established previously, she was now able to see how the design looked on paper, rather than simply trying to conceptualize it. If the patterns had proved unworkable—that is, if the format had interfered with usability or readability—the editor would have changed them even at this stage of production.

Field Test

When the editor and the writer had completed this second draft, they arranged to observe some typical manual users in action. This field test acknowledged the limitations of a paper review by technical or language specialists. Debra was responsible for the field test, but Elizabeth helped identify the people who would participate in the field test, and she reviewed the test plans with Debra. The users worked as Debra watched and listened; they stated aloud what they were thinking as they worked, identifying instructions or other features that were confusing. By keeping careful notes of troublesome places, Debra was able to apply the information from the field test to her next version.

Copyediting

The text was read for final editing before publication. Because content, organization, format, and style were already established, Elizabeth edited for correctness, consistency, completeness, and accuracy. She corrected any errors in grammar, punctuation, and spelling. She verified not only that the manual had a table of contents but also that the section names in the table of contents matched those in the text. She checked the accuracy of the page numbers in cross-references and reviewed the illustration numbers to ensure that they were sequential. She also watched for consistency in the use of terms, so that readers would not be told, for example, to "press" a key at one point but to "hit" it at another. Because she edited on **hard copy** (that is, on paper rather than on the screen), she marked any errors or inconsistencies she noted right on the paper using the appropriate copymarking symbols.

Debra then entered the changes into the computer, and another person on the staff proofread it—for a final check from a fresh pair of eyes.

If necessary, a substantial revision would have been a possibility at the copyediting stage had the draft not achieved the purposes established at the reviews and after the field test. For this particular project, however, the primary editorial tasks were matching and checking.

Production

Debra ordered a clean copy from the laser printer, one that had no pencil marks or dirt smudges and that would photocopy well. Elizabeth took the copy to the printer for printing and binding, being sure to include a statement of specifications for the final copy covering the paper weight and size, ink color, cover stock, binding plans, and number of copies. The copies were printed, stapled to their covers, delivered, and added to the inventory of ACS manuals.

COMMENT:
THE EDITORIAL
PROCEDURE AT ACS

At ACS, the editorial procedure was roughly equivalent to what it would be elsewhere, but specific editorial responsibilities and the relationship between editor and writer were determined in part by the smallness of the ACS organization and in part by its editorial policies.

Division of Responsibilities

The size of ACS (one editor, one writer), as well as the scope of the job (a 55-page manual), made the editor responsible for the full range of editing tasks, from project definition to production. The decision to use desktop publishing rather than a full-service printer further simplified the editing job. By contrast, in a larger organization or for more comprehensive projects, several editors would share the duties. One might be in charge of project definition, another would be responsible for substantive editing, yet another for copyediting, and a fourth for production. When the responsibilities can be divided, the editors with the least experience typically do the copyediting, while editors who have already demonstrated their ability to copyedit are given the further responsibility of substantive editing and management.

Collaboration The relationship between editor and writer at ACS was ideal though not necessarily typical. The editor was involved from the beginning with shaping the project, and the writer knew from the beginning what the editor's expectations were. Sometimes, however, the editor becomes involved in the process only after the first draft is complete, which increases the potential for conflict between writer and editor. The editor may have a different conception of the project and may wish to reshape it. A better project may result, but the procedure is inefficient as well as difficult for the people who must negotiate with one another.

The collaboration at ACS was also easier than it sometimes is because the writer was a writing specialist as well as a subject matter specialist. Often the writer's primary responsibilities are technical; that is, the writer may be an engineer or a manager who also has writing responsibilities. Such people may be excellent writers, but some are impatient with writing and do not fully understand or appreciate the special skills of the editors who help them.

EDITORIAL FUNCTIONS AND RESPONSIBILITIES

Why are there editors? What does an editor do? For technical editors, these questions can be answered by summarizing their two primary functions.

- **Preparing documents for publication**. The editor is the link between the typescript version and the published version of a document. Most writers (technical writers and others) lack the means for publishing and distributing their materials. Chances are they do not have much interest in the physical tasks of preparing the typescript for publication. So the editor coordinates production of the document, arranging for the preparation of the typescript in printable form and working with a printer to prepare the copies.

- **Making documents effective for readers**. A writer who is a subject matter specialist may write competently, but chances are that an editor, whose speciality is language and document design, can suggest ways to make the document easier for readers to understand and use. The editor knows how to use style, organization, and format to achieve specific document purposes.

Even when the writer is as sophisticated in the use of language as the editor, an editor can bring objectivity to the reading that the writer may lose in his or her involvement with the subject matter. In a sense, the editor takes the place of the intended reader, noting areas where clarification is needed or where material might be reorganized. Perhaps the editor will simply correct grammar and typos and thus eliminate a source of distraction for the reader. At whatever level the editor works with the document, he or she is serving as a readers' advocate.

The editorial responsibilities that follow from these functions may be classified as management and text editing.

MANAGEMENT

As manager, the editor arranges for the development, publication, and distribution of documents. The manager must not only coordinate tasks and draw up schedules but supervise staff as well. In addition, the manager keeps records and budgets and negotiates with suppliers such as printers and graphic designers. Specific responsibilities will depend, in part, on whether the editor works for a periodical and the writers are from other organizations or whether both the editor and the writers work within the same organization. Management responsibilities may include project definition, document acquisition and selection, scheduling and coordination, staff supervision and training, and production.

Project Definition

An organization that publishes in order to meet a specific need, such as for a user manual to accompany a piece of equipment that a company manufactures, defines the needs and the type of document that can meet them. The company may use a staff writer or may contract with a freelance writer. In either case, the editor may work with this writer to define readers and purpose and to establish scope, length, format, and style. An editor of an ongoing project, such as a newsletter, may also need to define the specific purpose of a special issue of the newsletter, perhaps an issue that explores one topic in depth.

Acquisition and Selection

The editor of a periodical or an anthology is responsible for acquiring articles for publication, a function that parallels the project definition task. The criteria for submission may be printed in the front matter of a journal. Sometimes the editor of such a publication will issue a **call for manuscripts** that will invite submissions from a broad reading public. Such a call may be published in the periodical or in other publications that potential writers might read, or it may be mailed directly to potential contributors. Sometimes the editor will invite specific writers to submit articles on particular topics.

After the articles are submitted, the editor will also oversee the selection of appropriate ones for the publication. Perhaps the editor will select the articles, or perhaps he or she may appeal to a board of reviewers to evaluate the articles and recommend certain ones for publication.

Scheduling and Coordination

Part of project management entails determining publication deadlines. Working backwards from a publication date, the editor establishes deadlines for completion of drafts, reviews, copyediting, and printing. In addition, the editor will coordinate the various people working on the project, such as writers, reviewers, graphic designers, technical experts, typists, proofreaders, and printers. If the document is a user manual being produced as the project is being developed, the editor will have to arrange a schedule to coordinate with the stages of development as well. The editor, in collaboration with others who will be involved in the project, will develop a management plan to assign specific responsibilities and establish due dates.

Staff Supervision and Training

Staff supervision relates to the coordination function. The editor will ensure that each person meets the deadlines, as well as seeing that each staff member has the resources and assistance necessary to do the job. There may also be explicit training functions, especially for new staff.

Production

The editor as production manager arranges for the publication of the document in the form in which it will be distributed. The production editor will either determine the graphic design of the document or work with a designer to establish it. **Graphic design** entails a number of duties: selecting typefaces and type sizes for both the **body copy** (the prose part of the text) and the **display type** (headings, titles); determining page size, margin size, and amount of space between columns if there are more than one; marking running heads, if any, for placement; and making any other decisions that affect how the document will look on the page. Graphic design also involves decisions about the weight, color, and type of paper and about the binding. If a graphic designer who is not an employee of the company works on the text, the editor will need to contract with the designer for the services and fee.

The editor will also need to know the length of the printed document in order to obtain bids and make decisions about binding. If the document will be prepared in camera ready form, the editor may just count pages; but if it will be typeset from a typescript, the editor will need to predict length by **copyfitting**, or estimating how many typeset pages will result from the typescript.

The production editor needs specifications such as number of copies, weight and type of paper, ink color, type of cover, and method of binding. The editor or graphic designer may make these choices. With these specifications, the editor may get an accurate estimate from a printer on how much the document will cost. If the cost estimate exceeds the budget, the editor will have to either modify some decisions about the publication, such as choosing cheaper paper, or negotiate for a larger budget if the choices made seem necessary. The editor will choose a printer on the basis of cost bids and scheduling considerations as well as reputation for doing quality work.

TEXT EDITING

The text editing function requires editors to ensure that the text of the document is complete, correct, and consistent and that the document achieves its overall purpose. Specific text editing responsibilities may be classified as **substantive editing**, when the editor works with the substance, or the content and meaning, of the text, and **copyediting**, when the editor's responsibilities are limited to text features such as grammar, punctuation, spelling, and labeling of illustrations.

Not all documents receive the complete editing that has been described so far. Some documents, especially if they will be used by very few readers and perhaps stay in house, may be printed (perhaps by photocopying) in their typescript stage. The editor may do nothing more than ensure that all the pages are present and correctly numbered.

Other documents are copyedited but not edited for style and substance. That is, the editor will check spelling, grammar, and consistency but not worry about completeness and accuracy of information, organization, or format.

When you are working as an editor, you need to know the expectations of your supervisor or the writer. If you are expected only to copyedit, you won't spend time reorganizing. But if you are expected to edit for style, you won't restrict yourself to correcting grammar errors. Knowing the expectations helps you work harmoniously and efficiently with others.

Substantive Editing

In substantive (sub′ stan tive) editing, the editor shares with the writer responsibility for document substance or content. This function includes selecting subject matter and making choices about adding and deleting material as necessary. When the text is interpretive or argumentative, the editor evaluates reasoning and evidence. Substantive editing also entails reviewing the document's organization, format, and style, each of which affects readers' ability to find the information they need and comprehend it. Thus, substantive editors look at overall document organization as well as the organization of sections and paragraphs. They also review formatting devices, such as headings and paragraphing, that reveal organization. In addition, they may edit for style, or the choices of words and sentence structures.

This substantive editing may occur at various stages of document development. Ideally, the editor helps to conceive the project before the first draft is written, so that writer and editor can develop a shared concept of the document in terms of its readers and purpose. Reviews of early drafts may enable necessary reshaping of the document before too much time has been invested in its development, but the editor may also edit for substance after the document is virtually complete. Substantive editing sometimes requires rewriting of sections as well as sentences.

A document may also be subject to a technical review, which differs from substantive editing though the functions may overlap. A technical review is a review by a subject matter expert rather than by a language expert. The technical review is for accuracy and completeness of subject matter, so the reviewer is less concerned than the editor with organization, format, and style. Sometimes the editorial review represents a sufficient technical review, particularly when the editor is a subject matter expert.

A **field test** provides a further evaluation of the document and a basis for revision. Representative readers use the document under the intended conditions of use. Thus, a field test occurs in the "field" rather than in the office, and the evaluators are typical readers rather than writers, editors, and technical experts. For this book, for example, the technical experts were teachers of technical editing and technical editors. The field tests took place in classrooms, with college students as the evaluators.

A good substantive editor understands how different text characteristics, such as organization, format, and style, affect reader response. This editor reads analytically and objectively and emends the text with specific goals in mind rather than according to personal preference. He or she interacts with writers in a professional manner. Because substantive editing addresses the content, the editor must know something about the subject matter.

Copyediting   Copyediting is the final stage of editing before the document is prepared in its finished form (typeset or typed as camera ready copy). The substance, including content, organization, format, and style, should already be established. The copyeditor makes sure that the document is not only correct in terms of spelling, punctuation, and grammar, but consistent in mechanics and from one part to the next. In addition, the copyeditor checks for document accuracy and completeness. And in some cases, the copyeditor may prepare the document for publication, marking the copy to indicate typeface and type size, column width, and page length.

Figure 1.1
Document Development
and Production

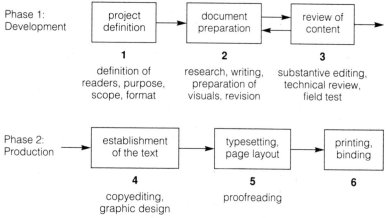

A good copyeditor has an eye for detail as well as a command of language. He or she is patient and willing to refer to handbooks, style guides, and other printed sources as well as to query the writer or a technical expert to resolve inconsistencies or other text questions.

The flowchart in figure 1.1 summarizes the document development and production process. The text beneath each box in the figure lists substeps in the process. The process is not entirely linear, as the two-way arrows between steps 2 and 3 imply. Writers draw on responses from editors, suggestions from technical experts, and results of field tests in their revisions. As the document develops, the project definition may change somewhat. Some documents develop more simply, without technical reviews and field tests, and are printed from typewritten rather than typeset pages.

THE "TECHNICAL" PART OF TECHNICAL EDITING

The management and text editing responsibilities are common to all kinds of editors: magazine and newspaper editors, academic journal editors, and the editors who work in commercial publishing houses on novels, trade books, and textbooks. All editors, whether technical or some other kind, share some responsibilities for helping to make writing effective and for arranging for the publication and distribution of documents. The adjective *technical* does, however, distinguish some defining characteristics of the specific type of editing that this textbook teaches.

Technical Subject Matter

Technical editors work on documents with technical subjects. *Technical* connotes technology, and typical subjects are computer science and engineering. However, technical editors also edit documents in medicine, science, government, agriculture, education, and business. The term *technical* suggests not only the subject matter itself but also the approach to the subject—to analyze, explain, interpret, inform, or instruct. The purpose of documents edited by technical editors is practical: readers will use the documents in some way other than for entertainment. A technical editor may thus be employed in any discipline for which the documents have practical aims.

Because of the specialized subject matter, editors ideally have technical (subject matter) expertise as well as language expertise. Thus, a technical editor working for an engineering firm would know some engineering, while a medical editor would have a fundamental knowledge of biology, chemistry, anatomy, and physiology.

Technical Genres   Technical editors typically work with the document genres that permit the transfer of information or that enable readers to act by making a decision or by following instructions. Examples of such genres include instruction manuals, proposals, feasibility studies, empirical research reports, and environmental impact statements. Note, however, that the documents are not always produced in print or on paper. For example, technical editors may edit online documentation for a computer program or a slide show that is part of an oral proposal for a grant. Instructions may be visual rather than verbal.

In-House Setting   Only a small percentage of technical editors work for large commercial or academic publishing houses—that is, places whose primary function is the publication of documents. Rather, technical editors are likely to work in the setting in which the writing is generated or is to be used. The primary function in such a setting is likely to be computer programming, engineering, scientific research, or business. Because the writers in these settings are likely to have primary responsibilities other than writing, the generation of documents is a secondary function.

THE ETHICS OF TECHNICAL EDITING   Technical communicators, like physicians, lawyers, professors, and clergy, consider themselves professionals rather than staff or laborers. Such classification brings privileges of status and material benefits—and some responsibilities as well. For example, professionals accept responsibility for their work rather than deferring to a superior. It is unprofessional in any setting to "pass the buck."

Because editors are the last people in the production process to emend a document before it is printed and distributed, they are directly responsible for quality control. Quality may be defined in textual terms as correctness and attractiveness. Like any other product, a document should meet company standards. More important from an ethical standpoint, it should also meet publication standards and laws. For example, editors must respect copyright laws and adhere to accepted standards for citation of sources.

The nature of the subject matter requires that the technical editor be ethical, because he or she is likely to be working with sensitive material. For example, documents produced under government contract projects may be classified, and private industries try to protect their new products from competitors. The editor is as responsible as anyone else working on the project for maintaining confidentiality.

Editors in research organizations have some responsibility for the accuracy and validity of the published reports as well. Thus, the editor who perceives that a report misrepresents research results or includes faulty data has an ethical obligation to hold up publication of the report in its incorrect form.

The potential for technology to affect health and welfare demands the highest ethical standards from technical editors. If instructions for a piece of equipment are unclear or incomplete, a user may misuse the equipment and be injured. The editor who perceives the lack of clarity or incompleteness must object out of concern for the users or others who may be affected by the technology.

The editor's ethical responsibilities increase along with other responsibilities—a substantive editor is more responsible than a copyeditor. Yet all editors can feel privileged to have a part in ensuring the quality and integrity of documents.

QUALIFICATIONS FOR TECHNICAL EDITING

Except in very small publishing organizations, editors are not likely to be individually responsible for the full range of editing tasks. Rather, the tasks will be divided among editors who specialize in different types of editing. A beginning editor will probably be assigned copyediting and manuscript coordination tasks. The editor can advance to greater responsibility for the text and for production as he or she demonstrates competence at the beginning level. As in all professions, expertise and responsibility grow with experience.

The primary qualification for copyediting is to understand language and know its rules. Editors also must be able to read carefully and focus on details. They need to have some knowledge of the visual characteristics of a text, such as spacing and type. With knowledge of language and a trained eye, people can qualify for copyediting jobs.

Editors with responsibility for document content also need to analyze and evaluate the subject matter and envision the context of and uses for documents. They can imagine readers using the documents, and they know something about how readers comprehend information. They are familiar with options for format and media. They are visually as well as verbally sophisticated. They have some understanding of the subject matter of the documents they edit. They accept responsibility for the quality and ethical integrity of the document. And they work well with others.

Editors with management responsibilities need to be organized and well disciplined. They encourage top performance from the people who work for them.

People who enjoy editing collaborate well with people and respect the contributions of people in different jobs. They set high standards for themselves, but when there isn't time to be perfect at everything, they set priorities and remain flexible.

SUMMARY

Technical editors have two primary functions: to manage the publication and distribution of documents (this is the management function) and to emend the writing of a subject matter specialist in order to increase its effectiveness for the readers (this is the text editing function). This textbook focuses on the text editing function, but it introduces management and production issues because the good text editor will understand the effect of editorial decisions and emendations in the context of the conception, development, and production of a document.

FURTHER READING

Wallace Clements and Robert G. Waite. 1983. *Guide for Beginning Technical Editors.* Washington, DC: Society for Technical Communication.

Arthur Plotnik. 1982. *The Elements of Editing: A Modern Guide for Editors and Journalists.* New York: Macmillan. See especially Chapter 2.

DISCUSSION AND APPLICATION

1. Using the flowchart in figure 1.1, relate the development and production of the SCRIPT manual to the different steps. What, for example, constituted research in the document preparation phase? What steps, if any, were omitted, and why?

2. Compare your perceptions of editing before reading this chapter with your current views. Have any perceptions changed?

3. Write three questions or comments you have as a result of reading this chapter. Be prepared to share them in class.

2 READERS AND DOCUMENTS

Just as writers begin their writing by considering who will read the document, in what setting, and for what purpose, editors should make editing decisions conscious of how the decisions will affect the reader's response to and use of the document. This understanding is especially necessary for those decisions that go beyond rules—that is, for editorial decisions that require judgment. However, even if your task is just copyediting (i.e., correction of typos and errors and establishment of document consistency), awareness of how apparently minor corrections can affect the readers' responses will give meaning to your task and incentive for high-quality editing.

This chapter describes how readers of technical documents respond to and use technical documents. It gives a theoretical framework for making decisions at all levels of editing by reviewing reading purposes and patterns, comprehension strategies and devices, access devices in documents, and the implications of all these for designing documents.

PURPOSES FOR READING TECHNICAL DOCUMENTS

Readers of technical documents, such as manuals, proposals, and feasibility studies, have purposes for and patterns of reading that differ from those of readers of other types of documents, such as novels or newspapers. Thus, the choices that technical editors make in terms of style, format, and organizational pattern may differ from the choices made by literary or newspaper editors.

Reading in Order to Act

Readers of technical documents often read in order to act. Reading is usually not an end in itself (as it may be for readers who read novels for pleasure or even for readers of newspapers). Rather, reading enables these readers to do something else, such as solve a problem, make a decision, or operate a piece of equipment. The reading is closely tied to work, whether it is work for a salary or work in the sense of completing a household task.

Often the action follows the reading immediately. In the case of instructions, the reading and action may even intertwine. If readers will perform a task while they read, editors will make it easy to get from the text to the task and back—perhaps by using numbers to identify steps in the task or white space on the page to set off the steps.

Because reading is linked to work, we can assume, in general, that readers are busy, that they have other responsibilities that compete for their time, and that they are more interested in the task than in the document. They may be impatient with delays and distractions caused by reading. Thus, writers and editors should not divert readers from the task with unnecessary information, nor should they make the reading difficult with unnecessarily difficult words and sentence patterns.

The best writing and editing decisions facilitate the readers' practical aims. These decisions relate to substance (i.e., content, organization, style) and to the physical document (i.e., format, typography, paper, size, binding). Editors can anticipate the most essential information, for example, and make it easy for readers to find, perhaps by placing it at the front of the document and by labeling it clearly. If action is the expected outcome of reading, editors will be sure in particular that recommendations are accessible or that steps in a task are clearly marked with numbers or typography. Editors make it easy for readers to negotiate their way through the text, using access devices such as a table of contents, an index, headings, and typography to identify the location of material. They can choose size and binding to make sure the document will stay flat on a desk if it needs to or fit into a shirt pocket if readers are likely to place it there.

Reading to Get Information

Whatever the practical outcome of reading, one purpose will be to get information. In order to act, readers will have to know something. Information will empower the reader to act. This information may be conceptual; that is, readers may need to understand concepts and relationships between ideas. Or the information may be factual; readers may merely need to find a switch on a machine. Knowing that one broad purpose of reading is to get information, editors aim to make documents comprehensible. They make sure that terms are accurate, that conceptual information precedes detailed information, and that the level of detail is right for the readers.

Sometimes, as in the case of a research report, readers learn the information so they can draw it from memory for future action such as a follow-up study. If readers will need to remember the information, editors will prefer prose over tables of data because it is easier to remember prose. Editors will also make sure that new information in the document is related to known information and that it is organized logically, and they will remedy distractions from comprehension such as misspelled words.

PATTERNS OF READING TECHNICAL DOCUMENTS

Not only do people read for different reasons, they read in a variety of ways: selectively, creatively, even with pre-established expectations. Thus, as writers and editors envision the readers who will use documents, they should be aware of patterns of reading and make choices accordingly.

Reading Selectively

Because they have specific practical reasons for consulting technical documents, selective readers will not necessarily either read every word or read the whole document from beginning to end. They look for shortcuts and for the information they need at a given moment. For example, an experienced computer user may skip over introductory material in a manual and look up the directions for transferring a file from a microcomputer to a mainframe. A manager may read only the summary and recommendations of a feasibility study. Reading may be interrupted by a phone call or business meeting, and readers will have to find their place in the document when they resume. Thus, editors are concerned with the readers' ability to gain access to information as well as with the document's comprehensibility.

Explicit devices of access include tables of contents, indexes, and headings; these devices enable readers to refer to specific parts of the document. Placement of material is another device to make the most useful information the most accessible. Information of primary importance is placed in the body of the document. Within a section, such as paragraphs grouped under a heading, important information usually appears early so that readers who read only the beginning of the section will be sure to read the important material. By contrast, information of secondary importance may be placed in an appendix. Such placement decreases the odds that the material will be read, but it makes the information of primary importance more accessible by removing the clutter of secondary information.

Creating Meaning

Reading is interactive. The meaning comes not just from the words and other symbols on the page but from the knowledge that readers bring to the text and the way readers relate this knowledge to the information in the document. Two readers with different experiences and different memories of facts and concepts may create different meanings from the same text.

Readers also differ in their attitudes toward the material and the task, their emotional states at the time of reading, and their reading environments. They may be distracted from their reading by other thoughts, ideas, or tasks. Furthermore, their attitudes and environments influence their responses to the text.

Nevertheless, the document will shape the reader's interpretation. Precise terms, analogies, and background information can help readers make connections between familiar ideas and new ones. Placing key concepts in prominent places in the document (e.g., the first sentence in a paragraph or the independent clause of a sentence) will reinforce the importance of these concepts. The writer's interpretation of data will influence the reader's.

| Anticipating Familiar Conventions | Readers develop expectations for the structure, format, and style of documents, expectations that differ in different contexts. In one situation, a reader is a scientist reading a professional journal. Because of implicit and explicit standards for science writing, the reader will anticipate that the article will set forth the research problem, the methods of investigation, the results of the experiment, and a discussion of its significance. Furthermore, that reader will anticipate a formal writing style, references to other related research reports, and the author-date documentation style. A writer who fails to meet these expectations probably will not be published, and even if the publication reaches print, it will have to be extremely significant to overcome the liability of unconventional patterns of argument and presentation. That writer will not belong to the discourse community of people who write and read about science.

A **discourse community,** loosely defined, is a group of readers and writers with similar expectations for documents. The readers of a scientific journal and its writers may constitute a discourse community and may, in turn, belong to a broader community of writers and readers in one scientific field. They share similar educational and professional backgrounds and vocabularies; they read similar journals and share assumptions about the appropriate way to present information. This community may be quite different from the discourse community of managers in a specific corporation, who also share common backgrounds, vocabularies, and assumptions about writing. Furthermore, the scientist reading the professional journal belongs to a different community when he or she reads the evening newspaper or a user manual for a computer.

One of the ways a person establishes that he or she belongs to a group is by following its conventions. For example, different organizations have dress codes (explicit or understood); a member who ignores the codes risks being shunned by other members. Likewise, a person establishes that he or she belongs to a professional community by writing according to its conventions of discourse. There may be conventions for organization, for style, and for content (e.g., whether to include an abstract or a literature review). There may be conventions as well for vocabulary and for mechanics of citing references and labeling illustrations. Readers become aware of these conventions both consciously (e.g., in writing classes) and by experience.

All the people who will use a particular model of computer and read its manual form a more amorphous group than readers of a scientific journal. Such users may vary widely in education, age and other demographic characteristics, experience with computers, and attitudes. Their only characteristic in common is that they are users of one model of computer. The discourse conventions have to be defined for each document or document set. The documenters establish policies about organization, format, and style, and they maintain the policies consistently in all the manuals for the computer.

Variations in the conventions may distract readers from the meaning; worse, variations may make readers skeptical about the writer and, consequently, about the writer's information. Therefore, editors help to ensure that the document will be appropriate for the discourse community.

COMPREHENDING INFORMATION: CONTENT, SIGNALS, NOISE

Readers of technical documents will use the documents to get information so that they can perform a task or make a decision. They need to comprehend the information, whether the comprehension is at the level of understanding concepts or at the level of identifying facts. Readers also want easy access to information. Some technical documents will address other specific purposes, but they share the universal purpose of giving information. Thus, an underlying goal of technical writing and editing is to make the information comprehensible. All levels of editing, from checking for correctness to substantive revision, work toward the goal of comprehension.

Documents give two types of information to readers: the content and the signals that help readers interpret content. The content may be a review of research related to an experiment, a description of procedures or of a mechanism, a recommendation to make a purchase, or a parts list. Signals can relate either to the content or to the document itself. Signals include verbal signals, such as the phrase *in conclusion,* that show one's place in the document as well as the relationship of ideas. Signals can also be visual, such as boldface or italic type to indicate importance or emphasis and numbers to indicate steps in a series.

Content   For readers to comprehend the document, all the necessary information must be included, and it must be accurate. Furthermore, it must be organized to facilitate the correct interpretation.

Accuracy, completeness, and conciseness. Content must be accurate so that readers can achieve the intended results, whether comprehension or correct action. Because the amount of information also affects comprehension and action, writers and editors must exercise good judgment in selecting content. The content must be complete enough to make sense in light of the readers' previous experience and learning, as well as complete enough to enable the readers to do the task that motivates the reading. It must also be on the right technical level for the readers.

Assuming readers can comprehend and use the material, a concise document is more efficient than a lengthy one. These descriptors— *complete, concise,* and *efficient*—are all relative and cannot be prescribed. Writers and editors cannot know for certain how much information to include and at what level, but they will make better decisions if they imagine how readers will respond to the document as a whole and at each point of reading.

Relationship of new and familiar information. Readers come to a document with a great deal of knowledge and experience in memory. Learning takes place when readers associate the new information with remembered information and expand their memory networks; this is one way in which readers create meaning. Content of a document must relate to a reader's prior experience and knowledge if it is to be meaningful. Readers cannot learn the information if all the terms are new or if the context is totally unfamiliar. Analogy, background description, and reviews of literature are explicit ways of making the new information relate to something familiar. As new information is presented in the document, it becomes familiar or "old" once readers have absorbed and interpreted it. Then additional new information can be linked to information previously presented.

Organization. Knowledge is stored in memory in **schemata,** or structured patterns. Readers do not store separate facts but arrange them into structures that distinguish concepts from details and the relationship of parts. Readers need to organize information in order to learn it and to store it in schemata. The information in an organized document is easier to learn than that in a disorganized one. Thus, content will be easier to comprehend if readers can sense its structure.

Organization will reveal a hierarchy of information—the most important points and the supporting details. It should also indicate how pieces of information relate, as in a cause-effect relationship, a temporal (chronological) one, or a spatial one. (See Chapter 12 for a more detailed discussion of organization.)

Signals

Signals, as well as the content itself, communicate information about the content and the document. These signals can be verbal, structural, or visual. Readers use the information communicated by the signals to help interpret the content. Editors make sure the signals point readers to the correct meaning.

Verbal signals. Verbal signals about the content indicate verbally how to interpret the content. Introductions and overviews at the beginning of a document or a section of a document help readers understand the material by establishing a framework for interpreting details. They predict the broad structure of the information to follow and help readers form a mental outline of the key points.

The writer can signal the hierarchy of ideas with phrases such as "the most important fact is" or "the significance is." Verbal signals also include transitional words to indicate the relationship of ideas. Examples of such words are *however,* which signals contrasting information; *thus,* which signals a conclusion; and *then,* which signals a time relationship. Such signal words help readers understand the content by revealing the relationship of facts and ideas.

Structural signals. Structure refers to the arrangement of words into sentences, sentences into paragraphs, paragraphs into sections, and sections into whole documents. Accurate structural signals help readers interpret the content by showing the hierarchy of ideas and distinguishing main ideas from supporting details. Some explicit structural signals are the table of contents, which shows at least the main division of the document, and headings, which reveal major divisions as well as subdivisions.

The arrangement of words and sentences implicitly cues readers about the relative importance of the words and sentences. Some parts of documents are structurally stronger than others. For example, readers generally expect to find the topic sentence of a paragraph high in the sequence of sentences, and they expect to find the main idea of a sentence in the subject and predicate rather than in a modifying phrase. Thus, the first sentence in a paragraph generally is stronger than the following sentences, and the subject and verb in a sentence are stronger than the modifying phrases. Furthermore, an independent clause in a sentence is stronger than a dependent clause or modifying phrase.

The sequence of content items shows their relationships as well as hierarchy. Items may be ordered chronologically, spatially (e.g., top to bottom), in order of importance, or from general to specific. The sequence, along with the words themselves, helps readers interpret the material.

Visual signals. Visual signals can be seen on the page. A common visual signal is indentation to signify a new paragraph, which, in turn, leads readers to expect a new concept or piece of information. Numbers can also be used to identify sections of a document. A variation of type, such as boldface, indicates that the content set in bold somehow differs from the content set in regular type; the boldface type calls attention to the words and identifies them as words to learn or as labels. Visual signals in graphs, such as an incline or decline in a line graph, explicitly guide the interpretation of the data. Headings provide visual as well as structural signals about content.

Even the paper and the type quality are visual signals about the content. High-quality paper and typesetting signal that the document is important and encourage readers' attention and respect. Neat work, even if typewritten and on cheap paper, encourages readers to take the same care in reading that the writer and editor have taken in producing the document.

Undesirable Signals: Noise

A document sometimes includes verbal, structural, or visual signals that interfere with comprehension of the content or that create a negative response to it. These signals are **noise** in the document, in the way that static in a radio broadcast is noise that partly covers the music or talk. Just as listeners are annoyed and distracted by static, readers are annoyed and distracted by document noise. If the noise becomes too great, listeners will turn off the radio, and readers will stop reading. Thus, editors try to eliminate noise that interferes with readers' comprehension and use of the document.

Verbal noise can be misspelled words and grammar errors, which distract readers from the content. Inconsistencies in the use of terms or in capitalization also represent noise because readers have to interrupt their reading in order to interpret whether the inconsistency signals a distinction in meaning. This textbook, for example, tries to be consistent in using

the term *readers* rather than mixing the term with *audience* lest some
readers wonder whether a distinction is intended between the two terms.
As another example, a reader queried a medical columnist about the distinction in the meanings of *heart beat, heart rate,* and *pulse.* The columnist had used the terms interchangeably, but the reader presumed the
terms referred to three different things.

Noise can also consist of irrelevant information, such as a digression
from the main theme, unnecessary background information, or too many
definitions. In addition, an inappropriate writer voice, or **persona**, can
cause distracting noise in a document. For example, if the writer offends
readers by seeming to be prejudiced or uninformed, readers will transfer
some of their negative reaction to the content. They may object to the content, or they may not "hear" it at all.

Noise can be structural and visual as well as verbal. Structural noise
could result from the arrangement of content in a text that inaccurately
reflects its arrangement in reality (e.g., placing steps in a task out of
chronological order). Visual noise could be smudges on the page or an
exaggerated mixture of typefaces that calls so much attention to itself that
readers see only the chaos, not the content.

Although verbal, structural, and visual signals can help readers interpret and find information, too many signals can create noise. Not every
sentence needs a transition word, nor does every paragraph need a heading. If readers are constantly processing signals rather than content, they
will soon come to focus on the signals themselves. Signals should be relatively unobtrusive — integrated logically into the document and recognizable only when readers consciously seek them.

Noise interferes with comprehension by distracting readers or by making interpretation more difficult. It also increases the chance of errors in
interpretation. When noise becomes so great that it dominates the content,
the noise *is* the content, and the document has failed.

ACCESSING INFORMATION   Because readers are likely to read selectively, an effective document
includes devices to help them find the information they need. Some parts
of the document, such as a table of contents and an index, explicitly aid
accessing. Chapter titles and headings provide ways to locate specific sections on the page, as well as offering structural and visual signals to meaning; the use of color and tabs on pages are more expensive options.
Numbering and use of space or rules between sections are visual signals
about meaning, but they also aid in accessing.

A forecasting statement in the introduction tells readers in prose what will be covered and where. A sentence could state explicitly, for example, that the document will begin with an overview of a piece of equipment followed by an alphabetical list of applications. Readers who know what to expect will waste less time hunting through the text.

DESIGNING DOCUMENTS FOR USE

The more writers and editors know about how readers will read and use a document and about the readers' prior knowledge and expectations, the more likely they will be to design useful products. Just as architects design buildings and engineers design roads, tools, and machines, technical writers and editors design documents. Design is more than a visual or aesthetic concept; a good designer considers the people who will use the building or the road or the document and plans his or her design accordingly. A conception of the functional whole leads to choices about specific features, such as materials and space. **Document design** parallels architectural and engineering design in its scope and purpose.

Document designers (i.e., writers, editors) begin their work with an awareness of how the document will be used. Even if you edit a document that has been completed when you receive it, a good editorial practice is to think of the document in use before you begin making specific emendations. This conception of the whole helps editors choose and modify specific components as they design the document for use.

A document designer's tools are words, sentences, and paragraphs; but they also include organization, style, mechanics, grammar, format, typography, paper, size, and binding. Good design results in documents that readers can use efficiently and successfully—and with pleasure.

SUMMARY

Documents enable readers to solve problems, complete tasks, or add to their knowledge. Readers interact with the document by using their prior knowledge and established reading patterns and by seeking specific information. The complexity of documents and the active role of readers explain why the editor's job is a significant one. The editor, as readers' advocate, language expert, and designer, is an essential member of the publication team.

FURTHER READING

Ann Hill Duin. 1988. "How People Read: Implications for Writers." *The Technical Writing Teacher* XV: 185–193.

Janice C. Redish. 1988. "Reading to Learn to Do." *The Technical Writing Teacher* XV: 223–233.

1. The material shown on pages 28 and 29 appears in the owner's manual for an iron.* Discuss how it reflects one or more of the following concepts from Chapter 2.
   a. Readers of technical documents may read in order to act. (What specifically in the example encourages or enables action?)
   b. Readers may read selectively. (What are the aids to selective reading?)
   c. Readers anticipate familiar conventions. (What in the language, structure, or format makes the document suitable for its readers?)
   d. Verbal signals help readers understand the hierarchy of ideas. (What verbal signals give clues to the hierarchy of ideas?)
   e. Visual signals help readers understand information as well as locate it. (What are the visual signals, and how do they help readers locate and understand information?)
   f. Document noise may interfere with the message of the text. (Does this document contain noise? If so, how does it interfere with the message?)

2. Locate a document of a technical nature, such as a textbook, proposal, or user manual. Find examples in it that illustrate the writer's and editor's awareness of one or more of the concepts discussed in Chapter 2. Depending on your instructor's directions, either elaborate on how the document illustrates one of the principles or show how the document's designers were aware of several design principles.

   If your document fails to acknowledge one or more of these principles, show where and how it fails. Bring your examples to class for sharing.

3. Check the introductory paragraphs of the chapters in a textbook for forecasting statements—statements that tell what the chapter will cover and in what order. How will students use these verbal signals?

4. Verbal signals indicate relationships of pieces of information. Some categories of relationships are listed below with an example for each category in italics. Extend the list of examples for the categories.

Contrast	on the other hand
Time	after
Space	above
Continuation	furthermore

---

* From User's Manual for "Sears Counter Craft Iron." Reprinted by permission of Sears.

ABOUT YOUR TEMPERATURE CONTROL
Set accordingly for fabric, for steam or for dry ironing.

ABOUT YOUR REVERSIBLE CORD
Cord may be located on either side of handle for left or right hand use. See "LEFT-HANDED IRONING" section for switching cord.

ABOUT YOUR SAFETY HEEL REST
When iron has cooled, wrap the cord around the front of the iron then around the heel rest for convenient cord storage.

ABOUT YOUR FABRIC IRONING GUIDE
This guide is designed to help you select the best setting and method for the fabric you plan to iron. Check garment labels and follow recommendations given by the fabric manufacturer. The correct setting for your use may be slightly higher or lower than the marking on your iron. For blended fabrics use setting for fabric in blend requiring the lowest temperature.

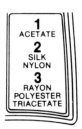

SELECTING THE CORRECT TEMPERATURE
When ironing, it is best to use the temperature setting recommended for the type of fabric being ironed. Garments requiring low temperature settings should be ironed first. This will help avoid damaging garments with a too hot iron. If you are not sure of the fabric content of a garment, first test the temperature of the iron on an area of the garment where it will not show, such as a seam or facing.

For your convenience, the following page has a chart indicating the temperature setting to be used for various types of fabrics, and ironing recommendations for that fabric.

USING DISTILLED WATER
In extremely hard water areas use demineralized (Kit available at most larger Sears stores) or distilled water. Do not use water passed through home water softening systems because such water contains minerals that may be harmful to the iron. Demineralizers are not as effective on water that has been processed through a water softening system. If tap water is used a demineralizer is suggested. See back page for ordering instructions.

TEMPERATURE AND FABRIC CHART

	FABRIC	FABRIC DIAL SETTING	IRONING RECOMMENDATIONS
PERMANENT PRESS	Acetate	1	Dry iron on wrong side while damp.
	Silks†, Nylons†: Nylon C, Caprolan*, Antron* Acrylics: Acrilian*, Creslan*, Orlon*, Zefran* Metalics: Lurex*, Mylar*	2	Dry iron. May also be steam ironed at steam setting if fabric manufacturer directs.
	Polyesters: Dacron*, Fortel*, Kodel*, Vycron* Rayons† Triacetates: Arnel*	3	Dry iron. May also be steam ironed at steam setting if fabric manufacturer directs. Dry iron to touch up collars, cuffs, pockets, etc. Iron Rayon and Metallic fabrics on wrong side.
STEAM/JET OF STEAM	Permanent Press and Wash & Wear Fabrics if Fabric Manufacturer directs. Cotton Play Clothes, Sleep Wear, Bed Linens, Tea Towels, Denims, Unstarched Cottons, etc.	"STEAM"	Steam iron or dry iron to touch up collars, cuffs, pleats, etc.
	Woolens	"WOOL"	Steam iron on wrong side or use pressing cloth on right side.
	Cottons (Not Permanent Press or Wash & Wear Type)	"COTTON"	Dry iron while damp or sprinkled. Iron dark fabrics on wrong side to avoid shine.
	Linens	"LINEN"	Dry iron while damp or sprinkled. Iron each section until entirely dry. Iron dark fabrics on wrong side, table linens on right side.

*Designations trademark of the fiber manufacturer.   †Best ironed while slightly damp.

SETTING DOWN HOT IRON

Your Sears Counter Craft™ iron is designed to rest on the Safety Heel Rest as shown. Be careful, however, that the Steam or Dry button is never on steam or that the Jet of Steam button is never depressed when the iron is in this position. The powerful steam pressure could be hazardous if someone is close by in line with the steam vents. Do not leave the iron unattended. Do not set the hot iron on an unprotected surface, even if it is set on its safety heel rest.

Frequency	sometimes
Example	for example
Conclusion	in conclusion
Cause-effect	because
Explanation	that is

5. The following paragraphs are from a series of guidelines on public relations (PR) for volunteer associations. Underline the verbal signals, and classify the type of relationship indicated. Trace your own mental processes as you read a verbal signal. That is, what expectations do the signals create?

Why did the writer use two paragraphs for the first point rather than running paragraphs 1 and 2 together? Paragraphing is a structural signal that may shape your interpretation of content.

The first principle of effective PR is that there is no "general public." Rather, there are a variety of publics defined by combinations of factors such as income, interests, profession, and geographical location. Most people belong to several publics. The crucial first step in any PR strategy is to select a specific audience-- teachers, students, parents, doctors, agency personnel, legislators, potential employers--and then to design a message that will interest this group. Many people have explored the question of how to get people to take the action or adopt the attitude you support. They all find, in essence, that effective communications aim at people's self-interest. That is, you tune in to your audience and point your message at the things they consider important. Only when you have selected a specific audience can you tailor your PR message to their interests.

This approach is clearly contrary to the shotgun approach of blanketing all media with the

same messages in an effort to reach as many
people as possible. These shotgun approaches will
not be nearly as effective as a carefully planned
message delivered to a specific audience. Use
mass media efforts only to complement specific,
targeted PR activities and not as the core of
your PR program.

The second principle of PR is that personal
contact is more effective than impersonal
communication. While you should use many kinds of
communication channels, try to include personal
channels (face-to-face discussions, speeches,
questions and answers with groups, conventions,
telephone, letters) whenever possible. Use other
media (newspaper, radio, television, billboards)
to complement personal efforts. Also learn what
members of the group you're trying to reach have
the most influence in the group. Gain the support
of these "opinion leaders."

6. How might a table and a bar graph visually invite readers to
   compare?

PART II COPYEDITING

3 COPYEDITING: AN INTRODUCTION

In the process of preparing a document for publication, copyediting takes place after the document's content, format, and style have been established but before the pages are prepared in final form, ready for printing. Thus, copyediting precedes typesetting, or the preparation of camera ready pages by computer.

The copyeditor's main task is to make sure the document meets standards of publication and that readers will be able to read it without being distracted by errors or inconsistencies. The copyeditor makes the document correct, consistent, accurate, and complete.

Correct: spelling; grammar; punctuation

Consistent: spelling (e.g., judgment vs. judgement); abbreviations; numbers (e.g., spelled out or figures); capitalization; labels on visuals; matching of numbers and titles on the visuals with the references in the text; format; documentation form

Accurate: quotations accurately restate the original; dates; model numbers; bibliographic references

Complete: all the parts are present (e.g., title page, table of contents, chapters, back matter); all the visuals that are referred to are in the document

In addition, the copyeditor provides the typist or typesetter with clear instructions about how to type or typeset the text. These instructions relate both to the words (e.g., whether to hyphenate, where to put punctuation) and to the form (e.g., whether to italicize, where to indent). The copyeditor marks the text using a uniform set of symbols for specific functions, such as insert or delete or italicize. These marks will appear on paper if the copyeditor is using hard (paper) copy. If the document is online, the copyeditor may mark using a markup program and may also insert electronic codes if the document will be transmitted to a printer online. The process of marking the choices is called **copymarking** or **markup**.

Copyediting is more than proofreading though both processes share the function of making sure the document is correct. Copyediting occurs before the copy is set in its final form, whereas proofreading occurs after the copy is set. The copyeditor chooses from acceptable alternatives of punctuation and mechanical style and gives instructions about the document to the typist or typesetter. The proofreader determines whether such instructions have been carried out.

The copyeditor plays an important role in producing a quality publication. A document that is full of errors or inconsistencies discourages a reader's trust and reduces comprehension. Good copyediting also saves a lot of time and money during production because changes become increasingly expensive to make in subsequent stages of typesetting, page layout, and printing. Good copyeditors are masters of grammar and spelling. They pay careful attention to the details of a document. They read closely and can tell when a change in punctuation or wording might change meaning. In addition, they are alert to possible ambiguities in language and are willing to check with both the writer and with printed resources to verify their choices.

This chapter provides an overview of copyediting. It describes specific features to check in making a document correct, consistent, accurate, and complete. It also identifies the resources copyeditors use most frequently, especially style manuals. Other chapters in Part II of this textbook give specific instructions on copyediting for grammar, punctuation, and spelling. Chapter 4 presents copymarking symbols and procedures.

DOCUMENT CORRECTNESS

A correct document conforms to **standard American English**—that is, to the grammar, spelling, and punctuation that are accepted by language specialists and the usage panels of dictionary publishers. This function of copyediting is widely understood by writers and managers to be its most essential function. Errors in language use are more apparent to readers than are errors of argument or organization. Errors distract readers from the content, cause readers to misinterpret the content, and diminish readers' respect for the document—all of which can interfere with the effectiveness and usefulness of the document.

Chapters 5, 6, and 7 review spelling, grammar, and punctuation and give information on how to correct the text. The following list identifies some basic standards of correctness.

- Groups of words punctuated as sentences are complete sentences.
- The punctuation is right for the content (e.g., the colon and the dash are used in their best contexts and not merely substituted for each other).
- Punctuation is complete: sentences end with punctuation; quote marks and parentheses are closed.
- Subjects and verbs agree in number.
- Pronouns agree with their referents.
- Modifiers attach logically to a noun in the sentence (they do not "dangle").
- Words are spelled and capitalized correctly.

Exceptions to the standards of correctness are rarely acceptable in technical documents, though errors are sometimes intentional in literature (e.g., a novel for teens in which nonstandard speech patterns are replicated in print). Technical documents are conservative in their use of language and require the highest standards of copyediting.

DOCUMENT CONSISTENCY

Consistency means that the same text or the same type of text or visual is treated in a uniform or harmonious way. For example, a term that is hyphenated once in the text is hyphenated throughout the text, assuming that it is used in the same way. In this textbook, for example, the compound modifier *computer-assisted* is hyphenated throughout when it is used before the noun it modifies. Similar constructions of noun plus past participle are likewise hyphenated. The form of the headings in this textbook is also consistent: all level-one headings are set in 9-point type, all caps, and in the margin; level-two headings are set similarly but cap and lowercase; level-three headings are set in 10-point type, boldfaced and italicized, and run into the text. (The Helvetica typeface for level-one heads appears as large in 9-point size as the Times Roman typeface for level-three headings appears in 10-point size.)

In part, consistency is simply tidy and professional. It reassures readers that the document was produced by careful people. More important, the consistency gives useful information to readers as they process the text. For example, the hyphen in *computer-assisted* identifies the combination of noun plus past participle as an adjective phrase and therefore aids in correct reading. The consistent type style and placement of headings helps readers perceive the organizational pattern.

Four types of consistency apply to a document: verbal, visual, mechanical, and content. Table 3.1 lists the various subcategories for each of these document consistency types, as well as noting what each subcategory entails.

Verbal Consistency   Verbal consistency refers to words and their arrangement into sentences and paragraphs, as well as to meanings of words, structures, and style. Verbal consistency, whether semantic, syntactic, or stylistic, will help to clarify meaning.

Semantics. **Semantics** refers to meaning. Semantic consistency means that one term is used to represent a meaning. For example, users will not be told to flip a "toggle switch" in one paragraph and an "on-off switch" in the next paragraph if the same switch is being referred to. The variation in terms confuses because the two terms indicate two switches. Beginning writers sometimes insert semantic inconsistency because teachers have told them to vary their writing and to avoid repetition. In technical writing, where terms should represent specific meanings, the desire for variety often conflicts with the need for clarity. Technical writers and editors prefer consistency over variety for its own sake. Semantic consistency refers to abbreviations and actions as well as to terms denoting things.

Syntax. **Syntax** refers to the structure of phrases and sentences. Syntactic consistency means that the structure of related terms, phrases, and sentences are parallel. In the sentence you just read, the choice of nouns for the items in the series reinforces their relationship. The parallel structure is an example of syntactic consistency in a sentence. An alternative might read: " . . . terms, phrasing, and whether sentences are parallel." The alternative seems sloppy, however, and the inconsistency of noun, gerund,

TABLE 3.1 TYPES OF DOCUMENT CONSISTENCY

Type	Meaning
Verbal	
Semantics	Meanings of words: one term represents one meaning
Syntax	Structures: related terms, phrases, and clauses use parallel structure
Style	Diction, sentence patterns, and writer's voice: the document is consistent in its level of formality and sophistication and relationship to readers
Visual	
Typography	Typeface and type style are the same for parallel items, such as level-two headings
Layout	Repeated or sequential items, such as running heads and page numbers, appear in the same location on a series of pages
Tables, figures	Labels, titles, callouts, captions, and cross-references are treated the same for all similar visuals; visuals match content and purpose in quality, taste, and seriousness

and clause makes it more difficult to form a mental list of the levels at which structure matters. A series of steps in a procedure should be expressed either as commands or as statements but not as a mixture.

Style. **Style** refers to diction, sentence patterns, and the writer's voice. Stylistic consistency means that the document does not mix either formal language with casual language or a sophisticated approach to a subject and reader with a simplistic, childlike one. A variation in style surprises a reader and calls attention to itself rather than to the content. It forces readers to make repeated adjustments in their sense of who they are in relation to the document and to the writer.

Visual Consistency   Visual consistency refers to anything a reader can see on the page, including typography, spacing, and visuals. Although some visual inconsistencies will not show at the typescript stage, a copyeditor is careful to mark the typescript to ensure its consistency when it is prepared in camera ready form. This careful attention to visual consistency can reduce potential errors for the proofreader to catch at a later stage. The copyeditor's function in establishing visual consistency may overlap with the graphic

TABLE 3.1 (continued)

Type	Meaning
Mechanical	
Spelling	One spelling is used for the same term
Capitalization	Terms are capitalized the same on each related use
Hyphenation	Hyphenation is consistent for the same term and for like terms
Abbreviation	Use and identification of abbreviations follow a pattern
Numbers	Related numbers are consistent in punctuation, use of words or numerals, abbreviation, and arrangement
Punctuation	Items in a series and lists follow a pattern of punctuation; possessives and accents are the same on repeated uses of the same term
Cross-references	All cross-references follow the same patterns of capitalization, abbreviation, and punctuation
Documentation	References conform in arrangement, abbreviation, capitalization, underlining, and spacing to one acceptable pattern
Lists	Related lists match in capitalization, punctuation, spacing, signals such as numbering and bullets, and phrases or complete sentences
Type style	Variations such as italics, capitalization, and boldface signal specific meanings such as emphasis or terms used as terms
Content	References to the same object or event do not contradict one another

designer's function in designing the text, but even if the copyeditor does not make the decisions about typography and layout, he or she will mark the typescript for visual consistency.

Typography. Typographical consistency means that parallel parts of a document use the same typeface and type style. Levels of headings are distinguished by their spacing, typography, and capitalization. Typefaces, type styles, and type sizes are not altered except for a specific purpose. The principle of typographical consistency is increasingly important as more people gain access to computers with multiple fonts and type styles.

Amateurs play with their machines and create a visual hodgepodge that only distracts from the message.

Layout. **Layout** refers to the location of related items on the page and to the use of space. For consistency, page numbers appear in the same location on all pages, and the amount of space following a level-one heading is the same for each use. Figures are labeled consistently at the bottom or at the top, not sometimes at the top and sometimes at the bottom. If the document uses numerous visuals paired with text, the spacing between text and visuals is consistent. For example, all the visuals in a manual might appear on the left column with related text to the right, or the visuals might appear above the text; whatever the pattern, it will remain constant throughout the document. The top, bottom, left, and right margins as well as the space between columns, if any, are uniform from page to page. Indentation is the same not just for paragraphs but for other text elements, such as lists and block quotations. If the location of related items varies, it does so according to a pattern (e.g., page numbers may appear in the upper left corner on a lefthand page but in the upper right corner on a righthand page).

Figures and tables. Figures and tables, like text, should be treated consistently. Patterns of using numbers and titles and of placing them on the visuals should be established and followed. Callouts (i.e., names of parts), captions, and cross-references will be like others for similar visuals in typeface and type style, capitalization, and placement. (See the section on copyediting visuals later in this chapter for more details.)

The content and reproduction of figures and tables should also be consistent with the overall purpose and quality of the document. If a document is typeset and printed on quality paper, a poor reproduction or an amateurish drawing is inconsistent. The insertion of a cartoon is inconsistent with the goals of a serious financial report.

Mechanical Consistency **Mechanical style** refers to the mechanics of the document, such as capitalization, hyphenation, abbreviations, numbers, and type styles. Mechanical style should be consistent. For example, if a comma appears after the thousands position in a number (e.g., 1,000 rather than 1000), numbers throughout the document should use commas in this position. Copyeditors probably spend as much time with mechanical consistency as with any other type. They can often choose among acceptable alternatives, so to edit for mechanical consistency is not necessarily to apply a rule, as it is in editing for grammar, but to make the best choice for the specific document and its readers. Copyeditors depend on dictionaries and style manuals to help them make their choices. (Style manuals are described later in this chapter, following the discussion of consistency.) These guides help copyeditors make style choices objectively and avoid tampering with a writer's style to suit their own preferences.

- **Spelling.** Dictionaries often provide alternative spellings for words. Sometimes the first choice is preferred, but sometimes the choices are merely listed alphabetically. Spelling of terms should be uniform throughout the document. Editors choose one from alternatives such as these:

```
acknowledgment    acknowledgement

ensure            insure

copy editing      copyediting
```

- **Capitalization.** Copyeditors determine what terms should be capitalized according to rules and convention. Different discourse communities use different rules for capitalization. For example, government writing capitalizes *federal* and *state* used as modifiers, whereas most other writing would not. Some organizations capitalize the generic part of their name when it is used alone (e.g., the Company or the Society) although style manuals generally agree that such a term is capitalized only when it is part of the entire name. An editor might question capitalization in the following examples:

```
Crohn's Disease    Crohn's disease

Federal            federal

French fries       french fries

Helvetica          helvetica
```

- **Hyphenation.** The rules for determining when to hyphenate are summarized in Chapters 5 and 7. Because they can be complex, it is a good idea to record choices on a style sheet.

```
computer-assisted

end-of-year report

community-based
```

- **Abbreviation.** Copyeditors need to decide whether to abbreviate, what abbreviation to use if there are alternatives, and how to identify the abbreviations for readers. A list of abbreviations at the front or back of the document or a parenthetical explanation after first use are the typical ways to identify what the abbreviations stand for. The following sentence identifies the abbreviation parenthetically:

```
The Council of Biology Editors (CBE)

prefers . . .
```

After the abbreviation is thus identified, this group can be referred to subsequently as CBE. Some terms are better known by their abbreviations than by the spelled-out version. For example, more readers will recognize *PBX* than *Private Branch Exchange*. No parenthetical or list definition is necessary for such abbreviations in most instances unless publication policies require the definition. Copyeditors need to make choices about abbreviations such as the following and then to be consistent in using them.

```
a.m.          A.M.    A.M.

inches        in.     "

Pennsylvania  PA      Pa.
```

- **Numbers.** The various possibilities for expressing numbers require an editor to make choices.

Commas	1000	1,000
Numerals or words	five	5
Dates	12 April 1989	April 12, 1989
Inclusive numbers	411-414	411-14 or 411-4
Time	eight o'clock	8 a.m. or 8 A.M.
Equation numbers	eq. 2.2	equation 2
Illustration numbers	figure 1.1	figure 1

- **Punctuation.** All of the following text features require decisions about punctuation.

Items in a series: Should there be a comma before the final item?

```
The four types of consistency are verbal,
visual, mechanical, and content.
OR: The four types of consistency are verbal,
visual, mechanical and content.
```

Lists: Should there be punctuation after each item?

```
1. spelling;              1. spelling

2. capitalization;        2. capitalization

3. hyphenation;           3. hyphenation

4. abbreviations; and     4. abbreviations

5. numbers.               5. numbers
```

Possessives: Should an *s* be added following the apostrophe?

```
Paris' museums    Paris's museums
```

Accents: Should accents be used?

```
resume    résumé
```

- **Cross-references.** Cross-references within the text should be consistent in use of abbreviations, capitalization, and parentheses.

```
See figure 1    See fig. 1
(see fig. 1)    (See fig. 1.)
```

- **Documentation.** The styles for citing works consulted differ from discipline to discipline. All citations should conform to the appropriate style for the discipline or publication. The style establishes the arrangement of items in an entry, capitalization, abbreviation, punctuation, and the use of italics. Styles are usually variations of the author-date and footnote/bibliography styles. The following two entries conform to the author-date styles of the American Psychological Association and the Modern Language Association, respectively.

```
Benson, P.J. (1988). The expanding scope of
document design. Technical Communication,
36, 352-355.
```

```
Benson, Philippa J. "The Expanding Scope of
Document Design." Technical Communication,
36 (1988), 352-55.
```

- **Lists.** Lists should be consistent in these respects:

  punctuation, numbering, capitalization of the initial word in the item

  words, sentences, or phrases

- **Type style.** Type style is often a matter of visual consistency, but where it has to do with terms, it relates to mechanical consistency. For example, will terms used as terms be italicized or placed in quote marks?

  ```
  The word proofreading is no longer
  hyphenated.
  ```

  ```
  The word "proofreading" is no longer
  hyphenated.
  ```

All these types of mechanical consistency eliminate some document noise and contribute to the readers' impression of a quality publication. Mechanical consistency can also save production costs by reducing the need for expensive changes later.

Content Consistency   The check for content consistency eliminates contradictory information. For example, if a part of a mechanism is said to be made of steel at one point, it should not be described subsequently as made of aluminum. If the initial date of a five-year project is given as 1987, readers will be confused if the ending date is identified as 1993. If readers are told to find a reference on page 18 of a document when that reference actually appears on page 19, they will be frustrated or may not find the reference at all. If a forecasting statement in an introduction establishes four major divisions in a document with five divisions, readers will have to revise their sense of the document, an unnecessary and confusing step in processing the document and its information.

Inconsistencies in a document often result from revision or from legitimate changes in a project where the writer did not catch all the references that related to the changes. Inconsistencies can also result from typographical errors or carelessness.

The check for content consistency somewhat overlaps substantive editing, but copyediting is particularly concerned with the details of content whereas substantive editing focuses more on the larger issues of organization, completeness of information, and style.

A Foolish Consistency . . .

The aim for consistency is an important one in copyediting because consistency aids interpretation and because it communicates quality. However, copyeditors can go too far in their pursuit of consistency and create errors and clumsiness. One editor, reading the following sentence, saw that two of the three items in the series ended in -al.

```
The reasons for the change are philosophical,
technological, and economic.
```

Aiming for parallel structure, the editor added -al to "economic."

```
The reasons for the change are philosophical,
technological, and economical.
```

The structure is parallel—but the use of the word is wrong. Changes might be economical, but reasons (which have no price tag) are economic.

Ralph Waldo Emerson once observed: "A foolish consistency is the hobgoblin of little minds." A foolish consistency would be to insist that all the visuals in a document be of the same type—for example, to refuse to use both photographs and line drawings. Such a consistency would be foolish because the two types of illustrations have different purposes. A photograph shows realism, context, and depth, whereas a line drawing might work better to show how parts are assembled even though it sacrifices some realism and the background. The goal of providing readers with the information they need in the most effective way supercedes any goal of making related parts of the document uniform.

STYLE MANUALS

Editors make choices about mechanical style based on conventions established for the document, the organization, and the discipline, as well as on conventions of standard American English. The preceding section on mechanical consistency indicates the range of choices in spelling, capitalization, abbreviation, and so on.

Copyeditors use **style manuals** accepted in their discipline or organization in order to help make choices for a particular document. The style manuals establish conventions. Furthermore, they save a copyeditor from wasting time and effort thinking through each situation in order to make a decision or from merely guessing. Once an editor makes a choice based on a style manual, he or she records it on a style sheet for the document. Subsequent choices can then be consistent with the first choice.

Style manuals can be classified into three categories, ranging from very complete to very selective: comprehensive, discipline, and house or organization. In addition, and most selective of all, is the individual document style sheet, which will be discussed later in the chapter.

Comprehensive Style Manuals

Comprehensive style manuals cover style choices that might apply in any publishing situation, no matter what the discipline or document. Three style manuals widely used in technical communication are these:

The Chicago Manual of Style, 13th ed. 1982. Chicago: University of Chicago Press.

The GPO Style Manual, 28th ed. 1984. Washington, DC: U.S. Government Printing Office.

Words into Type, 3rd ed. 1974. Englewood Cliffs, NJ: Prentice-Hall.

The contents page from *The Chicago Manual of Style* (see figure 3.1) shows how comprehensive and thorough is the manual's coverage. The guidelines for using numbers, for example, take 18 pages. An editor willing to hunt through a comprehensive style manual should find the answer to almost any style question.

Discipline Style Manuals

Some disciplines publish their own style manuals, mostly as a guide for researchers who publish in academic journals. Nevertheless, any other publication that is linked in subject matter to these disciplines or is read by readers familiar with the discipline should try to conform in style to the style manual for the discipline. For example, an in-house research report in a psychological research center should conform to the *Publication Manual of the American Psychological Association.* An editor should definitely consult a discipline style manual not only for documentation style but also for conventions on such matters as labeling visuals and hyphenating terms. Some of the widely used manuals are these:

CBE Style Manual, 5th ed. 1983. Bethesda, MD: Council of Biology Editors. Used also in agricultural sciences.

Mathematics into Type, rev. ed. 1979. Providence, RI: American Mathematical Society. By Ellen Swanson.

The New York Times Manual of Style and Usage. 1975. New York: New York Times Books. Edited by Lewis Jordan.

Publication Manual of the American Psychological Association, 3rd ed. 1983. Washington, DC: American Psychological Association. Used widely by other disciplines, including business.

Style Manual, rev. ed. 1973. New York: American Institute of Physics.

Figure 3.1
Contents Page from *The
Chicago Manual of Style*.
Reprinted by permission
of The University of
Chicago Press.

Contents

The *GPO Style Manual,* listed previously, is also a specialized style manual, "intended to facilitate Government printing." It appears in the list of comprehensive manuals because its coverage is broader than that of the typical discipline style manual.

Two specialized style manuals useful for editors who work with technical and quantitative material are these:

American National Standard Guidelines for Format and Publication of Scientific and Technical Reports. 1974. New York: American National Standards Institute.

Guidance for Using the Metric System—SI Version. 1975. Washington, DC: Society for Technical Communication. By Valerie Antoine.

Other disciplines have specialized style manuals as well, many of which are identified by John Bruce Howell in *Style Manuals of the English-Speaking World: A Guide* (Phoenix: Oryx Press, 1983). To identify others, you can check reputable journals in a discipline to determine from the instructions for authors what style manual is preferred. Reference librarians can also assist in locating either a professional association that may publish a style manual or the manual itself.

House or Organization Style Manuals

An organization that publishes frequently, whether or not it is a commercial publishing house, will make similar choices for most of its documents. Certain technical terms will appear frequently in many of the publications, and some patterns of punctuation and formatting will be consistent. Choices that will be appropriate for all publications from that house can be listed in a house style manual. These choices probably incorporate the preferred choices in a comprehensive or discipline style manual, but because the house manual is more selective, it is easier to use, and it answers specific questions. Instead of 18 pages on the use of numbers, for example, there may be only 2 pages that list those instances in which the organization will use numbers. Digital Equipment Corporation, Bell Laboratories, and the publishers of *Oil and Gas Journal* are three organizations that have prepared their own style manuals, but such manuals are common wherever publication is frequent. Because they are used by a limited number of writers and editors, these manuals are likely to be photocopied and stapled rather than printed and bound. Figure 3.2 shows a page from the *Software Publications Style Guide* of Digital Equipment Corporation (Maynard, MA: 1980).

In establishing a style for a particular document, you will probably consult the house style manual first, because it is likely to address specifically the choices that have to be made for that document. Once you make the choices, record them on a document style sheet, specific to one document.

Figure 3.2   Sample-page from *Software Publications Style Guide,* Digital Equipment Corporation

3.7 Hyphenating Numbers

Use a hyphen between a number and word combined to form a unit modifier.

> This field must contain a 6-character file name.
> The project continued after a 14-week delay.
> The PDP-11™ has an 8-bit byte and a 16-bit word.

Hyphenate a fraction written as words.

> Approximately three-fourths of the programs executed without error.
> This procedure gives you three and one-half times the normal available memory.

Section 1 contains further information on forming compounds and hyphenation.

3.8 Ranges of Numbers

In text, use the word *to* to indicate a range of numbers in the following cases:

- If you write the numbers in the range as words

  > Enter one to three characters.
  > The program prints one to four different reports.

- If an expression of range occurs infrequently in text, even if the numbers are expressed as figures

  > Enter 12 to 20 characters.

- If the numbers in the range are part of a modifier containing a hyphen

  > Enter a 1- to 6-character file name.

In tables and illustrations, use a hyphen or en dash (defined in Section 4.6) to indicate a range of numbers.

Text	Table
1977 to 1999	1977–1999
columns six to nine	col 6–9
pages 5 to 18	pp 5–18
one to three characters	1–3 characters
1- to 6-character file name	same as text or file name (1–6 characters)

Figure 3.3
Style Sheet
for a Document

A–D	E–H	I–L
backup copies camera ready	halftone half title	
M–P	**Q–T**	**U–Z**
online mark up (v) markup (n)	type style typeface reread	
numbers	**style – spacing**	**miscellaneous**
Spell out one through nine	cross-references visuals– see figure 3.1 chapters– see Chapter 9 italicize new & unfamiliar terms	text = prose part of document document = the entire publication

Document Style Sheet

The document style sheet records choices made for a particular document that may influence subsequent choices. It should not list every editorial change, but it should list choices for which the editor had to consult a dictionary, handbook, style manual, or other source, as well as terms or situations for which several options are available. For example, because you know that state names are always capitalized, you would not list your marking of a lowercase *c* in *California.* But if you were unsure of the spelling and capitalization in *Alzheimer's disease,* you would include the term on the style sheet. The style sheet is less a record of changes than a guide to editing the pages that follow in the document.

In addition to listing spelling, capitalization, and hyphenation, the style sheet includes choices about punctuation, abbreviations, and other matters of consistency. The style sheet may be only one page long if the document is fairly short. One convenient way to prepare a document style sheet is to begin with a grid into which you can pencil the choices as you make them (see figure 3.3). You can incorporate page numbers of the first instance of occurrence so that you will always have an example in context to refer to. Or you can include page numbers for all occurrences if you think you may need to change your mind later. You will be able to find the choice quickly because the words are roughly alphabetized.

If your treatment of a term will differ depending on its form, as from noun to adjective, be sure to specify on the style sheet how you are using the term. For example, the phrase *top-down* as an adjective is hyphenated, but as an adverb it is not. To illustrate the application of this difference, one might say, "Top-down editing helps an editor make decisions in light of the whole," and then be consistent in saying "That person edits top down." The style sheet would look like this:

```
top-down (adj.)
top down (adv.)
```

In addition to listing terms in the alphabetical sections, you can include sections on the sheet for punctuation, numbers, and miscellaneous formatting.

A second way to prepare a style sheet is on computer. With a sophisticated word processing program, you will be able to open your style sheet file while your document remains open. You can alphabetize as you add entries, or you may be able to ask the computer to alphabetize for you. The alphabetical list for your document will let you locate the choices you have made easily when a question about style arises. Page numbers of occurrences are not so important with this method because of the computer's search and locate capability.

Part of the style sheet for this textbook appears in figure 3.4.

Either way you prepare your document style sheet, by hand using a grid or on the computer, you will have an easy way to determine choices you have made previously, enabling you to be consistent throughout the document. The style sheet will accompany the document through subsequent stages of production, including typesetting and proofreading. Other people working on the document will then have a basis for making decisions when questions arise.

DOCUMENT ACCURACY

"Accuracy" refers here to content, while "correct," as used previously, refers to the use of language. Errors in content, such as using the wrong term, date, or model number, can make a document partially or totally

Figure 3.4
Alphabetized Style Sheet
Prepared by Computer

PARTIAL STYLE SHEET: TECHNICAL EDITING

backup copies
camera ready (adj.)
Chapter 9 (capital letter for cross references)
computer-assisted (adj.)
copyediting
double-spaced (adj.)
double-spaced (pred. adj.) 12.7
doublespacing
half title
in-house (adj.)
in house (pred. adj.)
lefthand
metric system 8
online
overformatting 12
reread, rereading 5.12
résumé
righthand
roman type (not capitalized)
subpart
type size
type style
typeface
walk-in (adj.); walk-in customer
The Chicago Manual of Style (title); *Chicago Manual*
Words into Type (title)

punctuation:
comma after introductory phrase or term (Thus, In fact,)

terms:
document = the entire publication, including prose, visuals, mechanical
   parts, and binding
text = prose part of the document

visuals:
cross-references in text: lc (figure 3.1, or, see figure 3.1)
labels: double numeration (figure 3.1)

worthless to readers, legally incriminating, and even dangerous. Copyeditors should check carefully those places in the text where errors are likely to occur:

- **Quantitative data:** model numbers, formulas, calculations (e.g., addition of figures in a column), measures, dates

- **Prose data:** names, titles, terms, abbreviations, quotations

- **Visuals:** labels, cross-references, callouts

A copyeditor may need to check these things even after a substantive edit or technical review because often the editor and reviewer have focused on the larger text structures—the argument, the gist of the meaning, the organization—and only scanned details such as those listed previously. Furthermore, the more atypical the text is, the more likely it is that errors will occur and not be noticed by the editors. Prose paragraphs are easier to copyedit than quantitative data and names and titles. But writers are likely to be impatient with the details of the text, having expended a great deal of energy creating and organizing the content and wishing to be finished with the writing task. Therefore, errors are more likely to occur in tables, reference lists, and other atypical text.

A complete check for accuracy requires familiarity with content. Even if a copyeditor is not a subject matter expert, he or she can be alert to probable errors. For example, in one long article on relationships between people, the writer referred to "dynamic" relationships. However, the quotations from other sources on the subject referred to "dyadic" relationships (i.e., relationships of dyads, or two people). Noting the inconsistency, an alert copyeditor wondered whether "dynamic" and "dyadic" relationships differed or whether the writer (or the writer's typist) used one wrong term. Even without knowing advanced psychology, the copyeditor could spot an apparent discrepancy.

Not knowing for sure the meaning of the terms as used in the article, the copyeditor would have been premature in changing one term or in querying the writer immediately. A change could simply make the text wrong, and constant queries to the writer without sound basis can irritate and raise some questions about the copyeditor's competence. Instead, she looked for other text signals about meaning, such as parenthetical definitions of the terms or some other explanation of the difference. The copyeditor might have consulted a psychology text index or glossary or a specialized dictionary of psychological terms to find definitions. If no explanation appeared in the document or could be found in other sources, the copyeditor would note the instances when the terms were used for possible change later. As the copyeditor read further, she noted additional signals indicating that one term was incorrect. For example, in a quotation the writer substituted "dynamic" for "dyadic." Then there was enough evidence to warrant a check with the writer or other content expert.

Inconsistencies, facts that seem to contradict logic, and omissions are clues to potential errors. Note the inconsistency in the following model numbers:

JC238-9Y

JN174-2Y

R2472-3

Noting that the third item does not end in a letter as the first two do, you would verify the numbers, perhaps by checking with the company catalog or even the product itself.

As another example, a reference to a photographic process in 1796 raises a question about the date—you suspect (even if you do not know) that photography came later in history. Likewise, a call for one tablespoon of salt in a recipe for a dessert that serves eight makes you suspect that a teaspoon is the correct measure.

An error in one type of text alerts you to pay close attention to all instances of similar text. For example, a reference list entry that cites a date and an author's initial(s) incorrectly is a clue to look carefully at the other entries. The error in one entry suggests the possibility that the writer was not careful in compiling the list. Likewise, an error in addition in one column of figures in a table requires a check of the other columns.

You rely on careful, alert reading more than on rules you can learn in a handbook when you copyedit for accuracy. Do not dismiss your quiet hunches that something may be wrong; do not take for granted that simply because a reputable writer and editor have previously reviewed the text that it is free from errors—or that they are incompetent for having missed errors. They were concentrating on other text features. Be especially careful in your check of atypical text, such as numbers and dates, reference citations, and headings.

DOCUMENT COMPLETENESS

A complete document contains all its prose and visual parts as well as the necessary front matter and back matter. The copyeditor provides the quality control check to make sure that a document doesn't get published lacking its index or a table cited in the text. The copyeditor also checks that all the pages are included and in order, including blank pages, before the typescript goes to the printer or is prepared in camera ready form.

Parts of a Book, Manual, or Long Report

Books, manuals, and other long documents have three major sections: the preliminary pages or front matter, the body, and the back matter. Within these major divisions are subparts, some of which are optional. A part should be included only if it is functional.

Decisions about what parts a document will include are generally made before the copyeditor works on the copy. If the document is part of a set, other documents in the set help to establish the pattern. Or the editor who has worked on development and substantive editing will determine document specifications and list them for the copyeditor. The copyeditor, then, does not decide whether to include abstracts or a glossary but makes sure that the wishes of the writer and the substantive editor are carried out.

When the document includes many parts, it's good to have a checklist, based on the specifications. Only long documents will include all the parts identified in the discussion that follows here. Simple documents contain only some of these parts. You can consult a comprehensive style manual, such as *The Chicago Manual of Style* or *Words in Type*, for specific guidance on how to prepare these parts and for information on other, less common parts, such as epigraphs and dedications.

An editor has some choice about where to place some materials. For example, a list of references in a book may appear at the end of each chapter, or all the references for all the chapters may appear in the back matter.

Preliminary Pages The preliminary pages appear before the text begins. The title and contents pages are included in virtually all books, manuals, and long reports. Roman numerals identify their page numbers, with the half title (a short version of the title page) being page *i*. Blank backs of pages are counted in the numeration even if the number does not appear on the page. Parts other than the title and contents pages are optional.

- **Cover.** Includes both the type and the artwork, if any. It identifies the title and subtitle and may identify the author or editor and place of publication. On reports, it may also include the date and other information.

- **Half title page.** Includes only a short title or the main title without a subtitle, immediately inside the cover. The type is generally smaller than it is on the title page, and the back usually is blank.

- **Title page.** Includes the title and subtitle; may include the name of the author or editor. Title pages of reports generally contain more information; for reports or other short documents, the cover and title page may be the same page.

- **Copyright page.** Generally falls on the back of the title page; includes, at the least, the copyright symbol, year of publication, and copyright holder. Here is an example:

© 1991, Wadsworth Publishing Company
All rights reserved
Printed in the United States of America

No periods appear at the end of the lines. The copyright page also includes the address of the publisher and the ISBN (International Standard Book Number) for commercial publishers. This number identifies the country of publication and the publisher according to an international code.

- **Table of contents.** Lists main divisions and their page numbers; usually is labeled simply "contents."

- **List of tables and figures.** Lists the title, number, and page number of the visuals; tables and figures may be listed separately and on separate pages as a "list of tables" and a "list of figures."

- **List of contributors.** Lists the authors' names and other identifying material, such as position and place of employment; appropriate for anthologies of articles by different authors or for journals. Alternatively, this information may appear for each contributor on the first or last page of the article or as a list in the back of the document.

- **Foreword.** Written and signed by someone other than the author or editor; introduces the document by indicating its purpose and significance. It is more common in academic and literary texts than in technical documents.

- **Preface.** Written by the document's author or editor; introduces the document by indicating its purpose, scope, significance, and possibly history. It often includes acknowledgments.

- **Acknowledgments.** Usually incorporated into the preface; names people who have helped with the publication, such as reviewers and typists, and their contributions.

Body   The first page of the body of the document is numbered page 1 (arabic numeral). Whether the document contains all or just some of the prose parts listed below depends on the nature of the document.

- **Chapters or other subdivisions.** All should be present, in order; all pages for each subdivision should also be present and in order.

- **Titles/identifying information.** Each major subdivision of the document should begin with a title, author's name in a multi-author book, and other identifying information that is standard for all the subdivisions.

- **Abstract.** Summarizes or describes the contents of the chapter or subdivision at the beginning.

- **List of references.** Identifies the sources mentioned in the chapter or division.

- **Half titles.** Sometimes placed between major parts of the document (groups of related chapters); identifies the part title.

- **Blank pages.** May be inserted in the typescript that goes to a printer to signal blank pages in the printed document. These blanks will probably be **verso** (back or lefthand) pages; they are especially useful when all chapters or divisions begin on a **recto** (righthand) page. When editing electronically, insert page breaks for the blank pages, especially if you are using an automatic page numbering system.
- **Running heads.** Headers in the top margin that name the chapter, author, or part title. They help people find their place in the book; sometimes they are different on the recto and verso pages.
- **Visuals.** These elements (tables, figures) warrant a separate check when you check for completeness. If the document contains a list of tables and figures, you can compare the items on the list to the visuals included with the typescript. All the items listed should be included, and all those that have labels and titles should be listed.

Back Matter The back matter contains supplementary information and information that lets a reader search either in the document itself or in other sources. Page numbers continue sequentially from those in the body, in arabic numerals.

- **Appendix.** Provides supplementary text material, such as research instruments (e.g., a questionnaire) or tables of data. Each appendix is labeled with a letter or number and titled (e.g., Appendix A: Survey of Users).
- **Glossary.** Defines terms used in the document; a mini-dictionary that applies just to the document and its specific topic.
- **References.** The complete publication data for the materials cited in the document, unless this information appears after each chapter; sometimes references are grouped by chapter at the end of a book.
- **Index.** Lists the key terms used in the text and the pages on which they are discussed or referred to; useful for readers who want to read selectively.

COPYEDITING VISUALS Visuals require copyediting for the same reasons that text does: to make the visual correct, consistent, accurate, and complete. A copyeditor does not evaluate whether the visual is suitable for content and purpose (a task of substantive editing) but does make sure the visual meets accepted standards of communication.

The marks used in copyediting visuals are the same as the marks for text. Thus, the symbols identified in Chapter 4 for deletion, insertion, transposition, alignment, and so forth work the same for visuals as for prose.

Correctness, Consistency, Accuracy, and Completeness

The verbal information on a visual requires copyediting for correctness. Spelling and punctuation errors can be made as easily on visuals as in paragraphs, and the illustrator may not be able to use a spelling checker. Thus, you will check any words that appear on the visuals. The identifying features of visuals, including titles, numbers, callouts, and other features discussed in the following section, require editing both for correctness and for consistency.

Accuracy checks are especially necessary for visuals that present quantitative information and when a procedure or piece of equipment poses safety hazards. You can spot-check numbers on graphs to see if they make sense in their context. Sometimes you will check simple calculations, such as addition, if the totals seem questionable or if you know a writer or graphic artist frequently makes mistakes in details. You can compare line drawings to the actual object.

In checking the visual for completeness, you will look to see that parts are identified on illustrations and that base measures (e.g., percent, liters) are on tables and graphs. Dates and other identifiers may also be necessary. Sometimes parts of the visual are shaded, as when the columns of a column graph are shaded differently to represent different products or other elements. The meaning of the shading should be clear, either on or next to the column or in a legend. Also, all the visuals must be present.

The information in the title must match the information on the visual. If the title promises records from 1987 to 1991, the visual cannot stop with the 1990 records. Likewise, references to the visual in the text must match the identifying information on the visual. Finally, if the visual itself or information in it are borrowed from other sources, the source must be cited.

Labels, Numbers, and Titles

For labeling purposes, visuals are classified as either tables or figures. A **table** presents information in tabular form, that is, in rows and columns. The information in the rows and columns may be quantitative or verbal. All other visuals are considered **figures**, whether the visual is a photograph, line drawing, bar graph, flowchart, line graph, or other graph. As copyeditor, you need to be aware of the functions of identifying features of tables and figures, including labels, numbers, and titles.

Labels. If the visual will be referred to in more than one place in the document or if the visual will not set directly following the text that discusses it, labels (e.g., "table" and "figure") and numbers are useful. Small and informal visuals, however, may not need to be labeled and numbered if they appear right at the point where they are mentioned.

Some pattern of labeling visuals should be established, and style guides may help. The American Psychological Association, for example, requires table titles and numbers at the top of the table and figure titles and numbers at the bottom. Not all documents in other disciplines will follow this particular pattern, but readers should be able to anticipate where to find specific kinds of information in visuals throughout the document. You should record your choices about placement of labels and titles on your style sheet and be sure that you follow your own style.

In addition, labels on the visuals themselves must be consistent with the references to them in the text. Thus, you must check that the reference to figure 1 in the text really does refer to the visual labeled "figure 1."

Numbers. Visuals are numbered sequentially through the document, but tables and figures are numbered independently. Thus, a document may include a table 1 and a figure 1. Double numeration is common in documents with multiple sections. Thus, "table 12.2" indicates that the table is the second numbered table to appear in Chapter 12 (as with figures, not all tables in a document are necessarily numbered).

A series of illustrations, particularly in visual instructions, may be numbered right on the illustration itself. These numbers show the sequence of steps and are analogous to the numbers for the steps of prose instructions. The numbers are not joined with a label because the illustrations will be referred to elsewhere only as steps (e.g., step 1, step 2).

Titles. The primary function of titles is to let readers identify the visual without reference to the text. Because some readers will try to take shortcuts by reading only the visuals, the visuals should be as self-contained and self-explanatory as possible. The words in the title should refer to the content of the visual in concrete terms. For example, "Sales of Chip #A422, First Quarter 1991" answers *what* and *when* questions and informs more specifically than "Sales" would. In addition, titles of line drawings and photographs may require information on point of view, such as top view, side view, cross section, or cutaway view. Finally, it is never appropriate to name the type of visual (e.g., photograph, line graph) in the title—the type is evident from the visual itself.

Visuals may also contain a number of other identifying elements, such as callouts, legends, captions, and footnotes. As copyeditor, you need to become familiar with the uses of these devices.

Callouts. A verbal identifier, such as a part name, on an illustration is known as a **callout**. Callouts supplement the visual information by giving a name for a part or procedure, and they link the visual with the text. Callouts should be used selectively. If readers do not need to identify a part or procedure, delete the clutter of unnecessary identifying words. Check with the writer, however, before you make such decisions about what is necessary.

The callouts on the visual must match the terms used in the text. If a part is a "casing" in the text, readers will search the visual for a part called a casing, not a cover. Generally all parts that the text names should have callouts, and all the parts identified with callouts on the illustration should be referred to in the text.

The callout should be next to the part or procedure it identifies. If necessary, a straight line can connect the part and the callout. If the object has major and minor parts, that structural relationship can be shown by callout placement or type style. For example, all major parts might be identified on the left of the object while minor parts are identified on the right, or major parts could be named in capital letters while minor parts are set in lowercase letters. If the object has many parts crowded together, the parts may be numbered, with a numbered list of parts following. This type of callout is common in an owner's manual that identifies all parts of the mechanism.

For aesthetic purposes and also for the sake of readability, a standard typeface and size may be used for callouts on all visuals in the document. The type must be large enough to be read but not so large as to overwhelm the visual. Alignment of a vertical series of callouts, when practical, helps give the visual a neat appearance.

Legends. A **legend** explains shading or other visual ways to distinguish the elements on a graph from one another. For example, it may list the different types of lines—solid, dashes, dot-dash—on a multiple-line graph, indicating what each line represents. The legend generally appears in a corner of the visual. Because legends are separate from the elements

they identify, they require an extra step in processing for readers. Therefore, you should restrict their use to avoid repeating the same information
and cluttering up the visual.

Captions. Brief explanations (a few lines of text) beneath (or above) the
visual are called **captions**. They let readers identify significant features
and interpret the visual without referring to the text. The caption should
present efficiently specific points of information; long and complex
interpretations belong in the text itself. The caption appears below the
label, number, and title.

Footnotes. Explanatory and source information notes, or **footnotes**, may
appear on visuals for the same reasons they appear in text: to explain or
to give credit. A superscript number or letter can identify a footnote. The
note itself appears at the bottom of the visual, above the label, number,
and title if they are also placed at the bottom. If footnotes appear on more
than one visual, a consistent pattern of superscript numbers or letters
should identify them.

If the information in the visual or the visual itself comes from another
document, cite the source, including author, title, publisher, date, and
pages, at the bottom of the visual. If the title is at the bottom, place the
source note above the title. If a visual is reprinted from copyrighted material, make sure the copyright holder has granted written permission to
reprint. Add to the source statement the words "Reprinted with permission" or other words that the copyright holder cites. This statement also
appears above the title but below the explanatory footnotes.

Placement The text should refer to the visual before the visual appears. Otherwise,
readers look at the visual and wonder what they are looking at and why.
For maximum effect, however, visuals should appear as soon after the first
mention as practical, given the limitations of page size and page makeup.
If readers have to flip pages to find the visuals, they may not bother, and
the visuals will be wasted. If no reference to the visual appears in the text,
insert, at an appropriate spot, "see figure 1," or whatever the label and
number are.

Visuals should face in the same direction the text faces; readers should
not have to flip the document around to read the visuals. If the visual is too
wide to fit on the page, however, it may be turned sideways. Sideways visuals on facing pages should face the same way so that readers have to turn
the document only once. If a visual appears on a verso (lefthand) page,
place it with its bottom in the **gutter** (by the binding). On a recto (right-

hand) page, place the top of the visual in the gutter. Readers will rotate the document clockwise a quarter turn to see any visuals displayed at right angles to the text.

Before production of the document, visuals may be appended to the end of a typescript rather than inserted to allow an appropriate placement when the pages are made up in camera ready form. You will mark the text to show where the visuals are to be inserted by writing the placement instructions in the margin. For example, write "Insert figure 4.2 about here."

Quality of Reproduction

If the typescript includes camera ready visuals, the copyeditor may have to determine whether the visuals are suitable for printing. For example, photographs need a high contrast of darks and lights. Line drawings need to be drawn professionally or printed from a laser printer, because amateur drawings done with poor-quality pens produce lines with feathers and jags that printing exaggerates. Poor-quality visuals cheapen the overall quality of the document. For best reproduction, all visuals other than photographs should be drawn or printed in black ink.

Sometimes editors prepare the artwork, especially when the document and budget do not warrant full-scale printing. If no artist is available to prepare the illustrations, an amateur can, with careful work and ready-made tools, achieve professional results. Some graphics programs for computers store templates for graphs and illustrations that a user adapts for the particular situation. If you do not have a computer, you can use clip art and adhesive materials for lines and shading. **Clip art** consists of camera ready pictures of a variety of subjects that can be cut from the package you buy. To make line graphs or boxes, you can purchase strips of adhesive tape that can be pressed in place; the tape comes in a variety of widths and patterns. These materials are available in art supply stores.

HOW TO COPYEDIT

Copyediting demands careful and close reading. Because it requires attention to so many details, it will also probably require more than one editorial *pass* through the typescript. That is, in one reading, you will not be able to keep your attention focused on grammar and spelling and all the elements of consistency, accuracy, and completeness, as well as attending to format and instructions for a printer, especially if the text is long and complex. So you may plan on going through the text perhaps three times, or making three passes, looking for different things each time.

You can copyedit effectively either on hard copy or on a computer, or using a combination. Even if you copyedit electronically, though, it is a good idea to see the whole document on hard copy before you begin, to get a sense of the whole.

1. **Gather information; prepare a style sheet and parts checklist.** A good way to begin is by gathering information on the document, including the intended readers, purpose, and conditions of use. Any document specifications that are available will also help you with your copyediting choices. Specifications may include styles for the various levels of headings, parts to be included in the completed document, and decisions about printing and binding. Some decisions about mechanical style may already have been made. Your supervisor may provide you with this information, or you may need to inquire about it. These specifications will help you draw up your checklist for the completeness check and your document style sheet. The checklist and the preliminary style sheet should be ready when you begin editing.

   You should also be clear about the production schedule and about your specific duties. For example, will the writer have the chance to review the editing once you have finished it? If so, by what date? If you are editing on the computer, can you make corrections "silently"–that is, with no record of the changes–or should you insert comments that point to the changes?

2. **Survey the document.** When you are ready to look at the document itself, begin by scanning the entire typescript, perhaps reading a few pages in detail. This quick initial reading will identify particular features that need editorial attention, such as an extensive use of tables or an inconsistent documentation style. You will see, at least cursorily, the variations of visuals, headings, and lists. You can apply these preliminary impressions to help you make thoughtful line-by-line decisions. Even if you will copyedit on a computer, a survey of the complete typescript on hard copy will give you a sense of what elements are included and how they are treated.

3. **Edit for correctness, consistency, and accuracy.** At this point, you will pay close attention to the words themselves, reading for meaning and making necessary emendations to ensure that the text is correct, consistent, and accurate. You will keep your style sheet handy, adding to it as you confront new situations, and revising both the style sheet and the text emendations already made as needed. If you don't understand the meaning, you should ask the writer, either in person or with a written query, before you guess at a change.

   If the text contains an unusually large number of errors, you

may need to make more than one pass to complete the correctness, consistency, and accuracy checks.

4. **Edit the visuals and other nonprose text.** Without the distraction of verbal content, check the typescript visually. Are the
levels of headings, indentations, and type styles consistent?

You should also complete the check of visuals. Are all visuals cited in the text and in the list of illustrations present? Are
they numbered in sequence, and do they correspond to the references to them? Are all visuals marked by label, number, and
title? Are callouts marked? Are spelling and type style correct
and consistent? Are points for insertion of the visuals in the text
marked?

A graphic artist may provide instructions for treatment of
visuals—screening, doing color separations, cropping, or reducing visuals. Attach these instructions to the hard copy—perhaps
with a note paperclipped to the visual or with a Post-it™ note or
query slip.

If the document contains numerous equations, a separate
pass just to examine the equations may increase your accuracy.
The principles for copyediting mathematical text are similar to
those for editing visuals. You will check the equations themselves for accuracy and clarity, and you will also check the
enumeration of equations, if any, to make sure all the equations
are present and in order and that the references to them in the
text match the numbers on the equations. (See Chapter 8 for
more information on editing quantitative and technical material.)

5. **Prepare the typescript for the printer.** At this point, you
check that the document is complete—that all the parts are present and in order. You may also be responsible for marking the
copy to let the printer know exactly what to do at each point in
the document. (Alternatively, a graphic designer may mark the
copy for the graphic design.) You may need to include a page of
specifications about type and layout, as well as marking individual pages that may require special treatment. Unless you have
some training or experience in design, you will probably not
have to make the design decisions but only record them.

If you are transmitting text electronically, you may need to
insert some codes that will enable typesetting in a variety of
styles as specified by the graphic design.

At the point when the typescript is delivered to the printer, or to the page layout specialist in desktop publishing, copyediting is completed. The editing from this point forward is production editing, which entails coordinating the rest of the production process, including proofreading and making sure schedules are kept. The copyeditor may share some of these responsibilities as well.

SUMMARY

Copyediting renders a document more functional for readers by making it correct, consistent, accurate, and complete. It thereby improves the quality of the document. Copyediting is a useful process in preparing a document for publication because it allows specific attention to the details of the text, which may be neglected in writing and substantive editing.

The copyeditor's best resources are knowledge of the language, alertness to possible errors, and willingness to check when questions arise. Even the most experienced copyeditors have not memorized all points of grammar and the spelling of all terms; therefore, copyeditors have on their desks the most essential reference materials: a good desk dictionary; perhaps a specialized dictionary, such as a dictionary of scientific and technical terms or a medical dictionary; a handbook of grammar and usage; and style manuals. Editors keep these books at hand in order to consult them when they have questions.

FURTHER READING

Rudy Domitrovic. 1977. *How to Prepare a Style Guide.* Washington, DC: Society for Technical Communication.

David K. Farkas. 1985. The Concept of Consistency in Writing and Editing. *Journal of Technical Writing and Communication* 14(4): 353–364.

Karen Judd. 1990. *Copyediting: A Practical Guide,* 2nd ed. Los Altos, CA: Crisp. See especially Chapters 1 and 3.

DISCUSSION AND APPLICATION

1. Find a book from a major commercial or academic press and identify the parts of it. Bring it to class and be prepared to point out its parts and their functions for that book. What parts have been omitted, and why? Are the parts labeled and ordered correctly?

2. Compare a book and a technical manual. Find the book, as directed above. Also find a technical document, such as a computer manual or technical report. How do the two types of documents compare in the variety and arrangement of parts?

3. a. Distinguish between a preface and a foreword in the front matter by identifying their functions and writers. Note that both differ from an introduction, which is a substantive part of the book's body.

   b. Distinguish between a glossary and an index in the back matter.

4. Locate two discipline style manuals from the list in this chapter or by asking a reference librarian. Compare the directions for citing references in the two manuals. What similarities and differences do you note?

5. Explain why a document style sheet should not list every editorial change made in a document.

6. What features in the following two paragraphs will require a decision about mechanical consistency? Assuming that the paragraphs are just the introduction to a 10-page report, make a 1-page grid-type style sheet for these paragraphs so that subsequent decisions may be consistent. If you have questions about some of the choices, determine what printed resources you could use to find answers.

Ignitron Tubes were first used in dc-arc welding power supplies. An ignitron tube is a vacuum tube that can function as a closing switch in pulsed power (using a pulse of current rather than a continous current) applications. A closing switch is a switch that is not <u>on</u> or will not pass current until it is triggered to be on. When the tube is triggered to be "on," it provides a path for the current. The ignitron tube is turned on by a device called an "ignitor." The ignitor sits in liquid mercury inside the vacuum tube. The ignitron tube creates a path for the current by vaporizing mercury. More mercury will be vaporized as the current crosses the tube. When there is no current the vaporized mercury goes to the bottom of the tube and turns back into liquid.

When an Ignitron Tube turns on and passes

current, this process is referred to as a shot. The greatest amount of current that ignitrons can presently handle is nearly 1,000,000 amps. The tube can handle this amount of current for five shots before the tube fails. Industry wants a tube that will handle 1000 shots before it fails.

4 COPYMARKING

When an editor reviews a draft of a document, either to make suggestions to the writer for revision or to direct the typing or typesetting before printing, he or she marks the document with instructions. These instructions tell the next person who works on the copy how to incorporate the editing. The person who uses the editor's marks may be the writer (in revision), typist, graphic designer, or typesetter.

The editor's instructions, marked on the document itself, are written with a special set of symbols. Marking the document with these instructions in symbolic form is known as **markup** or **copymarking.**

An editor may mark a document for the writer's revision. Such marks include instructions about substantive revision, such as reorganization, insertion of new information or deletion of existing information, and revision of style. The marks may also include queries to a writer when the editor is uncertain about meaning or purpose.

If the substance of the text has been established and revisions approved by the writer, the editing marks are primarily copyediting marks, to establish correctness, consistency, accuracy, and completeness. The primary reader of these marks is a **keyboard operator** (typist, word processing specialist, or typesetter), who incorporates the information when preparing the text for publication. In addition, the document may contain instructions for graphic design, type specifications (face, size, and style), line length, page depth, and other design features. Copymarking is usually considered to refer to these copyediting and graphic design marks placed on the document after substantive editing is completed.

The computer is changing some traditional ways of marking copy as transmission of text is increasingly done through electronic means rather than on hard copy. Instead of marking the hard copy so that another person (keyboard operator) can key in the changes, the editor may simply make the changes or insert the suggestions for revision electronically. However, even with the possibilities for onscreen editing and transmission of text, many editors prefer to work with hard copy at some point in production, especially for substantive editing. Thus, all editors should know the accepted symbols of copymarking.

This chapter gives examples of copymarking symbols for copyediting and for graphic design. This chapter covers only copymarking on hard copy; Chapter 16, "Computers as Editorial Assistants," covers electronic copymarking.

THE SYMBOLS OF COPYMARKING

Editors, printers, and graphic designers all understand a special set of symbols to indicate corrections and design choices. Some of the symbols and methods of giving instructions may seem cryptic to you at first, and you may be tempted to write out fuller instructions. However, such variations in conventions will confuse rather than help designers and keyboard operators—you will earn their respect and enhance their comprehension by using the conventional symbols. Table 4.1 shows the symbols for indicating changes in letters, spacing, and type style of words. Table 4.2 shows symbols for copymarking punctuation. Table 4.3 shows how to mark for spacing.

Placing the Marks on the Page

Copyediting marks appear within the lines of the text. Typically, typescripts are double spaced to leave room within the lines. Interlinear marks assume that the next reader will read every word of the text. Interlinear marks help a keyboard operator because they appear right where the change must be made. If marks were in the margin (as they are for proofreading), the reader's eyes would have to move from the margin to the point of correction and back.

Instructions to the keyboard operator other than for corrections appear in the margin. These directions cover line length, justification (whether

TABLE 4.1 COPYMARKING SYMBOLS: WORDS AND LETTERS

Symbol/Meaning		Example	Result	Comment
ℯ	delete	dele*t*e	delete	Use the closeup mark, too, if the word could be spelled as two words.
ℰ	delete, close	proof/reading	proofreading	
—	delete a word	in the ~~the~~ back	in the back	
∧	insert	in*s*ert	insert	
/ or #	insert space	insert/space mark/up a text	insert space mark up a text	Usually the line alone will suffice; use the space symbol if there could be a question.
∾	transpose	tra*sn*pose *Australia* ~~Au~~s~~tra~~lia	transpose Australia	If multiple transpositions in a word make the edited version difficult to read, delete the whole word and print the correction above it.
⌒	close up	cl⌒ose	close	
≡	capital letters	ohio; ibm	Ohio; IBM	
=	small caps	6 a.m.	6 A.M.	Because not all fonts include small caps, make sure they are available before you mark them.
/	lowercase	/Federal	federal	
WORD	lowercase, whole word	FEDERAL	federal	
WORD	initial cap	FEDERAL	Federal	

the margins are to be aligned on the right or left or both), and typeface. They may also cover math symbols, extra leading, special design material, instructions for handwritten material—anything not covered by standard copymarking symbols. Such directions often apply to whole blocks of text rather than to single words or phrases, which is why they are marginal rather than interlinear.

Sometimes content insertions that are too long to fit between the lines of the text can be written in the margin, if there is room. Longer insertions should be typed and labeled with identifying letters. For example, a paragraph that needs to be inserted on the first page might be labeled "A." At the point of insertion, you write "insert A" and circle the direction. The

TABLE 4.1 (continued)

Symbol/Meaning		Example	Result	Comment
___	italics	Star Wars	*Star Wars*	Underline to change the type style from roman to italic or vice versa.
___	roman type	*Star Wars*	Star Wars	Roman type is the opposite of italic, with straight rather than slanted vertical lines.
or *rom*		*Star Wars*	Star Wars	To convert from italic to roman, you underline, just as you do to convert roman to italic. You can also write and circle "ital" or "rom."
～～	boldface	emphasis	**emphasis**	
∨	superscript	Master's degree	Master's degree	Use the superscript sign to identify apostrophes, quotation marks, or exponents.
		A2	A^2	
∧	subscript	H2O	H_2O	
' ' ' '	delete an underline	revelry	revelry	OR: White out the line. Be careful not to cover up descenders or punctuation.
◯	spell out an abbreviation or number	② Assn. hp	two Association horsepower	Circle an abbreviation or number you want spelled out. Spell the word as well as circling if the spelling may be in question.
. . . . or *stet*	"let it stand"; ignore the editing	precede	precede	If you have edited incorrectly or have changed your mind, direct keyboard operator to set the copy in its original unedited form.

paragraph labeled "A" may be placed on a separate page following page 1. Sometimes it is taped to the edge of the page, like a flap, so that the keyboard operator can find the original by lifting the flap. Or you may literally "cut and paste." That is, you might cut the original text with scissors, paste or tape the insertion into place, and then attach the rest of the original. If, however, you need to move existing blocks of text, you circle the block,

TABLE 4.2 COPYMARKING SYMBOLS: PUNCTUATION

Symbol/Meaning		Example	Result	Comment
⊙	period	...forever⊙	... forever.	Circle the period to call the keyboard operator's attention to this small mark. Do not circle other punctuation.
⌄	comma	copper⌄ iron⌄ and silver	copper, iron, and silver	Place an inverted caret over the comma. Do not place it over other punctuation.
⊙	colon	following⊙	following:	The oval makes the colon more clear.
⌄	semicolon	following⊙ following⊙ following⌄	following; following; following;	To create a semicolon from a comma or colon, draw in the dot or tail and place an oval around it. Otherwise, simply insert the semicolon.
⊱ ⊰	parentheses	⊱1986⊰	(1986)	The lines in the parentheses won't be typeset, but they do reinforce your intent to include parentheses rather than other lines.
⊏ ⊐	brackets	⊏word⊐	[word]	Be sure to square the lines if the writer has used parentheses.
⹀ or ⌄	hyphen	light⹀emitting diode computer⌄ assisted	light-emitting diode computer-assisted	The underline or checking of the hyphen reinforces your intent to include a hyphen at that point. Mark end-of-line hyphens for clarity.
(eq)	equal sign	a=b (eq)	a=b	Because the equal sign can look like the underlined hyphen, write "eq." by the mark and circle it to show that the information is an instruction.
$\frac{1}{M}$ or M	em dash	a pejorative$\overset{M}{=}$ disparaging$\overset{M}{=}$ word	a pejorative— disparaging— word	An em dash is as wide as the base of the capital letter *M* in the type size and typeface used. It is used to set off parenthetical material or a break in thought.
$\frac{1}{N}$ or N	en dash	1989$\overset{1}{\underset{N}{}}$91	1989–91	An en dash is as wide as the base of the capital letter *N* in the typeface and type size used. Its primary use is in numbers expressed as a range.

TABLE 4.3 COPYMARKING SYMBOLS: SPACING AND POSITION

Symbol/Meaning	Example	Result
⁋ begin a new paragraph	...other design features. ⁋The editor's...	...other design features. The editor's ...
⌐ begin a new line	numbers;⌐abbreviations;	numbers; abbreviations;
⌇ run together (do not create a new paragraph)	...other design features.⌐ ⌐ The editor's...	other design features. The editor's ...
⌐ or ⒧ flush left or justify left	⌐ The editor's choice...	The editor's choice ...
⌐ justify right	Book Title ⌐	Book Title
⌐ ⌐ center	⌐——————⌐	————————
⊢ fill out the line	...form your marks. not the ——————⊣ time to express your	...form your marks. ...not the time to express your ...

‖ align	‖ ————————
	  ————————
	  ————————
		————————
		————————
		————————

⧠ indent one em	⧠————————	————————
⧠ or ⧅2 indent two ems	⧅2————————	————————

⧅2 indent the whole block of text two ems	⧅2 ————————
	   ————————
	   ————————
		————————
		————————
		————————

⌐⌐ transpose a group of words	transpose of words⌐a group	transpose a group of words
(close up vertical space (e.g., when an extra space has been skipped between paragraphs)	...too many lines skipped. (Close up vertical space.	...too many lines skipped. Close up vertical space.
⌇ set as a paragraph rather than as a list	numbers;⌐ ⌐abbreviations;⌐ ⌐spelling.	numbers; abbreviations; spelling.

identify the place where the block is to move by a letter, and write in the margin "move to B." Be sure to mark the "B" location.

Marks must be neat and easy to read. They should not be too small to see nor so big that they make the whole page look messy. In addition, you should train yourself to form your marks in conventional ways. Copymarking is not the time to express your personality in handwriting with such quirks as small circles substituting for dots over the letter *i*. Be careful when you mark not to obscure the correct type on the page. Clean copy will increase the chances of error-free copy at the next stage of production, so taking the time to mark neatly will ultimately save both time and money in production.

You can help the keyboard operator or other reader locate specific points of change by using a bright-color pencil, such as red or green. Not only are faint pencil marks difficult to read, but, because they suggest timidity or lack of self-confidence, they may make the reader question your authority or competence. If you are marking the hard copy of an electronic file, be especially careful to make the marks noticeable. The person who corrects the file will not be reading line by line, so that person needs to be able to find the specific instances of error to correct.

If the document is on a computer, corrections will normally be incorporated into the electronic copy before the document goes to a typesetter, either on hard copy or electronically. The copy will therefore be as clean as possible. Copymarking on corrected hard copy that goes to a typesetter is likely to be limited to information about graphic design, and this will appear in the margins.

If the document is not on a computer, taking the time to retype messy sections will increase the chance of accurate typesetting. You can type paragraphs or other sections and paste or tape the retyped version over the original messy part.

Figure 4.1 shows a marked typescript, and figure 4.2 shows how the same typescript looks after being typeset.

Marking Consistently   Generally you will mark each occurrence of changes rather than depending on the keyboard operator to remember what you have done on previous pages. If you mark erratically, the keyboard operator may assume you intend some distinction among marked and unmarked items and therefore set the text exactly as marked — or not marked. Furthermore, especially with a long document, more than one keyboard operator may work on the job. Finally, the operators are trained to type what they see rather than to edit as they go along. The editing is your job.

If, for example, you are changing the spelling of "judgement" to "judgment" throughout, mark each instance where the word occurs. If para-

Figure 4.1   Marked Copy

KEEPING PRODUCTION COST DOWN

Good editing in the early stages of document production saves time and money later on. When the document is still in the manuscript stage (or, more accurately, the typescript stage, the corrections cost only the editors time. The costs increase geometrically thereafter; each error costs not only the editor's or proof reader's time but also the typist's or typesetter's time. A 50 cent error at copyediting time may cost $30 after the plates have been burned. After the document is typeset, the materials costs of galleys or page proofs are added to the labor costs. If the document reaches the blue line stage with errors and must be corrected, the printer will charge the the costs of stripping and plate making again. Once the document is printed, the costs of paper and press time must be added. If an error is the printer's fault, he or she is responsible for the cost of correcting errors.

But the publisher is responsible for all other errors. A printer's error at the galley stage becomes a publisher's error if the publisher accepts the galleys as correct before page proofs are prepared.

Editor's work carefully when they mark a text for a typesetter, paying close attention to detail, and consulting a dictionary, handbook, or style guide when they have questions. They read for meaning to make sure the writer has not made careless errors, such as inadvertently substituting in for on or leaving out words. They are also careful to mark the text clearly and accurately so that both text and instructions can be read correctly. Thus, they can increase the changes of getting clean galleys from the typeseter and of saving production time and costs.

Figure 4.2
Copy Set as Marked
in Figure 4.1

Keeping Production Costs Down

Good editing in the early stages of document production saves time and money later on. When the document is still in the manuscript stage (or, more accurately, the typescript stage), the corrections cost only the editor's time. The costs increase geometrically thereafter; each error costs not only the editor or proofreader's time but also the typist or typesetter's time. After the document is typeset, the materials costs of galleys or page proofs are added to the labor costs. If the document reaches the blueline stage with errors and must be corrected, the printer will charge the costs of stripping and platemaking again. A 50¢ error at copyediting time may cost $30 after the plates have been burned. Once the document is printed, the costs of paper and press time must be added.

If an error is the printer's fault, he or she is responsible for the cost of correcting errors. The publisher is responsible for all other errors. A printer's error at the galley stage becomes a publisher's error if the publisher accepts the galleys as correct before page proofs are prepared.

Editors work carefully when they mark a text for a typesetter, paying close attention to detail and consulting a dictionary, handbook, or style guide when they have questions. They read for meaning to make sure the writer has not made careless errors, such as inadvertently substituting *in* for *on* or leaving out words. They are also careful to mark the text clearly and accurately so that both text and instructions can be read correctly. Thus, they can increase the chances of getting clean galleys from the typesetter and of saving production time and costs.

graph indentations are not clear in the typescript, mark each change. Mark each heading that must be boldface, and note the type size and typeface where appropriate. If spellings are unusual, you may write and circle "stet" next to the unusual spelling to indicate that the unusual spelling is intentional.

You should also keep a record of copyediting choices on your style sheet so that you can maintain consistency and save yourself the time of rechecking prior decisions or of reconsulting a style manual. Do not record every change on your style sheet; just include items for which more than one option was available or for which you had to consult a dictionary or other reference book for proper spelling.

Consistency is especially important with spacing and graphic design marks if the design itself includes variations. Some designers, for example, specify indenting all paragraphs except those that follow headings. You would check all paragraph indentation and mark any places where the pattern had been deviated from.

Distinguishing Marginal Notes from Text Emendations

Sometimes marginal notes will be necessary to clarify your marks on the text. For example, if you want an equal sign but the marked text looks just like a hyphen with an underscore, you should write "equal sign" in the margin. Be sure to circle this note to identify it as a note rather than as words to be inserted.

If you need to include marginal messages to both writer and keyboard operator, you may distinguish these by using different colors of pencil for each category of message. You may also preface the note with a label identifying the audience for the message—usually "au" for author and "comp" for compositor or typesetter.

```
Pierce's philosophy
```

(circled marginal note:) au: correct?

```
"Influences on Darwin's Origin
of Species"
```

(circled marginal note:) comp: set rom

Remember to circle these messages to distinguish them from text insertions.

Marginal notes may also give instructions for the placement of visuals if those instructions are not clear in the text.

SPECIAL PROBLEMS OF COPYMARKING

Though the copymarking symbols discussed previously will be clear in most situations, you must be particularly careful in marking text where multiple interpretations of the marks may be possible. Specifically, you may need to insert additional instructions when marking ambiguous letters and symbols, when distinguishing between hyphens and dashes, and when marking nonprose text and visuals.

Ambiguous Letters and Symbols

Some letters and symbols look similar. On the typewriter, some look the same, though typesetting can distinguish them. Thus, the editor should clarify anything about which the keyboard operator may have to make a judgment. One example is the numeral 1 and the letter *l*. On many typewriters, the same key types both, but in a font for typesetting, they have different shapes and are inserted with different keys. Sometimes context will establish which is meant, and the editor does not need to clarify. For example, if you have to insert an *l* in *galey*, the keyboard operator will know that you don't mean the numeral 1. But in the following example, it will be a good idea to clarify by writing "el" by the letter (circled to indicate that this is information for a keyboard operator rather than text to insert). In this example, the editor has indicated a capital letter *L* as an abbreviation for liter, not the numeral 1. The keyboard operator, thinking "numeral" after typing the 2, may type in a numeral unless the note clarifies the editor's intent.

```
Evaporate a 2-1 sample.
```

Likewise, the letter *O* and the numeral 0 may be confused. You may need to write "zero" by the number and circle the word to show that you mean for a zero to be typed in that place. And in equations, the *x* (indicating a variable or an unknown) must be shown to differ from the multiplication sign ×. (See Chapter 8 on editing mathematical material for more information on copymarking equations.)

Hyphens and Dashes   Although hyphens differ in use and size from dashes, the distinction between hyphens and dashes is not always clear on a typescript and thus should be marked. *Hyphens* are the mark for combination words. They also appear in words that are broken at the end of one line and continued on the next.

A line inserted under a hyphen during copymarking indicates that the hyphen should be set as marked. If the hyphen is already typed correctly, however, you don't need to underline it unless the word is hyphenated at the end of a line on the typescript. Here, you need to clarify whether the hyphen should be retained if the word breaks differently in typeset copy. Underline an end-of-line hyphen that should be retained. Likewise, if the word is not normally hyphenated but conceivably could be, use the closeup mark with the hyphen at the end of the line on a typescript to show that the word should be set closed.

```
Marking the document with instructions is called copy-
marking. The copyeditor marks with the assumption that
the keyboard operator will enter text exactly as it is
marked, letter for letter and mark for mark. End-of-
line hyphens are particularly confusing and should be
marked.
```

You can minimize the confusion of end-of-line hyphens by preparing typescripts without hyphens except for words that are always hyphenated. Instruct writers to turn off the hyphenation on their word processors; then no hyphens will appear at the end of the line. In the preceding example, "copymarking" could have been typed on the second line without a hyphen, saving copymarking time.

Em dashes separate words or phrases from the rest of the sentence — they function like parentheses in casual style. They are about the length of a capital letter *M* in the typeface in which they are set. On a typewriter, they are formed with two hyphens. *En dashes*, which are the length of a capital letter *N* in the relevant typeface, are mostly used in numbers, to show a range. If there can be ambiguity in interpreting which dash is intended, you should mark each occurrence.

```
Place two lead weights--each weighing 4-7 grams--

on the model car body between the rear wheels.
```

Hyphens and dashes are set without space on either side. If a typist has typed spaces around them, mark the copy to close up the space.

```
Dashes -- marks of punctuation used to set off

parenthetical material --are longer marks than

hyphens, and on a typewriter they are typed with

two hyphens. Sometimes a typist uses just one

hyphen. The copyeditor must mark such instances

as em dashes.
```

You can provide a style sheet for the keyboard operator for uses that appear frequently in the document. For example, if the document contains many dates expressed as ranges (e.g., 1974–1976), include an example on the style sheet with a note that all use an en dash. For isolated or infrequent uses, you should mark each occurrence rather than expecting the keyboard operator to remember every item on the style sheet. In general, you must prepare the typescript as though the next person to read it will begin reading only at the point of the mark you are making, rather than at the beginning. If there can be any doubt about how to interpret the text, you should clarify.

Marking Nonprose Text In copyediting, you are likely to read the prose parts of a document most carefully because you are a language specialist and because you are interested in content. You will pay attention to the paragraphs, but you may read less closely other types of text, such as the headings, tables, and list of references. Yet errors are more likely to be made in the nonprose parts of the text. The writer, too, will devote more attention to the prose parts and may overlook errors in the nonprose parts. Not only is it easier to make both content and typing errors in a reference list than in a table, it is more difficult to catch errors there. Thus, you must check for the accuracy and completeness of the information in these parts of the text. Be sure also to mark such text carefully, checking details such as type style (e.g., italics, roman, bold), accuracy of the numbers, and spacing. Also, pay close attention to lists, watching for incorrect end-of-line punctuation and indentation as well as for spelling, grammar, and punctuation errors.

Marking Visuals   As editor, you are responsible not just for the text but for the entire document, including tables and figures. The symbols used to mark visuals are the same as those for marking text. You may need to correct spelling by deleting or inserting letters, to adjust spacing, or to request alignment of numerals on their decimal points. Pay careful attention to headings, labels, and titles when you mark visuals, looking for correctness but also for mechanical and visual consistency and completeness of information. For example, is the capitalization of titles of visuals consistent from visual to visual? Do titles all use the same type style (e.g., regular, bold, italic)? You should also add numbers to make sure their totals match what is displayed. If you discover an error, you will need to check with the writer to determine whether the addition or one of the figures is wrong. (Checking by simple calculations is analogous to looking up the spelling of a word in a dictionary.)

If the visuals are attached to the end of the typescript for insertion at the time of page layout, mark the place where they are to be inserted. You can do this in the margin if the text does not already indicate the location. Simply write "insert figure 1 about here." You can only specify an approximate location because the page may not have enough room for the visual at the exact point where you have marked.

MARKS FOR GRAPHIC DESIGN   The editor or graphic designer or the printer's staff may mark the document for its graphic design—that is, the face, style, and size of type, the spacing, and the line length. If you have some training in graphic design, you may make the decisions about design and mark them too. Or you may place marks on the document according to a graphic designer's instructions. You can mark boldface, italics, and capitalization using the marks displayed in table 4.1.

The marks for typeface, type size, and line length will make more sense to you once you are familiar with typeface names and with the printer's measures of points and picas (see Chapter 17). But the example following will illustrate how you will mark such information, assuming a graphic designer provides it to you. The instructions direct the typesetter to set type of a particular size and face on a line of the specified length:

set 10/12 × 24.5 Times

Here is what this note means:

set = set type

10/12 = 10-point type on a line 12 points deep (there will be some
        extra space between the lines of type)

× 24.5 = the line length—24½ picas

Times = the typeface—Times Roman

In fact, these instructions would produce type just like what you are reading here. Once again, be sure to circle such instructions to clarify that they are not part of the text. Place them in the left margin so the keyboard operator will see them before typing the letters.

If your document uses more than one face and size for display type (the headings) or more than one face and size for body copy (the paragraphs), mark each instance. For example, your level-one headings may be 12-point bold centered while the level-two headings are 10-point bold left-justified. Mark each instance so that the keyboard operator can determine the level of heading. Likewise, if the body copy changes, say, from 10-point type to 9-point type in an indented section, mark the size for the indented section, and then mark the return to 10-point type.

QUERIES TO WRITERS

Sometimes you will not be able to make copyediting decisions until you contact the writer for further information. At other times you may mark the text but wish to confirm that the marks are correct or explain a change that will not be obvious. A question to a writer is called a **query**. The term is also used to refer to all comments from the copyeditor to the writer. Marginal notes can work for simple queries, but some questions and explanations are too elaborate to be phrased as marginal notes on the text. For these—or for all your queries, even simple ones—you can attach query slips to the typescript that can be removed before the typescript is forwarded for typesetting. The query slips prevent the clutter of notes on the typescript itself that could distract the compositor; the slips also provide space for the writer to respond.

Post-it™ notes work well as query slips. They can be attached to the edge of the typescript, with the sticky part on the back, and folded over the edge of the page. They should be attached to the typescript at the place where the question arises. When the writer opens the slip, he or she reads the query and responds by revising the text or confirming that the editing is correct. The slip remains in place until the copyeditor checks the response and makes the necessary changes. (Figure 4.3 shows a marked page with a query slip attached.)

You should not question or comment on every mark you place on the page but should use your queries to acquire information that you need to edit or mark correctly. You may also attach explanations of marks that may puzzle a writer. In phrasing your queries, write directly and courteously, and avoid evaluative statements, especially when the evaluations are negative. For example, instead of writing "unclear" or giving the vague directions to "rewrite" or "clarify," tell the writer exactly what you need to know. Some examples follow:

- **Requests for information:**
  (to check a discrepancy in an in-text citation and a reference list)

  ```
  Page 16 cites the date of 1986 while the
  reference list cites 1987. Please check the
  date and indicate the correct one.
  ```

  (to verify an unclear use of quotation marks and capitalization)

  ```
  May I assume that the quote marks signal a
  quotation and that ABC should be capitalized?
  ```

  (to clarify the reference for a pronoun)

  ```
  I'm not sure whether "it" refers to the program
  or to the previous step. Please clarify.
  ```

  (to verify format)

  ```
  Do you have any special instructions for this
  figure-e.g., single or double space, paragraph
  indentations or flush left? Please advise.
  ```

- **Explanations:**

  (to explain why a numbered list has been converted to text with headings)

  ```
  Other numbered lists in this book present very
  short discussions for each item. The importance
  and development of each of these topics warrant
  the use of two-level headings. The headings
  will emphasize each topic more than the
  numbered list does. OK?
  ```

  (to explain changes in headings)

  ```
  I expanded the main heading and deleted the
  subheadings to parallel the pattern in other
  chapters. OK?
  ```

Ask the writer to indicate by initialing or checking the slip or by a verbal response that he or she has considered the query.

It's a good idea to note the typescript page number on the query slip so that you will know where it belongs if it is accidentally detached. If you are writing queries to a designer or production editor as well as to the writer, also note on each slip who should read it. The note "au/24" identifies a query to the author on page 24 of the typescript. Some copyeditors attach the slips for the writer on the right side of the page and slips for the designer on the left. That practice helps the designer and writer determine which slips to read and which to ignore.

Figure 4.3 illustrates a copyedited typescript page with marginal notes for the compositor, alignment marks on the tabular material, and marks to identify typeface, type size, and type style. The flag at the right of the page is a query from the copyeditor to the writer. It asks for the writer's approval of a possible change in the examples if small capital letters and italics are not available in the compositor's typewriter font.

The straight vertical lines and the circled letters at the left indicate specific design elements. BL means "bulleted list," LT means "list text," TYP means to use typewriter font for the examples, MCL means "multicolumn list," UL means "unnumbered list," and AC means "art callout." The circled note by the abbreviation for inches directs the compositor to use the symbol for inches, not for quotation marks. The note in the right margin tells the compositor to use the text font for the items in the left column and the typewriter font for the other columns (the examples).

Figure 4.3

Copyedited Typescript Showing Notes to a
Compositor and Marks for Graphic Design

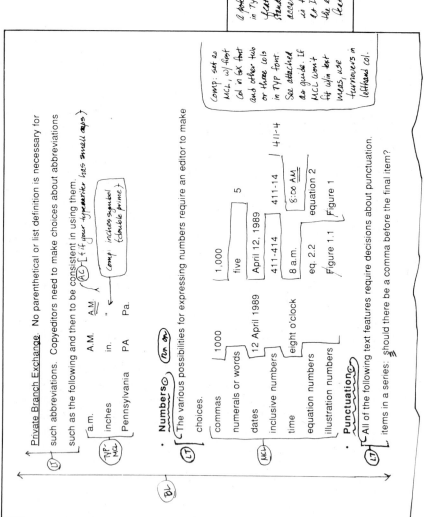

Turnovers would be phrases in the first column spilling onto a second line. The irregular vertical lines within the columns specify alignment for the three columns of examples. You can see the results of these marks by looking back to page 42.

SUMMARY

A version of a document that follows the typescript can only be as good as the copymarking. If the copymarking is incomplete or ambiguous, you are likely to encounter errors in the proof copy. Such errors will cost time and money because they will require doing at least part of the job more than once. Conversely, thorough and accurate copymarking should result in clean proof copy, and the production of the document will continue on schedule.

FURTHER READING

Mary Stoughton. 1989. *Substance & Style: Instruction and Practice in Copyediting.* Alexandria, VA: Editorial Experts.

DISCUSSION AND
APPLICATION

1. Mark the words in the first column so that they will be printed like the words in the second column.

developement	development
interogation	interrogation
emphasis	*emphasis*
italic	italic
1/2	one-half
three	3
teh	the
ambivalance	ambivalence
on going	ongoing
tabletennis	table tennis
2mm	2 mm
semi-colon	semicolon

CHAPTER TITLE	Chapter Title
Cpr	CPR
Research Laboratory	research laboratory
testing confidential	confidential testing
Tavist D	Tavist-D
referees decision	referee's decision
m2	m^2
M2	M_2
We finished quickly - we had more errands to complete.	We finished quickly--we had more errands to complete.
end of sentence	end of sentence.
end of clause,	end of clause;
introduction	introduction:
quote	"quote"

2. Mark the first paragraph so that it will be printed like the second paragraph. The second paragraph is set in the typeface Helvetica, and the measures are 10/12 × 23, flush left, ragged right. The title is Helvetica 12.

FIRST AID
It is always wise to be cautious and aware of infectoin
control measures when asisting trauma victims. If contact
with human
blood, urine, feces or other body secretions occur, through
washing withsoap and water is importent; and soiled
clothing should be changed as soon as practicle. We know,
for example that the Aids virus
   is readily killed by soap and water and by common
   disinfectants. You should avoid touching your mouth or

eyes with your hands or any items contaminated by glood, feces, or other body secretions, personal with wounds or abrasions on exposed body surfaces, such as the hands or face, should try to protect those areas from contact with blood or secretions when emergency treatment is being given. It is good practice to wear disposable gloves while handling items contaminated, this is especially important for personnel with wounds or abrasions on the hands.

First Aid

It is always wise to be cautious and aware of infection control measures when assisting trauma victims. If contact with human blood, urine, feces, or other body secretions occurs, thorough washing with soap and water is important, and soiled clothing should be changed as soon as practical. We know, for example, that the AIDS virus is readily killed by soap and water and by common disinfectants. You should avoid touching your mouth or eyes with your hands or any items contaminated by blood, feces, or other body secretions. Personnel with wounds or abrasions on exposed body surfaces, such as the hands or face, should try to protect those areas from contact with blood or secretions when emergency treatment is being given. It is good practice to wear disposable gloves while handling contaminated items; this is especially important for personnel with wounds or abrasions on the hands.*

3. Your job is copyeditor—to make the document correct, consistent, accurate, and complete. You do not alter word choices or organization. Yet, you know enough about style to object to the use of the passive voice in the second sentence of the paragraph in exercise 2. You argue to yourself that readers would identify more with the instruction and be more likely to follow it if the sentence read, "... wash thoroughly with soap and water, and change soiled clothing as soon as practical." What can you do?

---

* Source: Theodore M. Hammett. 1987. *AIDS in Correctional Facilities: Issues and Options,* 2d ed. Washington, DC: U.S. Department of Justice, 112.

4. Circling an abbreviation instructs the compositor to spell it out. Assume you want the abbreviation *STC* spelled out. Why might circling be inadequate? What should you do instead?

5. You personally prefer to spell *proofread* as a hyphenated compound *(proof-read)* rather than solid. Do you have the choice of spelling it according to preference if it appears in a document you are editing? Why or why not?

5 SPELLING, CAPITALIZATION, AND ABBREVIATIONS

If you have ever come across a spelling error in a printed document, you know the feeling most readers have when they discover errors. Making (or missing) errors in spelling and capitalization is like having a piece of spinach stuck between your front teeth when you ask your boss for a raise — the person responds by laughing, inwardly or outwardly. Such errors mean something is amiss; someone was not careful. Credibility suffers. Readers' comprehension may suffer, too, if only because they are distracted from the content.

Finding that lone error in a printed document is easier than finding all of the errors in copyediting a typescript. The error sticks out in a printed document because most of the rest of the document is correct and perhaps attractive. In a typescript, however, you are distracted from one error by others and even by the mess of a heavily copyedited page. Or you may become so familiar with a typescript that your eye reads the words as correct even when they are not.

Even if you are a good speller and know the rules of capitalization and abbreviation, you will have to work at perfecting a typescript. One way to do so is to become aware of the issues. A second way is to check resources when you have questions, especially dictionaries, including a desk dictionary and specialized subject matter dictionaries, and style manuals, such as *The Chicago Manual of Style* and *The GPO Style Manual*. After checking, you record the correct version (or your choice when there are alternatives) on the document style sheet so that you will make the same choice consistently throughout the document and so that you will save the time of rechecking resources when the word occurs again.

This chapter identifies ways to recognize misspelled words and alerts you to times when you should check capitalization and abbreviations.

SPELLING

Spelling is notoriously difficult in English because of the many irregularities and inconsistencies. Imagine trying to teach a non-native speaker how to spell and pronounce these words: *tough, though, through.* Or try to explain to someone why the *sh* sound in English can be spelled in at least 10 different ways, as illustrated by the words *shower, pshaw, sugar, chaperone, special, tissue, vacation, suspicion, mansion,* and *ocean.* Nevertheless, guidelines and tools are available to help editors correct spelling.

Basic Guidelines and Tools

The following list outlines some of the resources available, as well as some of the "tricks of the trade," that you can draw on as you address spelling issues.

1. **Use a spelling checker on your computer.** One of the most valuable tools the computer offers editors is the spelling checker. By matching words in the document with words stored in the memory, a computer can recognize words that do not match and that may be misspelled. You simply load the document file into the computer, load an electronic dictionary from a word processing program or a spelling check program, and then wait for the computer to identify mismatched words. For each mismatched word, you must choose whether to change the spelling or to let it stand. Some spelling checkers will suggest alternative spellings, but sometimes the user must key in the change.

    A computerized spelling check is a good first step in editing any document in electronic form. If spelling errors can be corrected at the beginning, they will not distract the editor from correcting other errors. Running the check as the last step in editing can also help to catch errors that have been introduced in editing.

    A computerized spelling checker will not relieve you of responsibility for checking spelling. Because it matches only characters and does not read for meaning, it will not know, for example, whether *there* is correct or whether *their* was intended. It will approve *type script* even though you meant *typescript* because the two words match words in its memory, and it will not catch *in* substituted for *on*. A computer would approve the spelling in this sentence.

Their our know miss steaks in this sent ants.

The memory may also not contain all the words in the document. A typical desk dictionary contains 200,000 words, whereas a typical computerized dictionary stores only 80,000 words, including variations (such as different tenses) of the same word. Thus, the computer may question words that are spelled properly, especially technical terms and names.

Don't depend entirely on the computer for your spelling check, but do use it to save time and to catch misspelled words that you might otherwise miss. The spelling check can also clean up your copy and make it easier to find the errors that remain.

2. **Use a dictionary.** Look up the spelling of a term that is unfamiliar to you. Use a subject dictionary (e.g., a dictionary of medical terms) for specialized terms. When you look up a word, mark it in your dictionary to encourage review when you are using the dictionary another time. You can also add the word to your own list of commonly misspelled words and to the document style sheet to enable a quick check another time you are uncertain about the spelling.

3. **Keep a list of frequently misspelled words.** Even good spellers have difficulty learning the spelling of certain words. Table 5.1 lists some words that are frequently misspelled; you may have other words to add to your individual list. (In addition to these frequently *misspelled* words, see the list of frequently *misused* words, later in the chapter.) The list itself reveals some problem areas:

endings *(-ar, -or,* or *-er; -ment* or *-mant; -able* or *-ible; -ance* or *-ence; -ceed* or *-cede; -ary* or *-ery)*

consonants — single or double

the schwa ("uh") sound — created by *a, e, i, u*

ie and *ei*

When you are checking spelling, check especially the endings and consonants and the schwa sound. Spelling rules and mnemonic devices, like those in guidelines 4 and 6, will help you spell these words.

TABLE 5.1 FREQUENTLY MISSPELLED WORDS

accommodate (a double *m*)	changeable	liaison	receive ("*i* before *e* except after *c* . . . ")
achievement	convenient	license	separate (note the *a* in the second syllable)
acknowledgment (no *e* before the suffix)	defendant	lightning	
acquire	embarrass (double *r* and double *s*)	maneuver	severely (keep the final *e* before the suffix)
a lot (two words, like *a little*)	feasibility, feasible	miniature	
all right	forty (not *fourty*)	mischievous	
analysis	gauge	misspell	sincerely
approximately	grammar (the ending has an *a* in it)	occurred	subpoena
argument	grievous	parallel	resistance
assistance	harass	pastime	subtly
basically	inasmuch as	personnel	surveillance
category (note the *e* in the second syllable)	indispensable	plausible	undoubtedly
	irrelevant	precede (compare *proceed*)	
	irresistible	questionnaire (note the double *n*)	
	judgment		

4. **Develop mnemonics.** A *mnemonic* is a memory device, usually an association. By remembering the association, you can remember the spelling. Here are seven examples:

accommodate: When you accommodate someone, you do more than is expected; there are more *m*s than you expect.

all right: It's two words, like *all wrong*.

liaison: The "eyes" on either side of the *a* look both ways, the way a liaison looks to both sides.

principal (a school official): The principal is (or is not) your pal.

stationery (writing paper): Remember, *er* as in pap*er*.

dessert (sweet food): More of the letter *s* than in *desert* (a dry region); a dessert tastes so good that you want more.

affect, effect: Effect is usually a noun, while affect is usually a verb.

An auditory mnemonic: the effect (long *e* for both words); *the* precedes a noun, not a verb.

A visual mnemonic: an *e*ffect is the result or the *e*nd.

5. **Learn root words, prefixes, and suffixes.** Words are frequently formed from basic words and from the addition of suffixes and prefixes. Recognizing the structure of the words can help you spell them. Here are some examples:

subpoena: Although you don't hear the b when you pronounce this word, you can recognize the prefix *sub-,* meaning "under." A *subpoena* requires a person to give testimony in court, *under penalty* if he or she refuses.

misspell: Instead of wondering whether the word has one *s* or two, consider that the prefix *mis-* is added to the root word *spell.* The structure of the word explains the double consonant. The words *misfortune, mistake,* and *misconduct* have only one *s* because their root words do not begin with *s.* The same principle applies to words with the *dis-* prefix: *dissatisfied* and *dissimilar,* but *disappear* and *disease.*

inanimate: One *n* or two? The root of this word is a Latin term, *animalis,* meaning "living." The prefix *in-* means "not." An inanimate object is not living. There is only one *n* in the prefix, and the root word does not begin with an *n,* thus the single *n* in the first syllable. There is only one *n* in the root word, as in *animal.*

millennium: The root *mille* means "thousand." A second root is the Latin *annus,* meaning "year," as in *annual.* Those roots can help you remember that the vowel sound in the second syllable is formed with an *e* and that the consonant *n* is doubled, just as it is in *annual.*

Common roots in English are sometimes similar enough to be confused. You should be familiar with these pairs:

ante (before); *anti* (against): *ante*bellum (before the war); *anti*dote

hyper (above, over); *hypo* (less, under): *hyper*active; *hypo*glycemia (low blood sugar)

macro (large); *micro* (small): *macro*cosm; *micro*scope

poly (multiple); *poli* (city): *poly*gamy (multiple marriage); metro*poli*tan

6. **Learn spelling rules.** The spelling rules treat especially the addition of suffixes to words. You can find a more complete discussion of rules in a spelling textbook, such as *Spelling 1500.*

final *e:* A word ending in a silent *e* keeps the *e* before a suffix beginning with a consonant: *completely, excitement, sincerely.* Exceptions: *acknowledgment, judgment, argument, truly.* If the suffix begins with a vowel, the silent *e* disappears: *loving, admirable. Changeable,* however, keeps the *e* to establish the soft *g* sound.

final consonant: When a word ends with a consonant, the consonant is doubled before a suffix beginning with a vowel: *planned, transferred, occurrence, omitted.* If the final syllable is not stressed, the final consonant is not doubled: *inhabited, signaled. Busing/(bussing)* and *focusing/(focussing)* are correctly spelled with one consonant or with two.

able/ible: The suffix *-able* generally follows words that are complete in themselves, such as *remarkable, adaptable, moveable, changeable, readable, respectable,* and *comfortable.* The suffix *-ible* follows groups of letters that do not form words. There is no *feas, plaus,* nor *terr;* thus, we write *feasible, feasibility, plausible,* and *terrible.* Words that end in a soft *s* sound also take *-ible: responsible, irresistible, forcible.* A mnemonic: words that are *able* to stand alone take the suffix *-able.* Some exceptions to the general rule: *inhospitable, indefensable, tenable.*

ie/ei: The familiar rhyme works most of the time: *i* before *e* except after *c* and when sounded like *a* as in *neighbor* and *sleigh.* Exceptions should be memorized: *neither foreigner seized the weird financier at leisure on the height.*

7. **Respect the limits of your knowledge.** Editors have made mistakes by substituting familiar words for similar but unfamiliar words. You can imagine the impatience of a writer in psychology whose editor changed *discrete behavior* to *discreet behavior,* not knowing the term *discrete* was defined to mean "separate." Or the frustration of the writer in a social service organization whose editor changed *not-for-profit* to *nonprofit* when *not-for-profit* was the legal term used in the application for tax-exempt status. Or the writer in biochemistry whose editor changed *beta agonists* to *beta antagonists.* In all cases, the first term was correct in its context; the editor substituted a term that was more familiar but incorrect.

A wise person respects the limits of his or her knowledge and checks a reliable source, such as a dictionary or the writer, before changing the spelling of an unfamiliar term.

Frequently Misused Words   The following groups of words are so similar in appearance or meaning that they are frequently confused.

affect, effect: Both words can be nouns, and both can be verbs. Usually, however, *effect* is a noun, meaning "result," and *affect* is a verb, meaning "to influence."

```
Your training in writing will have an effect
on your performance in editing.
```

```
The Doppler effect explains the apparent
change in the frequency of sound waves when a
train approaches.
```

```
Class participation will affect your grade.
```

assure, insure, ensure: All three words mean "to make secure or certain." Only *assure* is used with reference to persons in the sense of setting the mind at rest. *Insure* is used in the business sense of guaranteeing against risk. *Ensure* is used in other senses.

```
The supervisor assured the editor that her
salary would be raised.
```

```
The company has insured the staff for health
and life.
```

```
The new management policies ensure greater
participation in decision making by the staff.
```

complement, compliment: A *complement* completes a whole; a *compliment* expresses praise.

```
In geometry, a complement is an angle related
to another so that their sum totals 90
degrees.
```

```
The subject complement follows a linking verb.
```

```
Your compliment encouraged me.
```

continually, continuously: *Continually* suggests interrupted action over a period of time; *continuously* indicates uninterrupted action.

```
We make backup copies continually.
```

```
The printer in the lab stays on continuously
during working hours.
```

discreet, discrete: Discreet means "prudent;" *discrete* means "separate."

```
A good manager is discreet in reprimanding an
employee.
```

```
We counted seven discrete examples of faulty
reporting.
```

farther, further: Farther refers only to physical distance; *further* refers to degree, quantity, or time.

```
The satellite plant is farther from town than
I expected.
```

```
The company cannot risk going further into
debt.
```

fiscal, physical: Fiscal refers to finances; *physical* refers to bodily or material things.

```
The tax return is due five months after the
fiscal year ends.
```

imply, infer: Imply means "to suggest;" *infer* means "to take a suggestion" or "to draw a conclusion."

```
These figures imply that bankruptcy is
imminent.
```

```
We inferred from the figures that bankruptcy
is imminent.
```

its, it's: Its is a possessive pronoun; *it's* is a contraction for *it is.*

```
The company is proud of its new health
insurance policy.
```

```
It's a good idea to accept the major medical
option on the health insurance policy.
```

lay, lie: Lay is a transitive verb that takes an object; that is, you lay something in its place. *Lay* can also be the past participle of *lie. Lie* is always an intransitive verb followed by an adverb.

```
A minute ago, I lay the flowers on the table,
and they lie there still. I will lay the
silverware now. Then I will lie down.
```

personal, personnel: Personal is an adjective meaning "private" or "one's own"; *personnel* is a collective noun referring to the persons employed or active in an organization.

```
The voltage meter is my personal property.
Take the job description to the personnel
manager.
```

principle, principal: A *principle* is a basic truth or law; a *principal* can be a school official (noun), or it can mean "first" or "primary" (adjective).

```
Our company is managed according to democratic
principles.
Writing ability is the principal qualification
for employment.
```

stationery, stationary: Stationery refers to writing paper; something *stationary* is fixed in place or not moveable.

```
Our business stationery is on classic laid
paper.
The projection equipment in the seminar room
is stationary.
```

their, there, they're: Their is a possessive pronoun; *there* is an adverb designating a place (note the root *here*) or a pronoun used to introduce a sentence; *they're* is a contraction for *they are*.

```
Their new book won a prize for design.
There are six award-winning books displayed
over there on the table. They're all
impressive.
```

whose, who's: Whose is a possessive pronoun; *who's* is a contraction for *who is*.

```
Whose house is this? Who's coming to dinner?
```

your, you're: Your is a possessive pronoun; *you're* is a contraction for *you are*.

```
I read your report last night. You're a good
writer.
```

CAPITALIZATION

Most people know the basic rules of capitalization: to capitalize the first word of a sentence, titles of publications and people, days, months, holidays, the pronoun *I,* and proper names. Proper names include names of people, organizations, historical periods and events, places, rivers, lakes, and mountains, names of nationalities, and most words derived from proper names.

As an editor, however, you must be even more particular about capitalization decisions. For one thing choices about capitalization may vary from discipline to discipline. For example, if you work for the government, conventional usage dictates that you capitalize *Federal, State,* and *Local* as modifiers, but in other contexts, such capitalization would be incorrect. Furthermore, you will sometimes have choices about capitalization; you will record those choices on your document style sheet. Your primary resources in determining capitalization are a dictionary and style manuals.

One principle of capitalization is to capitalize titles and places that refer to specific people and places but not general references. For example, capitalize names of specific regions (e.g., the Midwest) but not a general point on the compass (e.g., the plant is west of the city). Capitalize adjectives derived from geographic names when the term refers to a specific place (e.g., Mexican food) but not when the term has a specialized meaning not directly related to the place (e.g., french fries, roman numerals, roman type). Capitalize the specific name of an organization (e.g., Smith Corporation) but not a reference to it later in the document by type of organization rather than by specific name (e.g., the corporation). Capitalize a title when it precedes a name (e.g., President Morales) but not when it is used in general to refer to an officer (e.g., the president). Finally, capitalize names of disciplines that refer to nationalities (e.g., English, Spanish) but not to other disciplines (e.g., history, chemistry).

Over time, the trend has been to less capitalization. In the eighteenth century, many nouns, not just proper nouns, were capitalized. The use of capitalization has declined in part because excessive capitalization distracts readers and interferes with **readability.** Capitalizing for emphasis encourages word-by-word reading rather than reading for overall sense. The repeated capitals also look like "hiccups" on the page. Typing words in all capital letters destroys the shape of the word (all words become rectangles) and therefore obscures some information that readers use in identifying words. Other techniques of typographic emphasis, including boldface type, a larger type size, white space, and boxing, are more effective.

Distracting Capitalization

```
Visitors Must Register All Cameras with
the Attendant at the Entry Station.

VISITORS MUST REGISTER ALL CAMERAS WITH
THE ATTENDANT AT THE ENTRY STATION.
```

Preferred Style

```
Visitors must register all cameras with
the attendant at the entry station.
```

```
Visitors must register all cameras with
the attendant at the entry station.
```

ABBREVIATIONS

An editor considers whether to use abbreviations or to spell out the terms, as well as ensuring that unfamiliar abbreviations are identified. A related editorial task is to make consistent decisions about capitalization and periods within abbreviations.

The best reason for using an abbreviation is that readers recognize it; perhaps it is more familiar than what it represents. Abbreviations may also be easier to learn than the full name, and they save space on the page. *NASA*, for example, is now more familiar to readers, and also was easier to learn when first coined, than is the spelled-out title, *National Aeronautics and Space Administration*.

When an abbreviation becomes a word in its own right, it is an *acronym*. For example, *PABA*, an ingredient in some sunscreen lotions, is an acronym for *Para-aminobenzoic acid*. Most readers, except possibly chemists, will know the ingredient by its acronym rather than by its full name.

In making decisions about whether or not to abbreviate, you should always respect the spelling of a name that uses abbreviations. For example, if a company is known as Jones & Jones (with the ampersand appearing on company signs and on the company letterhead), do not spell out the "and" in an attempt to make it more formal.

Identifying Abbreviations

Many abbreviations are not familiar to readers and must be identified the first time they are used. A parenthetical definition gives readers the information they need at the time they need it. After the initial parenthetical definition, the abbreviation alone may be used.

> Researchers have given tetrahydroaminoacridine
> (THA) to patients with Alzheimer's disease. THA
> inhibits the action of an enzyme that breaks
> down acetylcholine, a neurotransmitter that is
> deficient in Alzheimer's patients. The cognitive
> functioning of patients given oral THA improved
> while they were on the drug.

If the abbreviation is used in different chapters of the same document, however, it should be identified parenthetically in each chapter, because readers may not have read or may not remember previous identifications. Documents that use many abbreviations may also include a list of abbreviations in the front or back matter.

Periods with Abbreviations   Some abbreviations include or conclude with periods (e.g., U.S., B.A.); others, especially scientific and technological terms and groups of capital letters, do not (USSR, CBS, cm). The trend in print media is to drop the periods. For example, *NAACP* is more common now than the older form *N.A.A.C.P.* When an abbreviation contains more than one period, no space is set between the period and the following letter except before another word.

The conventions about whether to use space after the periods vary from abbreviation to abbreviation. At end of sentence, one period identifies both an abbreviation and the end of a sentence. Thus, you use only one period.

> While working as a technical editor, she is also
> completing courses for a Ph.D.

Because they represent complete "words," initials substituting for names and abbreviations of single terms also require spaces after the periods (e.g., Mr. A. L. Bustamantes, 2-in. nail). But single abbreviations consisting of multiple abbreviated words do not have spaces within them (see the next section, on Latin terms). When in doubt, you should check a dictionary for the conventions of capitalization and punctuation for an abbreviation. Most standard desk dictionaries include a list of abbreviations as part of the back matter.

Latin Terms   Many common abbreviations represent Latin terms, and you need to be cautious in using them. Some, such as *e.g., et al.,* and *cf.,* are used primarily in scholarly documents and may therefore be unfamiliar to readers or seem pretentious outside a scholarly context. The overused *etc.* should be restricted to informal writing — or omitted altogether. It is often a meaningless appendage to a sentence, added when a writer is unsure whether he or she has given enough examples. It may thus signal incomplete thinking rather than useful information for readers. In addition, it is redundant if a writer has also used *such as,* which indicates that the list following is representative rather than complete.

Abbreviations of Latin terms use periods following the abbreviated term. Here are some common Latin abbreviations with which you should be familiar:

A.M. (*ante meridiem,* before midday); *P.M.* (*post meridiem,* after midday): these abbreviations may be set in capital letters, lowercase letters, or small caps. The periods distinguish A.M. from the abbreviation for *amplitude modulation.*

ca. (*circa,* about): used in giving approximate dates

cf. (*confer,* compare): used for cross-references

cwt. (*centum-weight,* hundred-weight): a hybrid of Latin and English

et al. (*et alii,* and others): used primarily in bibliographic entries in humanities texts. Note that *et,* being a complete word and not an abbreviation, takes no period.

etc. (*et cetera,* and other things, and so forth)

ff. (*folio,* on the following page or pages)

i.e. (*id est,* that is): used in adding an explanation

e.g. (*exempli gratia,* for the sake of an example; for example)

N.B. (*note bene,* note well)

Ph.D. (*Philosophia Doctor,* Doctor of Philosophy): the Latin terms explain the capitalization and use of periods in this abbreviation.

v. or vs. (*versus,* against)

Measurement and   Three systems of measurement are widely used: the U.S. Customary Sys-
Scientific Symbols   tem, the British Imperial System, and the International (metric) System. Specific abbreviations are recognized for the units of measure in all three systems. Thus, one editing task is to check that abbreviations used for measurement conform to the standards; another is to check capitalization.

The metric system, which provides a system of units for all physical measurements, is used for most scientific and technical work. Its units are called SI units (for *Système International,* in French). The abbreviations for the metric system do not use periods. In the U.S. and British systems, the conventions about periods with abbreviations vary. For example, the abbreviation for *inch* may or may not include a period (in. or in). The abbreviation for *pound* (lb.) uses a period because it stands for the Latin word *libra.* In addition, the abbreviation is always singular even if the quantity it stands for is multiple. Thus, *3 lb.* is correct; *3 lbs.* is not. Check a list of abbreviations in a dictionary or style guide to determine the use, and record it on the style sheet.

Because the abbreviations for measurements are standard, they do not require parenthetical identification. Within sentences of technical and scientific texts, measures used with specific quantities may be abbreviated or spelled out. When measures are used alone, without specific quantities, they are spelled out. Thus, we would write "The weight is measured in kilograms." In tables and formulas, however, abbreviations are preferred. As always, the document should be consistent.

Like the abbreviations for measurements, scientific symbols for terms in chemistry, medicine, astronomy, engineering, and statistics are standard. Consult a specialized style guide to determine the correct symbols. (Chapter 8 discusses quantitative and technical material in detail.)

States

The United States Postal Service recognizes abbreviations consisting of two capital letters and no periods for the states and territories (e.g., CA, NC). The old system of abbreviations for the states—usually consisting of capital and lowercase letters with a period—is rapidly becoming obsolete. Use the postal service abbreviations on envelopes because both human and machine scanners recognize them quickly. In the headings of letters, either the abbreviation or the spelled-out state name is appropriate, but be consistent. Within the text of a document, spell out names of states.

SUMMARY

Correct spelling, capitalization, and abbreviations increase the accuracy and clarity of writing. Experience with language and understanding of its rules will help editors work quickly and accurately on these aspects of a document, but good editors will also depend on dictionaries and style manuals. These resources establish conventions and aid in consistency.

FURTHER READING

J. N. Hook. 1986. *Spelling 1500,* 3rd ed. San Diego: Harcourt Brace Jovanovich.

1. Use copymarking symbols to mark spelling corrections in these paragraphs.

A feasability study is a way to help a person make a decision. It provides facts that help a researcher decide objectively weather a project is practical and desireable. Alot of research preceeds the decision.

An invester deciding whether to purchase a convience store, for example, must investigate issues such as loans, lisences, taxes, and consummor demand. One principle question for a store in a residentail nieghborhood concerns the sale of liquer. People who come into the store might be asked to compleat a brief questionaire that inquires about there wishes.

Undoubtably, the issue of personal is signifigant as well. Trustworthy employes are indispensible. The investigator can check employmant patterns at the store and in the area overall.

After the study is complete, the investigator will guage the results and make a judgement. Some times the facts are ambigous. Intuition and willingness to take risk will influence the decision. If the project looks feasible, the recomendation will be to procede with the purchase.

2. Which of the spelling errors in the paragraphs in exercise 1 would a computerized spelling checker *not* catch? Why?

3. From the lists of frequently misspelled and misused words in this chapter, or from your own list of difficult words, select three, and develop mnemonics for remembering their spelling or use. Alternatively, analyze the spelling of these words by analyzing their roots.

4. Get acquainted with your desk dictionary as editorial assistant. Everyone knows that a dictionary is a resource for correct spelling, but what other information does it provide an editor? Check the front matter and the appendixes. Also look for help within the word lists on measurements and on symbols and signs. Name your dictionary, and cite at least three editorial resources other than help with spelling and usage. Compare your dictionary with a classmate's to get a sense of how different dictionaries may help an editor.

5. Correct the following sentences for spelling, misused words, capitalization, and abbreviation. Consult a dictionary and style manual when you are uncertain. Use copymarking symbols.

   a. Development will continue in the Northern part of the city.

   b. Do not spill the Hydrochloric Acid on your clothes.

   c. Do swedish meatballs go well with French fries?

   d. A research project at the sight of a major city landfill has shown how slowly plastic decomposes; i.e., a plastic bottle takes 100-400 years to decompose.

   e. The Society for Technical Communication has planned feild trips to three Hi Tech company's. Later in the year some students will attend the Annual Conference of the STC. All of these plans for travelling requie some extensive fund raising this Fall. The sponsers have proposed the establishment of an Editing Service. Student edtors would aquire jobs thru the Service and return 15 per cent of there earnings to the group.

   f. A minor in computor science in combination with a major in english can make a student an attractive canditate for a a job in technical communication.

g. Capitol investmant in the company will raise in the next physical year.

h. A prevous employe was the defendent in an embarasing and costly law suit charging sexual harrasment.

i. Only 10 m. seperates her house from mine. I wish it were further.

6 GRAMMAR AND USAGE

As a technical editor, you are expected to be an expert on grammar and usage. The need to establish your credibility is one good reason to master grammar and usage. Although you will probably not know all the rules, you should know enough to complete everyday editing tasks without constant reference to handbooks. You should also recognize when your knowledge is inadequate and know how to get the information you need.

Grammar refers to the rules that govern the construction of sentences from words. Thus, it concerns the functions of different types of words (the parts of speech) and their relationships in sentences. Using the rules of grammar is a way to achieve clarity in sentences. For example, in order to understand a sentence, readers must find in it a subject and verb, and they will look for the parts of speech in predictable places. Otherwise, the words may seem to be arranged in a random string. Although the rules of grammar change over time, they are firm enough and used widely enough so that following them is necessary for clarity.

Usage refers to acceptable ways of using words and phrases. Matters of usage include, for example, whether *access* is acceptable as a verb, what the distinctions among *assure, ensure,* and *insure* are, and when to use *fewer* and *less.* The conventions of usage change more rapidly than the rules of grammar and are more a matter of choice. To establish some consensus about usage and to monitor the trends in language, in the mid-1960s the editors of *The American Heritage Dictionary* formed a "usage panel" consisting of language experts. These experts are polled to determine whether new words or words used in new contexts are acceptable.

In your role as readers' advocate, you can appreciate how errors in grammar may result in misreading or misunderstanding. Because errors are relatively easy for readers to identify, they can diminish your company's reputation—and yours. Errors in usage are less serious than errors in grammar, but they also raise questions about the reliability of the document and your competence as an editor.

The ultimate authorities on grammar and usage are handbooks for writers and dictionaries. Most major publishers offer a handbook. If you do not have one, find out if one is preferred in your organization or in your discipline before you select one. Otherwise, use a current edition of a handbook from a major publishing house.

This chapter reviews basic concepts and vocabulary of grammar that all editors should know. It begins by defining words as parts of speech and continues by defining parts of a sentence. These sections focus on the building blocks of sentences. The chapter then discusses the common rules governing the relationships of words in sentences and the errors that result from breaking those rules. Terms are sometimes used before they are defined because of the assumption that this chapter reviews material you have learned previously. If you encounter unfamiliar terms, please consult the glossary or a handbook.

PARTS OF SPEECH

English words are grouped into eight main parts of speech: noun, verb, adjective, adverb, pronoun, preposition, conjunction, and interjection. Other parts of speech, such as gerund and participle, are subdivisions of these main parts. These terms are important to the discussion in a later section of this chapter on the relationships of words to one another in sentences.

- **Noun.** A noun names a person, place, thing, or idea. *Roberto, Canada, machine, life,* and *Marxism* are all nouns. A noun can function in a sentence as subject, object of a verb or preposition, complement, appositive, or modifier.

- **Verb.** A verb denotes action or state of being. A verb functions as the predicate in a sentence. Verbs may be **transitive,** meaning that they need an object to complete their meaning, or **intransitive,** meaning that they do not need objects. An intransitive verb is followed by an adverb or subject complement. Most verbs are transitive. Intransitive verbs include the *to be* verbs and verbs such as *appear, become, seem, look, go, wait,* and *sit.* They are also called **linking verbs.**

Transitive:

```
Vermont raised the minimum age for drinking.
subject    verb          object
```

Intransitive:

```
The child sat quietly.
     subject verb adverb
```

Some verbs can be either transitive or intransitive, especially the verbs of sense *(taste, feel, smell, hear, touch, see).*

```
She tasted the ice cream. (transitive)
```

```
The ice cream tastes good. (intransitive)
```

The subject **complement** that follows an intransitive verb is either an adjective modifying the subject or a noun that can substitute for the subject.

```
The reports are complete.
     subject    verb  subject complement
                      (adjective)
```

```
The letter is a proposal for funds.
     subject   verb  subject complement
                     (noun that can substitute for "letter")
```

- **Adjective.** An adjective modifies (i.e., describes or limits) a noun or pronoun. Words such as *contaminated, careful, flexible, thorough, clean,* and *strong* are adjectives. Adjectives may show comparisons with the suffixes *-er* and *-est (strong, stronger, strongest).* The articles *a, an,* and *the* are adjectives.

- **Adverb.** An adverb modifies a verb, adjective, other adverb, or even the entire sentence. Adverbs are frequently formed by adding the suffix *-ly* to an adjective.

The surgeon stitched <u>carefully</u>.

<u>Surprisingly</u>, the rates declined.
"Surprisingly" is an adverb modifying the entire sentence.

The team played <u>very well</u>.
Both "very" and "well" are adverbs; "well" modifies "played," and "very" modifies "well."

- **Pronoun.** A pronoun substitutes for a noun that has already been named. Pronouns may be personal *(I, you, he, she, they)*, relative *(who, whoever, which, that)*, indefinite *(each, one, neither, either, someone)*, interrogative *(which, whose, why)*, or other types as well.

- **Preposition.** Prepositions show relationships between other words. Common prepositions are *about, after, among, at, below, between, from, in, of, on, since,* and *with*. Some prepositions consist of more than one word, such as *in addition to*. The word following the preposition is its *object*. The preposition plus its object and modifying words form a *prepositional phrase*. A prepositional phrase is a modifier, used either as an adjective or as an adverb.

The disk <u>between the fourth and fifth vertebrae</u>
is herniated.
The prepositional phrase is adjectival, modifying "disk."

The surgery began <u>after midnight</u>.
The prepositional phrase is adverbial, modifying "began."

- **Conjunction.** A conjunction joins words, phrases, or clauses. The **coordinating conjunctions** *(and, but, or, for, yet, nor, so)* join elements of equal value. The **subordinating conjunctions** *(although, because, if, since, unless, while,* etc.) make the group of words following the conjunction dependent or subordinate to a main clause in a sentence.

- **Interjection.** An interjection is a simple exclamation, such as *yes, no, well,* and *Oh!* A mild interjection is followed by a comma; a strong interjection is followed by an exclamation point.

Some words can serve as different parts of speech depending on their context and use. For example, the word *effect* can be both a noun and a verb. Dictionaries identify the part of speech of a given word. When a word can be more than one part of speech, the dictionary will distinguish the meanings for the different uses.

This classification of words as parts of speech differs from the grammatical divisions of a sentence, including subject, predicate, object, and subject complement. The parts of speech and grammatical divisions are related, however, because only certain parts of speech can function in the grammatical divisions. For example, the subject is a noun, pronoun, or other noun substitute, such as a gerund; the predicate requires a verb; the object can be a noun or pronoun; and the subject complement is a noun or adjective.

PARTS OF A SENTENCE

Words and groups of words are defined according to their functions within the sentence as well as by parts of speech. The two main parts are the subject and predicate. The various parts of a sentence can be identified in the following example.

```
The computer that we purchased last month
subject

has increased productivity by 40 percent.
predicate
```

- **Subject.** The subject of the sentence identifies the agent or recipient of the action in a sentence — it names what the sentence is about. The subject is a noun, pronoun, or verbal (gerund, participial phrase, infinitive phrase). The simple subject is the subject without its modifiers. In the example sentence, "computer" is the simple subject.

- **Predicate.** The predicate tells what the subject does or what happens to the subject. It makes a statement or asks a question about the subject. The predicate always includes a verb; it also includes the object or complement of the verb. The simple predicate is the verb or verb phrase. In the example sentence, "has increased" is the simple predicate.

- **Object.** The object completes the meaning of a transitive verb. It answers the question *What?* posed by a transitive verb. In the example sentence, "productivity" is the object of the verb; it tells what has increased. The object is part of the predicate.

- **Complement.** A complement completes the meaning of an intransitive verb. The complement is sometimes called a *subject complement* because it describes or substitutes for the subject of the sentence. In the sentence "All members are present," the complement "present" describes "members." In the sentence "A virus is a pathogen," the complement "pathogen" could substitute for "virus."

- **Modifier.** A modifier describes and limits the meaning of the word or phrase it modifies. Modifiers may be adjectives and adverbs, but they may also be clauses and prepositional phrases. The example sentence includes several modifiers: "The" is an adjective modifying "computer"; "that we purchased last month" is a clause modifying "computer"; "by 40 percent" modifies "increased" because it tells how much the increase was.

Groups of words within sentences may be defined according to their structure as well as according to their function. The basic structural units of sentences, in addition to words, are clauses and phrases. (These parts are defined in more detail in Chapter 7.)

- **Clause.** A clause is a group of words that contains both a subject and a verb. The example sentence contains two clauses: the main clause ("computer . . . has increased") and a subordinate clause ("that we purchased last month"). You should be able to find a subject and a verb in both of these groups of words. The relative pronoun "that" makes the second clause subordinate, or unable to stand alone as a complete sentence. All sentences must contain at least one main clause.

- **Phrase.** A phrase is a group of words that does not contain both a subject and a verb. Phrases are frequently identified by the type of word contained in them. For example, a noun phrase contains a noun and its modifiers (e.g., the feasibility study); a prepositional phrase contains a preposition (e.g., to the director).

RELATIONSHIPS OF WORDS IN SENTENCES

The rules of grammar specify the accepted ways of using words in relationship to one another to form sentences. Their aim is clarity. Although following the rules will not ensure that the resulting sentences can be understood, sentences that break the rules will be difficult or perhaps impossible to understand.

Subjects and Verbs

The most basic rule for forming sentences is that each sentence must contain a subject and a verb. A group of words that lacks both a subject and a verb is only a phrase. If the phrase is used to substitute for a sentence, it is a sentence fragment. Fragments are generally more difficult to understand than complete sentences because some essential information is missing. Subjects and verbs must agree with one another in number.

Subject-verb agreement. A sentence will be easier to understand if the subject of the sentence agrees in number with the verb. A singular subject takes a singular verb; a plural subject takes a plural verb.

- **Singular subject, singular verb:**

  ```
  The Twenty-First Amendment gave states the
  right to set minimum age requirements for
  purchasing alcohol.
  ```

  ```
  Adolescent drinking is sometimes an expression
  of rebellion against the paternal authority
  figure.
  ```

- **Plural subject, plural verb:**

  ```
  Age limits on drinking may encourage
  clandestine drinking by the young.
  ```

  ```
  Correlations between stress and alcoholism are
  high for all age groups.
  ```

When a singular noun is modified by a prepositional phrase whose object is plural, the singular noun determines that the verb will be singular.

```
The column of numbers was misaligned.
NOT: The column of numbers were misaligned.
```

Collective nouns, such as *staff* and *committee,* may be regarded as either singular or plural, depending on whether you think of the group as a single entity or as a collection of individual members.

```
The committee is prepared to give its report.
```

```
All staff are responsible for completing their
sick leave forms.
```

When the demonstrative pronoun *there* begins a sentence, the verb agrees in number with the noun that follows the verb.

```
There have been thefts in this location.
```

```
There has been talk of hiring an all-night
guard.
```

The term *data* is frequently misused as a singular noun. *Datum* is the singular form; *data* is the plural. Thus, *data* is used with a plural verb.

```
The data are convincing.
```

Faulty predication. Sentences must make sense. S
work together logically as well as grammatically. W
ition tell you that the sentence doesn't make sense
subject can do what the verb says. If not, the erro

```
These observations have concluded
percent of new employees will be
three years.
```

The sentence doesn't make sense because an observation cannot conclude; only a person can. The writer meant that the observations have *shown* or that, on the basis of the observations, *researchers* have concluded. In the following sentence, the same problem is evident.

```
In some cases, a Master's degree can fill the
position.
```

A degree cannot fill a position; only a person can. The writer meant that in some cases a person with a Master's degree can *qualify* for the position.

Tense sequence and consistency. The **tense** of a verb refers to the time when the action takes place—present, past, or future. The six tenses in English are present, past, future, present perfect, past perfect, and future perfect.

Present	`I edit, I am editing`
Past	`I edited, I was editing`
Future	`I shall edit`
Present perfect	`I have edited`
Past perfect	`I had edited` Places the action before another action in the past
Future perfect	`I shall have edited` Indicates an action that will be complete before some other event in the future

Use the present tense for action that occurs in the present or for timeless actions. Most descriptive writing is in present tense.

```
The hard drive speeds up movement among files
and programs.
```

The past tense is identified by the past participle of the verb (formed by adding *-ed* to the verb unless the verb is irregular). It can also be identified by the helping verb *was*. Use the past tense only for action that occurred at a specific time in the past.

```
I was waiting for the morning mail when the
accident occurred.
BUT: Newton illustrates the concept of gravity
with the example of an apple falling from a
tree.
```

The future tense is identified by the helping verbs *will* or *shall*. Use the future tense for action that will take place in the future.

```
When the new equipment arrives, we will convert
to desktop publishing.
```

Unnecessary shifts in tense disorient readers by requiring them to move mentally from present to past and to future. On the other hand, tenses may be mixed in a document for good reason. For example, a trip report may include statements in the past tense that recount specific events on the trip and also statements in the present tense that describe processes, equipment, or ongoing events.

```
In our meeting, President Schober told us that
STC plans a new recruiting drive this fall. The
organization presently attracts technical
communicators who are well established in their
jobs. The recruiting drive will target new
hires.
```

The paragraph includes verbs in the present, past, and future tenses, but the tenses all identify accurately when the action occurs. A confusing shift is an arbitrary shift among tenses.

Objects and Complements

Objects and complements complete the sense of the verb. An object follows a transitive verb. It includes a noun or noun substitute.

A *subject complement* follows a linking (intransitive) verb. The *to be* verbs, such as *is, are, was, were, will be,* and *have been,* are linking verbs; other verbs, such as *appear* and *sit,* are linking verbs that are followed by subject complements rather than by objects. They link the subject of the sentence to a modifier in the predicate. In the sentence "The tea tasted good," for example, "good" is the complement.

A *faulty complement* occurs when the modifier or noun in the predicate cannot modify or substitute for the noun in the subject.

```
The application of DDT is one of the best

chemicals to eradicate the rootworms.
```

"Application" is the subject, and "one of the best chemicals" is the complement. However, "application" is not a chemical, so the complement is faulty. A simple revision eliminates the redundant "application."

```
DDT is one of the best chemicals to eradicate

the rootworms.
```

Another revision eliminates "chemicals." It also changes the structure of the sentence by using a transitive verb ("eradicate") and an object rather than an intransitive verb and a subject complement.

```
The application of DDT could eradicate the

rootworms.
```

Look for faulty complements especially when the sentence contains a *to be* or other intransitive verb.

Pronouns   A pronoun is a part of speech that substitutes for a noun that has already been named or is clear from the context. Pronouns relate to other words in the sentence by number, case, and reference.

Pronoun number: pronoun-antecedent and pronoun-verb agreement. The noun that precedes the pronoun is the *antecedent*, meaning that it "comes before" the pronoun. Pronouns may be singular *(he, she, it, him, her, one)* or plural *(they, their)*. Pronouns must agree in number with their antecedents. If the antecedent is *people*, the pronoun will be *they;* but if the antecedent is *person*, the pronoun will be *he* or *she* or possibly *he or she.*

The pronouns with "one" in them, including *everyone, anyone, none,* and *no one,* are singular. So are pronouns with "one" implied, such as *each, either,* and *neither.* In formal usage, they should be used with other singular pronouns.

```
Everyone should complete his or her report by

Monday.

NOT: Everyone should complete their report by

Monday.
```

Informally, however, *their* is increasingly accepted when following a pronoun with "one" in it, especially as a way of avoiding the generic *he.* Unless you know your readers and co-workers approve of this usage, however, it is safer to be conservative – or to avoid the problem altogether by using plural subjects.

```
All applicants should submit their transcripts.
```

When used as subjects, pronouns with "one" included or implied take singular verbs.

```
Neither is satisfactory.

None of the students was prepared.
```

Relative pronouns *(who, which, that)* used as subjects take the number of their antecedent.

```
Applicants who send samples of their writing
will have the best chance to be called for
interviews.

The editor who is my supervisor has helped me
learn how to estimate time for various tasks.
```

Pronoun case. Pronouns may be subjects of clauses, as with *I, we, you, he, she, they, anyone, each;* objects of prepositions, as with *us, me, him, her, them;* or possessives, as with *my, mine, your, yours, their, theirs.* Some pronouns can serve as either subjects or objects, as with *it, everyone, anyone, one.* Their role in the sentence, whether subject, object, or possessive, is their **case.**

Objects and subjects must be used as such, not as substitutes for one another. You may have been chastised as a child for saying "Her and me are going out," using pronouns in the objective case for the subject position. The rule governing case requires "She and I are going out." Likewise, saying "The coach picked he and I" uses pronouns in the subjective case as objects. The transitive verb requires objects: "The coach picked him and me." If the pronoun is the subject of a sentence, use a pronoun that serves as a subject; if the pronoun is the object of a verb or preposition, use a pronoun that serves as an object.

People seem especially self-conscious about using *I,* and errors follow from this hesitancy. "Carlos and myself will conduct the study" errs because the personal pronoun in the subjective case is "I." The pronouns containing *-self* can only appear when the noun or pronoun they refer to has already been named in the sentence. "Carlos and I myself will conduct the study" is correct.

Who and *whom* also create confusion. *Who* is a subject; *whom* is an object. If the person does what the verb says, use *who*. If the person receives the action of the verb, use *whom*.

```
The person who trained the new computer operator
was sent by the computer company.

The person whom we trained can now perform all
the necessary word processing functions.
```

Pronoun reference. The pronoun must "refer" clearly to the noun it represents—there must be no ambiguity about the meaning of the pronoun. Pronouns with more than one possible antecedent may cause confusion.

```
Cytomegalovirus (CMV) is a danger to those whose
natural immunity has been impaired, such as
persons with transplanted organs. Their immune
system is deliberately weakened to prevent it
from attacking the donor tissue.
```

Is "it" the virus or the immune system? Rereading will aid interpretation, but readers, more conditioned to thinking of viruses attacking tissue than the immune system attacking tissue, may read "it" as "virus."

Modifiers   Modifiers (adjectives, adverbs, and modifying phrases) are meaningless except in combination with the words they modify. Readers must be able to perceive the relationship of the modifier to what it modifies. Some uses of modifiers obscure the relationship of modifier to words modified. Common misuses include *misplaced modifiers* and *dangling modifiers.*

Misplaced modifiers. A modifier, in English, generally precedes the noun it modifies. Readers would expect to read "tensile strength," for example, but would be startled and confused by "strength tensile." Adverbs generally follow the verbs or adverbs they modify.

If modifiers are placed too far from the term they modify, the sense of their meaning may be lost, and they may seem to modify something other than what is intended.

> Based on annual usage, 458 copies would have to
> be purchased by walk-in customers to reach the
> break-even point <u>each day</u>.

The modifying phrase, "each day," seems to modify "to reach the break-even point." However, logic suggests that the writer is not concerned about breaking even each day but about the number of copies to be purchased each day by walk-in customers. Readers can figure out the meaning, but they shouldn't have to spend so much time doing so.

> Based on annual usage, 458 copies would have to
> be purchased <u>each day</u> by walk-in customers to
> reach the break-even point.

Dangling modifiers. Modifiers, by definition, attach to something. Sometimes, however, the thing they are intended to modify does not appear in the sentence; then, the modifiers are said to "dangle." Instead of attaching to what they should modify, they attach to another noun, sometimes with ridiculous results.

> By taking a course and paying court fees, the
> charge for DWI is dismissed.

The modifier, "By taking a course and paying court fees," can only logically modify a person who has committed a DWI offense, because only a person can take a course and pay fees. But no person is in the sentence, so the modifier "dangles." Structurally, it modifies "charge," the first noun to follow the modifier, which is absurd because a charge cannot take a course.

Dangling modifiers are likely to be phrases containing verbs used as nouns, adjectives, or adverbs. Verbs used for these functions are called *nonfinite verbs,* or **verbals**. Verbals may be **participles,** which are modifiers formed from a verb plus the suffix *-ing* or *-ed*; **gerunds,** which are noun substitutes formed from a verb plus the suffix *-ing*; or **infinitives,** which are formed from a verb plus *to* and are used chiefly as nouns.

> Changing the oil, a worn radiator hose was
> discovered.
> dangling modifier with a gerund

> To complete the application, the tax return must
> be attached.
> dangling modifier with an infinitive

One way to correct a dangling modifier is to insert the missing subject into the sentence.

```
By taking a course and paying court fees, a DWI
offender may have the charge dismissed.
```

An alternative is to rephrase the sentence altogether to eliminate the modifier.

```
The court will dismiss a DWI charge if the
offender takes a course and pays court fees.
```

Although rearranging sentence elements may disguise a dangling modifier, it will not correct the problem, because the item modified is still not in the sentence.

```
The charge for DWI is dismissed by taking a
course and paying court fees.
```

One frequent cause of dangling modifiers is a modifying phrase in combination with the passive voice. **Passive voice** means that the subject of the sentence receives the action of the verb rather than performing the action. "Charge" in "The charge may be dismissed" receives the action of dismissal; that is, the sentence is in passive voice. In passive voice, the agent of the action frequently is unnamed; thus, modifiers that refer to the agent of the action will dangle. One way to reduce the possibility of dangling modifiers is to use active voice rather than passive voice.

CONVENTIONS OF USAGE

Although a document may contain usage errors and still be understood, applying the conventions of usage increases clarity and decreases noise. A few conventions that technical communicators use frequently and that relate to the expression of quantities and amounts, the use of relative pronouns, and the treatment of idiomatic expressions are reviewed here.

Quantities and Amounts

The adjectives *fewer* and *less* and the nouns *number* and *amount* have specific uses and are not interchangeable. The use is determined by whether they refer to measurable quantities, such as pounds, dollars, or liters, or to indefinite amounts, such as weight, money, and milk. *Fewer* and *number* are standard usage when the reference is to measurable quantities.

> Fewer people attended the trade show this year
> than last, but the number of products sold was
> greater.

When the reference is to indefinite amounts, *less* and *amount* are standard.

> The amount of gasoline consumed rose 50 percent.

> This shipment of apples shows less contamination
> from pesticides than the shipment in April.

Relative Pronouns

The relative pronouns, *who, which,* and *that,* are used in specific ways. *Who* refers to persons; *which* and *that* refer to things. It would be incorrect to say "The people that came to the meeting brought tape recorders." The correct version would be "The people who came . . ."

In formal usage, *which* and *that* are distinguished according to whether the clause they begin is restrictive or nonrestrictive. A **restrictive clause** limits the noun's meaning. A **nonrestrictive clause** provides additional information about the noun, but it does not restrict the meaning of the noun. Some usage experts specify the use of *that* with a restrictive clause and *which* with a nonrestrictive clause. (See also Chapter 7.)

- **Restrictive clause:**

> The supplies <u>that we ordered yesterday</u> are out
> of stock.
> Only those supplies ordered yesterday, not all supplies, are out of stock.

- **Nonrestrictive clause:**

> Murray Lake, <u>which was dry only two months ago,</u>
> has flooded.
> Even without the information about the dryness of the lake, readers would know
> exactly which lake the sentence names.

Idiomatic Expressions

Some expressions in English cannot be explained by rules alone. In fact, the usage may contradict logic or other conventions. It would be difficult, for example, to explain according to what rules we say *by* accident but *on* purpose, or why we could be excited *about* a project, bored *with* it, or sick *of* it. Such expressions are *idiomatic.* The use of prepositions, in particular, is idiomatic in English. One simply learns the idioms of the language through reading and conversation. Idioms are especially difficult for writers for whom English is a second language. These writers may be perfectly competent in English grammar but have too little experience with the language to know all its idioms. A copyeditor quietly helps.

SUMMARY

Editing sentences to conform to the rules of grammar and the conventions of usage is a basic job for a copyeditor because correct grammar and proper usage increase clarity. Editors need to know how different types of words function in sentences. Editors also need to recognize and correct errors in usage. Memorizing basic rules speeds up editing, but editors also need the help of dictionaries and handbooks.

FURTHER READING

Theodore M. Bernstein. 1984. *The Careful Writer.* New York: Atheneum.

Roy H. Copperud. 1980. *American Usage and Style: The Consensus.* New York: Van Nostrand Reinhold.

DISCUSSION AND APPLICATION

1. Identify the parts of speech of all the underlined words in the following sentences. If necessary, refer to a dictionary or a handbook of grammar and usage. Note with regard to sentence 3 that a gerund (noun formed from a verb) can take an object just as a verb can.

[1] Genomes are complete sets of genetic instructions for assembling and sustaining the life of an organism. [2] Not surprisingly, the human genome is overwhelmingly complex. [3] Biotechnology will soon be capable of mapping and sequencing the human genome. [4] A genome map will show scientists precisely where genes are located on a chromosome. [5] This map will provide a basis for predicting genetic diseases. [6] This project will be expensive. [7] It will cost millions of dollars each year.

2. Identify the following sentence parts in each of the sentences in exercise 1: simple subject, complete subject, complete predicate, and modifiers.

3. Determine which of the following groups of words are phrases, which are clauses, and which combine a phrase with a clause.

genetic instructions

have recently determined

researchers have determined the cause

on the bottom

in the event that the program crashes

4. According to traditional grammarians, the adverb *hopefully* is misused as a substitute for "it is to be hoped." Thus, it would be misused in the sentence "Hopefully, we will finish before Friday." Consult a dictionary and a handbook to determine the recommendations for the use of *hopefully*. Also, define the grounds on which the use of *hopefully* could be considered a matter of usage rather than of grammar.

5. Identify and correct grammar errors in the following sentences. There may be errors in subject-verb agreement, pronoun-verb agreement, pronoun-antecedent agreement, and pronoun case as well as faulty predication, faulty complements, dangling modifiers, misplaced modifiers, and misuse of pronouns and expressions of quantity.

   a. The nitroglycerin patch provides continuous absorption of the medicine without taking a pill every so many hours.

   b. The interaction between the chemical mechanism and the dynamic mechanism appears to be the two important factors behind the depletion of the ozone layer.

   c. The purpose of this section of the report is to increase the fatigue strength of an already welded joint.

   d. When preparing copy for the typesetter or when correcting errors on the screen, the cursor can be easily moved with the mouse.

   e. Rather than make marks on the copy, the change can be placed in the computer for a faster and neater job.

   f. The cost of production can be reduced by

purchasing software and hardware for desktop publishing.

g. The exterior and interior conditions of the house is in need of some repair.

h. As a technical communicator with your ambitions set on the upper ranks of management, the ability to communicate, coordinate, facilitate, motivate, and lead is important.

i. Shipment of factory sealed cartons are made from our warehouse via the cheapest and fastest way.

j. The engineers that worked on the project protested the amount of contaminants permitted by the EPA.

k. Use the express lane if you have less than 10 items.

l. A mosquito bit Lord Carnarvon on his left cheek five months after entering King Tut's tomb.

m. Growing up to five feet long and weighing over 600 pounds, natives on the Moluceas Archipelago use the shells of the giant man-eating clam as children's bathtubs.

n. Like most daycare centers, there is a waiting list.

o. By using lead-free gasoline, harmful lead oxides and lead chlorides and bromides are not released into the atmosphere as is the case with leaded or regular gasoline.

p. Please excuse this informal manner in replying. By doing so, it enables us to give you lower prices, faster service, and responding promptly.

6. Edit this paragraph with particular attention to verb tense.

We take great pleasure in welcoming you to our
staff. We hope our relationship is one of mutual
understanding and support. The owners had many
years of experience in the operation of
successful and profitable businesses. We were
fortunate in the past with our choices for our
staff, and we sincerely hope that you will follow
in this path.

7 PUNCTUATION

Minimum competency for a copyeditor entails the ability to edit for punctuation as well as for grammar, spelling, and mechanics. You must know sentence structures and the corresponding rules of punctuation. Such knowledge—more than your ear or intuition—provides a secure basis for editing. Your best sources of detailed information about punctuation are a writer's handbook and other books about using language.

This chapter will not take the place of a handbook, but it will provide a review of basic sentence patterns and points of punctuation. It will also help you retrieve essential vocabulary and concepts that may be hidden in the recesses of your memory. A specific goal is that you will understand these terms: clause (independent or main and dependent or subordinate), phrase, conjunction (coordinating and subordinating), relative pronoun, restrictive and nonrestrictive modifier, and parallel structure. You should be able to use these terms in making decisions about emendations for punctuation and, if necessary, defending them.

The chapter begins by explaining why an editor should care about punctuation rules. It then illustrates sentence patterns and their punctuation as well as the punctuation of sentence elements other than clauses. Finally, it reviews mechanics of punctuation. If you learn the basic principles and terms in this chapter, read closely for meaning when you edit, and consult a handbook when you have questions, you should be a good editor for punctuation.

WHY BOTHER TO MASTER PUNCTUATION?

Editors and writers sometimes feel that rules of punctuation are annoying and even arbitrary. Because there are many rules, more than one can memorize, it is tempting to dismiss their importance and to rely, instead, on the ear, on habit, and on intuition. Many of us have not used the language of grammar since our elementary or junior high school days, and yet our own writing is reasonably correct from the standpoint of rules of punctuation. Why bother with the rules? Why bother to use punctuation precisely?

For one thing, correct punctuation helps readers perceive meaning even if they are not conscious of punctuation and its rules. Punctuation clarifies the meaning of sentences because it signals sentence structure. It shows where the main structural parts begin and end, and it helps to show relationships between parts of a sentence. Correct punctuation helps readers to read a sentence accurately.

Structures also reveal relationships of ideas. Readers look in sentences for answers to their unstated questions: What happened? Who did what? What was done? The sentence core should provide the answer to these questions. The core—the simple subject plus the simple predicate—is the strongest part of the sentence structurally (because the sentence could not exist without it); thus, whatever information is contained in the core seems to be the most important. Likewise, a subordinate clause in the sentence signals that the information is subordinate to (or less important than) the information in the main, or independent, clause. In a series, parallel structure, or consistent phrasing of sentence elements that are related in content, will help readers recognize the number of elements in the series. (These terms will be defined in more depth later in the chapter.)

End-of-sentence punctuation (period, question mark, exclamation point) shows where a new thought will begin. But internal marks of punctuation also reveal sentence patterns and relationships. Accurate signals facilitate accurate interpretation of meaning.

Incorrect punctuation also diminishes comprehension because it creates document noise. Many readers can readily recognize common errors of punctuation. Although they may overlook the occasional error or tolerate debatable usage in uncommon situations, frequent errors will diminish their respect for the writer. Readers may not pay attention to the content if they lose respect for the writer.

Editing is likely to be more accurate if editors know *why* they are emending. Our ears are good tools for editing, but they are limited. That's especially true if we offer vague explanations for our punctuation choices. We may be satisfied to place commas where we would "breathe" or "pause"; yet, if we do, we may be sending out faulty signals about structure and making arbitrary editorial decisions. Punctuation is logical—not biological!

Finally, writers will respect you more if you use the technical terms of the profession. The explanation that you inserted a comma because the sentence consisted of two independent clauses joined by a coordinating conjunction is more convincing than saying that the place where you inserted the comma was a good place to breathe or to pause. You are a technical expert on punctuation just as the person whose work you edit may be a technical expert on computer hardware. Editing and speaking like the expert you are encourages others to respect you as an expert.

BASIC SENTENCE ELEMENTS

The ability to edit for punctuation depends on a knowledge of how sentences are constructed. Punctuation corresponds to sentence structure. The terms that describe structural parts of the sentence, including *clause, phrase, conjunction, relative pronoun,* and subcategories of these sentence parts, are defined and illustrated in this section.

Clauses

A **clause** is a group of words containing a subject and a predicate. The subject is a noun or noun substitute; the predicate tells what is said about the subject and must contain a verb. The clause is the fundamental unit of a sentence—all sentences must contain a clause in order to be complete. (There are some exceptions to this statement, particularly in advertising copy and informal writing, but most technical writing follows conventional rules.)

Clauses may be independent or dependent. An **independent clause** (sometimes called the **main clause**) includes the subject and predicate and can stand alone as a sentence. A **dependent clause** (sometimes called a **subordinate clause**) contains a subject and predicate, but it also begins with a subordinating conjunction or relative pronoun. The inclusion of a subordinating conjunction or relative pronoun makes the clause dependent on an independent clause. The following list summarizes the definitions and gives examples.

- **Clause = subject + predicate**

- **Independent clause = subject + predicate:**

  The editor proofread the text.
  subject   predicate
  noun   verb

- **Dependent clause = subordinating conjunction or relative pronoun + subject + predicate:**

```
Although the editor proofread the text,...
subordinating        subject    predicate
conjunction
```

Subordinating conjunctions and relative pronouns are defined and discussed on the next few pages. For now, note that the dependent clause, because of the subordinating conjunction "although," makes us as readers expect that the thought will be completed elsewhere. This clause is dependent on the independent clause that presumably will follow.

When you are determining whether a group of words is a clause, make sure the verb is a verb and not another part of speech formed from a verb. Gerunds and participles, for example, are formed by adding *-ing* or *-ed* to a verb, but they function as nouns and modifiers rather than as verbs. Thus, "The experiment being finished" is not a clause because it contains no verb. How would you turn this group of words into a clause?

In sentences in the **imperative mood** — phrased as commands — the subject of the sentence *(you)* is understood. Thus, "Turn on the computer" is an independent clause because it means "[You] turn on the computer."

Phrases   In addition to containing an independent clause, a sentence may (but does not need to) include one or more phrases. A **phrase** is a group of related words, but it does not contain a subject and predicate. Phrases and clauses are punctuated differently.

Different types of phrases may be defined by the type of words in them. For example, a **prepositional phrase** is introduced by a preposition, such as *by, from, to, for,* or *behind*. A **noun phrase** includes a noun and modifiers. An **infinitive phrase** includes the infinitive form of a verb, identified by *to*. A **participial phrase** includes a participle (a verb with an *-ing* or *-ed* ending that functions as a modifier). An **appositive phrase** renames the term just mentioned. Some common types of phrases are illustrated here:

Prepositional phrase	The package arrived <u>from New York City</u>.
Noun phrase	We obtained <u>the required papers</u>.
Infinitive phrase	We will try <u>to complete the proposal tomorrow</u>.

Participial phrase	The technician <u>taking readings</u> discovered a faulty procedure yesterday.
Appositive phrase	OKT3, <u>a monoclonal antibody</u>, helps to prevent a rejection crisis in kidney transplants.

In order to punctuate sentences correctly, you must be able to distinguish a clause from a phrase. Phrases function in a sentence as the subject or predicate, as modifiers, or as objects of the verb. Because they do not contain both a subject and verb, however, they cannot be punctuated as independent clauses (or as sentences).

Conjunctions

When a sentence contains more than one clause, the clauses are often joined by a **conjunction.** As the root word *junction* suggests, the purpose of the conjunction is "to join."

Conjunctions may be **coordinating,** joining independent clauses or other sentence elements (such as the terms of a compound subject) of equal grammatical value. Only seven words can function as coordinating conjunctions, all with three or fewer letters. You should memorize them.

- **Coordinating conjunctions:** and, but, or, for, yet, nor, so

Conjunctions may also be **subordinating,** joining a dependent clause to an independent clause. They establish that one clause is less important than another, or subordinate to it. If a clause contains a subordinating conjunction, it is a dependent or subordinate clause. You probably won't memorize this list, but you should be familiar with it.

- **Subordinating conjunctions:** after, although, as, because, if, once, since, that, though, till, unless, until, when, whenever, where, wherever, while

Recognizing conjunctions and their type will help you determine whether the clause you are punctuating is independent or dependent.

Relative Pronouns

Relative pronouns relate to a noun already named in the sentence. They introduce dependent clauses (dependent because readers must know the noun already named in the sentence to understand the meaning of the clause). Like subordinating conjunctions, relative pronouns make clauses dependent.

- **Relative pronouns:** that, what, which, who, whoever, whom, whomever, whose

Clauses beginning with relative pronouns may be the subject of the sentence, or they may be modifiers.

Whoever comes first will get the best seat.

The library book that Joe checked out is
overdue.

These groups of words introduced by relative pronouns are called clauses, not phrases, because they contain subjects and predicates. Can you explain why they are dependent clauses?

BASIC SENTENCE PATTERNS AND PUNCTUATION

Sentences may be constructed according to four basic sentence patterns, distinguished by the number and type of clauses they contain. The punctuation of sentences will depend on the basic pattern, which might be any one of the following:

- **Simple.** Contains one independent clause (subject + predicate).

Rain fell.

- **Compound.** Contains two independent clauses.

Acid rain fell, and the lake was polluted.

- **Complex.** Contains one independent clause plus one dependent clause.

Because the factory violated emission
standards, its owners were fined.

- **Compound-complex.** Contains two independent clauses, one of which includes a dependent clause.

The factory that violated emission standards
was fined; therefore, the owners authorized
changes in procedures and equipment.

Punctuating Simple Sentences

Simple sentences contain one independent clause. The punctuation of simple sentences is end punctuation only unless there are introductory phrases or interrupting elements within the sentence. No single commas should separate the subject from the predicate although a pair of commas may enclose an interrupting modifier or appositive. Paradoxically, while a single comma separates, a pair of commas does not—the comma pair functions like parentheses.

> WRONG: Some student editors with good grades in English, assume they know grammar well enough to edit without consulting a handbook.
>
> CORRECT: Angie Gantner, a good student in English, edits effectively for grammar.

Sometimes simple sentences look like compound or complex sentences because they contain a compound verb or object. Nevertheless, they are still simple sentences and should be punctuated as such. If a comma is inserted before a second verb appears, it separates this verb from its subject.

> WRONG: This draft prunes away some wordiness, and attempts to present the remaining information more efficiently.
>
> WRONG: The writer prepared the draft of the text on the computer, but drew in the visuals by hand.
>
> WRONG: The copyeditor marked the typescript for grammar, but not for graphic design.

The separation of subject from verb interferes with the reader's perception of the sentence core. Perhaps the commas in the three incorrectly punctuated sentences appeared because the writer expected to breathe after the long beginning. Perhaps "and" or "but" seemed to begin a clause rather than the second part of a compound verb or object. However, it is illogical to separate parts of the sentence that belong together. The sentence type is simple; the comma should be deleted.

Punctuating Compound Sentences

Compound sentences contain two independent clauses. Internal sentence punctuation (comma, semicolon, colon, or dash) reveals the structure of the sentence, signaling the end of one clause and the beginning of another. These punctuation marks thereby cause readers to anticipate a new subject and a new verb.

If the independent clauses are joined by a coordinating conjunction, separate them with a comma.

    Joe catches typos when he proofreads galley
    proofs, but he is less careful about word-
    division errors.

If the sentence contains no coordinating conjunction, however, insert a semicolon or colon between the two clauses. The semicolon should be used to separate statements relatively equal in importance.

    Good proofreaders check for omissions as well as
    for typos; they also note details of typeface,
    type style, and spacing.

    The dynamic mechanism theory explains sudden and
    drastic concentration changes of ozone; the
    chemical mechanism theory cannot account for
    these huge depletions.

The colon should be used if the first clause introduces the second or if you could insert "namely" after the first clause. A colon creates a sense of expectation in the reader that some additional, qualifying information will follow.

    One fact remains clear: the field of editing
    lacks a consistent vocabulary.

    Substantive editing is rhetorical: it begins
    with an editor's understanding of the document's
    audience, purpose, and context of use.

One troublesome group of words for writers and editors punctuating compound sentences are the conjunctive adverbs such as *consequently, however, moreover, besides, nevertheless, on the other hand, in fact, therefore,* and *thus.* They are called *conjunctive adverbs* because they join and modify. They are often confused with subordinating conjunctions. *However* and *although* are easily confused because they both signal contrasting information. You must be able to make the distinction in punctuation. If you use only a comma between clauses in a compound sentence whose second clause begins with a conjunctive adverb, you will have a "comma fault" error. A semicolon must be used with a conjunctive adverb in a compound sentence.

> COMMA FAULT: Our organization transmits text to
> the printer electronically, therefore, we save
> the costs of rekeyboarding.
> CORRECT PUNCTUATION: Our organization
> transmits text to the printer electronically;
> therefore, we save...

The first sentence in the following pair consists of two independent clauses (i.e., a compound sentence); because the sentence has no coordinating conjunction, the clauses are separated with a semicolon. The second sentence in the pair consists of an independent plus a dependent clause introduced by the subordinating conjunction "although." Because the sentence pattern is complex rather than compound, it requires no internal punctuation.

> We have no leather recliners in stock; however,
> we do have vinyl ones.

> We have no leather recliners in stock although
> we do have vinyl ones.

If *however* does not introduce a clause but is only an adverb, it will be set off in the sentence with commas.

> We have no leather recliners in stock. We do,
> however, have vinyl ones.

Note that the second sentence is a simple sentence (with one independent clause) and therefore requires no semicolon.

You will make the right decision about punctuating clauses within a sentence if you can identify which clauses are independent and which are dependent. Although you do not need to memorize the entire list of subordinating conjunctions, you may need to memorize the common conjunctive adverbs and recognize that they are *not* subordinating conjunctions.

Punctuating
Complex Sentences

Complex sentences contain both an independent and a dependent clause. There may be no punctuation between the clauses, or they may be separated by a comma. Semicolons and colons should not be used to separate independent from dependent clauses.

If the dependent clause is made dependent by a subordinating conjunction, a comma is appropriate between clauses. A comma should be used if the dependent clause comes first in the sentence. A comma is not necessary if the dependent clause follows the independent clause.

Although we use a computerized proofreading
program, we also depend on a human proofreader
to correct errors that the computer cannot
identify.

We depend on a human proofreader although we
also use a computerized spelling checker.

We depend on a human proofreader because the
computerized spelling checker does not
comprehend meaning.

Dependent clauses formed by relative pronouns may be modifiers. Whether a modifying clause should be separated from the main clause with a comma or not depends on whether the modifying clause is restrictive or nonrestrictive.

Restrictive clause. A **restrictive clause** restricts the meaning of the term it modifies. The term may suggest a class of objects, but the restrictive modifier clarifies that the term in this sentence refers only to a subclass.

Concrete that has been reinforced by
polypropylene fibers is less brittle than
unreinforced concrete.

In this sentence, the term "concrete" refers to all concrete. The clause "that has been reinforced by polypropylene fibers" clarifies that the sentence is not about all concrete but just the concrete that has been reinforced. The clause therefore restricts the meaning of "concrete" as it is used in the sentence.

To put it another way, the circle in the illustration below represents all concrete. The shaded pie slice represents the subject of the sentence—the concrete that has been reinforced.

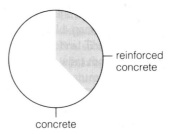

Because the restrictive modifier must be understood in conjunction with the term it modifies, it would be illogical to separate it from the term with a comma. If the clause is restrictive, do not use a comma.

Nonrestrictive clause. A **nonrestrictive clause** adds additional information, but it does not restrict the meaning of the term it modifies. Although removing the clause from the sentence would cost the sentence some meaning, a reader would still understand the meaning of the term. Because the term can be identified on its own, it does not need to be joined to its modifier. Use a comma (or commas) to separate a nonrestrictive clause from the term it modifies. Use a pair of commas if the dependent clause falls within the sentence rather than at the beginning or end.

```
Research in the reinforcement of concrete with
polypropylene fibers led Shell Chemicals to
develop their "caracrete" material, which
essentially consists of polypropylene fibers and
concrete.

Caracrete, which consists of polypropylene
fibers and concrete, can be used in...
```

Usually a proper name or specific term will be followed only by a nonrestrictive clause. "Caracrete" defines a material that is not further subclassified. The nonrestrictive clause that follows tells readers something about the material, but it does not define just one type of caracrete. On the basis of the information in the restrictive clause, we could not draw a circle representing "caracrete" and identify a pie slice that represented just one type of caracrete.

Strict rules of usage dictate that a restrictive clause begins with *that*, while a nonrestrictive clause begins with *which*. Because most writers do not know or do not apply that distinction, it is an unreliable clue about whether the clause is restrictive or nonrestrictive. Usually you can determine whether the clause is restrictive or nonrestrictive by close reading of the sentence on its own and in context. If you cannot determine whether the clause is restrictive or nonrestrictive, ask the writer for clarification of meaning.

When the relative pronoun in a restrictive or nonrestrictive clause refers to people rather than to objects, use the pronoun *who* rather than *that*. Never use *which* to refer to people.

```
The proposed computer center would benefit walk-
in customers, who would receive inexpensive and
quality service.
```

Punctuating Compound-Complex Sentences

When you punctuate sentences that contain two independent clauses, one of which includes a dependent clause, you will apply the rules both for punctuating compound sentences and for punctuating complex sentences. Begin with the biggest structures, the two independent clauses. If the clauses are joined by a coordinating conjunction, separate them with a comma preceding the conjunction; otherwise, use a semicolon. Next look at the clause that contains a dependent clause. If the dependent clause introduces the clause, place a comma after it. If the dependent clause modifies the subject, determine whether it is restrictive or nonrestrictive, and punctuate accordingly.

The preceding sentence is a compound-complex sentence. The subject and verb of the two independent clauses are "[you] determine" and "[you] punctuate." (*You* in both clauses is the understood subject because the verbs are in the imperative mood.) Because the coordinating conjunction "and" joins the clauses, a comma is sufficient to signal that the new clause begins. One dependent clause within the first clause contains the subject and verb "clause modifiers." The subordinating conjunction "if" makes the clause dependent. Because the dependent clause introduces the independent clause, a comma signals the end of that clause and the beginning of the new one. A second dependent clause includes the subject and verb "it is"; the subordinating conjunction "whether" makes it dependent. This clause functions as the object of the verb "determine." Because punctuation should not separate parts of the sentence that logically belong together (such as verb and object), no comma precedes this dependent clause.

Punctuating Items in a Series/Parallel Structure

A series is a list within a sentence of three or more items such as terms, phrases, or clauses. **Parallel structure** means that items with related meanings share a common grammatical form. The items in the list may be a series of prepositional phrases (e.g., by planning, by scheduling tasks, and by evaluating), or nouns, or adjectives, or infinitive phrases, or clauses, or other structural units that may reasonably appear in a series. The structural similarity helps to identify the items in the list and to establish that they are related. Sentence structure will guide your punctuation of series.

Series comma and semicolon. Unless the items in the series are long and complex, they are generally separated by commas, with the conjunction *and* preceding the final item. The commas signal to readers where one item ends and another begins. In fact, conventions about whether to place a comma before the final item in the series have changed over time and differ, to some extent, among disciplines. However, major handbooks of punctuation and grammar today concur in recommending the comma before the final item in the series. The comma clarifies the sentence structure by indicating that the series is about to end. The comma is especially important for clarification purposes when one item in the series includes a conjunction. If commas are not routinely used before the final item in the series, a reader has only the coordinating conjunction to signal the end. Because a coordinating conjunction may also signal that one of the items in the series has two components, the conjunction alone may give misleading information.

Consider how some readers may stumble over the following sentence.

```
Good hygiene, such as sneezing into a tissue,
washing hands before handling food and cleaning
utensils and cutting boards thoroughly,
eliminates most of the risk of transmitting
bacteria in food handling.
```

On first reading, a reader may regard "food and cleaning utensils" as objects of "handling." Rereading and logic will confirm that the writer is not advising washing hands before handling cleaning utensils, but reading time has been wasted. One problem is that the series is built on *-ing* words ("sneezing," "washing," "cleaning"), but other *-ing* words ("handling," "transmitting") interfere with the recognition of their relationships. A comma before the final item could eliminate the need to reread.

```
Good hygiene, such as sneezing into a tissue,
washing hands before handling food, and cleaning
utensils and cutting boards thoroughly,
eliminates most of the risk of transmitting
bacteria in food handling.
```

The two sentences in the following example may require a reader to reread. In the first sentence, if readers depend only on the coordinating conjunction *and* to signal the end of the series, they may, on first reading, assume that "research" is the third area and "special programs" the fourth. In the second sentence, the item "information systems and quantitative sciences" may be read erroneously as two teaching areas, and "management and marketing" may be read as one. The practice of using a comma before the final item will reduce the reader's dependence on the coordinating conjunction alone to signal the end.

> Today the College of Business Administration includes four functional program areas: undergraduate programs, graduate programs, research and special programs and the Center for Professional Development. The teaching areas of the college are accounting, finance, information systems and quantitative sciences, management and marketing.

With the insertion of series commas, however, the sentences are likely to be read correctly the first time through.

> Today the College of Business Administration includes four functional program areas: undergraduate programs, graduate programs, research and special programs, and the Center for Professional Development. The teaching areas of the college are accounting, finance, information systems and quantitative sciences, management, and marketing.

Journalism, unlike technical communication and educational publishing, advises writers not to use the comma before the final item in the series. Thus, if you are editing according to journalistic style, you will not use the comma as recommended here. Appreciation of the possible confusion resulting from its absence, however, should cause you to structure sentences to minimize the possibility of misreading.

Semicolons may be used to separate the main items in the series when these items contain subdivisions separated by commas.

> The editing course covers sentence-level issues such as grammar and spelling; whole-document issues such as style, organization, and format; and design and production issues such as typography and printing.

When you check the punctuation of a structurally complex series, look at the main divisions first and then consider the smaller divisions. Be sure to include a comma and conjunction before the final item in each series of three or more.

Faulty parallelism. Faulty parallelism results when the structure of items in a series shifts. Faulty parallelism creates confusion for readers because the structural signals contradict the meaning of the words. Because of faulty parallelism, readers may not interpret the sentence correctly.

```
The major steps in changing spark plugs are
setting the gap on the new plugs, remove the
spark plug wire, and install the new plugs.
```

The shift from the noun form, "setting," to the verb form, "remove" and "install," reveals a shift from description to instruction, inappropriate in a list of steps. The noun form is the correct one to follow the *to be* verb, because the information that follows such a verb either modifies or substitutes for the subject of the sentence.

```
The major steps in changing spark plugs are
setting the gap on the new plugs, removing the
spark plug wire, and installing the new plugs.
```

What appears as faulty parallelism is often incorrect punctuation. You may recognize faulty parallelism first but fix the sentence by restructuring. For example, does the following sentence identify two research tasks or three?

```
In researching the career of an agricultural
scientist, I consulted the Occupational Outlook
Handbook, Standard and Poor's Index of
Corporations, and interviewed a research
associate at the Agricultural Experiment
Station.
```

The punctuation suggests three research tasks, but analysis reveals that the signals are misleading.

As you analyze the structure of sentences in order to punctuate, it may help to list key terms in outline form. Note how the first outline, which preserves the three-part series signaled by punctuation and conjunctions, reveals the faulty parallelism in the sentence.

```
I

    consulted
    Standard and Poor's
    and interviewed
```

The first and third items are verbs, but the second is the name of a book. Thus, you might try a second outline.

```
I

    consulted a and b
    and interviewed...
```

The second outline reveals how the basic series includes two items, with the first item consisting of two objects. According to the rules, two items are joined by a coordinating conjunction, without punctuation.

```
In researching the career of an agricultural
scientist, I consulted the Occupational Outlook
Handbook and Standard and Poor's Index of
Corporations and interviewed a research
associate at the Agricultural Experiment
Station.
```

Thus, the punctuation identifies the structure of the sentence as a simple sentence with a compound verb. The verbs are joined by the coordinating conjunction "and," without punctuation. However, because of the complexity (compound object and compound verb), it will help readers if you create two independent clauses here by repeating the "I."

```
In researching the career of an agricultural
scientist, I consulted the Occupational Outlook
Handbook and Standard and Poor's Index of
Corporations, and I interviewed a research
associate at the Agricultural Experiment
Station.
```

A series of three is often easier to understand than a double compound. If you can preserve the meaning accurately by converting a double compound to a series of three, choose the series of three.

Original (Faulty Parallelism)

```
Thousands of openings will occur each year
resulting from growth, experienced workers
transferring, or retiring.
```

Double Compound

```
Thousands of openings will occur each year
resulting from growth and from experienced
workers transferring or retiring.
```

Series of Three

```
Thousands of openings will occur each year
resulting from growth, transfers, and
retirements.
```

When the items in a series are prepositional or infinitive or noun phrases, the word that introduces the phrase (e.g., the preposition *to* or the article *the*) may or may not be repeated for each item. The choice depends on the complexity of the sentence. It may be sufficient to use the introductory word just once, in the first item.

```
The accountant is responsible for preparing the
balance sheet, analyzing the data, and ̶f̶o̶r̶
reporting findings to the manager.
```

The series is short, and the three responsibilities are evident. In a more complex series, however, the repetition of the introductory word with each item will help readers recognize when they have arrived at subsequent items on the list.

```
Damaged O-rings have been tested in order to
determine the extent of failure in the material
and the temperature at which failure occurred
and to evaluate the effect of joint rotation.
```

Be consistent in your choice.

PUNCTUATION WITHIN WORDS

The punctuation discussed thus far reveals sentence structure. Punctuation within words also gives readers useful information. This category of punctuation includes the apostrophe and the hyphen.

The Apostrophe   Apostrophes show either possession or contraction. The apostrophe before a final *s* distinguishes a possessive noun or pronoun from a plural. For example, *engineer's report* and *Bachelor's degree* show that the second term in some way belongs to the first. Whenever you could insert the conjunction *of* in a phrase, the noun or pronoun is likely to be possessive and should have an apostrophe. Although we probably wouldn't say "report of the engineer" or "degree of a bachelor," it would not be wrong to do so, and the "of" points to the need for an apostrophe.

Words can be both plural and possessive. In these cases, you should form the plural before you show the possessive. For nouns whose plural ends in *s*, the *s* will precede the apostrophe, as in "students' papers" (more than one student) or "pipes' corrosion" (more than one pipe). Irregular plurals are the exception: "women's studies."

As an editor, you will have plenty of chances to fix the use of apostrophes to show possession. Many writers ignore the apostrophe altogether; many others use them incorrectly to indicate plurals. You may have seen signs like the one in the grocery store announcing "banana's for sale" or the building directory identifying an office for "Veterans Adviser's."

Its and other pronouns (*his, hers, theirs, whose*) are the exceptions to the rule to use an apostrophe to show possession. If this word shows possession (that something belongs to it), there should be no apostrophe, as in "its texture" or "its effect." The word *it's* is the contraction for "it is"; *who's* means "who is."

Do not use an apostrophe with years or abbreviations (the *s* simply forms a plural):

the 1920s, the late 1800s

IQs, YMCAs

Finally, with a compound subject, use the possessive only on the second noun.

Mark and Steve's report

The Hyphen   The hyphen shows that two words function as a unit. Often new terms introduced into the language are formed from two familiar words. These new terms are compound nouns and compound verbs, such as *cross-examination* and *cross-examine*. Compound terms may be hyphenated, "open" (i.e., two words, unhyphenated, such as *type style*) or "solid" or "closed" (i.e., a single word, such as *typesetting*). Hyphens are also frequent in modifiers when two terms join to modify another, but not all modifiers are hyphenated.

You can often determine which compounds are hyphenated by consulting a dictionary. Check the dictionary, for example, to determine whether to hyphenate "cross" compounds. You will find inconsistencies: *cross section* but *cross-reference* and *crosscurrent; crossbreed* but *cross-index; halftone* but *half note* and *half-truth*. Where the dictionary is incomplete, you will have to apply general principles, such as those discussed here and in more detail in a style guide.

Noun forms. Noun forms are more likely to be open or solid than hyphenated. Noun phrases formed from two nouns are usually open or solid. The nouns *problem solving* and *decision making,* for example, are not hyphenated; the nouns *lovemaking* and *bookkeeping* are closed up as one word. Nouns phrases formed from a noun and an adjective are more likely to be hyphenated or solid. Thus, the "self" compounds — for example, *self-service, self-study,* and *self-treatment* — are hyphenated; so are the "vice" compounds — *vice-president. Hydrochloric acid,* however, and many other compounds of noun plus adjective, are open. Finally, fractional numbers, such as *one-half* and *two-thirds*, are hyphenated.

Adjective forms. Compound adjectives are hyphenated if they precede the word modified and if they are formed in the ways listed below:

- **Adjective or noun + past participle** (if the compound term precedes the noun):

  ```
  country-smoked ham
  ```
  BUT: The ham was country smoked.

  ```
  computer-assisted editing
  ```
  BUT: The editing was computer assisted.

  ```
  dark-haired girl
  ```
  BUT: The girl was dark haired.

- **Noun + present participle:**

  ```
  decision-making procedures
  ```
  BUT: decision making
      (noun)

  ```
  interest-bearing account
  ```

- **Compounds with "all," "half," "high," or "low"** (whether they precede or follow the noun):

  ```
  all-purpose facility, all-or-none reaction,
  all-out effort, all-around student
  ```

  ```
  half-raised house, half-blooded Indian
  BUT: halfhearted effort, halfway house
  ```

  ```
  high-energy particles, high-grade disks
  BUT: high blood pressure
  ```

- **Compounds with "well"** (if they precede a noun):

  ```
  well-researched report
  BUT: The report was well researched.
  ```
  Compounds with "well" are not hyphenated in a predicate.

Do not use a hyphen in compound adjectives in these situations:

- **The suffix -ly:**

  ```
  highly motivated person, recently developed
  program
  ```

- **Two proper names:**

  ```
  Latin American countries
  ```

- **Two nouns:**

  ```
  blood pressure level
  ```

Unit modifiers with numerals. When a numeral forms part of a compound adjective, it should be hyphenated when it precedes the noun it modifies. Thus, we would write "two-unit course" or "six-foot fence." The hyphen is particularly important if two numerals are involved.

```
three 2-liter bottles
```

A predicate adjective, however, is not hyphenated.

```
The fence is six feet tall.
```

Make sure that the phrase is a modifier and not simply a measure.

```
a two-semester course
```

BUT: `a course lasting two semesters`

If you have a series of unit modifiers, repeat the hyphen after each numeral.

```
The foundation offers two- and three-year
scholarships.
```

Finally, spelled-out fractions are hyphenated.

```
three-fourths full, one-half of the samples
```

Color terms. If one color term modifies another, do not hyphenate.

```
bluish gray paper
```

If the two color terms are equal in importance, however, insert a hyphen.

```
blue-gray paper
```

Prefixes and suffixes. Generally, prefixes and suffixes are treated as part of the word and spelled solid although some prefixes are hyphenated to prevent misreading. For example, the prefix *re* is frequently hyphenated if the word that follows begins with an *e—re-enter, re-enact, re-examine, re-educate*. The dictionary will show both hyphenated and solid alternatives for some of these types of words. In that case, you should choose one form and place it on your style sheet so that you can be consistent in future choices.

When in doubt, leave it out. If you judge that readers will read accurately without the hyphen, chances are you don't need one—except for unit modifiers with numerals. This principle also acknowledges a trend in language development away from hyphens. In the history of a word's development, the two familiar words that form a new compound may be hyphenated initially so that readers will see their relationship. When, over time, the compound becomes familiar, the hyphen isn't needed for this information and often disappears. This trend is one reason why *copyediting* is spelled solid in this book though you will see it spelled elsewhere both as *copy editing* and *copy-editing*. *Proofreading*, an older term, has become a permanent compound spelled solid though it began as *proof-reading*. Likewise, the words *longterm* and *fulltime* (and even *shortterm* and *parttime*) are increasingly spelled solid. Within a document, you will always hyphenate consistently.

MECHANICS OF PUNCTUATION

All the discussion in this chapter so far has emphasized punctuation as a clue to meaning. As an editor, you also need to know the conventions of placing the marks of punctuation. This section reviews common occurrences; a handbook or style guide will give you more detailed and complete information.

Quotation Marks

Place quotation marks outside a comma or period but inside a semicolon or colon.

```
The prosecutor described the defendant as
"defiant and uncooperative."

The defendant was described by the prosecutor as
"defiant and uncooperative"; however, the
defendant's behavior changed once he took his
place on the witness stand.
```

Do not use quotation marks with a block quotation (one that is indented and set off from the rest of the text). In such a situation, they are redundant, as the block form identifies the material as a quotation.

Parentheses

If parentheses enclose an entire sentence, include the end-of-sentence punctuation within the parentheses. But if parentheses enclose only part of a sentence, place the period or other punctuation outside the parentheses.

```
Twelve reports in the library deal with air
pollution and acid rain in various ecosystems
(e.g., the urban environment, streams, forests,
and deserts).

Twelve reports in the library deal with air
pollution and acid rain in various ecosystems.
(Examples of ecosystems are the urban
environment, streams, forests, and deserts.)
```

Keep parenthetical cross-references and references to visuals within the sentence. That is, do not let a parenthetical cross-reference "float" in a paragraph; attach it to the previous sentence.

> The survey revealed that 40 percent of the
> employees favor a profit-sharing plan for
> retirement (see Table I).

**Commas:
Introductory Phrases
and Internal Phrases**

Unless an introductory phrase is quite short, use a comma after it.

> In the appendix to our style guide, we have
> listed the correct spellings for specialized
> terms that are frequently used in our
> publications.

If a word or phrase is set off within the sentence, use a pair of commas
(just as you would use a pair of parentheses).

> Natural fibers, such as cotton, silk, and wool,
> "breathe" better than fibers manufactured from
> oil byproducts.

> On May 3, 1990, we introduced our first
> accounting software at the convention.

If the internal phrase, such as an appositive, is restrictive, don't use any
commas.

> Plants such as poison ivy may cause allergic
> dermatitis.

"Such as poison ivy" identifies a small category of plants. It restricts the
meaning of "plants" to those that are like poison ivy. Other plants do not
cause allergic dermatitis.

**Comma with
Adjectives in a Series
(Coordinate Adjectives)**

If adjectives in a series both or all modify the noun, use a comma between
them but not after the final one.

> The older, slower models will be replaced.
> (The models are both older *and* slower.)

Sometimes one adjective must be understood as part of the term modified.
The phrase *theoretical research* identifies a type of research that differs

from, say, *empirical research*. The phrase *recent theoretical research* does not use a comma between the two adjectives, "recent" and "theoretical," because "recent" modifies the whole phrase "theoretical research" rather than "research" alone.

Dash   A dash—typed as two hyphens without space around them—can substitute for parentheses or can show a break in thought. In the sentence you just read, they function as parentheses. Commas could have been used instead, but the dashes are more emphatic. Dashes also signal additional information at the end of the sentence that helps a reader interpret the significance of the primary information in the sentence.

```
Some state prison systems apply the policy of
risk-group screening for AIDS only to pregnant
women—a very small number of inmates.
```

Dashes have their proper and formal uses, but overuse will diminish their power to emphasize, and constant breaks in thought will make the writer seem immature or disorganized. Therefore, you should use dashes judiciously. There are no rules about how many are too many; you will have to trust your hunches and common sense.

Colon   The colon is used to introduce a list, but it is often used superfluously and therefore incorrectly. Do not use a colon between a preposition and its object nor between a verb and its complement or object. (See Chapter 6 and the glossary for definitions of these parts of speech.)

```
WRONG: Natural fibers, such as: cotton, silk,
and wool, are comfortable next to the skin.
WRONG: Three types of communication are:
written, oral, and graphic.
CORRECT: A complete technical communicator is
competent at three types of communication:
written, oral, and graphic.
```

Note that in the sentence labeled "correct," the verb and complement are complete before the colon.

Type two spaces after a colon, just as you would type two spaces after a period.

Ellipsis Points   Ellipsis points indicate that some words have been omitted from a quotation. They are rarely used at the beginning or end of the quotation. Ellipsis points are typed as three spaced periods. If the ellipsis comes at the end of a sentence, also type a period (four periods total).

SUMMARY   Correct punctuation is a way of clarifying meaning because it reveals structures in sentences and relationships of ideas. To punctuate correctly, an editor must understand basic sentence patterns and the corresponding punctuation rules. For detailed guidelines and answers to specific questions, editors should consult a handbook or book on grammar.

FURTHER READING   Theodore M. Bernstein. 1984. *The Careful Writer.* New York: Atheneum.

Roy H. Copperud. 1980. *American Usage and Style: The Consensus.* New York: Van Nostrand Reinhold.

DISCUSSION AND APPLICATION

1. Identify the sentence type—simple, compound, complex, or compound-complex—for each of the sentences following.

    [1]Since 1974, thousands of papers have addressed the subject of ozone depletion. [2]The first hard evidence that proved a problem existed did not surface until 1985; in that year, Dr. Joe Farman of the British Antarctic Survey team reported finding a hole in the ozone directly over Antarctica. [3]In order to learn more about this Antarctic ozone phenomenon, scientists around the world have joined forces to create the National Ozone Expedition (NOZE). [4]Each year since 1986, these scientists have braved the cold of Antarctica in order to study the ozone depletion patterns that occur there every spring.

2. Punctuate the sentences to clarify the structure of clauses and phrases within them. Articulate the reason for each mark of punctuation you insert or the reason for deleting a mark.

a. I had hoped to find a summer job in the city however two weeks of job hunting convinced me that it was impossible.

b. We came to work today in the rain; although we all preferred to stay in bed.

c. Most of our studies have focused on the response of cultured mammalian cells to toxic inorganics such as cadmium, these in vitro studies benefit from the ease and definition with which cultured cells may be manipulated and from the absence of complicating secondary interactions that occur in vivo. Perhaps the greatest advantage of working with cultured cells however is that it is often possible to derive populations that vary in their response to the agents in question. Because the mechanisms involved in cell damage or protection are often altered specifically in such cells; they provide tools invaluable to identification of these mechanisms and to a definition of their importance in the overall response of the cell.

d. This intentional fragment appears in a college catalog course description. Explain why the colon won't work, and suggest alternative punctuation.

The study of contemporary techniques of music: modes, synthetic scales, serialism, vertical structures, with a term project.

  e. Since computer skills, including page design
     have become essential to professional writers,
     college writing courses include a computer
     component.
  f. Other substances inhibit digestion of insects,
     alter insect reproduction to make it less
     efficient or interfere with insect
     development.

3. In the following sentences, identify the dependent clauses that
   begin with a relative pronoun. Determine whether the clause is a
   restrictive or nonrestrictive modifier, and punctuate accordingly.
   Change "which" to "that" when the modifying clause is restrictive.
   When you cannot tell for sure, explain the difference in meaning if
   the modifier is restrictive rather than nonrestrictive.

  a. Adding polypropylene fibers to concrete
     increases its resistance to dynamic loading
     which is characterized by high strain rates
     that result from explosive impact or earth-
     quake loading.
  b. The death of 3,000 white-tailed deer in 1962
     resulted from heavy overpopulation and range
     abuse which led to malnutrition and its vari-
     ous side effects.
  c. Americans admire intelligence, which has prac-
     tical aims, but intelligence which ponders,
     wonders, theorizes, and imagines is suspect.
  d. The photoconductive cells measure the amount
     of radiant energy and convert it to electrical
     energy which is then interpreted by the com-
     puter and displayed on the meter.
  e. Present lab equipment allows pulse energy
     experiments, which require 300,000 kW or less

of electric power. New equipment would
increase the potential of the lab.

f. A high deer population which continuously
feeds on the seedlings of a desired tree
species can severely retard the propagation
of that species.

g. Pulse welding can join many metals which are
impossible to join by conventional welding
methods.

4. Each of the following sentences contains faulty parallelism or a
double compound punctuated as a series of three. The present
punctuation and item structure do not accurately reveal the overall
sentence structure. Punctuate and use parallel structure to clarify
the relationship of the items. If you cannot determine the writer's
meaning well enough to punctuate, write a query to the writer to
elicit the necessary information.

a. The rehabilitation center is raising funds to
purchase Hydro-Therapy bathing equipment,
wheelchairs, and to renovate the Hydro-Therapy
swimming pool.

b. The disease is typified by a delay in motor
development, by self-destructive behavior, and
it leads to death.

c. The virus may cause AIDS, cancer, or even kill.

d. The literature component of the professional
writing major allows students to develop their
sensitivity to language, texts, and their
ability to read critically.

e. This anthology is for psychologists, students
of psychology, and of other related fields.
The articles deal mostly with contemporary
problems in psychology, minority, cultural,
and other underrepresented groups.

f. These instructions are written for automobile owners who do their own minor repairs, know the primary parts of an engine, and the use of tools.

5. For each of the following, make sure all related items in a series have parallel structure.

   a. The old copiers produce copies of inconsistent quality, sometimes too light and at other times a black smudge of toner.

   b. Some qualities that are needed are the ability to communicate orally and written, and possess good judgment and tact.

   c. We have investigated ways of raising capital for building the Ronald McDonald House. We have spoken to banks about loans, to a foundation about getting grants, as well as fundraisers.

   d. Please send information on the following:

      - the national office's program for low-interest loans

      - the matching funds program

      - any other helpful advice on funding

   e. The ten-year cost is $5,000 for renting and $3,864 if they were to buy.

   f. Be careful, this one is tricky. Hint: A verb plus -ing can form a participle (adjective) or gerund (noun substitute).

      A teenager may reveal a drug habit by skipping classes, falling grades, and losing friends.

6. Which of these phrases require an apostrophe to show possession?

   a. bears paw

   b. two years experience

c. two years ago

d. jobs requirements

e. requirements for the job

f. its colors

g. joints rotation

h. Steves Café

i. Masters degree

j. two months allowance

k. policies cash value

l. employees cafeteria

7. Correct the punctuation in the following sentences, and explain why each change was necessary. Some sentences may require more than one change. If the sentence is punctuated correctly, cite the principle that verifies its correctness.

a. The copy center, like the check cashing service and the convenience store would be open 24 hours each day.

b. Harris/3M offers a 36 month leasing plan. For the proposed copiers for the center, the 6055 and the 6213. Lease costs would be $702 per month which includes maintenance.

c. If the target goal of 36,000 copies per month billed at $.045 is met the equipment will pay for itself in 2.5 years sooner if the monthly allowance is exceeded.

d. The fixed costs involved with this project; electricity, ventilation and floor space are not considered.

e. There are two types of ultraviolet (UV) radiation; UV-A and UV-B. UV-A radiation which is frequently used for tanning beds, is lower in energy (longer in wavelength) than UV-B there-

fore it is considered safer than UV-B radiation. Some experimenters; however, believe
that UV-A is just as damaging as UV-B;
although higher doses of UV-A are required.

f. Many theories about the depletion of ozone
have been proposed but at present, two main
hypotheses are widely accepted; the chemical
mechanism and the dynamic mechanism.

g. Chlorofluorocarbons (CFCs) such as the
refrigerant freon, are very inert compounds,
however, when CFCs drift into the upper
atmosphere ultraviolet light will activate
them.

8. Determine whether the compound terms and modifiers in the following sentences should be hyphenated, solid, or open.

a. While studying day to day read outs from the
Total Ozone Mapping Spectrometer, Dr. Wilson
discovered that drastic depletions of ozone in
a short period of time are not at all out of
the ordinary.

b. The manual includes step by step instructions.

c. We took a multiple choice exam.

d. The grant requires a semi-annual progress
report.

e. Type the sub-headings left justified.

f. The left justified headings are not recognizable as level one headings.

g. The pipe is two meters long.

h. The valves in the two, three, and four meter
pipes have corroded.

i. Cross fertilization joins gametes from different individuals. The parents may be different
varieties or species.

```
   j. This text book also serves as a reference
      book.
   k. The architect designed a multi purpose cafete-
      ria for the school.
```

9. The following pairs of sentences differ only in punctuation. Explain the difference in meaning that results.

```
   a. A style sheet is a list of the general style--
      spelling, capitalization, abbreviation,
      hyphens--and unfamiliar or specialized terms.
      A style sheet is a list of the general style--
      spelling, capitalization, abbreviation,
      hyphens, and unfamiliar or specialized terms.
```

```
   b. When you make an entry on your style sheet,
      write the page number of the first occurrence
      (or every occurrence if you think you may
      change the style later). You will then be able
      to check your choice in its context.

      When you make an entry on your style sheet,
      write the page number of the first occurrence,
      or every occurrence, if you think you may
      change the style later. You will then be able
      to check your choice in its context.
```

10. Examine a sample of your own writing, and determine the following:
    a. Sentence patterns: What types of sentences do you use the most?
    b. Punctuation: Is your work punctuated correctly?
    Prepare some goals for yourself for structuring sentences and/or punctuating them.

11. Word play: tell why these terms are named as they are.
    a. Why is there a "junction" in a conjunction?
    b. Why are some pronouns "relative"?
    c. Why are some clauses "subordinate"?

d. How is "punctuation" related to "punctuality"?
e. How does a "period" relate to time?
f. How is a pronoun "pro" the noun?
g. What does a restrictive modifier "restrict"?
h. How does a modifier "modify"?
i. What is "semi" about a semicolon?
j. How does a "dash" dash?

8 QUANTITATIVE AND TECHNICAL MATERIAL

When the material is mathematical, statistical, or technical, the copyeditor's job is the same as when the material consists solely of words. The object is to establish that the material is correct, consistent, accurate, and complete. In addition, the copyeditor prepares the text for typesetting by marking for italics and capitalization, distinguishing letters from numbers, and indicating spacing and other unusual elements.

Mathematical, statistical, and other technical documents require even more attention than do paragraphs and sentences. Because of the potential complexity of quantitative and technical material, which may contain many symbols and unusual type devices, the chances of errors occurring in the typescript are greater than with a prose typescript. Copyeditors with expertise in words rather than numbers can be especially helpful in establishing correct grammar and proper punctuation in mathematical and other technical documents. As a copyeditor of quantitative and technical material, you do not have to understand fully the meaning of equations and statistics. However, you must be aware of the implications of changing symbols or capitalization or punctuation and of the need to mark clearly for typesetting.

This chapter introduces some principles for using numbers in math and statistics as well as basic standards of measurement and some scientific symbols. It also introduces guidelines for displaying and marking mathematical material. The chapter will not make you an expert in math and statistics, but if you learn the principles outlined here and check the applicable style manuals as you work, you can be competent in and confident about marking this type of text.

USING NUMBERS

The conventions for the treatment of numbers in technical texts differ from those in humanities texts, and to some extent, they differ among the technical disciplines. The conventions concern questions of style such as whether to spell out a number or use a figure and whether to use the metric, British, or U.S. system of measurement. A style guide will provide specific guidelines within a discipline, but some generalizations about using numbers in technical documents should be noted.

1. Use figures for all quantifiable units of measure, no matter how small, rather than spelling out the numbers. Also, use a figure whenever you abbreviate the measure.

```
2 m   1.5 in   0.3 cm
12 hours   $1 million   18 liters
```

Figures aid readers in comprehending and in calculating. In documents that are not scientific or technical, however, you should spell out both the number and the measure if the number is lower than 10 or possibly lower than 100.

2. Do not begin a sentence with a figure. Either rearrange the sentence to avoid the figure at the beginning or spell out the number.

3. Given a choice, use the metric system of measurement rather than the British or U.S. system, and don't mix systems. For example, do not describe something in both inches and centimeters. Readers may be confused or misled by the dual usage and may misjudge the measures.

4. Set decimal fractions of less than 1.0 with an initial zero (e.g., 0.25, 0.4). An exception is a quantity that never equals 1.0, such as a probability or a correlation coefficient.

Check a comprehensive or discipline style manual for specific directions on the treatment of numbers in dates, money, and time.

MEASUREMENT   Three systems of measurement are widely used: the U.S. Customary System, the British Imperial System, and the International (metric) System. In the U.S. and British systems, the standard measures are the yard and the pound, but these systems vary in some measures and in the expression of them. For example, a billion in the British system equals a million million, whereas in the U.S. system it equals a thousand million. The metric system is used for most scientific and technical work.

The International System of Units, an extension of the metric system, comprises a standard system of units for all physical measurements. Its units are called SI units (for *Système International,* in French). The International System has seven fundamental units, listed here.

Quantity	*Unit*	*Symbol*
length	meter	m
mass	kilogram	kg
time	second	s
electric current	ampere	A
temperature	kelvin	K
luminous intensity	candela	cd
amount of substance	mole	mol

Other measures, based on these fundamental units, are derived units—that is, they are multiples or parts of the fundamental units. Because the metric system is a decimal system, all the derived units are multiples of 10. The prefix indicates the multiple: a *kilo*meter equals 1,000 meters, while a *centi*meter equals 0.01 meter. Use only numbers between 0.1 and 1,000 in expressing the quantity of any SI unit; use the derived units for smaller or larger numbers. For example, 10,000 m equals 10 km.

SI units established for other physical quantities are used primarily in science and engineering. The following list presents a few of these units. The SI units and symbols pertinent to a given field are likely to be listed in that field's handbook.

Quantity	*Unit*	*Symbol*
acceleration	meter per second squared	m/s^2
electric resistance	ohm	Ω
frequency	hertz	Hz
power	watt	W
pressure	newton per square meter	N/m^2
velocity	meter per second	m/s

As copyeditor, you ensure that the symbols used for these measurements are correct and that they are used consistently. Whereas the *units* are lowercase, even when they represent names, some *symbols* include capital letters, especially if they represent names. Note, for example, the capitalization style for watt and newton as units as opposed to symbols. Note, too, that the units and symbols are set in roman type and without periods.

The symbols are never made into plurals. Thus, six watts would be written as "6 W," not "6 Ws." However, if the measures are written in prose, the words are formed into plurals according to the same rules that govern other words. Thus, "6 watts" is correct in a sentence. Fractions of units are always expressed in the singular whether they are expressed in symbols or in prose—0.1 m and 0.1 meter.

A hyphen is used between the measure and the unit when they form a modifier but not when they simply define a measure. Thus, both "The trial lasted 10 seconds" and "the 10-second trial" are correct.

MATHEMATICAL MATERIAL

Documents that include fractions, equations, or other mathematical expressions require close copyediting attention. Sometimes, to save space, stacked fractions must be converted for inline presentation. Equations may have to be displayed, numbered, or broken. In addition, copymarking must clarify characters that could be confusing (e.g., the number 1 and the letter l, the number 0 and the capital letter O, the unknown quantity x and the sign for multiplication) and indicate the position of subscripts and superscripts on the page, as well as noting italics and capitalization. Because mathematical material is expensive to copyedit, typeset, and print, good copyediting can save expense later in production. Fortunately, the computer has eased the copyeditor's job—writers are likely to submit material that is already formatted with a scientific and technical word processing program. Copyeditors use these programs, too, saving time with marking. (See the section on computer programs later in the chapter.)

Fractions

Fractions may be set "stacked" or "solid" (inline). The inline version substitutes a slanted line, or **solidus**, for the horizontal line of the stacked fraction.

Stacked	*Solid (Inline)*
$\dfrac{1 + (x - 3)}{y + 2}$	$[1 + (x - 3)]/(y + 2)$

The stacked version is preferable for comprehension because it conveys visually the relationship of the numbers. However, it takes more space in typesetting. Particularly if a fraction appears in a sentence, it may have to be converted to inline form in order to avoid awkward line breaks and extra space between the lines. Complexity in fractions, however, will justify the extra space for stacking.

When fractions are converted to inline form, parentheses may be necessary to clarify not only the numerator and denominator but also the order of operations, which will affect the result obtained. (Remember, operations within parentheses are completed before other operations.) In the previous example, the denominator is the *quantity* (or sum) of $y + 2$. Thus, $y + 2$ will be added before the sum is used as a divisor; otherwise, the numerator of the fraction would be divided by y and then 2 would be added to the total. The entire numerator is enclosed in brackets to establish that those operations must be performed before division. Both the square brackets and the parentheses, as well as braces, are *signs of aggregation* or *fences*. The preferred order for these signs is parentheses, square brackets, and braces:

$$\{[(\ )]\}$$

Fractions containing square root signs can be set inline if the sign is converted to the exponent ½. The square root sign may also be set without the top bar, thereby allowing it to fit within a normal line of type. All three of the following expressions say the same thing.

$$\frac{a + b}{\sqrt{\dfrac{2a - 12}{6}}} \qquad (a + b)/[(2a - 12)/6]^{1/2} \qquad \frac{a + b}{\sqrt{[(2a - 12)/6]}}$$

Mark a stacked fraction for inline presentation by creating a "line break" mark using the line in the fraction.

$$\frac{1}{2} \quad \text{marked} \quad \frac{1}{2}\diagup \quad \text{becomes} \quad ½$$

Equations   Equations are statements that one group of figures and operations equals another. Equations can contain known quantities (expressed as numbers), variables (often expressed as a, b, and c), and unknowns (often expressed as x, y, and z). Equations always include an equal sign.

Displaying and numbering equations. Equations may be set inline, or they may be displayed (set on a separate line). If multiple equations in a text are displayed, they should be either centered or indented a standard amount from the left margin.

Displayed equations may be numbered if they will be referred to again in the document—the numbers provide convenient cross-references. If an equation is to be numbered, it must be displayed, but not all displayed equations are numbered. Generally, the equation number appears in parentheses to the right of the equation.

Equations are numbered sequentially either through the work or through a division of it. A system of double numeration (chapter number followed by a period and the equation number) can save time and labor if an equation number must be changed (perhaps because one equation was deleted). With double numeration, only the equation numbers in that chapter must be changed. The possibility that equation numbers may change during copyediting and revision is also a good reason for numbering only the equations that must be referred to, not all those that are displayed.

Let there begin the value of the y_0, y_1, ..., y_n of the function $y = f(x)$ at the $(n + 1)$ points x_0, x_1, ..., x_n. A unique polynomial $P(x)$ whose degree does not exceed n is given by the equation

$$P(x) = a_n x^n + a_{n-1} x^{n-1} + \cdots + a_0, \quad (2.2)$$

for which $P_n(x)$ at x_i must be satisfied by

$$P_n(x_i) = f(x_i) = y_i, \quad i = 0, 1, \cdots, n. \quad (2.3)$$

The conditions in (2.3) lead to the system of $n + 1$ linear equations in the a_i:

$$\begin{aligned} a_0 + a_1 x_i + \cdots + a_n x^n \\ = y_i i = 0, 1, \cdots, n. \end{aligned} \quad (2.4)$$

Note that equation (2.3) is referred to again by its number. The parentheses identify the figures as an equation number. Some disciplines, such as the American Psychological Association, prefer that the text read "Equation 2.3" rather than (2.3).

Breaking equations. Equations that are too long to fit on one line should be broken before an operational sign (e.g., $+$, $-$, $\times$, $\div$) or a sign indicating relations (e.g., $=$, $\leq$, $\geq$, $<$, $>$). However, you should never break terms in parentheses. Note, for example, that equation (2.4) in the preceding example is broken before an equal sign. Use the line break mark to indicate a break in the equation.

$$a_0 + a_1 x_i + \cdots + a_n x^n \!\!\!\diagup\!\!= y_i i = 0, 1, \cdots, n.$$

In a document with a series of related equations, the equations should be aligned on the equal sign, regardless of the amount of material to the right and left of the equal sign.

```
The mathematical formula for computation of the
mean is
```

$$\overline{X} \;=\; \frac{\Sigma X}{N}$$

```
where
```

$$
\begin{aligned}
\overline{X} &= \text{mean of the scores} \\
\Sigma X &= \text{sum of the scores, and} \\
N &= \text{number of scores.}
\end{aligned}
$$

Punctuating equations. Equations are read as sentences when they appear in prose paragraphs, with the operational signs taking the place of verbs, conjunctions, and adjectives. Thus, $a + b \geq c$, where $b = 2$, would be read aloud as *a* plus *b* is greater than or equal to *c*, where *b* equals 2.

Practice in punctuating equations varies. Some publishers omit punctuation such as commas and periods on the grounds that the marks are potentially confusing if read as part of the equation rather than as punctuation. They would also argue that when the equation is displayed, the space around it signals its beginning and end, making punctuation redundant. Other publishers, however, follow the same rules for punctuating equations as for punctuating prose sentences: displayed equations are punctuated as though they appear in sentences. Thus, they may be followed by commas or periods as the structure of the sentence requires. Note, for example, that in the following examples, no colon appears after "by" in the first equation, but a colon appears after "as follows" in the second equation. The words that introduce the displayed equation are not followed by a colon unless they would be followed by a colon in the same circumstances if all the text were prose. The sentences in which the equations appear end with periods.

```
Let the polynomial be given by
```

$$P(x) \;=\; a_0 + a_1 x + a_2 x^2 + \cdots + a_n x^n,$$

```
where the coefficients a_i are to be determined.
```

If the center of a circle is at the origin and
the radius is r, the formula can be reduced as
follows:

$$x^2 + y^2 = r^2.$$

Grammar. Mathematical copy, like prose copy, should follow accepted rules of grammar: subjects and verbs must agree, nouns take articles, and clauses contain subjects and verbs.

You do not need to understand the following equation to edit the subject-verb agreement error, to place a comma before the nonrestrictive clause, and to conclude the sentence with a period.

There exists a unique polynomial $P(x)$ whose
degree do not exceeds n which is given by $P(x)$
= $a_n x^n + a_{n-1} x^{n-1} + \cdots + a_0$.

A common error in mathematical copy is the dangling participle.

Constructing interpolation polynomials, the
inverse can be explicitly calculated.

By solving $x = 12 - y$, a contradiction can be
obtained.

Dangling participles occur in mathematical text for the same reason they occur in prose: the subject to be modified is absent from the sentence, often because the passive voice omits the agent. Revisions must insert the agent or delete the modifier.

The inverse can be explicitly calculated with
the construction of interpolation polynomials.

Solving $x = 12 - y$, we obtain a contradiction.

Solving $x = 12 - y$ yields a contradiction.

Copymarking for Typesetting Copymarking clarifies type style (italic, roman, or bold), spacing, subscripts and superscripts, and ambiguous characters. Unknowns and variables in expressions and equations are set as lowercase italic letters. These are usually letters in the English alphabet, but sometimes they are Greek letters. If they are not typed in italics on the hard copy, they should be marked with an underline to denote italics. A slash through a letter indicates lowercase when the letter is typed as a capital. Numbers, symbols, and signs are set in roman type. Vectors are set in bold.

Operational signs (e.g., $+$, $-$, $\times$, $\div$) and signs of relation ($=$, $\leq$, $\geq$, $<$, $>$) are set with space on either side. Note that the sign for multiplication is roman, not italic as for the unknown x.

Copymarking should clarify the intent when characters are ambiguous. For example, a short horizontal line may be a minus sign, hyphen, en dash, or em dash. It could even indicate polarity (a negative charge). Some, but not all, possible ambiguities are listed here.

0	zero	ß	Greek beta
O	capital "oh"	B	capital "bee"
o	lowercase "oh"		
°	degree sign	e	exponent
		e	charge of an electron
1	number one	Σ	summation
l	lowercase "el"	ϵ	element of
×	multiplication sign	m	symbol for meter
x	unknown quantity	m	unknown quantity
χ	Greek chi		

If the text contains just a few of these ambiguities, they may be marked as in any other copymarking. A clarifying statement may be circled next to the character. For example, you might write and circle "el" next to the letter that could be misread as the number one. For the unknown quantities, just be sure they are marked as italic if they are not typed in italic.

$$\underline{a} = 0 \text{ (zero)}$$

Even when the typist has been careful to use symbols, italics, and spacing correctly, marks can clarify the intent for the compositor and leave no doubt as to how the elements are to be set. For example, you might mark the superscripts and subscripts, even if they are typed correctly, to confirm that the positions should be retained in typesetting, and you might write and circle "minus sign" next to a minus sign so that it will not be mistaken for an en dash. The extent of your marking for clarification will depend, in part, on your company's practice and on your compositor's expectations, but it is better to err on the side of overclarification than to leave interpretation of elements up to the compositor and spend time—and money—correcting errors after typesetting.

Sometimes you may not be able to tell for certain which characters the writer intended. If characters are handwritten, they are probably Greek letters or others that are not standard on a keyboard. If you have questions, check with the writer.

Computer-Assisted Typesetting — A number of programs are available for typing and typesetting mathematical text. The advantages of the specialized programs for mathematical applications over a regular word processing program are its characters (including Greek symbols and signs of aggregation that span several lines), its ease of formatting subscripts and superscripts, and its automatic generation of displayed and numbered equations.

A regular keyboard is used for typing, but special codes that give directions on spacing, characters, and format are typed in. In the following example, the codes __ and ∧ indicate subscripts and superscripts, respectively.

Input	*Output*
x∧{2y}	x^{2y}
x_{2y}	x_{2y}

If you want to display and number an equation, you simply type in code characters to trigger the display and number. The program can indent and vertically space the equation, break it where appropriate, and number it. If you subsequently change the equation number (by deleting or inserting equations), the computer renumbers the equations automatically.

Input
\begin{equation} x' + y∧{2} = z∧{2}\end{equation}

Output
$$x' + y^2 = z^2 \quad (3)$$

Note that the backslash indicates instructions rather than text that is to be printed. The word "equation" in braces tells the program to number the equation and where it begins and ends. The symbols ∧ and __ indicate superscript and subscript. The conversion from roman type to italic is automatic for unknowns.

With a laser printer connected to a computer, it is even possible to type camera ready mathematical copy with such a program, thereby bypassing copymarking on hard copy altogether.

STATISTICS

Statistics is a system of procedures for interpreting numerical data. The science of statistics governs the collection of data (as by sampling), the organization of data, and the analysis of data by mathematical formulas. Using statistics, researchers learn the significance of "raw" data, or figures that have not been analyzed, as well as make predictions. Statistics is widely used in any empirical research, or research that relies on observation and experiment. Thus, it is used in the natural, physical, and social sciences and in engineering. You may copyedit material based on statistical analysis if you work in any of these fields and if you edit research proposals and reports. The results of product testing or field testing of documentation may also be analyzed statistically.

Two usage notes: the word *statistics* is singular if it refers to the system of interpreting numerical data; the word is plural if it refers to numbers that are collected. "Statistics is a science" is the correct usage because the reference is to the science. "The statistics are misleading" is correct as a reference to specific numbers. Also, the word *data* is plural; thus, "data are" is the correct usage, in spite of what your ear may tell you.

If you work extensively with statistical material, you should learn more about it than this chapter will tell you. But this chapter will introduce some of the more common terms and symbols to enable you to copyedit.

Letters used as statistical symbols are italicized, whether they appear in prose or in tables, unless they are Greek letters. If they are not italicized or underlined in the typescript, they will have to be marked. Some of the common symbols and abbreviations and their meanings follow.

ANOVA	analysis of variance
r	correlation
df	degrees of freedom
F	F-ratio
μ (Greek letter mu)	mean
n	number of subjects
N	number of test results
p or ϕ (Greek letter phi)	probability
SD	standard deviation
S; Ss	subject; subjects
t-test	test of differences between two means

Equations are placed on the page according to the same rules that govern mathematical material. Thus, related equations are aligned on the equal sign, and operational or relational signs are set with space on either side (e.g., $\mu = 92.55$, not $\mu=92.55$). Remember, too, to place a zero before a decimal in a quantity of less than 1, except for correlation coefficients and probabilities, which are always less than 1. Form plurals of symbols by adding *s* only, with no apostrophe (e.g., *Ss,* not *S's;* IQs, not IQ's).

One other note: capitalize *experiment* or *trial* when these words refer to specific tests. Thus, "The results of Experiment I revealed that . . . " but "the experiment."

TABLES

Tables represent an efficient way to present quantitative data, enabling readers to refer quickly to specific numerical (or verbal) information. Tables often require close scrutiny by the copyeditor for correctness, consistency, accuracy, and completeness. A copyeditor should be alert to misspellings and other errors; inconsistencies in capitalization, spelling, and abbreviation; clarity of identifying information, such as whether the numbers represent percents or totals and whether the measures are meters or feet; correctness of arithmetic, such as whether totals are correct and whether percentages total 100. Apparent inconsistencies in numbers or other data may signal inaccuracy. In addition, the copyeditor should check visual characteristics of the table, such as the amount of space between rows and columns and variations in type style (bold, italic, capitalization) to indicate different levels of headings. A reference to the table in the text should precede the table. Tables should be numbered sequentially in the chapter, and each table number should match the number used in cross-references. The title should accurately reflect the contents.

General Guidelines

Tables should be constructed to enable accurate reading and comprehension. You can find guidelines to aid you in copyediting tables in textbooks on technical writing and in some handbooks and style manuals. The following points briefly summarize these guidelines.

- Visuals that are tabular are called **tables;** other visuals, such as line drawings, graphs, and photographs, are called *figures.* The information in the rows and columns of tables may be quantitative or verbal or even pictorial. The table title and number are identified at the top of the table, although informal tables that lack titles and numbers are also permissible. Some disciplines specify roman numbers for table numbers.

- Items compared in a table are listed down the "stub" (left) column, while points of comparison are listed across the top.

This arrangement allows easy comparison of related numbers down rather than across the columns.

- Vertical and horizontal lines (rules) separating rows and columns are discouraged except for highly complex tables because the lines clutter the table with visual noise. White space is the preferred method for separating rows and columns. Too much space between columns, however, may result in inaccurate reading because the eye may skip to a lower or higher row. Tables do not need to be spaced to fill the same width as the text. Figure 8.1 depicts a table that requires vertical lines to distinguish different levels of information.

- To increase accuracy of reading across the rows of long tables, a space may be used between groups of five or so rows, or alternate groups of five rows may be lightly shaded.

- Columns of numbers should be aligned on the decimal.

- Headings for columns should identify the measure (e.g., $, %, m) that is represented by the numbers in the column. The tables are cleaner (less noisy) if the abbreviation is not repeated for each entry. Another method is to insert the symbol (e.g., $, %, m) before or after the first number in each column. This method reduces clutter in column heads.

- Notes to clarify information or to cite sources may be necessary, just as they are in prose text (see figure 8.1). When the table as a whole comes from a single source, a footnote number appears on the table title, and a note that cites author, title, and publication data appears at the bottom. The form of the note corresponds to the form used for the reference list.

- All tables must be referred to in the text.

Application: Copyediting a Table

Copymarking right on the table is sufficient for simple corrections. You can specify capitalization, deletions, and insertions on the table and supplement these marks with marginal instructions. When the changes are extensive, however, the table may have to be retyped.

Figure 8.2 illustrates a copyeditor's marking of a table for correction before printing. The table was created for a report on AIDS in correctional facilities. It shows the results of screening to determine how many inmates test positive for the HIV antibody, which would indicate that they have been exposed to AIDS. At the time of the screening, only four states had mass screening programs; other jurisdictions rejected mass screening because of questions about the usefulness of the information when

Figure 8.1   Table with Footnotes and Multiple Levels of Headings. Source: U.S. Bureau of the Census. 1989. *Statistical Abstract of the United States, 1989*. 109th ed. Washington, DC: Government Printing Office, 150.

No. 269. Total Graduate Student Enrollment and Degrees Conferred in Selected Fields, by Race/Ethnicity: 1984

[As of fall. Excludes outlying areas. Totals may not agree with other published data because of newly classified schools for which racial/ethnic data were not imputed. For methodological details, see source]

ITEM	NUMBER				PERCENT DISTRIBUTION			
	Total	Minority [1]	White [2]	Non-resident alien [3]	Total	Minority [1]	White [2]	Non-resident alien [3]
Graduate enrollment..................	1,113,113	111,625	892,091	109,397	100.0	10.0	80.1	9.8
Degrees conferred. [4]								
Masters	280,421	29,841	223,628	26,952	100.0	10.6	79.7	9.6
Doctorates	32,307	3,056	23,934	5,317	100.0	9.5	74.1	16.5
SELECTED FIELD								
Agribusiness/agri. products:								
Masters	786	56	520	210	100.0	7.1	66.2	26.7
Doctorates	198	35	111	52	100.0	17.7	56.1	26.3
Agriculture sciences:								
Masters	2,062	136	1,434	492	100.0	6.6	69.5	23.9
Doctorates	822	62	519	241	100.0	7.5	63.1	29.3
Business and management:								
Masters	66,531	6,106	54,623	5,802	100.0	9.2	82.1	8.7
Doctorates	847	57	587	203	100.0	6.7	69.3	24.0
Computer and info. systems:								
Masters	6,942	930	4,303	1,709	100.0	13.4	62.0	24.6
Doctorates	240	20	150	70	100.0	8.3	62.5	29.2
Engineering:								
Masters	20,145	2,265	12,186	5,694	100.0	11.2	60.5	28.3
Doctorates	3,165	398	1,370	1,397	100.0	12.6	43.3	44.1
Mathematics:								
Masters	2,831	273	1,873	685	100.0	9.6	66.2	24.2
Doctorates	686	65	372	249	100.0	9.5	54.2	36.3
Physical sciences:								
Masters	5,661	430	4,133	1,098	100.0	7.6	73.0	19.4
Doctorates	3,369	268	2,420	681	100.0	8.0	71.8	20.2
Social sciences:								
Masters	10,197	1,065	7,333	1,799	100.0	10.4	71.9	17.6
Doctorates	2,828	262	1,969	597	100.0	9.3	69.6	21.1

[1] American Indian/Alaskan native, Non-Hispanic Black, Asian/Pacific Islander and Hispanic.   [2] Non-Hispanic   [3] A person who is not a citizen or national of the U.S. who is in the country on a temporary basis and does not have the right to remain indefinitely.   [4] Includes degrees conferred in fields not shown separately.

Source: U.S. National Center for Education Statistics, *Education Data Tabulations*, January 1988.

therapeutic drugs are not available and about confidentiality and discrimination.

The copyeditor has marked several types of changes, not only in the familiar copyediting realms of correctness, consistency, accuracy, and completeness but also with an eye to visual considerations.

- **Correctness.** A check for correctness reveals several problems. The visual was inappropriately labeled as a figure, but because

Figure 8.2   Copyedited Table

Table U.7

RESULTS OF MASS SCREENING AND RISK-GROUP SCREENING PROGRAMS

A. Mass Screening

Jurisdiction	Number Tested	Inmate category(ies)	Number Seropositive	HIV Seropositive (%)
Colorado	2847	all new inmates	15	0.5%
Iowa	800	all new inmates	0	0.0
Nevada	2638	all new inmates	8	0.3
Nevada	3820	all current inmates	96	2.5
South Dakota	1124	all current inmates	2	0.2

B. Epidemiological Studies

| Michigan | 457 | All new inmates | 4 | 0.8 |

C. Risk-Group Screening

Alabama	301	unspecified risk groups	7	2.3%
New Hampshire	128	homosexuals and IV drug users	5	3.9
Orange County, CA	978	female prostitutes	28	2.9
Minneapolis, MN	260	homosexuals and IV drug users	2	0.8

the material is tabular, its label is changed to *table*. Also, the numbers in columns 2 and 4 are marked to align on the decimal, and the misspelling in the fifth row under "Mass Screening" is corrected.

- **Consistency.** Several changes are required for consistency. The column headings are marked for left justification. Capitalization in headings and in the third column is made consistent. And, because "number" is spelled out in the heading for column 4, the "percent" is also spelled out in the heading for column 5.

One potential troublespot is the "jurisdiction" column. First, note that, even though two jurisdictions in the third category include names of states, this information is not inconsistent because all the other jurisdictions are states. State names thus remain for these two entries. Second, although the jurisdictions are alphabetized in the first section, the alphabetical arrangement is less clear in the third section. The pattern seems to be to name the jurisdictions that are states first and then to include the cities, arranged according to the alphabetical order of the states in which the cities exist. Other patterns of order may be just as rational. For example, the first letter of the jurisdiction may establish the order, or the entries may be ordered according to the state name rather than the city name. However, with such a short list, the order does not particularly matter—a reader will see at a glance what jurisdictions are included. Thus, a change in the order of entries is not necessary and might seem arbitrary.

- **Accuracy/completeness.** In checking for accuracy and completeness, the copyeditor notices several things. The selection of states might raise questions about completeness, but the prose part of the text verifies that only a few jurisdictions have screening programs. Also, the numbers are consistent enough to suggest that they are accurate.

  A copyeditor may legitimately question the middle category, "Epidemiological Studies," because the title names only the first and third categories, and the middle category contains only one study. The table may in fact be complete without this information. However, a deletion would be a content change and therefore beyond the expectations for copyediting. The copyeditor should query the writer before such a deletion, perhaps suggesting that the information on that single study be included within the text of the report where the table is discussed. Another alternative would be to change the title of the table to "Results of Screening Programs for the HIV Antibody in Inmates," which does not imply just two categories. However, a title change would also have to be approved by the writer, and all references to the table in the text and in preliminary pages would have to be changed accordingly.

- **Visual readability.** Perhaps the copyeditor's biggest task is adjusting the visual aspects of the table to make it easy to read and visually pleasing. The title is marked for lowercase letters rather than all caps; presumably, the other tables in the report do not use all capital letters in the title. The decision to use lower-case letters in table titles is also based on the fact that lowercase letters are easier to read.

Headings for the three major categories are aligned on a left margin that protrudes farther into the left margin than other data in the stub column. Such placement is conventional for tables as well as logical for the left-right reading pattern. The headings are printed in boldface type rather than italicized for greater typographic prominence. The letters "A," "B," and "C" are deleted as irrelevant because they are not used in the text references and because the three side headings establish visually that there are three categories of headings.

The headings for points of comparison (column headings) are placed above the heading for the first category because they head the columns for all three categories. In addition, they are marked to set lightface roman rather than boldface, which, in combination with underlining, interferes with reading. The visual prominence of those headings also conflicts with the category headings. Underlining alone sufficiently distinguishes the column headings from the body of the table.

The space between columns 4 and 5 is reduced so that the eye will not have to leap so far to get from one item to the next. In this case, the specific amount of space is left up to the compositor and will be based partly on how much space the column headings require; other times, the copyeditor specifies the space. The left and right margins of the table as a whole will increase as a result of the change in internal spacing.

Finally, the whole table is set in the same typeface as the rest of the text.

Figure 8.3 shows how the table will look when printed as marked by the copyeditor.

TECHNICAL SPECIFICATIONS

Specifications may have two meanings for a technical editor: standards for products and publications that specify qualities such as materials and size, or guidelines for a particular product to be developed that establish product uses and capacities, budget, and development schedule. The first type may govern the way documents are written; the second type is a document (a kind of blueprint for product development) that may have to be copyedited.

Figure 8.3   Printed Version of the Copyedited Table in Figure 8.2

Table U.7

Results of Mass Screening and Risk-Group Screening Programs

jurisdiction	number tested	inmate category(ies)	number HIV seropositive	percent seropositive
Mass Screening				
Colorado	2847	all new inmates	15	0.5%
Iowa	800	all new inmates	0	0.0
Nevada	2638	all new inmates	8	0.3
Nevada	3820	all current inmates	96	2.5
South Dakota	1124	all current inmates	2	0.2
Epidemiological Studies				
Michigan	457	all new inmates	4	0.8%
Risk-Group Screening				
Alabama	301	unspecified risk groups	7	2.3%
New Hampshire	128	homosexuals and IV drug users	5	3.9
Orange County, CA	978	female prostitutes	28	2.9
Minneapolis, MN	260	homosexuals and IV drug users	2	0.8

Specifications for technical materials and processes are published by both government and industry, including such organizations as the United States military, the Department of Defense, the American National Standards Institute (ANSI), and the Institute of Electrical and Electronics Engineers (IEEE). These standards cover many kinds of equipment and processes, including aircraft, computers, and quality assurance. They may specify, for example, the size and brightness of screens for visual display terminals and the interfaces for microprocessor operating systems. A technical document may include references to the relevant specifications and standards.

In addition to standards for equipment and processes, a number of standards, particularly in the military, govern publications. These specify standards for abbreviations, format, parts lists, readability, abstracts, and reports. The military specifications are identified in labels with the prefix MIL- and are commonly referred to as MIL-SPECS. Documents for all government agencies except the Department of Defense are governed by Federal Information Publication Standards. These specifications for publications will be particularly important if you work for the military, the government, or military and government contractors. Your supervisor will probably provide you with copies of the relevant standards. You may also consult Joseph Kleinman's book listed in the "Further Reading" section at the end of the chapter.

In addition to checking publications for conformity to applicable specifications, you may be asked to copyedit the written specifications for a product to be manufactured. Product specifications precede the development of a project and guide that development. They describe the product, requirements for its use, resources for development, and documentation needed. They also define the product's users and the environment of use. Good specifications help to produce quality products and good documentation. They also help the writers and editors who produce the documentation to begin their work while the product is being developed. Thus, the effort to make them complete and accurate is worthwhile.

Because specifications precede the product, they may be vague or incomplete. As copyeditor, you must check to see that all necessary specifications are included. A good example of specifications or an outline of parts for this document will help you evaluate completeness. In addition, the technical data is likely to appear in tables and graphs, and these will need your attention. Because these specifications are internal to the product developer and contractor, you will probably worry less about spelling, usage, and stylistic consistency than you do in a document that will be published for external use, but if ambiguity will result from errors or inconsistencies, they should be corrected.

SUMMARY

Quantitative and technical material may look alien to copyeditors, but to respond by ignoring it is to overlook an important copyediting task. Your knowledge about punctuation and grammar and about marking type for a typesetter are pertinent to copyediting material full of quantities and symbols. You do not have to be an expert in the subject matter to copyedit this type of material, but you must be diligent about checking details, cautious about marking changes, and willing to inquire when in doubt. Chances are you won't be expected to copyedit complicated technical material until you gain some experience on more familiar material.

FURTHER READING   Judith Butcher. 1981. "Science and Mathematics Books." Chapter 13 in *Copy-Editing: The Cambridge Handbook,* 2nd ed. Cambridge: Cambridge University Press. This book is oriented to British standards, but it is thorough in noting what needs to be marked in scientific and mathematical text.

Karen Judd. 1990. *Copyediting: A Practical Guide*, 2nd ed. Los Altos, CA: Crisp.

Jerry Kass. 1972. "Editing Mathematical Copy." *Journal of Technical Writing and Communication* 2(4); 307–330. This article is dated in its references to typesetting methods, but the editorial advice on mathematics is sound.

Joseph M. Kleinman. 1983. *List of Specifications and Standards Pertaining to Technical Publications.* Washington, DC: Society for Technical Communication.

Ellen Swanson. 1979. *Mathematics into Type,* rev. ed. Providence, RI: American Mathematical Society. The authority of the professional society makes this reference the first choice of a mathematics editor.

University of Chicago Press. 1982. "Mathematics in Type." Chapter 13 in *The Chicago Manual of Style,* 13th ed.

DISCUSSION
AND APPLICATION

1. Copyedit the sentences below to show the correct use of numbers, symbols, and abbreviations. You may need to refer to the discussion of abbreviations in Chapter 5 and to a list of abbreviations and a style guide. Prepare a style sheet if there are options.*

   a. When the electrode is fully in the spinal cord tissue, the resistance shoots up to 1000-ohms or more.

   b. There are two methods of applying a coagulating current. One uses a fixed time, eg, 30 sec, and varies the power applied, eg, 5-mA, then 10mA, 15mA, etc, up to a limit given by the manufacturer. The other method fixes the power, eg at 30 mA, and varies the time, eg 5 sec, then 10 seconds, 15 sec, etc.

---

* Sentences in la, b, and c are adapted from "Neurolytic Blocks Around the Head" (first draft), by Samson Lipton, M.D. Used with permission of the author.

c. The spinal cord at the C1-C2 level is about 15-MM across and 10- to 12-mm from front to back, so the maximum lesion needed is 6 mm x 4 mm. Furthermore, a cylindrical electrode with a 2-mm uninsulated tip will provide a lesion somewhat barrel shaped; an exposed tip of 3-mm. is also used and will provide a lesion of about 4.5 x 3.0 mm.

2. Copyedit the following sentences and equations to clarify punctuation, spacing, italicization of letters that represent unknowns, and grammar.

   a. Consequently an integer p is even if p^2 is even and is odd if p^2 is odd.

   b. Then, squaring we have:

   $$p^2 = 2q^2$$

   c. Hence: since 2 is rational, both p and q are even integers.

   d. Thus,

   $$|4| = 4, \qquad |-4| = -(-4) = 4 \qquad |0| = 0.$$

   e. Using the less than, equal to, greater than symbols, these three possibilities are written:

   $$a < b \qquad a = b \qquad a > b$$

3. Convert these stacked fractions for inline presentation.

   a. $\dfrac{1}{16}$

   b. $\dfrac{3}{a + b}$

   c. $\dfrac{x + 2}{2y}$

4. Mark this equation to show an appropriate line break.

$$H(-x) = -(-x)^4 + 3(-x)^2 + 4 = -x^4 + 3x^2 + 4 = H(x).$$

5. Mark these equations to align them on the equal sign. Clarify other spacing and italicization as necessary.

$$(2x^2 - 2)(x^2 - x - 12) = 0$$
$$2(x-1)(x+1)(x - 4)(x + 3) = 0$$
$$x = -1, 1, 4, -3$$

6. Mark these sentences from a statistical analysis to show italics, spacing, and capitalization.

a. The analysis revealed a significant effect of method in both experiments. In experiment I, F = 8.09 and p = .001. In experiment II, F = 8.58 and p = .0007.

b. Results of a two-tailed t test (t= .728, p< .20) indicate that the performance difference between the two groups is not significant.

9 PROOFREADING

Proofreading entails checking a version of a document against an earlier version, marking deviations from the earlier, marked version, and correcting errors. Proofreading may occur at any point in production when the document is prepared in a new form.

A typescript (prepared with a typewriter or computer) may be typeset, in which case the typeset document usually appears first as a galley proof. (A **galley proof** is printed on a long sheet of paper; type size and style and line length are fixed, but the text has not yet been broken down to form actual pages.) The galley is proofread according to the marks on the typescript. Next, **page proofs** are printed, showing page breaks. The page proofs are proofread to determine that corrections marked on the galley proofs have been made. Once page proofs are corrected, metal printing plates are made, and a **blueline** may be prepared. The blueline, a photographic print in blue ink of the pages as they will be printed and bound, is proofread to confirm that pages appear in the right sequence and that folds, if any, are correct. In desktop publishing, the document is proofread during word processing and again after page layout. At each stage, proofreading confirms that errors previously noted have been corrected and checks that new procedures (e.g., page breaks) have been completed correctly.

Proofs in printing are analogous to photo proofs in portrait photography: proofs are the unchecked version of camera ready copy that follows typesetting, computer-generated copy, or typewriting. Proofs show how the document will look and read with all the editing incorporated. Proof copy allows a final check before printing.

The term *proofreading* is sometimes used loosely as a synonym for *copyediting*. Though the procedures and symbols of the two functions are related, the processes differ not only in the stage of production at which they occur and in the purposes they serve but also in the placement of marks on the page. Copyediting prepares the text for printing; proofreading verifies that the text has been printed according to specifications. Copyediting takes place early in production; proofreading is done later. Copyediting marks are interlinear; proofreading marks are mostly marginal. Figures 9.3 and 9.4, which fall later in the chapter, compare copyediting and proofreading marks by showing the typescript and typeset stages of the same document.

Copyediting establishes spellings and capitalization where more than one option is available. Copyediting or graphic design also establishes type style and size, typeface, and spacing. Proofreaders do not change these choices but verify that they have been incorporated into the document. Proofreaders alter the text only where the copyeditor has overlooked some errors.

Proofreading verifies that a new version of the document matches an earlier version as corrected. The earlier version is **dead copy.** When the galleys are being proofread, the marked typescript is the dead copy; when page proofs are being proofread, the galleys are the dead copy. The proofreader compares the new version of the document with the dead copy to verify that the new version has been keyboarded according to directions on the dead copy. The dead copy indicates the established text. The proofreader does not copyedit or make changes other than to mark places where the proofs differ from the dead copy.

Proofreading marks appear in the margins of hard copy. Because the copy has already been keyboarded, the keyboard operator will only rekeyboard those places where errors have occurred. The marginal marks alert the keyboard operator to check specific lines. In addition, typeset copy leaves little room between the lines for marking. Thus, on proofs, interlinear marks are limited to indicating where the proposed changes, as identified in the margin, should be inserted. In contrast with the marginal marks of proofreading, copyediting marks are generally interlinear—that is, at the place where changes are to be made. Interlinear marks give the keyboard operator information about changes where the information is needed. Even if the text will be transmitted electronically, chances are the typescript is still double spaced, allowing interlinear marks in copyediting.

Editors often proofread, though large companies may hire people with the job title of proofreader. Even if editors only supervise a proofreader, they should be familiar with the nature of the proofreader's task and appreciate its importance. They should also appreciate the time and skill required to proofread well.

This chapter identifies goals of proofreading, symbols and their placement on the proof copy, and strategies for effective proofreading.

THE VALUE AND GOALS OF PROOFREADING

The two primary justifications for careful proofreading are dollars and credibility. The cost of fixing errors increases exponentially at each stage of production. If a correction costs $1.00 at the galley stage, it may cost $6.00 at the page proof stage and $60.00 after metal plates for printing have been made. Each stage of production provides a chance to correct the document, but efficient proofreaders do a good job early and thus save money down the line. Proofreaders ensure clean copy by checking for typos and punctuation errors as well as attractive copy by checking spacing and typography.

Clean Copy: Eliminating Typos

Figure 9.1 illustrates some failures of proofreading. A reader who recognizes these errors will probably laugh, gloat, and feel superior—counterproductive responses to a serious document from the writer or publisher's

(from a physician's advertisement)

LAURA WARD, M.D.
Obstetrician & Gynecologist
Diplomate American Board of Obstetrics and Gynecology
Fellow American, College of Obstetricians & Gynecology
Medical Director for Planned Parenthood

(from an investment firm's newsletter)

Mr. Alberts rises early every weekday for a busy day of investing. After a 35-minute drive into town, Mr. Alberts starts his day pouring over the morning papers at a nearby coffee shop.

(from a newspaper report of the Chernobyl disaster in the Soviet Union)

The first detailed Soviet description of the Chernobyl disaster and its aftermath was given by Moscow Community Party chief Boris Yeltsin. . . . "We are undertaking measures to make sure this doesn't happen again," said Yeltsin, who was attending a Communist Party in Hamburg.

(from a newspaper ad for a series of workshops for women)

Sexual Harassment - Petticost Wars - Time Management
Men's Rections to The Women's Movement - And More

point of view. Spotting the one error that remains in a printed document, the reader will not stop to think about the fifty errors that the proofreader found. See how quickly you can spot the errors in the examples in figure 9.1.

When readers find errors that proofreaders have missed, they lose respect for the document, writer, and publisher. Errors in numbers and names can confuse budgets, orders, sales, and management, as well as give faulty information. For example, is the part number 03262 or 03226? Have 20 or 200 parts been ordered? Is Andersen or Anderson in charge of arranging the meeting? Should the pressure be set to 22 psi or 32? Is the claim for $38 million or $3.8 million? Readers may forgive an error or two, but if errors are too common, readers will ultimately dismiss the whole document as carelessly prepared and no longer trust either the information in or the producer of the document.

Attractive Copy: Eliminating Spacing and Typography Errors

For the inexperienced proofer, errors in spacing, type, and capitalization are less easy to spot than spelling errors, but such errors also detract from the quality of the publication. Sometimes a spacing error signals an omission of type. Shifts in spatial patterns and typography can distract readers from content or even give false signals about meaning. See how quickly you can spot the errors in figure 9.2.

**Figure 9.2
Spacing and Typography Errors in Printed Documents**

(from an annotated bibliography. Why might this error have occurred?)

```
The metric system is increasingly the norm in

U.S. indus- try. The system is economical...
```

(from a technical report)

A well-constructed message prototype for an emergency is important to the quick dissemination of information. The system and content of a message can have a dramatic effect on public response. Enough research has been conducted to discern a poor message from a good one.

(from the printed minutes of an annual meeting)

1. **Report of the Secretary/ Treasurer**
   The treasurer reported a balance of $9,978.90 in the checking account, but observed that the expenses exceeded income in this fiscal year.
2. **Report of the   Journal editor**

   The editor presented a budget of $11,002 for 1991 for the journal. The Board advised her to investigate the feasibility of desktop publishing.

(from the headings for a project summary)

PROJECT: Multi-Enzyme Reactor Design

SPONSOR: State of Texas

PRIMARY INVESTIGATOR: F. Senatore

Graduate Students: A. Lokapur, P. Zuniga, T. Jih

(from a book on word processing. Note how the spacing error [no indentation for a new paragraph] can indicate a content omission.)

                                                            . . . This is easy
and the results far more convincing than simply adding one's name to someone else's style.
the whole essay into the computer in the first place. Some enterprising . . .

PROOFREADING MARKS
AND PLACEMENT
ON THE PAGE Table 9.1 identifies proofreading marks. If you compare these marks with those for copyediting (tables 4.1–4.3), you will recognize the similarity. The same marks are used in copyediting and proofreading for indicating changes in type and for correcting typos. However, they are placed differently on the page, and proofreading uses more marks than copyediting.

TABLE 9.1 PROOFREADING MARKS

General

Margin	In Text	Meaning	Result	Comment
	wo@rds to the ~~the~~ printer	delete	words to the printer	
	ed{ting to printer	insert	editing to the printer	
#	in{the	insert space	in the	
⌢	edit ing	close up	editing	
	type{face	delete and close up	typeface	
tr	typescrpit	transpose	typescript	
a	tolerence	substitute letter(s)	tolerance	Write just the letters to be substituted, not the whole word.
sp	%	spell out	percent	Spell the whole word if the spelling will be in question.
eq #	to a book	equal space between words	to a book	
stet	proceed	let it stand	proceed	

Punctuation

Note: All punctuation insertions are marked in the text with an insertion symbol (caret) at the point where punctuation occurs. The mark of punctuation appears in the margin as noted here. To replace one mark with another, show the insertion only, not the deletion.

Margin	Meaning	Margin	Meaning	Margin	Meaning
⌃	comma	;/	colon	⌄	quotation marks
⊙	period	/=/	hyphen	⌄	apostrophe
set ?	question mark	⊥M	em dash	[/]/	brackets
;/	semicolon	⊥N	en dash	(/)/	parentheses

TABLE 9.1 PROOFREADING MARKS (continued)

Typography

Margin	In Text	Meaning	Result	Comment
lc	TITLE	set in lowercase	title	
cap	title	set in capital letters	TITLE	
ulc	THE TITLE	set in upper- and lower-case letters	The Title	
sc	document	set in small caps	DOCUMENT	
ital	document	set in italic type	*document*	
rom	document	set in roman type	document	
bf	document	set in boldface	**document**	
lf	document	set in lightface	document	
wf	helvetica Times	wrong font	helvetica Times	Specify the font if you know it.
✗	broken	reset a broken letter	broken	
⌄	m2	set as superscript	m²	
⌃	H2O	set as subscript	H$_2$O	

To affirm that the proofs are correct and that production may proceed, the proofreader must review such visual features as alignment, spacing, and the clarity of individual letters. Thus, the proofreading marks include marks for alignment, space between letters and between lines, and broken or upsidedown letters. The copyeditor does not care so much about these visual characteristics of the document because the final form of the document will probably differ from the typescript.

Figure 9.4, the typeset version of the copyedited document in figure 9.3, shows that most of the proofreading marks appear in the margin. The marks in the body of the text only show where to make the correction requested in the margin. In figure 9.4, the caret in the second line signals that the marginal word, "calcium," should be inserted at that point.

When a line requires multiple corrections, they may be listed, left to right—in the order in which they appear—with a slash between the individual corrections. The title in figure 9.4 contains both a transposition and a capitalization error. Both are listed in the margin with a slash between the two circled instructions.

Corrections may be placed in either margin, but the marginal marks will be easier to match up with the body marks if they are in the margin closer to the error. Don't confuse the person making the corrections by placing in the left margin a note about an error on the right side of the line

TABLE 9.1 PROOFREADING MARKS continued

Spacing Marks

Margin	In Text	Meaning	Result	Comment
¶	sentence. A new . . .	start paragraph	sentence. A new . . .	
(run in)	sentence. A new . . .	run lines together	sentence. A new . . .	
⌐⌐	the first book	move type up	the first book	
⌐⌐	the second book	push type down	the second book	Use for words or letters within words.
↓	**Headings** No space after.	push the line of type down	**Headings** No space after.	Use for whole lines of type
( ) or (close up)	extra space between lines	close up the space between lines	extra space between lines	
⌐	word hangs out. Move it in.	move right	word hangs out. Move it in.	
⌐	⌐paragraph	move left	paragraph	
][	]Title[	center	Title	
‖	‖margin is ‖ not straight ‖ on the left	align horizontally	margin is not straight on the left	
═	baseline	align vertically	baseline	

while placing in the right margin a note about an error on the left side of the line.

Where the corrections within the body of the text might be confusing, particularly when there are multiple corrections within the same area, you may write out the correct version in the margin, as well as marking within the body. That is the reason for the marginal words in paragraph 4 of figure 9.4. Otherwise, it is sufficient to write just a single letter when there is an insertion or substitution, as you can see in paragraph 5. To write more than is necessary not only will make you look like an inexperienced proofreader but also will cause you to waste valuable time.

Usually, the typesetter will be able to distinguish instructions from modifications of the text, but if there can be doubt, circle your instructions. The circled "run-in" that appears beside paragraphs 2 and 4 is an instruction to the typesetter.

Figure 9.3   Copyedited Version of an Article for a Health Newsletter

12 pt. new Century Schoolbook

set 10/12 × 25 new Cent

MILK: NOT QUITE THE PERFECT FOOD

Many people think that milk is nearly a perfect food. However, while calcium is a necessary mineral in the diet, many adults cannot tolerate even small amounts of milk. A scoop of ice cream or a glass of milk can cause abdominal cramps, gas, and sometimes diarhea for about thirty million Americans. These people lack an enzyme, lactase, which is needed to digest lactose, the sugar in milk. After about the age of two, many people gradually stop producing this enzyme. ~~If is thought that~~ fully 70% of the world's population have this condition. People of Asian, Mediterranean, or African descent are more likely to be lactase deficient while those of Scandinavian descent rarely lose the enzyme.

When lactose, the sugar found in milk and milk products, is not digested, bacteria in the colon use the sugar ~~and~~ to produce hydrogen and carbon dioxide. The result is gas, pain, and ~~a number of~~ other symptoms *that are sometimes mistaken for* ~~Lactose intolerance is not hte same thing~~ as an allergy to the protein in milk or irritable bowel syndrome, ~~although the three conditions may produce similiar symptoms.~~ Because hydrogen gas is produced, a test that measures hydrogen in the breath can confirm lactose intolerance is the problem.

Since lactose digestion depends on the ratio of lactase to the amount of ~~lactose~~ *lactose* containing food eaten, many people can drink small amounts of milk or eat some ice cream. The type of milk product can also make a difference. While yogurt contains more lactose than milk, it is often better tolerated because the bacteria in live cultures of yogurt break down the milk sugars. The same thing appears to happen in hard cheeses such as cheddar or swiss.

Fortunately, ~~there are~~ some products on the market that can make life easier for those with lactose intolerance. Some foods are treated with the enzyme to break down the lactose into glucose and galactose. LactAid or Lactrase may be added to food 24 hours before consumption.

_____ Figure 9.4   Proofread Version of the Document in Figure 9.3

tr / *cap*

Milk: Not Quiet the perfect Food

calcium

Many people think that milk is nearly a perfect food. However, while is a necessary mineral in the diet, many adults cannot tolerate even small amounts of milk.

eg #

A scoop of ice cream or a glass of milk can cause abdominal cramps, gas, and sometimes diarrhea for about 30 million Americans. These people lack an enzyme, lactase, which is needed to digest lactose, the sugar in milk. After about the age of two, many people gradually stop producing this enzyme. Fully

c / *run in*
lc / *tr*

70 per cent of the worlds population have this condition. People of Asain, Mediterranean, or African descent are more likely to be lactase deficient while those of Scandinavian descent rarely loose the enzyme.

tr / *#* / *∧*
eg. #

When lactose, the sugar found in milk and milk products, is not digested, bacteria in the colon use the sugar to produce hydrogen and carbon dioxide. The result is gas, pain, and other symptoms that are sometimes mistaken for allergy to the protein in milk or irritable bowel syndrome. Because hydrogen gas is produced, a test that measures hydrogen in the breath can confirm that lactose intolerance is the problem.

rom

Since lactose digestion depends on the ratio of lactase to the amount of food eaten containing lactose, many people can drink small amounts of milk or eat some ice cream. The type of milk product can also make a difference. While yogurt contains more lactose than milk, it is often better tolerated because the bacteria in live cultures of yogurt break down the milk sugars. The same thing appears to happen in hard cheeses,

lc / *#*

#
¶ / *run in*
wf

such as Cheddar or Swiss. Fortunately, some products on the market can make life easier for those with lactose intolerance. Some foods are treated with the enzyme to break down the lactose into glucose and galactase. LactAid or Lactrase may be added to food 24 hours before consumption.

Use a colored pencil or pen to mark in proofreading so that the marks will be easy to see. Legible marks also increase the likelihood that the typesetter will be able to follow your proofreading instructions. For purposes of cost accounting, the responsibility for each correction should be identified. Obviously, the print buyer should not be charged for the printer's errors, nor should the publishing company absorb the expense of excessive changes by the writer after typesetting. If everyone involved in writing, editing, and designing the document is on the staff of a single company, it may be sufficient for the proofreader to use a different color pencil for errors made by the printer and errors made by the company buying print. When the company contracts with people outside the company for services, a more detailed accounting is necessary. Each correction may then be accompanied by a circled mark to indicate responsibility: "*pe*" for printer's error, "*ea*" for editorial alteration, "*da*" for designer's alteration, and "*aa*" for author's alteration. However, an uncorrected error that appeared in the previous version of the document becomes the proofreader's error even if it was a printer's error in the earlier version. Thus, if a typo was not corrected at the galley stage and remains in the page proofs, it is charged to the print buyer even if the printer made the error in the galley.

Generally, you will proofread to make the new version conform to the previous version. That is, you will not copyedit—because of the expense and because substantial changes will slow down production. However, if outright errors remain in the proof copy that were uncorrected in the dead copy, you will, of course, correct them rather than making conformity to the dead copy a higher aim.

STRATEGIES FOR EFFECTIVE PROOFREADING

Most of us have spotted proofreading failures in printed documents and may therefore feel confident about our proofreading ability. Yet even the best of proofreaders will miss some errors. Proofreaders may get caught up in content and overlook surface errors. Reading quickly, we are likely to identify words by their shapes rather than by their individual letters, yet the word shape will remain essentially the same with a simple typo, particularly one that involves a narrow letter such as *i* or a missing member of repeated letters, such as two *m*s. Note, for example, that the word shapes are identical for both the correct spelling of *evaluation* and its misspelling. *Evalvation* would be easy to overlook in proofreading.

| evaluation | evalvation |

You will increase your proofreading effectiveness if you follow these guidelines:

1. **Always check against the dead copy.** Proof copy can omit phrases or substitute words and still make sense. The dead copy is also the authority for spellings of names and other unfamiliar material as well as numbers.

2. **Pay special attention to text other than body copy.** Proofreaders frequently overlook errors in titles, tables, lists, and nonverbal text. The paragraphs of the document seem to be more important, and they are easier to read. Don't overlook the body copy, but make a special point of proofreading the other parts of the document.

   - **Titles and headings.** Look for typos; check for capitalization, type style, and typeface.

   - **Illustrations.** Look for typos; check for spacing, alignment, keys, and completeness.

   - **Numbers.** Check for accuracy (reversal of numerals and errors in addition are common). Look for alignment on the decimal. Numbers on illustrations should match the references to them in the text.

   - **Reference lists and bibliographies.** Check the spelling of authors' names and of titles; check for spacing, capitalization, and italics as specified by the appropriate style manual.

   - **Proper names and place names.** Check them against the dead copy; use reference books if the dead copy seems inaccurate.

   - **Marks of punctuation.** Check for closing of quote marks and parentheses.

3. **If you catch one error in a line or word, go back over the line to look for other problems.** It is easy to overlook an error that appears close to another one. You feel as though you have "finished" a line if you catch an error. Yet mistakes cluster, perhaps at points where the typist or keyboarder became confused or tired. In the following reference list entry, one proofreader noted the extra space and inappropriate italics—but forgot to check the date. The proper date was 1983, not 1982.

Studies in Short Fi ction, 20 (Winter 1982): 33-37.
(underlining changes italic type to roman)

Studies in Short Fiction, 20 (Winter 1983): 33-37.
(corrected version)

4. **Review at least once solely for visual errors.** Allow yourself a review just for spacing, alignment, type style, and typeface without the distraction of the actual text content. Some proofreaders turn the copy upsidedown to check spacing; others read right to left.

   • **Typeface, type size, type style.** Make sure type does not change arbitrarily.

   • **Spacing above and below headings.** Are headings set solid over the body copy, or does some space separate headings from the body? Is there more space before than after the headings? Measure the type from the baseline of one line of type to the baseline of the next if you don't trust your eyes.

   • **Centering vs. left or right justification.** Check all like headings (e.g., first level, second level) together to spot inconsistencies.

   • **Indentation.** Check systematically, especially after headings.

   • **Alignment.** Scan the left and right margins and any other aligned material.

5. **Check hyphenated words at the end of lines.** If hyphenation at the right margin is part of the design, check that word divisions conform to those in the dictionary, or at least that the divisions make sense. Note, for example, the difference between *thera•pist* and *the•rapist.*

6. **Use techniques to force slow reading.** Some errors will pop out when you skim, but most will not, especially because the eye recognizes and accepts word shapes even when some of the letters may be incorrect. Unless you can slow yourself down, you may simply be reading for content and not for correctness.

   • **Proofreading with a partner.** One partner can read aloud from the dead copy while the other checks the proof copy. Partners can take turns to keep from tiring at one task. If you don't have the time to work this way for the entire document, try at least to use a partner for difficult text, such as columns of numbers and reference lists.

   • **Reading out of sequence.** Some proofreaders read backwards or read pages out of sequence to avoid getting caught up in the content.

7. **Use multiple proofreaders and proofreadings.** Publishing houses that value high quality insist on multiple proofreadings for any important document—as many as 10 throughout the various production stages. Ideally, several proofreaders will work on the document, and preferably, someone in addition to the writer or editor will proofread. Proofreaders who are familiar with the document or its content are likely to miss errors because they see what they expect to see. A single proofreader can increase the number of errors he or she catches by reading the document for a specific feature (e.g., the visual features, as in guideline 3, or word division), then rereading for another feature.

8. **Minimize errors by transmitting text electronically.** The computer can help a great deal in proofreading, saving both time and money. Electronic transmission of text eliminates the need for multiple keyboarding. Spelling checkers will catch many typos, and proofreading programs will catch unclosed quotation marks and parentheses and some capitalization errors. Some word processing programs include format templates that allow one to code the type and spacing for different levels of headings and other variations of text. Assuming the coding is correct, the type and spacing will be correct.

    Incorporating corrections electronically allows the printing of clean copy for subsequent proofreadings. It is easier to catch errors on relatively error-free copy than on copy filled with errors.

    The disadvantage of computerized proofreading is that it is easy to trust it too much. The computer will miss some spelling errors, and it cannot recognize omissions in content or spacing errors. Use the computer for preliminary proofreading, but use a human proofreader to check the results.

9. **Quit when you are tired.** Try to schedule proofreading for times when you are alert, such as first thing in the morning, and work only so long as you are effective. Interrupt the proofreading to do other tasks, and then return to the proofreading refreshed.

SUMMARY   Proofreading provides a check of the document after copyediting but before printing. Good proofreading helps to ensure a high-quality publication, notable for the apparent care with which it has been produced and the absence of distracting errors. Proofreading is skilled work.

FURTHER READING   Peggy Smith. 1987. *Mark My Words: Instruction and Practice in Proofreading*. Alexandria, VA: Editorial Experts, Inc.

DISCUSSION AND
APPLICATION

1. Compare the copyedited newsletter article in figure 9.3 with the proofread version of the same document in figure 9.4. In your own words, distinguish the types of corrections made on each document, and explain how and why the marks differ.

2. During the preparation of an annotated bibliography on technical editing, two collaborators missed the typos in the following words after repeated checks of the hard copy. (The spelling checker on the computer identified them.) For each word or phrase, hypothesize why the collaborators overlooked the error. That is, what is it about the spelling, word shape, or other feature of the word that encouraged the collaborators to read it as correct?

gullability	edtors
indentification	embarassing
labortatory	responsibilites
manuscritps	comform
progams	comunication

3. With regard to exercise 2, discuss how the fact that the collaborators were proofreading their own document might have affected the quality of their proofreading.

4. A national insurance company mailed to shareholders a ballot for trustees and a booklet describing the qualifications of 27 nominees. Inside the printed booklet was a slip of paper entitled "Errata" that included these comments:

Robert C. Clark is 45, not 55, as appears on page 5 of the Trustee booklet.

William H. Waltrip is 52, not 62, as appears on page 6 of the Trustee booklet.

Uwe E. Reinhardt's name incorrectly appears on the ballot as Uwe E. Remhardt.

What is the meaning of *errata?* More important, speculate on why the proofreaders missed these particular errors. When the errors were discovered (after the booklet was printed), what were the company's three options? Why did the company choose to include the errata slip? What were the consequences of the proofreading failures to this company, in terms of money, time, and image?

5. Proofread the version of the document in the right column by comparing it with the version in the left column. Mark the typeset version to make it match the typescript version.

Times 10/12 × 13 RR

Ivory Trade Continues
Elephants at risk of extinction

   Recent studies have established that ivory poaching has reduced the elephant populations in East Africa by half in less than a decade. The same story is repeated for the rest of Africa except parts of southern Africa where rigorous management has actually made it possible for the elephant numbers to increase. Over much of east and central Africa, elephants are so heavily poached, even in previously secure sanctuaries such as Selous, Tsavo, and the Luangwa Valley, that it will not be long before the elephant is extremely rare or even extinct. There is little doubt that short-term profit-motivated poaching is responsible for the enormous decimation of the large herds of elephants. Conservation organizations of the world are now demanding immediate enlightened action, strong political will, and a high degree of international cooperation to avert a disaster.

Ivory Trade Continues
Elephants at risk of extintion
Recent studies have established that ivory paoching has reduced the elephant populations in East Africe by half in less than a decade. The same story is repeated for the rest of Afirca except parts of Southern Africa where rigorous managment has actually made it possible for the elephont numbers to increase. Over much of central Africa, elephants are so heavily poached, even in previously secure sanctuaries such as Selious, Tasvo, and the Luangwa Valley, that it will not be long before the lelphant is extremely rare or even extinct. There is little doubt that short term profit-motivated poaching is responsible for the enormous decim-ation of the large herds   of elephands. Conservation organizations of the world are now demanding imediate enlightened action, strong politicial will and a high degree of international cooperation to avert a disaster.

6a. Proofread the right column to match the dead copy on the left;
check especially for errors in type style, typeface, and spacing.

Ban on Ivory Imports Established   Ban on Ivory Imports Established

A moratorium on the importation
of African elephant ivory was
implemented through an announcement in the *Federal Register.*

A moratorium on the importation

of African elephant ivory was

implemented through an announce-

ment in the Federal Register.

A quota system for legal,
regulated trade in ivory was
authorized under the Con-
vention on International
Trade in Endangered Spe-
cies of Wild Fauna and Flora
(CITES).

A quota system for legal,
regulated trade in ivory was
authorized under the Con-
vention on International
Trade in Endangered Spe-
cies of Wild Fauna and Flora
(*CITES*).

The United States, Western
Europe, and Japan consume
two-thirds of the world's
"worked ivory."

The United States, Western
Europe, and Japan consume two-
thirds of the world's "worked
ivory."

6b. Correct spacing errors in this paragraph.

If the United States, Western Europe, and Japan   were concerned enough as parties to
CITES to agree to the appeal and pro hibit importation ofall ivory without exception,

the present enormous demand for ivory wou ld cease. IN turn, poached ivory would
 become less lucrative. CITES, the   one instrument   of international   standards
available, should impose a world wide ban on the ivory trade to stop the convention
 being used to channel hundreds of tons of illegal ivory into legal trade.

PART III SUBSTANTIVE EDITING

CHAPTER 10
Substantive Editing: Definition and Process

CHAPTER 11
Style

CHAPTER 12
Organization

CHAPTER 13
Format

CHAPTER 14
Visuals

10 SUBSTANTIVE EDITING: DEFINITION AND PROCESS

In Part II of this book, you learned ways to make a document correct, consistent, accurate, and complete. But a document may achieve all the standards you have learned and still not work—readers may not be able to use it or comprehend it. Usefulness and comprehensibility depend on a document concept that matches the need for the document and on organization, format, and style.

Substantive editing is the process of evaluating a document's concept and content, organization, form, and style. Ideally, the editor takes part in planning the document, before it is written, but frequently, the editor sees the document only after it is written. Working with the writer (or with the writing and editing team), the editor suggests ways of improving the document in all or some of these areas. The purpose of substantive editing is to make the document more functional and appropriate for its readers, not just to make it correct and consistent.

The job of substantive editing is challenging in a different way than copyediting because of the analysis and judgment it requires. Although some specific guidelines will help you, decisions about style, form, and organization more often represent judgments than applications of rules. Furthermore, you have to think with the writer's mind as well as with the reader's and with your own. While substantive editing will take more time and effort than copyediting, the reward of editing for substance is that you can make the document *work,* not just make it superficially correct. Analytically oriented people find great satisfaction in this kind of editing.

In this chapter, you will compare the copyediting and the substantive editing of a single document to illuminate the differences between the two editing tasks. The chapter will walk you through the process of document analysis and goal setting that precedes substantive editing. This chapter also will prepare you for the following chapters, which give specific guidelines on editing for substance.

EXAMPLE: COPYEDITING VS. SUBSTANTIVE EDITING

To compare the purposes, methods, and results of copyediting and substantive editing, let us consider the following scenario. You work in the communications department of a large medical center. Today you are editing a grant proposal, due in Washington in five days, worth $500,000 if it is funded. You also have an appointment with the graphics specialist to review the photographs for a slide show for which you are writing the script, to be completed in two weeks. The Director of Maintenance, with whom you have a cordial relationship, drops by with a memo (figure 10.1), written for immediate distribution throughout the medical center. He asks you to look it over. Although you can spare only about 15 minutes, you agree to check the memo. Actually, even the 15 minutes is precious, but taking a break from the proposal will help refresh your mind so that you can think more clearly when you return.

The punctuation and mechanics of this memo need attention, but the work will be fun. Doing something on this level will be a real relief to you after working on the grant proposal. And you can perform a service for the Director of Maintenance with little effort.

To participate in this scenario, imagine that you are the editor assigned to the editing task. Using correct copymarking symbols, edit the document in figure 10.1 for grammar and mechanics.

Your edited memo will look much like the marked-up version in figure 10.2. On most points your editing will agree with the editing shown in figure 10.2 because you are applying the same rules of grammar and spelling. Some editing for mechanics will depend on your assumptions about titles. For example, is "Maintenance Department" a proper name or a descriptive one? Is "manual" a part of a title or just a descriptor? Your answers to these questions will affect your decisions about capitalization. If you actually worked at this medical center, you would either know the answers to these questions or be able to check them quickly. Editing in a hypothetical situation, you either have to make an educated guess or make a note to check the information.

Figure 10.1
The Original,
Unedited Memo

TO: All Medical Center personnal
FROM: Tom Barker
DATE: January 2, 1991
SUBJECT: Service Calls

The Maintenance Department will initiate a Service Call system beginning Monday,January 7th, 1991, that is designed to provide an effective response time with equal distribution for all departments for work categorized as Service Calls. Service Calls are defined as urgent minor work requiring immediate attention, for example, loss of heat, air conditioning, water leaks, clogged plumbing, faulty electrical wiring, fire, safety or security hazards.

To initiate a Service call a telephone call to the Maintenance Department, (742-5438, 24 hours a day), is all that is required. A Service Call number will be assigned to the job and furnished to the originator if requested. This number may be used when referring to the status of the Service Call.

During the hours of 5:00 p.m. through 8:00 a.m. daily, all day week-ends and holidays, only one Maintenance Mechanic is on duty, who must insure total systems are oprational on his shift, in addition to accomplshing Service Calls. That will limit the amount of calls, but should not deter anyone from calling in a Service Call to insure it is accomplished when the manhours are available. If no one answers, please call again.

For urgent or emergency requirements, the PBX Operator must be notified to page Maintenance. Please do not use the paging system unless your request is justifiable.

Your cooperation in this matter would be greatly appreciated.

Service Call requirements are outlined in the Policies and Procedures Manual. Requests exceding these these requirements will be classified as Job Orders, and are also outlined in the Policeis and Procedure Manual.

| Figure 10.2 | Memo from Figure 10.1 Marked to Show Copyediting |

TO: All Medical Center personn*e*l
FROM: Tom Barker, *Director of Maintenance*
DATE: January 2, 1991
SUBJECT: Service Calls

Excess capitalization is distracting.

The Maintenance Department will initiate a ~~S~~ervice ~~C~~all system beginning Monday,January 7~~th~~, 1991, that is designed to provide an effective response time with equal distribution for all departments for work categorized as ~~S~~ervice ~~C~~alls. Service ~~C~~alls are defined as urgent minor work requiring immediate attention; for example, loss of heat *or* air conditioning, water leaks, clogged plumbing, faulty electrical wiring, *and* fire, safety or security hazards.

The punctuation in the list makes the examples confusing. Surely "air conditioning" and "safety" are not problems requiring service calls. ("Loss" and "hazards" are.)

To initiate a ~~S~~ervice call, a telephone call to the Maintenance Department, (742-5438, 24 hours a day), is all that is required. A ~~S~~ervice ~~C~~all number will be assigned to the job and furnished to the originator if requested. This number may be used when referring to the status of the ~~S~~ervice ~~C~~all.

A list of two items (daily hours and weekend hours) requires a conjunction.

During the hours of 5:00 p.m. through 8:00 a.m. daily, *and* all day *on* week~~ ~~ends and holidays, only one ~~M~~aintenance ~~M~~echanic is on duty, who must insure *that* total systems are op*e*rational on his shift, in addition to accomplishing ~~S~~ervice ~~C~~alls. That will limit the *number* ~~amount~~ of calls, but should not deter anyone from calling in a ~~S~~ervice ~~C~~all to insure it is accomplished when the manhours are available. If no one answers, please call again.

Use "number" with quantifiable amounts

Figure 10.2   (continued)

Leave the abbreviation "PBX" without spelling out its meaning. Readers will recognize the abbreviation more readily than they recognize "Private Branch Exchange."

Titles need to be underlined. The title of the manual needs to match the title on the manual itself.

Capitalization of "job orders" should be consistent with capitalization of "service call."

For urgent or emergency requirements, the PBX Operator must be notified to page Maintenance. Please do not use the paging system unless your request is justifiable.

Your cooperation in this matter would be greatly appreciated.

Service Call requirements are outlined in the Policies and Procedures Manual. Requests exceeding these these requirements will be classified as Job Orders, and are also outlined in the Policies and Procedure Manual.

Your editing may vary from the sample in figure 10.2 on some other capitalization questions. For example, you may have decided to capitalize "Service Call" each time it appears in order to emphasize the main topic of the document. Or you may have determined that the repeated capital letters distract readers. Either decision is legitimate, so long as you are consistent.

Some of your decisions require more thoughtful analysis. For example, in the last line of the first paragraph, the series ending in "hazards" is not clearly punctuated. Logic suggests that "safety" is not one of the problems requiring a service call, so it must modify "hazard." But then, where does the series end, and where should you insert the "and" to conclude the series? You have two options:

...wiring, fire, and safety or security hazards.

...wiring, and fire, safety, or security hazards.

The assumption of the second option would be that a "fire hazard" as opposed to a "fire" requires a service call. You can check with the maintenance department if necessary, but logic tells you that fire, as opposed to a fire hazard, would require a call to the fire department.

Apart from these possible variants, however, the results of copyediting by any two competent editors will be similar. Furthermore, the edited document, as shown in figure 10.3, will be similar in content, form, and style to the original. Copyediting has not substantially affected how well the document will achieve its purpose with its intended readers.

Figure 10.3
Copyedited Memo
from Figure 10.2

TO: All Medical Center personnel

FROM: Tom Barker, Director of Maintenance

DATE: January 2, 1991

SUBJECT: Service Calls

The Maintenance Department will initiate a service call system beginning Monday, January 7, 1991, that is designed to provide an effective response time with equal distribution for all departments for work categorized as service calls. Service calls are defined as urgent minor work requiring immediate attention; for example, loss of heat or air conditioning, water leaks, clogged plumbing, faulty electrical wiring, and fire, safety or security hazards.

To initiate a service call, a telephone call to the Maintenance Department (742-5438, 24 hours a day) is all that is required. A service call number will be assigned to the job and furnished to the originator if requested. This number may be used when referring to the status of the service call.

During the hours of 5:00 p.m. through 8:00 a.m. daily, and all day on weekends and holidays, only one maintenance mechanic is on duty, who must insure that total systems are operational on his shift, in addition to accomplishing service calls. That will limit the number of calls, but should not deter anyone from calling in a service call to insure it is accomplished when the manhours are available. If no one answers, please call again.

For urgent or emergency requirements, the PBX operator must be notified to page Maintenance. Please do not use the paging system unless your request is justifiable.

Figure 10.3
(continued)

Your cooperation in this matter would be greatly
appreciated.

Service call requirements are outlined in the
<u>Policies and Procedures</u> manual. Requests exceeding
these requirements will be classified as job
orders, and are also outlined in the <u>Policies and
Procedures</u> manual.

What, then, has copyediting accomplished? First, because the document is correct, readers will take the message more seriously than they would if they recognized errors. Readers, fairly or not, evaluate a writer's skill and overall competence on superficial text characteristics such as spelling and punctuation. Thus, editing has increased the chances that readers will respond to the memo in the intended way rather than being distracted by errors.

To some extent, copyediting has also increased clarity. For example, in line 7 of figure 10.2, the insertion of the conjunction *or* will establish that "loss" refers to "air conditioning" as well as to "heat." The insertion of the conjunction *and* in line 8 clarifies that "safety" modifies "hazards" rather than being a problem in itself. With these insertions, you have clarified the information. The reduction of document noise (in this case excess punctuation and capitalization as well as errors) also makes the message clearer.

From the perspective of your work load, the task has taken relatively little time and energy. If you edited electronically, you used the global change function to make the capitalization and spelling consistent, and you quickly deleted unnecessary punctuation and inserted necessary conjunctions. You can now return quickly to your more important task—the proposal.

From the perspective of your relationship with the memo's writer, you have clearly performed a service without challenging his competence. If you and he disagree on some specific emendations, you can confirm your choices by pointing to a handbook or style guide, or you can yield on issues when his choice is acceptable (if not preferable). If copyediting is correct, it should not cause conflict between writer and editor.

Substantive editing, on the other hand, looks beyond words and sentences to the way in which readers will read and use the document. The only valid reason for substantive editing is to make the document more usable and comprehensible. It is *never* acceptable to change the document arbitrarily, imposing your preferences and possibly making it different but not better. While you will use judgment in substantive editing, you must use *informed* judgment. That is, you must edit with a full awareness of principles of style, organization, format, and other factors of document design.

Substantive editing will take more time than copyediting, so if you have the same commitment to other pressing projects described in the previous scenario, you may have to decline this project or negotiate for a lower level of editing.

The process of substantive editing is also more complex than the process of copyediting. Instead of reacting line by line to the text, you must begin by skimming the document as a whole in order to determine how readers will use the document and to establish editing objectives. The actual editing is followed by an additional review. The discussion of the substantive editing process that follows will continue with the example of the memo on service calls.

THE PROCESS OF SUBSTANTIVE EDITING

Substantive editing is a multistage process that parallels the writing process. It begins with invention, discovery, or pre-editing—a time of analysis and planning. The editing itself follows pre-editing and is likely to require several passes through the document, just as writing requires review and revision. Finally, substantive editing requires a review with the writer to ensure that editing has not introduced content errors.

In pre-editing, the editor considers the document as a whole in its context—as it will be read and used. Just as brainstorming, researching, and outlining provide direction for a writer, pre-editing yields an overview of the editing task. This overview helps an editor work systematically toward goals that are consistent with the needs of the readers and the purposes of and uses for the document. Without pre-editing, an editor would be likely to read line by line, reacting to errors and sentence structure problems. The line-by-line approach works for copyediting, but it does not direct the editor's attention to content, organization, and style. A sense of the whole document in its context and a concept of what the document seeks to achieve are necessary for the editor making judgments about substance.

As editor, you are more likely to achieve the overall goal of improving the document's usability and comprehensibility if you edit with a plan. Before you begin to mark the page or edit on the computer screen, you should complete a four-part pre-editing process that will result in a plan.

1. Analyze the document's readers, purpose, and uses to determine what the document should do.

2. Evaluate the document's content, style, organization, and form to determine whether the document does accomplish what it should.

3. Establish editing objectives to set forth a specific plan for editing.

4. Review the plan with the writer to work toward consensus.

These procedures may overlap with one another and may not be as linear as the list suggests. For example, a review with the writer to determine document readers, purposes, and uses (procedure 1) may satisfy the review of the editing plan (procedure 4). However, you should complete the pre-editing process before editing in order to determine what the purpose of the document is and how well it is achieved, to establish editing objectives, and to arrive at some consensus with the writer. Because pre-editing requires you to be familiar with the document as a whole, you will have to read sample sections throughout the document to determine editing goals.

Once pre-editing is complete, you are ready to undertake the actual editing. Editing may require more than one pass through the document, and it will certainly include an evaluation of the editorial decisions (the editing itself may be edited). Finally, the editor reviews the edited document with the writer.

The steps in the process of substantive editing are discussed more fully in the following pages, and then the process is applied to the memo on service calls.

Analyzing the Document's Readers, Purpose, and Uses

Substantive editing always begins with an analysis of who will use the document and for what purpose and with an evaluation of how well the document in its present form will achieve its objectives. Ideally, this analysis (and substantive editing) should begin before the writing does, when the document is being conceived. This kind of advance planning can prevent a conflict of wills when the writer assumes different objectives and strategies than does the editor.

Analysis begins with questions. These are familiar questions—the ones writers ask before drafting documents. You can begin the substantive editing process effectively with these questions:

What is the purpose of this document?

Who will read it and why?

What should readers do or know as a result of reading it?

What do they already know about the subject?

In what circumstances will they read it? (In good light or poor? Inside or outside? While doing a task?)

Will they read it straight through or selectively?

Should they memorize the contents or just use the document for reference?

What will they do with the document once they have read it? (Throw it away? File it? Post it?)

What are their attitudes toward the subject of the document? (Will they be inherently cooperative? Unsure? Hostile?)

Only by analyzing what you want the document to do and by imagining it being used by readers can you make valid judgments about editorial emendations. For complex documents, you will need to interview the writer to determine answers to these questions. You can answer a number of the questions, though, by inference and from experience.

Evaluating the Document

The analysis represents an objective basis for evaluating the document. While the purpose of analysis is to determine what the document *should* do, the purpose of evaluation is to determine how well the document *does* it. An evaluation should systematically review these document features:

Content: completeness and appropriateness of information

Organization: order of information; signals about the order

Format: prose paragraphs, lists, or tables; paper size

Style: writer's tone or persona; efficiency of sentence structure; concreteness and accuracy of words; grammar, usage, punctuation, spelling, and mechanics

Illustrations: type, construction, placement

Establishing Editing Objectives

The process of setting objectives may begin with an evaluation of what is ineffective with the original document, but it goes beyond a critical evaluation to identify what you want to accomplish in editing. If you observed in evaluation, for example, that the writer's style is full of nouns and weak verbs, the editing objective may be to substitute strong verbs for weak ones. If you determined that readers would be likely to read selectively but that the document provided inadequate identifiers of sections, your goal might be to insert headings for major divisions.

It may help to make notes of your editing goals, just as you take notes on what topics you want to cover and how you might organize them (i.e., a rough outline) when you write. You can jot these notes on the original copy as you read it through, but if you collect them in one place before you actually begin the editing, you can ensure that specific objectives do not conflict with one another and that they work together.

The analysis, evaluation, and establishment of objectives let an editor know exactly how to proceed with the editing and make all editorial emendations serve an overall concept of how the document should function. The actual editing should also be relatively easy now.

Reviewing Your Editing Plans with the Writer

After you have analyzed the document and established editing objectives, consult with the writer about the editing plans. Whenever your intervention will be substantial, you will achieve more cooperation and support if you share your plans before implementing them. The writer will become your partner rather than your adversary. Furthermore, you will avoid surprising him or her and thereby avoid the negative response that surprise can provoke. You may also save yourself a lot of time, because if the writer does not approve your editing plan, you can prepare another one before wasting time editing and then having to do the job again. The review is particularly important when you can anticipate major changes in content, organization, format, and style.

Completing the Editing

Top-down editing is generally most efficient. You start with the most comprehensive document features, the ones that will affect others. These features include content, organization, and format, all of which need to be consistent throughout the document. *Bottom-up* editing, beginning with sentences, can waste time and divert your attention from the comprehensive goals. You could start by correcting sentences for grammar and editing them for style and then proceed to format and content; however, you might ultimately decide to delete many of those same sentences altogether. On the other hand, if the surface errors distract you from the content, it may make sense to clean up the document first by correcting spelling and other errors. With clean copy, you can pay closer attention to more substantive document features. A strategy for perceiving the document structure may be to make the headings consistent.

You will probably not be able to achieve all your objectives working just once through the document. On your first pass, you can smooth out the format and organization and begin editing for style. On the second pass, you can review the organization, polish style, and make sure the document is consistent and correct. With a longer document, you can expect to make three or more editorial passes to complete all your goals. Note, too, that as you see the document take shape, you may slightly revise your editorial objectives.

Evaluating the Outcome | What determines that the editing is good or right? The editing has produced a document that does a better job than the original of achieving its purpose with its intended readers. The document is not simply different. The editing has been based on a thoughtful analysis of document function and use and applies known principles of style and document design. The emendations are thoughtful and functional, not arbitrary. The editor can give a reason for each emendation, showing the logic of his or her decisions. The results can be tested, either objectively (as in a field test with sample users) or by informed judgment.

Reviewing the Edited Document with the Writer | Both as a courtesy to the writer and as a check on the accuracy of your editing, you should give the writer a chance to review the edited document and to approve it or to suggest further emendations. Because you and the writer have already agreed on editing objectives, you will not surprise him or her with these substantial emendations. You need not (and should not) come to the conference defensively, but rather should function as the writer's partner. You should, however, be prepared to explain why you have made the choices in content, organization, format, style, mechanics, grammar, and punctuation. The writer may have questions, and you need to be able to answer them intelligently. (See Chapter 15 for suggestions on how to confer productively with a writer.)

Even at this stage, you may suspect that the document has additional editing needs, and this review session is a good time to identify them. The outcome of the review should be either the writer's approval or identification of additional editing tasks.

APPLICATION: THE SERVICE CALL MEMO | You should remember the sample copyedited memo discussed previously in the chapter and depicted in figures 10.1–10.3. The process of substantive editing of that memo resulted in the specific emendations that you see illustrated in figures 10.4–10.6, which appear later in the chapter. This discussion will show how those versions of the document emerged in the various stages of the editing process—analysis, evaluation of the content, establishment of editing goals, and evaluation of the outcome.

Analysis | Even this short memo raises some questions that may require some input from the writer. However, common sense will let us make some initial judgments about readers, purpose, and uses.

- **Readers.** This memo is addressed to "all medical center personnel." That label only generalizes about readers, however. More specifically, the readers who will use the memo are people who will actually place service calls. Realistically, the readers are secretaries and charge nurses. Secondary readers may be people who need to know the procedure but who will not actually place the calls, such as department managers who will direct a support staff person to place the call. Readers will generally be open to the instructions, because they want to do their jobs correctly; they will be even more receptive if they can see how the new system will benefit them. But if they have had trouble in the past with the maintenance department or if they are constantly bombarded with procedure changes, they may be impatient or unreceptive.

- **Purpose.** The purposes are to give information and instructions. For the primary readers (those who will place the service calls), the primary function is to instruct. Thus, the style and format of the document should make it easy for readers to determine what to do. A secondary purpose is to encourage cooperation and goodwill. Perhaps the procedure has changed because the previous one alienated some departments. Whatever the situation, the procedure will work best if readers want to and can cooperate.

- **Conditions of use.** Readers will not use the instructions immediately upon receiving them by mail. Rather, they will skim the memo to get its gist and then file it for reference when they need to place a service call. Thus, the document should be designed for filing, easy reference, and selective reading.

Evaluation   A critical evaluation of the memo should yield the following observations:

- The sentences and words are unnecessarily long.

- The instructions are buried in the passive voice.

- Specific information (e.g., the hours in which the policies are in effect) is difficult to find and interpret.

- The memo shows the value to the maintenance department of the change, but a "you" attitude is missing; cooperation could be better motivated if the service itself rather than the justification for it were stressed.

- Excessive capitalization creates distracting document noise.

Establishment of   Based on the evaluation, the following objectives would be reasonable for
Editing Goals   the service call memo.

- **Content.** Ensure that the necessary information is present. In this case, no new information is needed, but some information may have to be deleted to fit the document on one page.

- **Organization.** Begin with an overview of the process; then give specific instructions. This order will provide information at the beginning that makes the instructions seem meaningful and important.

- **Format.** First, restrict the document to one page in length to prevent some instructions from getting lost and to force simplification of the instructions. Second, create a memo of transmittal to explain the document if necessary, but place the instructions that will be filed on a separate single page. Third, hole-punch the left side of the instructions on the assumption that readers will file the instructions in the *Policies and Procedures* manual and that the manual is in a three-ring binder. Finally, use white space, headings, and lists to make information accessible.

- **Style**. Use the language of instructions—verbs in the imperative mood.

- **Illustrations.** Do not add any illustrations. Because no equipment (other than the telephone) is necessary and no forms will be filled out, illustrations will probably not clarify the procedure.

- **Mechanical style.** Establish consistent capitalization style for "service call," "maintenance department," and the manual title.

Evaluation of the Outcome

Figure 10.4 shows the initial results of substantive editing based on the established objectives. Note that although the message is the same as the message in figure 10.3, this document will enable readers to read selectively and to follow instructions, the stated purposes of the document. However, this version still warrants evaluation. Any substantive change may reveal other needs in the document that were not apparent at first. Thus, this version should be read with the same critical eye. You may approve the document overall but determine that the wording or spacing may still be improved.

For example, because the document fits on one page, a separate memo of transmittal is unnecessary. However, in figure 10.4, the procedure in response to the question "How do I place a service call?" seems incomplete. Besides placing the call and requesting the number, the caller will have to give some information. Thus, some new content may be appropriate after all. This need became apparent only after the first editorial pass accomplished some primary objectives. The first editorial pass also

Figure 10.4   Memo After the First Pass for Substantive Editing

TO: All Medical Center personnel
FROM: Tom Barker, Director of Maintenance
DATE: January 2, 1991
SUBJECT: Service calls: New procedure

Beginning Monday, January 7, 1991, a new procedure for placing service calls will take effect. This procedure will allow the maintenance department to respond to all requests quickly and effectively.

Shorter sentences make comprehension easier.

What is a service call?

Service calls are for minor work requiring immediate attention. Examples are:

Headings in question form let readers read selectively.

    loss of heat or air conditioning
    water leaks
    clogged plumbing
    faulty electrical wiring
    fire, safety, and security hazards

List form lets readers skim the examples. It also clarifies that "fire" and "safety" modify "hazards" rather than being problems that require service calls.

How do I place a service call?

    Call 742-5438.

    Request your service call number. Use this number if you need to check on the status of your service call.

Imperatives direct a reader to act.

For emergencies

    Ask the PBX operator to page maintenance. Please request paging only when you have a true emergency.

When may I call?

    You may place service calls 24 hours a day.

    From 5:00 p.m. through 8:00 a.m. weekdays and all day weekends and holidays, only one maintenance mechanic is on duty. He or she can respond to a limited number of calls during those times. However, you can still place a

Figure 10.4   (continued)

```
        service call on nights or weekends to be
        completed when the mechanic is available.

For information on service call requirements:

        See the Policies and Procedures manual, page 18.


Thank you for your cooperation.
```

reveals some opportunities for more effective spacing. Specifically, the information about emergency calls requires more emphasis.

In addition, note that the information under the final heading is limited to one reference. Also, that information relates to the definition of service calls under the first heading and will be used then, if at all; some reorganization to group related material is thus warranted.

Furthermore, the deletions may have been too extreme. The writer may have reasons not apparent to the editor for including the statement about "all departments" in the introduction and about identifying job orders in the final paragraph. The deletions may have been sound if the information is understood, but if the maintenance department has been accused of favoring some departments, it may be politically prudent to leave the phrase in. Both items can be worked back in efficiently.

Finally, in the last section, the statement that service calls may be placed 24 hours a day seems to be contradicted immediately by the following sentence. One purpose of the memo is to encourage users to place their calls during normal working hours. Restructuring the sentence can diminish the appearance of contradiction while encouraging users of the service call system to place their calls, when possible, during working hours. Figure 10.5 shows these refinements to figure 10.4.

You may have imagined quite a different document. You can probably think of ways to improve the document in figure 10.5. Or you may believe the version in figure 10.6 would be easier to read. Differences in editing result from different initial assumptions. If you have assumed (in contrast to the analysis outlined here) that readers will read primarily for comprehension and that they will read most thoroughly when they remove the memo from the envelope, you will probably have planned for prose paragraphs rather than the highly formatted version in figure 10.5. The highly formatted version assumes selective reading at the time a service call is placed. Because so many judgments have been involved in this editing and nothing comparable to a style guide tells what form a memo giving instructions on placing service calls *should* take, any two editors might

Figure 10.5   Final Version of the Memo After Substantive Editing

TO: All Medical Center personnel
FROM: Tom Barker, Director of Maintenance
DATE: January 2, 1991
SUBJECT: Service calls: New procedure

Beginning Monday, January 7, 1991, a new procedure for placing service calls will take effect. This procedure will allow the maintenance department to respond to requests from all departments quickly and effectively.

Reinsertion of "all departments" may soothe some feelings that prompted the new policy.

What is a service call?

Service calls are for minor work requiring immediate attention. Examples are:
   loss of heat or air conditioning
   water leaks or clogged plumbing
   faulty electrical wiring
   fire, safety, and security hazards

The reference to the manual relates to the definition of a service call. Reorganization groups related information.

See the <u>Policies and Procedures</u> manual (page 18) for service call requirements. Requests exceeding these requirements are classified as job orders.

How do I place a service call?

A new piece of information clarifies the three-step procedure.

   Call 742-5438.
   Identify the nature of the problem and the location.
   Request your service call number. Use this number if you need to check on the status of your service call.

More space sets off and calls attention to the second-level heading, "for emergencies."

For emergencies

Ask the PBX operator to page maintenance. Please request paging only when you have a true emergency.

When may I call?

   You may place service calls 24 hours a day.
   From 5:00 p.m. through 8:00 a.m. weekdays and all day weekends and holidays, only one

Figure 10.5   (continued)

> maintenance mechanic is on duty. He or she can
> respond to a limited number of calls during
> those times. However, you can still place a
> service call on nights or weekends to be
> completed when the mechanic is available.
>
> Thank you for your cooperation.

edit in quite different ways. Careful analysis during pre-editing will help keep subsequent judgments sound. Consultation with the writer will reveal his or her assumptions.

DETERMINING WHETHER SUBSTANTIVE EDITING IS WARRANTED

Substantive editing requires a great deal more commitment to a project than does copyediting. The choice to edit substantively has significant consequences for the editor's time as well as for the document. Furthermore, the greater the editorial intervention, the greater the risk of changing the message and alienating the writer. The choice will depend on several criteria.

- **Limits in your job description.** You may not have a choice. Your supervisor or the writer may set limits on the extent of editing you can do. If you are charged only with correcting grammar and spelling and making mechanics consistent, you will stop there even if you can see how a different form will improve it. Of course, you can always present an argument for a higher level of editing, but sometimes you must be satisfied with doing less than you could.

  The one exception to this general guideline to edit according to your job description is a situation where there is potential danger to someone's health and welfare or violation of laws or ethics. You have an ethical responsibility to make sure the document will not result in harm to a reader. If you are only a copyeditor but can see that a safety warning ought to be added or that a warning about risks should be emphasized, you should make the recommendation anyway.

- **Time.** If you are pressed by more important projects and the task has not been previously scheduled, you will have to stop when you have no more time.

- **Importance of the document.** Substantive editing is more appropriate for important documents than casual ones. The memo on service calls is important because safety is an issue. It may be important as well if productivity in the maintenance department is low because callers are abusing the service call system. Other criteria of importance are money and number of users. If the document will be used by thousands of people or if it accompanies a product that accounts for a large percentage of your company's revenue, it's worth editing substantively.

- **Document anonymity.** Messages that are essentially anonymous (i.e., whose author doesn't particularly matter) can generally be edited more substantively than can personal authorial statements, such as editorials or persuasive essays. Editors should be cautious about intervention in a personal statement that could change content or emphasis. The memo on service calls, though it is signed, is essentially anonymous; it is not a personal statement but rather a procedure. On the other hand, an article for a professional journal reflects an individual's point of view.

Sometimes there is a middle ground between copyediting and complete substantive editing. Most often this means editing for style but not for content, organization, or format. The memo on service calls, for example, would be easier to follow in prose paragraphs, its original form, if it used imperatives rather than passive voice. Figure 10.6 is an example of a document edited for style but not for form, content, or organization. It accomplishes the objectives of shortening sentences and words, making the instructions friendlier and more "you" oriented, and clarifying the information. It pays less attention to the objective of facilitating selective reading.

Be sure to determine what outside criteria may limit your right to edit substantively, either before you begin or after you have evaluated the document and set objectives. And don't exceed the limits without permission or other good cause related to safety and ethics.

THE COMPUTER IN SUBSTANTIVE EDITING

The computer makes a good editorial assistant in substantive editing because of the ease with which the computer can insert and delete for content changes, cut and paste for reorganization or style changes, and reformat. The computer also enables editors to obtain clean copy quickly so that they can see the effect of their editing without the distraction of crossouts and paste-overs. Also, a quick spelling check and correction prior to substantive editing can eliminate some superficial distractions.

Yet pre-editing will almost always require a hard copy so that the editor can develop a sense of the whole document. The limited amount of text

Figure 10.6   Memo Edited for Mechanics and Style

TO: All Medical Center personnel
FROM: Tom Barker, Director of Maintenance
DATE: January 2, 1991
SUBJECT: Service Calls

On Monday, January 7, 1991, the Maintenance Department will begin a new service call system. This system will let us respond to all departments quickly and effectively.

Service calls are for minor work requiring immediate attention, such as loss of heat or air conditioning, water leaks, clogged plumbing, faulty electrical wiring, and fire, safety or security hazards.

The use of imperatives and "you" in this paragraph is consistent with the way in which you want readers to read this memo. They must identify themselves as actors. Elimination of passive voice clarifies who is to do what.

To place a service call, telephone the Maintenance Department (742-5438), 24 hours a day. A service call number will be assigned to the job. You may request this number and use it when checking on the status of your service call.

From 5:00 p.m. through 8:00 a.m. daily, and all day on weekends and holidays, only one maintenance mechanic is on duty. He or she can respond to a limited number of service calls during these times. However, you can still place a service call on nights or weekends to be completed when the mechanic is available. If no one answers, please call again.

Use of "we" and "you" throughout personalizes the memo and is consistent with the reality that this procedure involves people working together.

In an emergency, notify the PBX operator to page Maintenance. Please do not use the paging system unless your request is justifiable. We will appreciate your cooperation.

Service call requirements are outlined in the Policies and Procedures manual (page 18). Requests exceeding these requirements will be classified as job orders, which are also outlined in the Policies and Procedures manual.

that shows at any one time on a computer screen invites line-by-line editing rather than editing based on understanding of the whole document. Once you are familiar with the whole, you may be quite capable of substantive editing on the screen.

Hard copy also is necessary at certain points in the editing process if the document is reformatted, because the screen design does not exactly reflect page design. What appears satisfactory on the screen may not appear satisfactory on paper. Thus, seeing the text on hard copy can help editors make good editorial decisions about format as well as about content and organization.

Keeping track of editorial decisions is also easier on paper. Many organizations require each editorial emendation to be marked. Editors in such organizations may mark proposed deletions without actually making the deletions. Programs for commenting on a file electronically without changing it are described in Chapter 16.

Many editors report that they favor the computer for copyediting but prefer to work with hard copy at least at some points in the substantive editing process.

SUMMARY

Substantive editing makes a document more usable and comprehensible. Even though an editor uses judgment rather than simply following rules, he or she bases editorial decisions on a clear concept of the document's intended purpose and uses rather than on personal preferences.

The substantive editing process requires analysis of the document's readers, purpose, and uses; evaluation of the document; establishment of specific editing objectives; and consultation with the writer about the plans before the editing takes place. After the editing is completed, the writer still has review privileges.

Analysis should be top down: it should first consider the document features that influence comprehension and usability, including content, organization, and format. Top-down editing can also help an editor avoid wasting time. Editing for grammar, punctuation, and mechanics can follow.

FURTHER READING

Sam Dragga and Gwendolyn Gong. 1989. *Editing: The Design of Rhetoric*. Farmingdale, NY: Baywood.

DISCUSSION AND
APPLICATION

1. The following definition of open heart surgery is prepared for patients and their families.* It is intended to answer a frequent question in a way that permits patients to study and ponder the answer. It thus may save the surgeon time, and it may answer questions that patients neglect to ask during consultation. The definition is printed on an 8½ × 11-inch page and folded in half for a two-page look.

Analyze the document's readers and possible uses in more depth, evaluate the document, and establish editing objectives. Do not edit! As you analyze, focus on the readers and on the document rather than on the writer. Use "readers" and "documents" rather than the "writer" as the subjects of your analytical statements.

If your instructor directs you to, write a letter to the writer proposing the editorial emendations in general terms. That is, indicate the concept of the emendations you propose, but do not revise specific sentences except as an occasional example. Request the writer's response and suggestions.

WHAT IS "OPEN HEART SURGERY"?
By Donald L. Bricker, M.D.

This question is often asked perhaps more of patients who have experienced "open heart surgery" than of physicians. It is even posed in an argumentative fashion in some circumstances, and the author has been called more than once to arbitrate as to whether a given surgical procedure was or was not really "open heart surgery." The confusion surrounding the use of the term is quite understandable, since the term "open heart surgery" was coined over two decades ago and is very vague today when applied to the large area of cardiac surgery which it may be used to describe.

Perhaps the term was coined originally because the heart surgeon was concerned with methodology which would allow him to correct congenital heart defects which actually entailed opening the cardiac chambers for repair. Yet, this nosological consideration for procedures performed within cardiac chambers overlooked the true area of common ground which set cardiac surgery apart in terms of magnitude and risk. This area of common ground was simply the need to relieve the heart of his physiological burden while operating on it. In other words, heart operations of great magnitude are best grouped together by the necessity of providing an external mechanical support system to substitute for the function of the heart and lungs in pumping and oxygenating blood. Any heart operation, therefore, which requires that the heart either be stopped for the procedure, or undergo such manipulation that it cannot perform its

---

* Reprinted by permission of Donald L. Bricker, M.D.

designated function, would fit this classification. The external mechanical support system referred to is, of course, the "heart-lung machine." What is today implied by the term "open heart surgery" in common medical parlance, then, is any cardiac operation requiring the use of the "heart-lung machine."

What does the "heart-lung machine" do? First, let us exchange that term for "cardiopulmonary bypass" to aid in our understanding. Basically, cardiopulmonary bypass removes the heart and lungs as a unit from the circulatory system and temporarily bypasses them while performing their function. To accomplish this, blood is diverted from the heart by tapping into the great veins delivering blood from the upper and lower extremities. This blood flows by gravity into an oxygenating device which performs the lungs' function of adding oxygen and dissipating carbon dioxide. This blood is then pumped back into the circulatory system through a convenient artery, usually the aorta, the great artery that comes immediately from the heart. It can be seen then, that with this system functioning, appropriately placed surgical clamps on the venous and arterial sides of the heart and lungs would totally isolate them. This allows the surgeon to stop the heart if he wishes and perform his operation in a precise and unhurried fashion. Of course, the cardiopulmonary bypass unit pump-oxygenator, or if you insist, "heart-lung machine," cannot do this job indefinitely, but sufficient time is safely at hand with today's equipment that the surgeon need not hold the concern he once did for the time factor. Improvement in this equipment has, more than any other factor, led to the successes we routinely enjoy today. One question frequently asked is about the blood supply to the heart and lungs themselves during this period of "bypass." Their blood supply is markedly reduced since they are removed from the circulatory system, but since they are at rest, oxygen requirements are minimal, and for the duration of most procedures no problems are posed.

In conclusion, "open heart surgery" has come to be a less than literal term and in common usage implies a cardiac surgical procedure requiring use of cardiopulmonary bypass. It is this factor which sets the operation apart from other operations on the heart. If your operative procedure was or is to be done under cardiopulmonary bypass, rest assured you have undergone or will undergo "open heart surgery."

2. Locate a brief document or section of a document that may benefit from substantive editing. This document could be a letter, short instructions, flyer, brochure, announcement, or chapter from a text. Assume that you have been assigned to edit the document. Using the procedure for substantive editing described in this chapter, analyze, evaluate, and set editing objectives for your document. If your instructor requests, bring the document to class and share your analysis, evaluation, and objectives with the class orally.

11 STYLE

The rules for grammar and punctuation of sentences still leave writers with many choices about words and their arrangements. Sentences may be long or short; words may take form as nouns, verbs, or adjectives; verbs may be expressed in the active or the passive voice. All such choices, and many more like them, are governed only in limited ways by rules of grammar. The choices, rather, are matters of *style*. Style in this sense differs from *mechanical style* — choices about capitalization, spelling, and other such characteristics of the text.

People use subjective terms in describing style. We may say that a document is "dense," "clear," or "wordy" (terms that reflect the reader's response to the document itself); or we may call the style "formal," "stuffy," "pretentious," "informed," "casual," or "warm" (terms that reflect the writer's projected image). These overall impressions are created by specific, identifiable components of language, namely, words and sentence structures. Style in documents is analogous to style in clothing or music. For example, the western style in dress is the cumulative effect of such components as denims, plaid shirts, boots, and belts with big buckles; the formal style in dress is created from such components as tuxedos, tucked shirts, bow ties, and polished shoes. Different styles in music, such as classical and jazz, are created by choices of notes, rhythms, and instruments. As with dress and music, for written documents some styles are more appropriate in some contexts and for some people than are others.

Creation (and modification) of an overall style, whether in dress, music, or language, depends on knowledge of component parts and options for arrangement. Editing for style requires knowledge of how to manipulate components in order to achieve certain goals. To make a document less "stuffy" or "pretentious," for example, or to make it "informal" or "casual," you may shorten sentences and word length and convert verbs in passive voice to active voice.

Whenever you edit for style, you will influence the reader's response to the content. You may encourage a positive attitude because the style seems right for the situation and projects the image of a competent person. You will also affect the reader's comprehension of the material by matching structures of sentences and words with their meanings and by choosing precise terms. In addition, you will minimize distracting noise in the document.

This chapter will present guidelines to use in editing for style. It will begin with a fuller definition of style and proceed to guidelines about sentence structures, words, and discriminatory language. It will then apply the guidelines to the editing of a brief proposal. It will conclude with a review of the process of editing for style. The chapter will be more meaningful to you if you have reviewed the basic components of sentence structure (e.g., noun, verb, complement, clause, subordination) in Chapters 6 and 7.

DEFINITION OF STYLE

Style is the cumulative effect of choices about words, their forms, and their arrangement in sentences. Therefore, we work with style at the word and sentence levels although the purpose of editing documents at this level is to increase the effectiveness of the document as a whole. An effective technical document satisfies reader expectations (for information, structure, format, and style) and can be understood. Both conditions are necessary to increase the chances that readers will respond in desired ways (by making a decision, taking action, absorbing information). Readers may be distracted from meaning by a style that is inconsistent with their expectations, such as an excessively formal style in a user manual or a casual, flippant style in a research report. Readers may misinterpret a document if the signals about meaning in sentence structures are misleading. Editors aim for reader comprehension because a universal purpose of technical documents is to inform.

The choices about words and sentence structures project an image of the writer—a persona—that will influence a reader's response to the content of the document. The image may be of a person who is objective and detached rather than enthusiastic and persuasive, but such characteristics have a corresponding style. The writer's persona reveals his or her attitude toward the subject and readers. The writer may seem to be serious, superior and disdainful, indifferent, or intensely concerned. This attitude creates a document's **tone,** analogous to a speaker's tone of voice. The tone can be inappropriate enough to create noise in a document that distracts from meaning, or it can be so inappropriate that the reader does not "hear" the meaning at all. For example, a computer manual that goes too far in creating the image of writer as pal looking over the user's shoulder may irritate the user by the presumption. Even when we speak in subjective terms of making a writer's persona project the attributes desirable in a given communication situation, our practical purpose as editors is to help readers understand and use the information.

In addition to revealing a persona, style can affect a reader's comprehension of information. Certain structures and word choices are easier to comprehend than others. For example, readers usually understand subject-verb-object structures better than inversions, concrete terms more readily than abstract ones, and positive expressions more readily than negative ones. An editor must know these principles of structure and word choice to guard against arbitrary changes in style. The ear (what "sounds better") has limitations as a monitor. An editor must also recognize when inverted structures, abstract terms, and negative expressions have their own meaning and should be left alone.

Because choices about style are much more wide-ranging than are choices about grammar and punctuation, the bases for editorial emendation are less certain. Editing for style, compared with copyediting, requires more awareness of readers and purpose, more knowledge both about the subject matter of the document and about principles of communication, and more judgment. Editing for style can both clarify the meaning and distort it. Editing for style can help or interfere with communication. To guard against arbitrary editing and to back up judgments, an editor must be able to articulate reasons for stylistic emendations even more than to articulate rules for grammar and punctuation. Editing for style is really editing for meaning.

The effectiveness of a document depends not just on style but also on accuracy and completeness of information, organization, format, correctness, and consistency. To distinguish the effect of style, let us look at two versions of the same paragraph that differ in style but not in any other features. The paragraphs illustrate the ways in which words and structures create a style and affect a reader's response and probable action.

The original paragraph is the first paragraph of a proposal for a grant to fund some research on the effect of job complexity in workshops for retarded persons. Like all proposals, this one tries to persuade the funding agency both that the research will be worthwhile and that the person who proposes to do it is capable of completing the research. To understand the paragraph apart from the fuller context of the document, you should know that sheltered workshops are places where people with handicaps complete tasks comparable to those in any industry but in settings where the pressures are not so great. The assumption is that simplifying their jobs will improve the performance of these workers. The question this proposal will raise is whether the tedium that results from simplification hurts performance.

Original Paragraph

```
The field of job complexity in industry has a
varied history encompassing as it does
philosophy, economics, social theory,
psychology, sociology, and a myriad of other
disciplines. In the rehabilitation field, the
job simplification model has been the mainstay
in sheltered workshops for retarded persons
almost since their inception. As in industry,
the reasons for adopting the job simplification
model are varied, but it is the author's
contention that in the workshop the reasons are
philosophical and technological rather than
economic.
```

Before reading further, as editor, you should identify your own response to this paragraph by asking a few questions: Does the idea seem important? Does the writer project competence and other desirable attributes? If the answer to both questions is yes, you will probably not edit these sentences for style. They seem to be appropriate *for the readers* and *the purpose*.

If you have any negative responses to this paragraph, either to the idea or to the writer, test them by identifying them specifically and then trying to pinpoint what features of the style created that response. (This procedure is important in substantive editing, whether for style or for any other document characteristic. You respond as a reader both subjectively and objectively. To develop the subjective response into something useful—more than just a reaction—you try to correlate the subjective response with objective triggers.)

Some readers have described this writer as "windy" and "inflated." Such an image would be counterproductive in a proposal. Inflation gives the impression that a writer has to expand on a trivial idea to make it seem important. If the writer invites a negative impression, the proposal concept and method will have to be proportionally stronger to persuade the people at the funding agency to approve this project rather than another, competing one.

To verify and emend an inflated style, we look for stylistic features that create it. This writer uses *redundant categories,* words that restate a concrete subject with an abstraction. His category word is "field." A quick review will reveal other tendencies toward the use of meaningless words and phrases (e.g., "as it does" in sentence 1). The style is also heavy on nouns and light on verbs. Furthermore, all the verbs are *to be* verbs, inconsistent with a proposal writer's goal of projecting a person who can act and make things happen.

These initial observations may reveal additional stylistic features in the paragraph that interfere with its purpose. Maybe on first reading, you slip by the "myriad of other disciplines," but having observed the writer's inflation, you may question whether any issue can encompass a "myriad" of disciplines beyond the five named. This phrase, you may reasonably conclude, is a sophisticated "et cetera"—but not a meaningful one.

Having identified the choices that inflate the paragraph, we may edit for style.

Edited Paragraph

```
The issue of job complexity in industry
encompasses philosophy, economics, social
theory, psychology, sociology, and technology.
In rehabilitation, sheltered workshops for
retarded persons have used the job
simplification model almost since their
beginnings. As in industry, the reasons for
adopting the job simplification model vary, but
```

in the workshop the reasons are philosophical
and technological rather than economic.

While the editing began with some specific observations, the editing process itself revealed even more instances of an inflated style. The category word "field" in the first sentence is inaccurate, so "issue" was substituted. In the second sentence of the original, "their inception," because of its placement immediately following "retarded persons," could be interpreted to modify "retarded persons" rather than "workshops." Some phrases were rearranged, and "beginnings" substituted for "inception." "Are varied" was emended to "vary" to put the action of the sentence in the verb rather than in an adjective. Three of the *to be* verbs are now action verbs. The writer's reference to himself is deleted; the context and phrasing reveal the statement following to be a thesis rather than a fact.

What difference has editing made? It has helped the reader focus on the problem that needs to be solved. The image of the writer is more subtle, but for the problem statement of a proposal it is better to be invisible than to get in the way of the meaning. Note, too, that the edited paragraph is shorter than the original but that conciseness has been a happy consequence of editing to make sentences reveal their meaning rather than an end in itself. The paragraph was edited with an eye toward readers and purpose rather than according to arbitrary rules about style.

Some overt changes of meaning, especially the substitution of "issue" for "field" and the deletion of the "myriad" phrase, have resulted from an analysis of the style. One substantive addition in the first sentence, "technology," results from analysis of the "myriad" phrase and comparison of the list in the first sentence with the descriptors in the final sentence. Style editing may be considered substantive because modifying word choices and sentence structures almost inevitably affects the reader's perception of the meaning. Analysis of style also helps an editor to evaluate the content.

GUIDELINES FOR EDITING FOR STYLE

The possibility of changing meaning requires editors to read carefully and to edit cautiously. Although editors cannot depend on rules about style, they can use guidelines that have been established by experience and by research. These guidelines parallel the guidelines for effective writing style.

Context: make style serve readers and purpose.

Sentence structures: make structure reinforce meaning.

Verbs: convey the action in the sentence accurately.

Words: make words accurate, concrete, and understandable.

Nondiscriminatory language: make choices that show respect for all readers.

The guidelines must be used with good judgment—they are guidelines rather than rules. For example, to edit a scientific paper for peer review according to the same criteria for editing an article for a popular magazine is to ignore how much style relates to the context and to the readers. Sometimes the guidelines that work in general will be inappropriate in a specific situation. The following specific guidelines will help you, though, in identifying the components of style, evaluating style, and making style support document goals.

CONTEXT: MAKING STYLE SERVE READERS AND PURPOSE

An editor who works on style must begin by evaluating readers and purpose and by reading for meaning. Just as no one style in dress or music is suitable for all situations, neither does one style work for all technical documents. In the example on sheltered workshops, the justification for editing at the word and sentence levels was the need for the proposal to compete with other proposals. In contrast, a style for a computer manual for new users would have been less formal, characterized by the use of the *you* pronoun and short sentences.

Some organizations and disciplines have guides for style that parallel their guides for mechanical style. For example, some groups encourage the use of passive voice; other groups discourage passive voice. You must be aware of such conventions that the discourse community expects.

SENTENCE STRUCTURES: MAKING STRUCTURE REINFORCE MEANING

Like all structures, sentence structures are hierarchical. Some component parts, especially the subject and verb of the independent clause, are inherently stronger and more essential than other parts, such as modifiers. The independent clause, without which the sentence would be grammatically incomplete, is the strongest part of the sentence, with more inherent emphasis than dependent clauses or phrases. It is the structural core of the sentence. (See Chapter 7 for a review of these terms and identification of basic sentence patterns.)

The structural core is the logical place for the main idea of a sentence. The sentence structure is a signal about the importance of the words. Other structural signals about meaning are patterns of coordination and subordination. An idea that is structurally subordinate seems inherently less important than an idea in an independent clause. If two ideas are related and equal in importance, that relationship may be reinforced by coordination and parallel structure. When the main idea is buried in a dependent clause or phrase, or when parallel ideas do not have parallel structure, comprehension is more difficult because the reader has to overcome misleading structural signals about meaning.

These relationships between structure and meaning are the basis for the primary principle of editing for style: *make structure reinforce meaning.* We may approach this principle with several more specific guidelines.

The Main Idea of the Sentence

The main idea should appear in the structural core of the sentence. The structural core includes the subject and verb of the independent clause. Consider the following sentence:

> The <u>course</u> of the twentieth century <u>produced</u> a
> cancer death rate that rose parallel to the
> advances in technology.

The core sentence (subject and verb) are the underlined terms, "course . . . produced," but the meaning appears elsewhere. The sentence is not about the course of the twentieth century and what it produced at all but rather about how the rising cancer death rate paralleled advances in technology. "Course" and "produced" are the least important words in the sentence, but they take the strongest structural part. The meaning does *not* appear in the core sentence, and the structure does not reinforce meaning. Style interferes with comprehension.

A reasonable stylistic revision would be to place the main idea in the structural core of the sentence:

> In the twentieth century, the <u>rise</u> in the cancer
> death rate <u>paralleled</u> the advances in
> technology.

> In the twentieth century, the cancer death <u>rate</u>
> <u>rose</u> parallel to the advances in technology.

Both revisions guide readers to the main idea using structural signals.

As an editor, you, like other readers, will be influenced by sentence structures when you read for meaning. Editors reading the following sentence may recognize readily that it is wordy:

> The Department's policies related to standards
> of behavior must be firmly maintained and
> affirmed.

One wordy phrase is the subject, "policies related to standards." If the editor is aware that this writer uses many redundant pairs of words, he or she may simplify the subject. But what is the subject, "policies" or "standards"? The structural signal is that "policies" is the subject because "related to standards" is merely a modifier. But closer analysis will reveal that the real issue is standards, not the policies that define them. The Department wants good behavior. Standards define behavior, and policies define standards. The policies are one level of abstraction further from the desired behavior.

```
The Department's standards of behavior must be
maintained.
```

"There Are" and "It Is" Sentence Openers

Sentences that open with the words "there are" or "it is" often waste the core sentence on a simple declaration. As a result, the main idea of the sentence may be buried in a dependent clause. Furthermore, such openers delay the significant part of the sentence.

```
It is often the case that a herniated disc
ruptures under stress.

Often, a herniated disc ruptures . . .

It is possible to apply for the scholarship by
completing either of two forms.

You may apply for the scholarship . . .

There are two expenses to be justified.

Two expenses must be justified.
```

In each of these pairs, the core sentence in the revised version gives more information. The sentences are more efficient not just because they are shorter but also because readers can find the key idea by looking for the key structure.

Use this guideline judiciously, however. Don't use it as a justification for red penciling every "there are" you find without considering the whole situation. Sometimes "there are" and "it is" are preferable to alternatives, especially when one has to substitute "exist" for the verb. For example, compare "There are three reasons for this problem" with "Three reasons exist for this problem." The purpose of the sentence is to prepare readers to hear the three reasons; the first version does just that.

Subordinate Structures for Subordinate Ideas

When the sentence pattern is complex (a main clause plus a subordinate clause), the pattern itself communicates the relationship of ideas. The structure identifies the main and subordinate ideas. If structure and meaning conflict—that is, if the structure affirms one relationship but the words affirm another—comprehension will be more difficult. Or the words may lead the reader to one interpretation while the aim was another.

The following sentence appeared in a letter of application for a job as bank teller.

```
I was elected treasurer of a social fraternity,
which enabled me to collect and account for
dues.
```

The readers and purpose help an editor determine which facts are subordinate. "Was elected" affirms leadership ability and the confidence of peers. Yet a person hiring a bank teller may be interested more in whether the applicant can handle money accurately. For this reader, then, the information that appears in the subordinate clause is the main idea of the sentence. An appropriate stylistic revision to emphasize the skills that matter in this context would be:

```
As elected treasurer of a social fraternity, I
collected and accounted for dues.
```

Consider the way in which the following sentences might shape a reader's desire to purchase an old home in need of repair:

```
Although the beams show signs of dry rot, the
house seems structurally sound.
```

```
Although the house seems structurally sound, the
beams show signs of dry rot.
```

The second version of the sentence would be more likely to lead a reader to the conclusion that the purchase is a risky one. The idea of structural soundness is subordinate to the idea of needed repair.

Parallel Structure   When relationships between ideas are additive, as when there are items in a series or a compound sentence, the meaningful relationship will be reinforced by a structural relationship. The structure could be a part of speech (e.g., nouns, participles), infinitive phrases, verb phrases in active voice, independent clauses, or any other structure that can appear in a series.

```
We can help to keep costs down by learning more
about the health care system, how to use it
properly, and by developing self-care skills.
```

The faulty parallelism in this sentence makes it difficult to determine whether there are three ways to keep costs down (as the punctuation suggests) or two (as the parallel phrases "by learning" and "by developing" suggest). Two revisions are possible:

```
We can help to keep costs down by learning more
about the health care system, by using it
properly, and by developing self-care skills.
```

```
We can help to keep costs down by learning more
about the health care system and how to use it
properly and by developing self-care skills.
```

The editor can encourage the correct interpretation by using parallel structure along with appropriate punctuation. Which is the better sentence of the two possible revisions? Reasoning suggests that learning how to use the health care system in itself will not keep costs down, but using the system correctly will. This argument favors the first version, in which "using" is a separate strategy rather than something to learn. Furthermore, the first version is easier to read because it avoids the complex structure of a double compound (the two parallel phrases plus the compound object of the preposition, "learning") used in the second version.

S-V-O or S-V-C Word Order

The subject-verb-object (S-V-O) or subject-verb-complement (S-V-C) pattern is the most common one in English. Its familiarity makes it easy to understand. Inversions of the pattern require extra mental processing.

Recall that a transitive verb takes an object, while an intransitive verb takes a complement. Examples of intransitive verbs are *is, come, go,* and *sit.* The words that follow intransitive verbs can only be modifiers or restatements of the subject, not objects.

The sentence you just read is an example of S-V-O order:

```
A transitive verb takes an object.
 S        V        O
```

A complement is either a substitute for a subject or a modifier, as in this example of S-V-C order:

```
A complement is a substitute.
 S          V    C
```

Inversions of the order, because they use patterns that are less familiar to readers, call attention to themselves and possibly away from meaning.

```
The jurors will no favors grant.
  S            O      V
```

```
Favored by the members of the committee is the
C                                           V
```

```
plan to renegotiate his contract.
S
```

Positive vs. Negative Constructions

Positive constructions are easier to understand than negative ones. A double negative illustrates the extra steps required to process a negative construction:

```
It is not uncommon for employers to require
writing samples from applicants.
```

Readers have to use "not" to cancel "un" before they understand that requiring writing samples is common. They would comprehend more quickly if the sentence began, "It is common . . . " The extra steps also increase the risk of faulty comprehension: a reader may comprehend "uncommon" and fail to complete the process of canceling.

How long does it take you to figure out the meaning of the following sentence?

```
The elimination of disease doesn't guarantee
that we won't die according to genetic
timetables.
```

The three negatives ("elimination," "doesn't," "won't") are especially difficult because the concept of "genetic timetables" is difficult. Though the emphasis is somewhat altered in the following revisions, they are preferable because they are easier to understand. An editor may need to consult the writer to determine the meaning of "genetic timetables."

```
Even if we eliminate disease, people may still
die at the same age they do now because of
genetic timetables.
```

```
Elimination of disease doesn't guarantee a
longer life. Genetic timetables rather than
disease may establish the lifespan.
```

Simple negative constructions in two clauses also load extra interpretation responsibilities on readers:

```
It is not possible to reduce inflationary
pressures when the federal government does not
reduce its spending.
```

Note how much easier it is to understand these edited versions:

```
Inflation will continue if the federal
government keeps on spending at the same rate.
```

```
Inflation will decrease only if the federal
government reduces its spending.
```

In this next version, the negative construction remains in one clause, for emphasis. Even elimination of one negative construction, however, makes the sentence easier to understand.

```
Inflation will not decrease unless the
government reduces its spending.
```

Positive language has a psychological benefit, as well as being easier to understand. In the next example, the company that resolves a complaint with a letter may negate some of its efforts to help if the letter ends with a reference to the problem:

```
If you ever have any more problems with our
company, do not hesitate to call.
```

The edited version anticipates a positive future relationship:

```
If our company can serve you in the future,
please feel free to call.
```

Sentence Length　If sentences within a document all contain roughly the same number of words, the reading will become monotonous. The rhythm will lull the readers rather than keeping them alert. Variety for its own sake may be desirable, but variety in sentence length also can be used to emphasize key points. A very short sentence surrounded by longer ones will draw attention and thus influence a reader's perception of the significance of the content.

Long and complex sentences are generally more difficult to understand than short and simple ones because they require a reader to sort and remember more information and more relationships. Yet they can be easier to understand than a series of short sentences just because they establish relationships. They thereby help to interpret the data. For example, a complex sentence (with a dependent and an independent clause) could show a cause-effect relationship. The first two sentences in this paragraph do just that. Notice the childlike quality of the following series of simple sentences:

```
Long and complex sentences are hard to
understand. Short and simple sentences are easy
to understand. Long and complex sentences
require a reader to sort information and
relationships. They require a reader to remember
more information and relationships than short
and simple sentences.
```

Length is, however, relative to readers. Adult readers who know something about the subject appreciate the information they receive from complex sentences. But readers who have limited backgrounds on the subject will need to absorb the new information in smaller and simpler chunks. Also, "length" describes more than just a number of words. For example, sentences constructed out of a series of phrases become "too long" more quickly than do sentences constructed with several clauses. If the sentence core gets lost in a series of modifying or prepositional phrases, the sentence is too long for easy comprehension.

VERBS: CONVEYING THE ACTION IN THE SENTENCE ACCURATELY

The choice of verbs is based on many of the same principles that govern choices of sentence structure and of words. For example, when you evaluate the sentence core to make sure it conveys the essential sentence meaning, you will need to evaluate verbs. The need to be concrete and accurate applies to nouns as well as verbs. Verbs are discussed separately here because sentences often falter stylistically because of their verbs. Writers tend to be noun and "thing" oriented; more effort is required to figure out what the nouns *do*. When you edit for style, consider verbs after you evaluate context and sentence structure.

Action Verbs

Readers come to each sentence subconsciously asking the questions, "Who did what?" or "What happened?" The answer to "what" and "what happened" should appear in the verb. Sentences often lose precision or fail to communicate effectively because the action that should be conveyed by the verb is lost in imprecise or general substitutes or in other parts of speech, including nouns and adjectives. An editor can help writers find their verbs. They will be using structure to reinforce meaning because the structure (verb) will match the meaning (action).

In the following sentence, the verb does not tell the most important thing that the subject does:

```
A one-year warranty was placed on the tape deck
through March 1992, guaranteeing that all parts
and labor would be covered during this time.
```

The fact that the warranty "was placed" is less important than how long it lasts and what it covers. "Placed" is a weak, imprecise verb. A reader has to insert mentally the answer to the question of what the subject (the warranty) did. An appropriate stylistic revision would clarify the meaning by putting the action in the verb, the structure where readers expect to find the answer to their question.

```
This tape deck's one-year warranty extends
through March 1992 and covers all parts and
labor.
```

Note that the new verbs, "extends" and "covers," are stronger than the original verb, "was placed," because they tell more specifically what the warranty does. The action in the original sentence is buried in a past participle ("would be covered") in the case of the second verb and is only implied in the case of the first ("through March 1992"). The revision lets readers comprehend quickly and easily. It further reduces possible misinterpretation by eliminating the word "guaranteeing." A "warranty" and a "guarantee" mean different things, at least in a legal sense.

The way to determine whether the action is in the verb is to examine the core sentence. If the verb tells what the subject does or if it tells what happened, chances are it is acceptable. If the verb is imprecise or ambiguous, or if it does not logically work with the subject, you will need to edit to find a more specific choice.

Note how this sentence hides the action by using an imprecise verb.

```
The stream of air that escapes the larynx
experiences a drop in pressure below the vocal
folds.
```

An editor examining the sentence core might reasonably ask: Can air "experience"? Does this verb tell what the subject does? The verb works with the subject grammatically but not logically. An editor can spot the hidden verb in the noun "drop."

```
The stream of air that escapes the larynx drops
in pressure below the vocal folds.
```

If you can help writers find their verbs, chances are the sentences' structures will reinforce meaning because the main action will appear in the sentence core.

Strong Verbs   Many writers draw on a limited repertoire of verbs. Everything that happens in their writing may be described in these verbs:

is (or other variations of "to be": are, was, were, will be)	add
	involve
have (has, had)	concern
deal with	reflect
make	provide
give	become
do	use

These are weak verbs because the action they describe is general and abstract. Nothing much happens in these verbs. These all-purpose verbs work in many contexts because they describe many possible actions. As an editor, you won't eliminate all uses of these verbs; sometimes they are the best choice. But if such verbs predominate in any given writing, you will have to hunt for the real meaning and substitute the appropriate verb. Consider the following example:

```
The report will deal with the third phase of the
project.
```

Although this sentence tells the reader the general subject of the report, the reader might have learned more had the verb been more specific. Will the report *describe, evaluate,* or *give instructions for* the project's third phase?

You will have to read for meaning to know the main idea. You may find the verb buried in the sentence in a noun or adjective form. If so, your editorial task is to reveal the meaning by placing the action in the verb (making structure reinforce meaning). Or you may find that the writer hasn't really determined what he or she wishes to say, and the meaning is still waiting to be articulated. In that case, an interview with the writer will be necessary to probe for exact meaning.

Nominalizations One way to weaken verbs is to "bury" them in nouns or adjectives. A verb turned into a noun is a **nominalization.** Usually, suffixes, such as *-tion, -al,* and *-ment,* convert verbs into nouns; the following lists some common nominalizations.

Verb	*Suffix*	*Nominalization*
admire	-tion	admiration
agree	-ment	agreement
transmit	-al	transmittal
depend	-ence	dependence
rely	-ance	reliance
solder	-ing	soldering

Nominalizations do serve valid purposes in writing. They become problems only when they obscure what is happening, as when the action a sentence seeks to communicate is disguised as a thing. The form conflicts with meaning and therefore makes comprehension more difficult. Furthermore, sentences full of nominalizations are wordy and lifeless and therefore discourage reading.

Verbs can become adjectives, too, in their participle form (with the addition of the suffixes *-ing* and *-ed*).

```
Some magazines are more specialized than others
by dealing with just one topic, such as science
or art.
```

Note that the verb is the weak *to be* verb, "are." The writer threw in "dealing with" as well, sensing the need for a more specific action. The real action, however, appears in the past participle, "specialized."

```
Some magazines specialize in just one topic,
such as science or art.
```

If you edit to help writers find their verbs, the sentences will probably not be plagued with verbs disguised as nouns and adjectives. The verbs will clarify meaning and will enliven the prose with action.

Active vs. Passive Voice **Voice** refers to the relationship of subject and verb. In the **active voice,** the subject *performs* the action represented by the verb. The subject is the agent of action.

```
The board reached a decision.
    S         V
```

The subject of the sentence, "board," performs the action identified by the verb. In the **passive voice,** the subject *receives* the action identified by the verb. The subject is the passive object of action, or the recipient of action.

```
A decision was reached by the board.
  S          V
```

The subject of the sentence, "decision," does not do the reaching. Rather, it *receives* the reaching.

Don't confuse passive voice with past tense or with weak verbs. A sentence in passive voice always has these components:

a *to be* verb

a past participle

Some statements seem passive because nothing much happens in them, but they are not in passive voice unless they include a *to be* verb and a past participle.

Reasons to prefer active voice. The use of the verb "prefer" in this heading is intentional. Active voice is preferable in many situations, but editors should not arbitrarily convert passive voice sentences to active voice. You need to know the reasons why it is preferable — usually — and why it is not — sometimes.

- **Adds energy to writing.** Active voice conveys directly that people do things or that things happen. In passive voice, the emphasis is on the result, the thing rather than the action.
- **Establishes responsibility.** Active voice is also preferable in many situations for ethical reasons. Sometimes writers use passive voice because they do not want to reveal who the agent of the action was.

```
A decision was reached that you should be
fired.
```

The writer of that sentence may not want the reader to know who made the decision. The passive voice protects the agent from identification.

Passive voice can mask responsibility for future actions as well as for past ones. Consider the group that plans to place a microwave oven in the company lunchroom. One person asks about the effect on workers who wear pacemakers. "A sign will be posted," says one. By whom? Who will take responsibility for posting the sign? A sentence that does not declare responsibility is less likely to shape subsequent action than one that tells who will do the task. "The *supervisor* will post a sign" or "*I* will post a sign" gives a person a task and thereby increases the chance that the task will be performed. If responsibility is not assigned, then the members of the group may all assume that someone else will do the job.

Reasons to prefer passive voice. The arguments for active voice are persuasive, so the reasons for choosing passive voice—in some situations—must be strong.

- **The agent is insignificant or understood.** Sometimes it doesn't matter *who* has done or will do something. The proper emphasis, then, is on the recipient of the action rather than on the agent.

  ```
  Computer chips are made of silicon.
  ```
  Passive voice; emphasizes the object of the action, of making.

  The purpose of this sentence is to identify the material that forms computer chips, not who makes them. The agent is irrelevant (unless context tells us otherwise).

  ```
  Manufacturers make computer chips of silicon.
  ```
  Active voice; introduces an irrelevant agent.

  Sometimes the context makes the agent of action clear. A policy statement directed to supervisors, for example, may establish in an opening paragraph or heading that the statement identifies policies for supervisors. To write in active voice throughout the policy statement would require the repetition of "supervisors" as the subject in many of the sentences. This repetition would therefore subordinate the policy, and the action that results from the policy, to the agent.

- **Readers expect passive voice.** Sometimes a publication or an organization has established passive voice as the preferred style. Some of the sciences, for example, maintain the convention of passive voice sentences, with the writer's voice, or at least the "I," invisible. The reason for minimizing the "I" is to convey a sense of the writer's objectivity—the facts rather than the interpreter predominate. Thus, a science writer may write

  ```
  It was determined that . . .
  ```

  rather than

```
We determined that . . .
```

A number of studies have challenged the presumed objectivity of the passive voice and even of empirical investigation. However, if the discourse community for which you are editing expects passive voice, you will acknowledge their expectations in your decisions about editing for style. Readers will be distracted by variations from the norm and may discredit the findings of a writer who does not use the language of the community and therefore seems not to belong to it.

WORDS: USING CONCRETE, ACCURATE WORDS

Words are the smallest building blocks of discourse. Readers depend on accurate words for the details as well as for forming concepts. If the words are inaccurate or difficult to understand, the reader must either apply extra mental effort to substitute the correct word or "learn" incorrectly. Nouns and verbs, even more than modifiers and articles, deserve your closest attention. You must constantly watch for writing that features abstract rather than concrete nouns, phrases or pairs rather than single words, and complex rather than simple words.

Concrete vs. Abstract Nouns

Concrete words evoke one of the senses — sight, sound, taste, touch, odor, motion. Because we learn through our senses, words that help us "sense" the meaning are easier to understand than are abstractions. Technical writing is often more concrete than philosophical writing because the subject matter is objects and specific actions (though it can be philosophical and abstract as well).

All-purpose nouns are the close cousin of all-purpose, weak verbs. Because they are general rather than specific, they often fail to convey a precise meaning. Consider these common examples:

areas

aspects

considerations

factors

matters

Now try to imagine what the following sentence, which includes several of these all-purpose nouns, means:

```
These aspects are important considerations for
this area.
```

The abstractions are functional, however, when they introduce a list. The concreteness appears in the list that follows the category.

Single Words vs.
Phrases or Pairs;
Simple vs.
Complex Words Anytime a writer unnecessarily complicates information, it places an additional comprehension load on the reader.

Phrases vs. single words. Some writers try to sound sophisticated and knowledgeable by using phrases in place of single words and multisyllabic words when simpler words are more accurate. A restroom may be referred to as a "guest relations facility," and a hammer as a "manually powered fastener-driving impact device." Such a style may please a writer, but it rarely pleases a reader. In *1984,* George Orwell called such circumlocutions "doublespeak." The National Council of Teachers of English (NCTE) each year gives out doublespeak awards for the "best" examples. The military and government have won in the past with these creations:

Phrase	*Translation*
unlawful or arbitrary deprivation of life	killing
controlled flights into terrain	airplane crashes
permanent pre-hostility	peace
violence processing	combat
collateral damage	civilian casualties in nuclear war
frame-supported tension structure	tent

However, military and government writers are not the only inventors of phrases when a word would do. A hospital described "death" as "negative patient care outcome." In finance, a "negative investment increment" means "loss."

These examples illustrate that a negative subject may motivate inflation of language: the phrases are euphemisms for unfortunate or tragic outcomes. But even without this motivation, writers often wander around a specific subject without ever identifying it clearly. The problem with a style that inflates and abstracts in this way is the subsequent loss of comprehension. Such violations of clarity may even cause harm to the readers who need clear, precise information if the subject matter involves potentially dangerous mechanisms or chemicals.

Multisyllabic words. Not only are multisyllabic words more difficult to understand than their one-syllable synonyms, they also take up more room on the page and take longer to read. They may create the appearance of pretense rather than of sophistication. Here are a few common examples of multisyllabic words and their one-syllable counterparts:

Multisyllabic Word	*Synonym*
utilize	use
effectuate	do
terminate	end

Won't readers respect the writer who is able to use the multisyllabic word more than the writer who uses the single-syllable synonym? This is a question you may be asked by a writer who objects to editing for simplification of words. The answer is not easy: writers must be able to use the terms of their discipline just to belong to their discourse community. This guideline does *not* advise you as editor to substitute imprecise generic terms for specific technical ones. It does *not* insist that you eliminate jargon. It does *not* advise you to edit all documents to the same simple reading level. However, it does advise you that writers rarely gain respect on the basis of an ability to use inflated words. They are respected because they have gathered and interpreted data in a credible way, or because they have solved a problem, or because they have helped a reader perform a task accurately. Writers are more likely to rely on multisyllabic words when their substance is weak and they need to impress in some other way. Readers appreciate being able to move through a document without artificial barriers of extra syllables.

Redundant pairs. Sometimes writers can't focus on the exact subject, verb, or modifier, so they insert two or more, hoping to cover all the possibilities. A writer may announce the "aims and goals" of a meeting, for example, not to distinguish between aims and goals but to avoid choosing just one of the words. A computer manual may instruct a user to "choose or select" a command without really meaning that the user has an alternative. The result is wordy, unfocused writing that may confuse readers because "and" and "or" signal multiple possibilities. In your initial analysis of a writer's style, you may note numerous pairs joined with the connectors *and* or *or.* The pairs may state legitimate alternatives, or they may indicate definitions in apposition. However, if they are merely synonyms, they are redundant.

Redundant categories. Redundant categories are abstract restatements of concrete words. The abstraction merely puts the more concrete word into a class without adding meaning. The weather announcer, for example, may predict "thunderstorm *activity.*" "Activity" is a class or a category of actions, only one of which is thunderstorms. The person planning whether to carry an umbrella to work that day imagines thunderstorms, not "activity," which is not something from which one needs the protection of an umbrella. Yet, because of the redundant category, the thunderstorm in the sentence is merely a modifier. The weather announcer could more directly predict thunderstorms.

The category is redundant if the specific term establishes the class.

```
Joe expects to set up a business in the Los
Angeles community.
```

Los Angeles, by definition, is a "community," so the word is redundant.

```
Joe expects to set up a business in Los Angeles.
```

Redundant categories demote key terms from noun to modifier, as well as adding extra words.

Redundant	*Edited*
a career in the medical profession	a career in medicine
hospital facility	hospital
time period	time
red in color	red
upright position	upright
money resources	money; resources
field of industry	field; industry

THE LANGUAGE OF DISCRIMINATION

Our word choices, as they relate to human subjects, may imply bias against particular groups. Language may discriminate against any group that in a particular context may be disadvantaged based solely on their sex, age, race, religion, politics, or physical or mental disability.

Both writers and readers are sensitive to the issue of discriminatory language. Writers may insist that they intend no discrimination when they use the "generic" pronoun *he*. They may be incredulous to think that the phrase *the disabled* is in any way more negative than the phrase *people with disabilities,* or that the term *handicap* may be any more offensive than *disability*. How the writer (and editor) feel, though, is less important than how the readers feel and how word choices will affect their attitudes and comprehension.

Because writers and readers feel so strongly about negative connotations in language, intentional or not, you as an editor must be quite objective about the issue. You may have to suppress your own biases. However you feel about particular phrases or pronouns, you edit for neutral, unbiased language for two good reasons:

- Language that appears discriminatory to readers creates such significant noise in the document that it may block comprehension altogether. The reader will never hear the intended meaning if the discriminatory language interferes.

- Most professional associations and journals have policies to discourage discriminatory language, particularly as the language relates to the sexes. You edit the document to conform to these policies, just as you edit reference lists and punctuation to conform to the accepted form.

These reasons supercede your own feelings about the significance of word choices.

Unnecessary demographic information can also make language discriminatory. For example, the sentence "Dr. Alice Jones, paralyzed from the waist down, was named dean of the College of Home Economics" introduces information that is irrelevant to her appointment and to her ability to do the job. That information about paralysis would only be appropriate in a human interest story. Information that indicates race, age, sex, religion, politics, or attractiveness is rarely appropriate in professional situations because it does not relate to professional credentials. It discriminates by implying that a given age, sex, race, or physical status may affect competence or by conveying surprise that the achievement is inconsistent with the demographic characteristic.

Application: Discriminatory Language

The paragraphs in figure 11.1 appear in an architect's program for a visitor park design. The program is a report with recommendations for design based on analysis of the facility function, use, and setting. It guides the designer by establishing a concept of the facility as well as specific goals and criteria for design. In these paragraphs, the writer addresses specifically the issue of visitors who have disabilities and how the park should be designed to accommodate them.

The message of the paragraphs is positive: the architect is concerned not just with physical accommodations, such as wheelchair ramps, but also with the visitors as whole persons. However, the language contradicts the message by making "the handicapped" an abstraction, and by separating these visitors from others. The language can shape the designer's response to the message by subtly suggesting that "the disabled" are significant primarily in terms of their handicaps. Though the message discourages differentiation of handicapped and other visitors, the language permits it.

Figure 11.1   Original Visitor Park Report

Handicapped people have expressed that they do not
need or desire segregated outdoor activities. They
prefer not to be singled out, but instead,
appreciate efforts made to accommodate their
special needs. A sensitive approach without
differentiation is preferred, and demonstrations of
sympathy should be avoided.

The disabled possess different learning styles
which tend to focus on using the sensory
perceptions to the greatest extent possible.
Depending on their particular disability, they
utilize their hands, eyes, and ears to perform as
informational transmittors. To enhance the overall
experience for the disabled visitor, and encourage
his participation, all kinds of sensory experiences
should be incorporated into exhibit and facility
design.

Activities should be created which will enable
participation by the physically disabled. Easy
access to areas in the way of ramps, minimal
inclines, and railings should be provided.
Developing designs and activities that accommodate
the handicapped population can provide them with a
more enjoyable and secure experience.

An analysis of the style will reveal nominalizations and weak verbs as
well as some discriminatory language. Passive voice is appropriate to the
extent that the designer is understood throughout the program to be the
agent of implementing the concepts. Yet overuse of passive voice may
reduce readers' access to and acceptance of the ideas. Figure 11.2 shows
how this report might be edited for style.

Figure 11.2   Visitor Park Report from Figure 11.1 Edited for Style

Handicapped people with disabilities have expressed that they do not need or desire segregated outdoor activities. They prefer not to be singled out, but instead, appreciate efforts made to accommodate their special needs. A sensitive approach without differentiation is preferred, and demonstrations of sympathy should be avoided.

People with disabilities use their ~~The disabled possess~~ different learning ~~styles which tend to focus on using the~~ sensory perceptions to ~~the~~ a greatest extent ~~possible~~ in learning. Depending on their particular disability, they ~~utilize~~ use their hands, eyes, and ears to ~~perform as~~ transmit information ~~al transmitters~~. To enhance the overall experience for ~~the~~ disabled visitors, and encourage ~~his~~ their participation, all kinds of sensory experiences should be incorporated into exhibit and facility design.

Physical disabilities require ~~Activities should be created which will enable participation by the physically disabled.~~ Easy access to areas in the way of ramps, minimal inclines, and railings ~~should be provided.~~ ~~Developing~~ designs and activities that accommodate ~~the handicapped population~~ visitors with disabilities can provide them with a more enjoyable and secure experience.

Editing for a Nonsexist Style   The generic *he* has been established as improper by various professional associations and by research showing that readers do associate male images with the male pronoun far more often than they associate female images. One study required subjects to complete sentence fragments such as "Before a pedestrian crosses the street, . . ." and "When a lawyer presents opening arguments in a court case, . . ." Subjects also had to describe their images of the people in the sentences and give them names. People who used *he* in completing the sentences gave the subject a male name five times more often than a female name, and they imagined the subject as a man four times more often than as a woman. By contrast, people who used *they* or *he or she* selected a male name only twice as often as a female name and imagined the subject as a woman as often as a man.

The male bias in imagery caused by the generic *he* is especially inappropriate in evaluative situations. For example, following are guidelines from one company for supervisors evaluating employees. Supervisors are asked to classify employees into one of three rankings: "needs improvement," "good," and "outstanding." Definitions of performance levels for all three categories are briefly described. The first two descriptions contain no masculine pronouns, but the description of the outstanding employee contains four references to males. In a subtle, and probably unintentional, way, the writer encourages the identification of outstanding employees as male.

```
The employee is clearly superior in meeting work
requirements, and he consistently demonstrates
an exceptional desire and ability to achieve a
superior level of performance. His own high
standards have either increased the
effectiveness of his unit or set an example for
other employees to follow. This rating
characterizes an excellent employee who
consistently does far more than is expected
of him.
```

Various professional associations have specified guidelines for avoiding sexist language. The National Council of Teachers of English (NCTE) suggests these alternatives for terms that include "man":

Sexist Language	*Alternative*
mankind	humanity, human beings, people
man's achievements	human achievements
the best man for the job	the best person for the job, the best man or woman for the job
man-made	synthetic, manufactured, crafted, machine-made

the common man	the average person, ordinary people
chairman	coordinator, presiding officer, head, chair
businessman, fireman, mailman	business executive or manager, firefighter, mail carrier
steward and stewardess	flight attendant
policeman, policewoman	police officer

The NCTE advises these alternatives for masculine pronouns:

1. Recast into the plural.

2. Reword to eliminate unnecessary gender problems.

3. Replace the masculine pronoun with *one, you,* or *he or she,* as appropriate.

APPLICATION: EDITING FOR STYLE

So far we have been looking at sentences and words in order to define the components of style. The brief proposal that appears in figure 11.3 illustrates the cumulative effect of stylistic choices at the word and sentence levels. It also illustrates the effect these choices have on the reader's comprehension and attitude. Like most documents, its needs for editing are not limited to style. You should spot at least one grammar error, and the insertion of headings could aid both comprehension and access. However, the analysis will focus primarily on style.

Figure 11.3   Original Proposal

[1]This request to the United States Geological Survey is in reference to the $15,000 allocated by the Office of Coal Management to the Ames District for use in hydrologic assistance. [2]At this time and stage of access and interpretation of existing data on record in the form of computer storage and publications in print that we may not be aware of is our main concern. [3]Due to the U.S. Geological Survey having vast storage of and access to this

_____   Figure 11.3   (continued)

data we would like to suggest the available funds
be used in the following two areas if possible.

[4]The first area may be handled by the Geological
Survey district office in Wilson due to
accessibility and central locale to all literature
and data sources. [5]By compiling this data a
comprehensive interpretation of surface water,
i.e., quantity, quality, salinity etc. for site
specific coal leases or areas immediately adjacent
those leases can be provided to the Ames District
hydrologist. [6]Thus, due to time constraints, time
may be spent on analyzing these interpretations and
conducting on-site calculations.

[7]Secondly, another area we foresee as a positive
and very useful endeavor is the expertise that can
be provided by the Water Resource Division of the
Geological Survey in Mountainview. [8]Because the
subdistrict office and the White River Resource
Area office are both located in Mountainview, we
may obtain their help in the form of infrequent
consultations, informal review of tract analysis
and field reconnaissance on a one time basis of any
lease area lacking available hydrologic data.

[9]The foregoing should provide adequate
justification for requesting the U.S. Geological
Survey's assistance.

Analysis   Analysis should reveal specific editing goals so that the editing can be purposeful and systematic. It will begin with general responses based on
awareness of the context and work toward specific goals.

- **Context.** Readers (the people who can determine whether to grant the funds or not) are likely to read the proposal and wonder: How will the money be spent? Is this expense worthwhile? Are the proposers capable of doing what they propose? Readers need to be persuaded that the proposed expense represents the best use for their funds. They would prefer not to read the proposal twice or more to find out what it is about. Yet the proposal is confusing on first reading. The final sentence compliments the writer and document rather than anticipating what a reader will need to know or do at this point.

- **Sentence structure.** The sentences are long, and it is difficult to find the sentence core. Verbs are weak ("is" and "would like" in the first paragraph). The "due to" construction (sentences 3 and 4) substitutes a prepositional phrase for a clause.

- **Verbs.** In addition to overreliance on weak verbs, the writer uses passive voice frequently (sentences 4, 5, and 6), making it difficult to determine who is to do what, as well as creating a dangling modifier in sentence 5.

- **Words.** One word that is particularly difficult to interpret is "area" in sentences 4 and 7. Is it a geographic area or a subject area? The mention of specific sites ("Wilson," "Mountainview") suggests a geographic area, but "area . . . is . . . expertise" in sentence 7 suggests a subject area. The writer also creates some ambiguity with redundant pairs and categories ("time and stage of access and interpretation of existing data on record in the form of computer storage and publications in print" in sentence 2, "positive and useful endeavor" in sentence 7). Some modifiers are excessive ("immediately adjacent" in sentence 5, "available . . . data" in 8).

Editing Goals Based on the analysis, the following editing goals may be established.

1. Shorten sentences and emphasize the sentence core by placing it earlier in the sentence.

2. Use action verbs. Prefer active voice; clarify responsibility if passive voice remains.

3. Make terms concrete. Delete unnecessary repetitions.

4. Leave the reader with a good impression.

Figure 11.4 shows how the marked copy might look; figure 11.5 shows the clean copy.

Figure 11.4   Marked Copy from Figure 11.3

Subject and verb come early in the sentence so readers can process its core.

Publications are listed before computer data bases to clarify that "computer" does not modify "publications."

A phrase is converted to a clause for easier comprehension. The qualifier, which only weakens the proposal, is eliminated.

The core sentence comes early in both of these sentences for easier comprehension.

Active voice replaces passive voice to establish who will do what.

Core sentences come early. Unnecessary modifiers are deleted.

This ~~request to the United States Geological Survey~~ *justification*
~~is in~~ reference*s* to the $15,000 allocated by the
Office of Coal Management to the Ames District for
use in hydrologic assistance. ~~At this time and~~ *We are concerned*
~~stage~~ *about our lack* of access ~~and interpretation of~~ *to* existing data
in publications and ~~on record in the form of~~ computer *databases* ~~storage and~~
~~publications in print~~ that we may ~~not be aware of~~ *Since*
~~is our main concern~~ ~~Due to~~ *(USGS) has* the U.S. Geological
Survey ~~having~~ vast storage of and access to this
data, we would like to suggest the available funds
be used in the following two ~~areas if possible.~~ *ways*

~~The first area may be handled by~~ the Geological
Survey district office in Wilson ~~due to~~ *has*
access~~ibility and central locale~~ to all literature
and data sources. ~~By compiling this~~ *It could compile and interpret* data ~~a~~
~~comprehensive interpretation of~~ *on* surface water
~~i.e.~~ (quantity, quality, salinity etc.) for site
specific coal leases or areas ~~immediately~~ adjacent
to those leases ~~can be provided to~~ the Ames District
hydrologist ~~Thus, due to time constraints, time~~ *could then spend his or her*
~~may be spent on~~ *time* analyzing these interpretations and
conducting on-site calculations.

Secondly, ~~another area we foresee as a positive and~~
~~very useful endeavor is the expertise that can be~~
~~provided by~~ the Water Resource Division of the
USGS ~~Geological Survey~~ in Mountainview~~,~~ ~~Because~~ *could provide expertise with through* the
subdistrict office and the White River Resource
Area office ~~are both located in Mountainview~~ we
~~may~~ *could* obtain their help ~~in the form of~~ *through* infrequent
consultations, informal review of tract analysis,

252

Figure 11.4   (continued)

initial

and field ~~reconnaissance on a one time basis~~ *survey* of any

lease area lacking ~~available~~ hydrologic data.

Instead of complimenting themselves, the writers offer the reader further assistance.

Please consider our request carefully and ~~The foregoing should provide adequate justification~~ *contact us at extension 388 if* ~~for requesting the U.S. Geological Survey's~~ *you need further information* ~~assistance.~~

Figure 11.5   Clean Copy as Edited in Figure 11.4

This justification refers to the $15,000 allocated by the Office of Coal Management to the Ames District for use in hydrologic assistance. We are concerned about our lack of access to existing data in publications and computer databases. Since the U.S. Geological Survey (USGS) has access to this data, we suggest that the available funds be used in the following two ways.

The USGS office in Wilson has access to all literature and data sources. It could compile and interpret data on surface water (quantity, quality, salinity etc.) for site specific coal leases or areas adjacent to those leases. The Ames District hydrologist could then spend his or her time analyzing these interpretations and conducting on-site calculations.

Second, the Water Resource Division of the USGS in Mountainview could provide expertise both through the subdistrict office and the White River Resource Area. We could obtain their help through infrequent consultations, informal review of tract analysis, and initial field survey of any lease area lacking hydrologic data.

Please consider our request carefully and contact us at extension 388 if you need further information.

Evaluation and Review Because some of the sentences were so ambiguous, an editor should consult with the writer before sending the proposal forward. The copy is also heavily marked. Although the editor should preserve a record of editing, the writer may be able to follow it better if he or she sees the edited version without the marks on the page. The editor may provide both the marked copy and the clean version to the writer to achieve the goal of helping the writer see the effects of the editing as well as the specific emendations. The dual copies are easy to provide if you are editing with a computer and thus don't have to retype everything.

Some content and format questions arise as a result of stylistic editing. For example, proposals usually include specific budgets. The reader may reasonably wonder how much of the $15,000 will go for each purpose and how much each data search and consultation will cost. Headings or numbers could help to identify the two proposed uses of the money. The editor may raise these questions with the writer and suggest additional data. But this level of editing exceeds editing for style and should be approved before it is done. Even if this proposal is edited only for style, it will be easier to understand and therefore more persuasive.

METHOD OF EDITING FOR STYLE

Because editing for style is editing for meaning, not just correctness, you should follow the method of discovery described in Chapter 10. This method requires some consideration of the document as a whole and in context of its readers and purpose. If you merely react sentence by sentence, you risk applying principles without paying attention to meaning.

1. **Be sure the job allows this level of edit.** If you have been assigned just to fix grammar and typos, you don't have the privilege of editing for style. If you are convinced that the document needs to be edited for style, you may point out the need, and you may receive permission to edit for style, but don't just assume it.

2. **Know the document purpose and readers.** The best way to make editorial judgments when you can't depend on rules is to consider the choices about style in light of responses you can predict readers will make.

3. **Analyze the document's style to determine specific editing goals.** Specific editing considerations may include sentence structure, verbs, words, and bias. Determine undesirable characteristics, such as a tendency to use pairs of terms when one will do or to depend on passive voice. This knowledge will help you edit systematically.

4. **Edit.** Based on your pre-editing work, you are ready to edit. Check the sentence core and word choices. Check each stylistic emendation to be sure that the edited version means the same as the original. Consult with the writer if you have any questions. Edit with respect for the power of word and sentence choices to change meaning and to affect the reader's response.

SUMMARY

A document's style affects how receptive readers will be to it and how well they will understand it. A writer's sentence structures and words create a persona to which a reader will respond. They shape the way readers will structure the information contained in the sentences and the emphasis the words will convey. Editing for style requires careful interpretation of the sentences as well as sensitivity to the ways in which different words and arrangements can change meaning. Thus, a good editor reads carefully for meaning and follows established guidelines for effective style.

FURTHER READING

Walker Gibson. 1969. *Persona: A Style Study for Readers and Writers.* New York: Random House.

Richard A. Lanham. 1978. *Revising Prose.* New York: Scribner.

Joseph Williams. 1989. *Style: Ten Lessons in Clarity and Grace,* 3rd ed. Glenview, IL: Scott, Foresman.

DISCUSSION AND
APPLICATION

1. The following sentences do not use verbs effectively. Analyze each sentence to determine the source(s) of the problem (e.g., action not in the verb, passive voice, nominalization, separation of verb from its subject), and then edit to use verbs more effectively. Be sure to preserve the writer's meaning, or prepare a query to the writer if you cannot determine the meaning.

    a. Prolonged use of the battery can cause it to become drained of its energy.
    b. The crimper on the alfalfa mower breaks the stem every inch to allow the fluids in the stem to be released.
    c. (from instructions for playing tennis)
       Place your legs in a bent position with your toes pointing outward at an angle of 45 degrees.

   d. Because there is a trend toward fewer and
      larger farms, it will cause an increase in the
      demand for machinery, decreasing the demand
      for farm laborers.

   e. The report shows a recommendation toward sim-
      ple, cost-effective advertising with the aid
      of either an advertising agency or an account
      executive from a media service.

   f. Further research needs to be entailed into the
      project.

2. Distinguish passive voice sentences from those with weak verbs or
   past tense. (Look for the *to be* verb and past participle to identify
   the passive voice sentences. Verify your identification by determining whether the subject performs or receives action.) Convert the
   passive voice sentences to active voice.

   a. The report was written collaboratively by
      three engineers.

   b. The report was informative but too long.

   c. The engineers have sent the report to the
      editor.

   d. The report has been shortened by three pages.

   e. This method of writing and editing is effec-
      tive for us.

3. Describe the sentences below in terms of core sentence, use of
   verbs, and voice. Do they all mean the same thing? Which version
   is "better" stylistically? What are the bases for deciding the answer
   to that question?

   a. There must be thorough preparation of the
      specimens by laboratory personnel.

   b. Laboratory personnel must prepare the speci-
      mens thoroughly.

   c. The specimens must be prepared thoroughly by
      the laboratory personnel.

      d. Preparation of the specimens by laboratory
         personnel must be thorough.

4. Compare the following sentence pairs to determine how the revision for style has also inappropriately changed meaning. Define the change in meaning. Suggest a way to edit the first sentence in the pair to improve style without changing meaning.

      a. Technical writers are now finding themselves
         in roles in product design and managing the
         production as well.

         Technical writers now find roles in product
         design and production management.

      b. The problem involves derivation of objective
         methods for evaluating the effect of
         adriamycin on the heart.

         The problem derives objective methods for
         evaluating the effect of adriamycin on the
         heart.

5. Edit the definition of an outstanding employee that appeared in the "Language of Discrimination" section to remove sexist language.

6. Discuss the suitability of the persona and style of the following paragraph assuming that the passage appears in a manual for volunteers assisting the probation officer. Discuss the suitability of the persona and style assuming the passage appears in a law textbook. How do context and readers influence your description of the style? What particular stylistic features make the passage appropriate or not for the two contexts?

      Probation is a method of disposition of a
      sentence imposed on a person found guilty of a
      crime. It is a court-ordered sentence in lieu of
      incarceration. The offender remains in the
      community under the supervision of a probation
      officer for a predetermined period of time. If
      compliance with the terms and conditions of

```
probation set by the court is made by the
offender, he or she is discharged from the
court's jurisdiction and the debt to society is
considered paid. If compliance is not made,
another method of sentence may be imposed which
may include incarceration.
```

7. Locate examples of "doublespeak," and conduct a doublespeak awards contest in your class.

8. Select a passage from a technical document, such as a computer manual, or from a textbook on a technical subject. Analyze the style, using the terms and principles discussed in this chapter. Then, taking note of the presumed readers and purpose for this document, evaluate the style. What are its strengths? What, if any, editing goals would be appropriate?

9. Consult a professional journal and the style manual in your field. Do they give guidelines to authors for style?

10. Analyze your own writing style.

12 ORGANIZATION

Reorganization can often significantly improve a reader's accuracy as well as ease of reading. The structure of a document influences how well readers understand it. By editing for organization, you can make a document more comprehensible. Often, your review of structures will also reveal gaps and inconsistencies in the information. Thus, a second result of editing for organization may be to improve the content.

Because organization is such a powerful aid (or hindrance) to comprehension, you must be particularly sure of your principles and expected results when you reorganize, and you must stay in close touch with the writer of the document. As with any editing, your editing for organization will be more effective if you proceed in an informed and systematic way rather than arbitrarily, considering the document's readers and purpose and applying principles of effective organization.

This chapter begins by discussing research on how readers learn from printed documents. These principles are fundamental to document design in general and to editing for organization in particular. An editor who wants to be trusted with content has a responsibility to know why he or she proposes organizational emendations. Next, the chapter presents guidelines for editing for organization based on that research. Finally, the chapter traces the process of analyzing and editing a document that can function better after reorganization. The chapter emphasizes organization as it influences comprehension. Chapter 13, "Format," addresses the second major function of organization—to provide selective access to information—and outlines methods of revealing the structure.

LEARNING FROM TEXT

One purpose of a technical document is to give information. By extension, writers (and editors) expect that readers will learn from what they read, whether the purpose of learning is to make a decision, perform a task, or review research and results. Writers and editors can do a better job of helping readers learn from documents if they understand basic principles of learning. Researchers in cognitive psychology and instructional technology have studied the ways in which people learn; here, the focus is on how they learn from printed texts. A number of text features, including organization, format, and sentence structure, can influence learning. This chapter applies learning theory specifically to overall document organization.

The Schema Theory of Learning

The most widely accepted theory of learning is *schema theory.* Basically, the theory proposes that people store information in long-term memory by creating structures, or *schemata* (sing., *schema*), for concepts and facts. We organize information in order to understand and remember it.

The word *schema* comes from the Greek word for *form.* You are probably familiar with one variation of the word as used in the term *schematic diagram,* which outlines the form of an object without representing it realistically. You might find such a diagram pasted on the back of your refrigerator to show the wiring pattern. Our schemata in memory resemble schematic diagrams for our stored concepts.

Even an abstract and simple concept such as "give" has a structure in memory. *Give,* even out of a context, always implies certain components, including a *giver, recipient,* and *gift.* These components remain constant even when the specific examples of giving change. (See pages 101–103 of the selection by Rumelhart and Ortony in the "Further Reading" section at the end of the chapter for an elaboration of this example.)

Each stored schema becomes a pattern or template against which new information can be matched. These templates help us learn new information because we can relate the new to old information. When we use the stored schema to process new information, we may modify the existing schema and make it more complex, or we may create a new schema. Thus, the schema for *give* may develop over time. For example, a child's concept may be limited to the experience of receiving gifts at Christmas and for a birthday. The adult's concept, based on broad experience, is more complex and may include giving of service and love as well as tangible gifts. Nevertheless, the basic components of *giver, recipient,* and *gift* remain constant.

The schema theory explains why analogy is such a useful teaching tool. The analogy attempts to relate new information to familiar information, or to tap into an existing schema and to modify it or to create a new schema with the additional information presented. It also explains why learners with expertise on a subject can learn new material on the subject more quickly than can equally intelligent learners with limited knowledge of the subject. The experts have more schemata, and more complex schemata, stored in memory on which they can draw to process new information.

Organization and Comprehension

Schemata are hierarchical—that is, they have major components and subordinate components. A person creating a new schema first creates the *macrostructure,* or arranges the major points. Then the person fills in the *microstructure,* or the details. This is called *top-down processing.* If we were to phrase this concept in terms that are familiar to writers and editors, we would say that most learners move from general to specific, or from the concept to the details. That is why documents begin with introductory material that establishes context and thesis, or some version of these. Writers and editors appreciate the readers' need to develop a concept (the macrostructure) within which to order the details (the microstructure). Readers also use the details to modify and develop the schemata. Thus, most reading moves two ways. Nevertheless, at least a rudimentary schema should be available early.

A document's organization affects how well and how easily readers learn the information contained in it. The structure of the document helps a reader locate the appropriate stored schema in memory and modify or create a new schema as needed. The major and subordinate points in the document should match the major and subordinate structures, and the sequence should facilitate top-down processing. If they do, the reader can place the details in the overall hierarchy. Likewise, a faulty structure can cause a reader to identify a minor point as a major point and thus to "learn" the new information incorrectly. Sometimes readers compensate for faulty structure by rereading and by imposing the correct order mentally. Each time the text demands that they do so, however, the chances increase that readers will comprehend incorrectly.

In summary, the overall structure of the document influences the reader's comprehension of the content. So do the reader's prior learning and other text characteristics, but at the very least we may say that *structure reinforces meaning.* A collection of facts has little meaning without a structure and a context. The order in which the information is presented (i.e., the sequence) and the emphasis given to various parts affect the reader's perception of the meaning and the schema he or she creates.

Analysis as a Means of Understanding

Writers and readers have in memory some templates for document structures. Good informative documents are organized in predictable ways, and their patterns of organization match the patterns in memory. Documents generally have three main parts: a beginning, a middle, and an end. The beginning (often called an **introduction**) presents the concept by identifying the topic and by placing it in its context (background, purpose, significance). The middle analyzes the overall topic by identifying component parts and develops the topic with details. The end, like the beginning, considers the topic as a whole, by summarizing, drawing conclusions, or anticipating applications of the information.

All patterns of development, or all ways in which you can arrange data in the middle of a document, are based on the principle of analysis. That is, the whole of the topic is analyzed (broken down) into its component parts. If the document contains instructions, the whole (the overall task) is analyzed into steps. If the document describes a mechanism, the whole mechanism is analyzed into functional parts. If the document is a feasibility study, the project is analyzed into topics of investigation, such as cost and availability of equipment.

Analysis is a means of understanding the whole, not an end in itself. Analysis gives meaning and coherence to a subject by revealing the structure of the information. However, to have meaning, a subject cannot be a series of isolated facts or objects; rather, the parts must cohere into a whole. Thus, the end of a document reassembles the material to force readers to look again at the topic as a whole. Instructions are an exception in the sense that they often have no formal conclusion; however, the completion of a task provides the reader with the sense of closure and completeness that a printed conclusion provides in a report. The beginning and end of a document, then, look at a topic as a whole, while the middle considers the component parts as a means of clarifying or supporting or enabling the whole.

As an editor who can manipulate organization to improve clarity and usability, you need to consider both the overall structure (beginning, middle, and end) and the structure within the middle section. To relate this observation to the cognitive theory just discussed, we may say that the beginning and the end focus on the macrostructure of a concept, item, or task. The middle focuses further on the macrostructure by naming components of the whole. The details within each section of the middle form the microstructure.

PRINCIPLES OF ORGANIZATION

Language is so complex, and documents are so varied in type and purposes, that we can only generalize about what constitutes a good organization. The organization that works in one situation may not work in another. You cannot rely on rules in editing for organization any more than you can rely on rules in editing for style. You can, however, apply principles of organization, using them with good judgment and remaining flexible enough to apply them differently in different situations.

This section of the chapter presents some principles that you should become familiar with before you try to improve a document's clarity and effectiveness by reorganizing. The principles suggest guidelines for editing for organization. The order in which the principles are presented also suggests a process for applying them. That is, if you consider the principles in the order that they are presented, you will work efficiently. Briefly, when editing for organization, you should do the following:

1. Follow pre-established document structures.
2. Arrange information from general to specific.
3. Apply conventional patterns of organization.
4. Group related material.
5. Use parallel structure for parallel sections (e.g., chapters, paragraphs).

Let us examine each guideline in more detail.

Pre-established Document Structures

Often the structure of a document is established by someone other than the writer. For example, an organization that publishes an **RFP** (request for proposals, a document that invites proposals for providing a service or solving a problem) may specify what components should appear on what pages. The RFP for the proposal in figure 12.3 specified, for example, that an abstract and a work schedule appear on the title page of the proposal. Some documents, such as a manual in a series of manuals, follow a structure established for the series (document set).

Certain organizational patterns are widely accepted for documents in different disciplines. Readers who know these conventions expect documents to follow them. For example, a research report in a scientific journal typically follows the pattern of problem statement, literature review, methodology, results, and discussion. These terms are likely to be section headings. Many business executives, especially those who manage according to management by objectives (MBO), expect that projects will be described in management plans in terms of goals (broad aims), objectives (specific aims), strategies (means of achieving the goals and objectives), and evaluation procedures (means of measuring whether the goals and objectives are achieved).

Minimal editing for organization should ensure that the document's structure conforms to any prescribed or conventional structure. The established structure sets up expectations in readers that they will find certain kinds of information in certain places. Variations will distract them from the content of the text and from their purpose for reading. In terms of learning theory, readers will need to redesign their schemata for the topic or else they will learn inefficiently because they will encounter information in a structure that does not correspond to the stored schema. Furthermore, the failure to follow conventions may cost the writer some credibility with his or her professional or discourse community.

Thus, your first task in editing for organization is to compare the structure of the document to be edited with any patterns to which it must conform. This comparison will help you spot missing parts as well as ineffective structure. For example, if you are editing a management plan that lacks evaluation procedures, you will suggest to the writer that he or she complete that section.

General-to-Specific Arrangement

Because readers process information top down, they need to know the underlying concept before being provided with details. General information in an introduction provides the concept. Readers who encounter the details before the concept may struggle with the details (because there is no context for understanding them), or they may form their own concept or schema (which may not be correct). Because this principle of top-down learning is so central to cognitive processing, this guideline is the second most important one for you to apply when you are evaluating organization.

You need to be sure that an appropriate amount of concept information is available at the beginning of the document to orient readers. Often writers omit such information because they are so familiar with the topic that they assume the points are clear even without explicit mention. As editor, you can look more objectively at the information from a reader's point of view. It is easiest to do this if your level of understanding matches the intended readers' level. (Sometimes you do your best editing when you are not a subject matter expert.) If you know more or less than readers probably will, you can still anticipate basic reader questions and evaluate opening paragraphs to see whether the questions are answered. Readers ask predictable questions when they first confront a document, such as "What is this about?" "Why is it important?" "Who is affected by it?" These are the investigative journalist's questions: who, what, when, where, why, how, and so what?

The amount of information to precede details will depend partly on the document's purpose. Instructions do not generally need to begin with detailed conceptual information. Readers are more eager to get on with the task than they are to analyze processes and principles. The general information in instructions may be as minimal as a definition of the scope of the task (what a reader will learn to do), expected competencies, and equipment and materials needed. Sometimes the introduction may also include a brief description or explanation of relevant processes if these will help the reader complete the task accurately, efficiently, and safely.

When the reader's task is comprehension rather than performance, the general information needs to orient the reader not just to the topic but to its context (background and significance) and to relevant principles. The amount of general information in such documents will depend on the expertise of the reader. Beginners are likely to need more explanation and background than are experts; and people who will use the information casually need less orientation than do people who will use the information in research. All readers learn new information best if it is prefaced with familiar information. The analysis of document readers and purpose described in Chapter 10 will help you assess the circumstances of use of the document you are editing and make editorial decisions accordingly. You will have to "get into" the intended reader's mind to assess likely questions and needs for information.

Your second task in editing for organization thus is to review the introductory material for the whole and for each major section. Does it orient the reader to the subject and purpose? Does it begin with information that is familiar to the intended reader?

Conventional Patterns of Organization

Readers have schemata stored for patterns of presenting information, such as chronological, spatial, comparison-contrast, and cause-effect. Unlike the scientific report and MBO patterns described previously, these generic patterns are used in all disciplines. As an editor, you can help make the document easy to understand by ensuring that it uses one or more of these patterns in a consistent and predictable way. A chronological structure is appropriate for narratives, instructions, and process descriptions. A spatial order (e.g., top to bottom, left to right, in to out) is useful when the text describes a two- or three-dimensional object. Comparison and contrast should develop consistently according to one of the two available patterns—point by point or item by item. A document organized to illustrate causes and effects should consistently move either from causes to effects or from effects to causes; a shift in pattern will disorient readers. All of these patterns help readers perceive meaning because they match the document structure with content structure. Shifts and variations in the document structure interfere with accurate storage of information in memory.

In a report to aid decision making, such as a feasibility study, the middle section addresses each of the topics that bear on the decision, such as cost, legal restrictions, available workforce, and competition. As you consider the organization of these topics, you can also assess whether they are complete. That is, are there other topics that will bear on the decision that are not discussed? The topics in such a report are arranged by importance and by relationship to one another. All financial topics, for example, would be grouped together.

Sometimes the pattern of organization is abstract, as when topics are presented according to their order of importance. Who is to decide what is more important than something else? The decision can be quite personal, based on one's own experiences and interests. It should, however, also take into consideration both the readers' needs and some objective measure of the relative importance of components to the overall subject. As an editor, you need to be particularly cautious about rearranging material to emphasize one point at the expense of another. Your perception about what is important may not be the same as the writer's. The writer, usually the subject matter expert, should have final say about rearrangement to suggest degree of importance.

All of these patterns—chronological, spatial, comparison-contrast, cause-effect, order of importance—are subordinate to the overall pattern of general to specific, as discussed in the previous section. As editor, you first ensure that the general information precedes the specific; then you check that patterns are used effectively in developing the parts. Many documents use more than one pattern. For example, a chronological narrative may also use comparison-contrast within the sections on various time periods. One pattern should predominate, however.

Grouping Related Material

This is a familiar concept for writers and editors. An editor tries to ensure that paragraphs stay on a topic rather than wandering, that chapters don't mix unrelated information, and that lists develop meaningfully rather than randomly. Even though the concept may be familiar, it is an important one in the editing process and a reminder to the editor to look for obvious, meaningful groups of information. Editors have to be concerned with grouping because writers often submit unrevised documents, and the order in their drafts may reflect their mental associations rather than any coherent structure. For many writers, the structure appears in revision, if at all.

The list in figure 12.1 illustrates the problem resulting from failure to group. The list appeared in the first draft of an employee handbook for a video rental store; its purpose was to delineate duties of the manager. The writer's free association is evident from the listing, and it causes problems for the reader. For example, does item 15, "filing on people," refer to filing in a file cabinet (as in item 16, presumably) or to filing in courts to pursue

Figure 12.1   Unedited List of Duties of Video Store Manager

Duties: Manager

1. waiting on customers
2. selling memberships
3. inventory of tapes, control cards, etc.
4. inventory of store
5. employee meetings
6. keeping employee morale up
7. accounts payable and receivable
8. computer input
9. computer reports--late, end of week, end of month, etc.
10. daily deposits
11. totaling time cards
12. payroll--total system done in store
13. checkbook balanced
14. hot check system
15. filing on people
16. filing system
17. ordering/merchandising
18. budget for store
19. prebooking
20. customer orders and order system
21. P.O.P. ordered and regulated
22. receiving
23. mail outs (free movie postcards)
24. static customer mail-outs
25. tape repair
26. cleaning VCRs
27. having anything that is broken fixed right away--the longer it sits the more money tied up
28. brown book--bookkeeping record

29. monthly report book
30. payroll book
31. schedule for employees
32. keep store appearance bright, eyecatching, clean, fun; movies playing by customer counter and children's movies in children's section at all times
33. keep coop checked on and updated
34. taking care of customer complaints or problems
35. taking care of employee problems
36. ordering computer supplies
37. ordering office supplies
38. keep plenty of paper supplies on hand
39. reshrinkwrap tape boxes that are getting worn out
40. Commtron bill
41. video log (introducing and explaining it to customers)
42. machine inventory every Wednesday--better control over what you have in the store; just in case one is stolen the time span isn't very long
43. promotions and marketing
44. know what's hot and new and learn the titles and actors
45. know your stock and what you have on hand--better control of movies and VCRs

writers of hot checks (as in item 14)? The lack of organization in the list would certainly cause problems for managers trying to develop a concept of their job and to identify and recall specific duties.

One task in editing this list, then, is to group various tasks under "umbrellas," such as finances (budget, accounting, and bookkeeping), personnel, marketing, customer relations, maintenance, and inventory/supplies. Under the topic of finances, one might include numbers 7, 9, 10, 12–15, 18, and 28–30. Marketing would include items 2, 17, 19, 21, 23, 24, 32, 33, and 43–45. Figure 12.2 shows an initial grouping based on these categories.

For your information, "Filing on people" (item 15) does in fact refer to filing charges against customers who fail to return the movies they have rented. "P.O.P." (item 21) is an abbreviation for "Point of Purchase" and refers to displays supplied by the wholesaler. "Coop" (item 33) refers to a cooperative advertising arrangement between the movie distributor and the retail store. "Commtron" (item 40) is the major supplier of movies to this store. This information was not obvious from the document; inquiries to the writer were necessary.

If the list appears on a computerized database, you can use your computer as an editorial assistant in sorting. You can identify each of the umbrella categories by a number and assign a group number to each item. Then you ask the computer to sort the items by number. You can try different arrangements with minimal effort.

Figure 12.2 shows how the list might look after one editorial pass. The editing is not yet complete, but the grouping will help the editor when reviewing the list with the writer. The grouping will probably reveal some holes, that is, missing duties. For example, will the manager train new employees? It may raise questions about whether the duties are really managerial duties. Might a subordinate handle orders, for example? Grouping may also encourage clarification of items. For example, is "promotions and marketing" (item 43) an umbrella term, or does it refer to a specific duty? Thus, editing for organization, using the guideline about grouping, should help the editor and writer make the content more complete and accurate as well as easier to comprehend. After the content is complete and meaningfully organized, the editor can work on consistency (e.g., "mail-outs," "mail outs," or "mailouts"?) and parallelism of phrases. (The example in figure 12.4 will illustrate the importance of grouping related ideas in paragraphs.)

Research has shown that memory decay begins after readers are asked to remember more than seven items, plus or minus two. That limit on memory is one reason why phone numbers have seven digits. If your groups contain more than seven items, as in the list of managerial duties

_____ Figure 12.2   Manager's Duties Grouped After One Editorial Pass

Duties: Manager

1. Finances
   accounts payable and
      receivable
   daily deposits
   checkbook balanced
   hot check system
   budget for store
   brown book--bookkeeping
      record
   Commtron bill
   filing system
   computer reports: late, end
      of week, end of month etc.
   monthly report book
   filing on people

2. Personnel
   employee meetings
   keeping employee morale up
   payroll--total system done in
      store
   schedule for employees
   taking care of employee
      problems

3. Inventory/Supplies
   inventory of tapes, control
      cards etc.
   inventory of store
   ordering computer supplies
   ordering office supplies
   keep plenty of paper supplies
      on hand
   machine inventory every
      Wednesday
   computer input

4. Marketing
   selling memberships
   P.O.P. ordered and regulated
   ordering/merchandizing
   mailouts (free movie
      postcards)
   static customer mailouts
   keep store appearance
      bright...
   keep coop checked on and
      updated
   know what's hot and new and
      learn the titles and actors
   know your stock and what you
      have on hand--better control
      of movies and VCRs
   prebooking
   promotions/marketing

5. Customer Relations
   waiting on customers
   customer orders and order
      system
   taking care of customer
      complaints and problems
   video log--introducing and
      explaining it to customers

6. Maintenance
   tape repair
   cleaning VCRs
   having anything that is
      broken fixed...
   reshrinkwrap tape boxes that
      are getting worn out

in figure 12.2, consider regrouping to shorten the list. The video store manager will have a better chance of learning and remembering the 45 duties grouped into six major categories with subduties than if the list remains 45 items long. Likewise, users performing a task can comprehend and remember six major steps more readily than 45 separate tasks.

The principle of restricting the number of chunks of information relates to prose as well as to instructions and lists such as the one in figure 12.2. Chunks may be the major sections in a report, proposal, or chapter as revealed by level-one headings. If such a document has many more than seven sections, however, readers may lose a sense of how the individual sections relate to one another and to the whole. Excessive efforts to reveal the structure of the information with divisions of text may actually diminish the coherence.

Parallel Structure for Parallel Sections

You are familiar with the principle of parallelism at the sentence level. The same principle is important for larger structures, too, such as paragraphs, sections of chapters, and chapters. The structure can clarify the content relationships of sections. For example, if you are editing a progress report that is ordered by tasks, each section probably will proceed from work completed to work remaining. The editor of this textbook looked for a pattern in each chapter of introduction, principles and theory, application or guidelines, and summary.

APPLICATION: THE PROBLEM STATEMENT FOR A RESEARCH PROPOSAL

This section illustrates the application of the principles and guidelines for editing for organization as well as the process of analyzing editing goals described in Chapter 10. Figure 12.3 shows the problem statement from a proposal for research on the bulb onion. The proposal was written by a graduate student competing for research funds distributed by the graduate school of a university. The graduate school distributed an RFP and promised to fund some—but not all—of the proposed projects.

The writer's goal, then, is to persuade the proposal evaluators that his project is feasible and worthy of being funded. To demonstrate worth, he has to show that the research will yield significant information. To demonstrate feasibility, he has to show that the work can be completed within the given time and that he has the facilities and skills to complete the research. (As a technical editor, you know these things because you are familiar with typical technical documents, such as proposals. If you do not know, you consult a technical writing handbook or textbook to orient yourself to the purposes and methods of proposals. You also consult the RFP to determine specific criteria for the grants.) The problem statement reproduced here is mostly concerned with demonstrating worth.

One problem the writer faces is writing for readers who are not expert in the subject matter. The evaluators are professors from various departments in the university; they are not necessarily experts in plant genetics. They are intelligent and well educated but possibly uninformed about the specific subject. Furthermore, they will be reading quickly through a

Figure 12.3
The Unedited
Problem Statement for a
Research Proposal

Isozyme Variability of <u>Allium cepa</u> Accessions

<u>Statement of the Research Problem</u>

Genetic variability is essential in the improvement of crop plants. Until recent years most of the single gene markers used in higher plant genetics were those affecting morphological characters, i.e., dwarfism, chlorophyll deficiency, or leaf characteristics. Molecular markers offer new possibilities of identifying variations useful in basic and applied research.

Proteins are an easily utilized type of molecular marker. Protein markers code for proteins that can be separated by electrophoresis to determine the presence or absence of specific alleles. The most widely used protein markers in plant breeding and genetics are isozymes.

Electrophoretic studies of isozyme variation within a plant population provide information on the genetic structure (Sibinsky et al. 1984) without depending upon morphological characters, which are easily influenced by the environment. Genetic studies of isozymes have been conducted on more than 30 crop species (Tanksley and Orton 1983). Considerable variation can exist among plant populations as well as among individuals within a given population. Domestic and wild barley accessions were assayed and substantial differences within and between accessions were found (Kahler and Allard 1981). Significant variation in allelic frequency and polymorphism has been detected in lentil collections (Sibinsky et al. 1984) as well as in <u>Zea mays</u> (Stuber and Goodman 1983).

Figure 12.3
(continued)

Researchers in the proposed project are
particularly interested in analyzing isozyme
variability within the bulb onion (Allium
cepa L.). The bulb onion is a major
horticultural crop in Texas with a cash value of
$75 million in 1982 (Tx. Veg. Stats. 1983). As
onions are a major crop, techniques are
continually being explored to facilitate the
breeding of superior varieties. However, a major
factor limiting advances in breeding is the
identification of selection criteria, i.e.,
genetic variation.

Electrophoresis as discussed above provides a
tool for selection. Electrophoretic techniques
for analyzing isozyme variability in onions have
been established (Hadacova et al. 1983; Peffley
et al. 1985). Isozyme markers have many
applications including introgression of genes
from wild species, identification of breeding
stocks, measurement of genetic variability,
determination of genetic purity of hybrid seed
lots, and varietal planting and protection
(Tanksley 1983).

This research intends to explore isozyme
variability of Allium cepa accessions with the
intent of identifying molecular markers useful
in onion breeding and genetics.

stack of proposals and will not have the luxury of rereading and mulling
over meanings. (As a technical editor, you discover this information
through queries to the writer or possibly to the contact person specified on
the RFP.)

Your analysis of the general communication situation is complete
enough at this point for you to assess the document itself. As editor, you
can probably act as a good stand-in for the intended readers. That is,

unless you have a good background in the study of plant genetics, the material will be new to you, as it will be for some evaluators. Your responses, therefore, will be useful in assessing likely responses from the evaluators.

Guideline 1 for the editing for organization will not apply here because you are looking at just part of the proposal. But guideline 2 — arranging information from general (concept) to specific (details) — will be very important.

Read the problem statement through. Note where you have difficulty understanding (i.e., where you find yourself rereading sentences or looking back in the text to verify assumptions). Also note where the meaning seems especially clear. These notes will be useful guides to you when you try to determine editing goals and to suggest useful emendations. After you have read and noted both the confusing and the clear places, you can set some editing goals. You can determine what you would need to do as editor to clarify the problem and its significance for intelligent but uninformed readers.

Chances are, unless you are a plant genetics expert, you found yourself lost before you got very far into the text. You probably understood the first sentence easily enough because of your general knowledge that crop scientists improve crops through genetic manipulation. You may have been relieved when you got to paragraph 4, where you can relate to the idea that onions are a major cash crop (even if you are surprised by this information).

If you stumbled over other parts, you may be thinking, as many editors do, that defining terms, either parenthetically or in a glossary, will solve the problem. In fact, the numerous technical terms can slow down nonexpert readers significantly. If you follow the principles and processes of editing described in Chapter 10, though, as an editor you may rightly choose to think first about organization and completeness of information. Just as readers process a text top down, you will edit top down. Your first task should be to define the concept of the research problem. Definitions may be an option later. If you are not convinced, look up a few of the terms that are repeated frequently—"electrophoresis," "isozyme variation," and "accessions." Once you know the definitions, does the significance of the problem statement become clear?

Your analysis of the document should identify the editing goal of reorganizing to make the concept and terms clearer. In particular, guideline 2 suggests that you place general or conceptual information before specific. Thus, the concept of the research (the need and purpose) should appear in the first or second paragraph. While considering organization, you may also have noted that the discussion of electrophoresis in paragraphs 3 and

5 is interrupted by paragraph 4 ("as discussed above" is a clue). Thus, an editing goal may be to group the sentences about electrophoresis together (guideline 4). Additional goals may include the definition of terms, correction of grammar and punctuation (especially the dangling modifier in paragraph 4), and other sentence- and word-level emendations.

To prepare for a thoughtful and systematic reorganization, begin with guideline 2: place general information before specific. To identify the general information (concept), look back through the problem statement to see if you can answer the basic question: What will the proposed research do that previous genetic research has failed to do? Repetition of key terms throughout, including "electrophoresis" and "isozyme variation," indicates that they are central to the meaning. The answer will provide the concept of the research and thus should appear early in the document.

The first paragraph contrasts two kinds of gene markers, those affecting morphological characters (the kind formerly used in research) and those affecting molecular markers (the kind to be used in the proposed research project). Why are molecular markers better? To answer that question, you may need to ask why morphological markers are limited. The answer to that second question is buried in a dependent clause in paragraph 3: ". . . which are easily influenced by the environment." If the morphological characters are easily influenced by the environment, the data generated by using them may be unreliable. These markers may measure environmental effects rather than genetic variation. This statement is implicit in the first paragraph, but it is not stated. Thus, this key information becomes available to uninformed readers only upon rereading (and mental reordering of the information).

This kind of questioning and probing for the central ideas that you do as an editor parallels a reader's questioning. Your editing task is to make the concepts so clear that a reader won't have to probe. Once you can answer the basic questions, you should have the conceptual information that should appear early in the document. This process of asking questions about concept, rather than questions about specifics, such as the meanings of specific terms, is central to top-down editing. Sometimes the questions cannot be answered from the existing text so you will pose them directly to a writer.

A simple paraphrase of this problem statement might be:

```
Researchers have been limited in their attempts
to breed superior bulb onions by an inferior
method of marking the genes. In this old method,
```

the markers were for morphological characters.
Because these characters could be influenced by
the environment, the data they yielded were
unreliable. A new method, electrophoresis,
allows the identification of protein markers,
specifically isozymes. In the proposed research,
electrophoresis will be used to analyze isozyme
variability in onions.

Figure 12.4 shows the problem statement reorganized to present conceptual information early and explicitly and to form paragraphs by topic. The sentences in boldface have been moved, and the two phrases in boldface italics (paragraphs 2 and 4) have been added to clarify information. No other editing has been done. The terms remain undefined, the dangling modifier remains in paragraph 4, and the writing style has not been improved. But the document is now more comprehensible to and persuasive for readers who are not genetics experts. The terms become more clear once the context is more clear. Given the hasty way in which the proposal will be read, it will be sufficient for readers to know that electrophoresis is a method and that an isozyme is a molecular marker, without knowing the specifics. Depending on how much time is available, the editor may work on sentences to achieve even greater clarity and persuasiveness. But even if he or she must stop now, the document will be more effective than it was in its original form.

As an editor, you may have other ideas for the organization of this problem statement—the version in figure 12.4 is not necessarily the "right" way. Because we are not applying rules, we cannot assert, without controversy, that one way is right and another is wrong. However, each emendation here can be explained in terms of how readers learn from a text. Nothing has been done arbitrarily. Furthermore, the editing is based on an analysis of the communication situation, including the purpose of the document, the intended readers, and the conditions of reading. Thus, decisions have been made to accommodate those readers and purpose. Had the problem statement appeared in the research report for publication, the organization would have been different. The review of literature in paragraph 5, for example, would have moved forward because of the established pattern in research reports of setting the research context with a literature review.

You may be interested to know that the edited proposal succeeded in winning funding!

Figure 12.4
The Problem Statement in
Figure 12.3 Reorganized

Code: Boldface indicates rearranged material. Boldface italic indicates inserted information. <> indicates material that should be deleted.

Isozyme Variability of <u>Allium cepa</u> Accessions

Statement of the Research Problem

The margin notes:

The original first sentence remains to establish the concept of the research. The familiar "genetic variability" also prepares for "isozyme variability." (See guideline 2.)

This easily understood information announces the significance in familiar and persuasive terms. This paragraph also establishes the context for the proposed research—the ongoing research at the university. (See guideline 2.)

The last sentence introduces the rest of the paper by stating the limitations of the old method of research.

The rearranged and new information states the specific limitation of the old method of research. By knowing the limits of the old, reviewers will see the importance of the proposed method.

Genetic variability is essential in the improvement of crop plants. **Researchers in this project are particularly interested in analyzing isozyme variability within the bulb onion (<u>Allium cepa</u> L.). The bulb onion is a major horticultural crop in Texas with a cash value of $75 million in 1982 (<u>Tx. Veg. Stats.</u> 1983). As onions are a major crop, techniques are continually being explored to facilitate the breeding of superior varieties. However, a major factor limiting advances in breeding is the identification of selection criteria, i.e., genetic variation.**

Until recent years most of the single gene markers used in higher plant genetics were those affecting morphological characters, i.e., dwarfism, chlorophyll deficiency, or leaf characteristics. **However, these characters are easily influenced by the environment, *so the data are unreliable.*** Molecular markers offer new possibilities of identifying variations useful in basic and applied research.

Proteins are an easily utilized type of molecular marker. Protein markers code for proteins that can be separated by electrophoresis to determine the presence or absence of specific alleles. The most widely

Figure 12.4

(continued)

used protein markers in plant breeding and
genetics are isozymes.

This paragraph and the next
one are rearranged to create
separate paragraphs on
electrophoresis and on
isozyme markers, rather than
mixing the subjects as the
original paragraphs 3 and 5
do. (See guideline 4.)

**Electrophoresis <as discussed above> provides
a tool for selection *of genetic characteristics.***
Electrophoretic studies of isozyme variation
within a plant population provide information on
the genetic structure (Sibinsky et al. 1984)
without depending on morphological characters.
**Electrophoretic techniques for analyzing isozyme
variability in onions have been established
(Hadacova et al. 1983; Peffley et al. 1985).**

This subject of isozymes could
precede the subject of
electrophoresis. However, the
material on isozymes is mostly
background material. The
material on electrophoresis
focuses attention on the
proposed project. (Remember
guideline 3: place important
information early in the
sequence.)

**Isozyme markers have many applications
including introgression of genes from wild
species, identification of breeding stocks,
measurement of genetic variability,
determination of genetic purity of hybrid seed
lots, and varietal planting and protection
(Tanksley 1983).** Genetic studies of isozymes
have been conducted on more than 30 crop species
(Tanksley and Orton 1983). Considerable
variation can exist among plant populations as
well as among individuals within a given
population. Domestic and wild barley accessions
were assayed and substantial differences within
and between accessions were found (Kahler and
Allard 1981). Significant variation in allelic
frequency and polymorphism has been detected in
lentil collections (Sibinsky et al. 1984) as
well as in Zea mays (Stuber and Goodman 1983).

This background information
can be skimmed; it basically
demonstrates the proposer's
knowledge rather than giving
information on the proposed
research.

The explicit purpose statement
leads nicely to the next
section of the proposal, a
statement of specific
objectives.

This research intends to explore isozyme
variability of Allium cepa accessions with the
intent of identifying molecular markers in onion
breeding and genetics.

SUMMARY | Organization affects comprehension by helping or hindering a reader in forming schemata, or structures for storing the information read. Thus, reorganizing can be a powerful editing tool—either for improving or for distorting the document.

Editing for organization is an example of top-down editing, in which the editor, before editing sentences, analyzes the communication situation and determines that the concepts and details are presented in an order that will facilitate learning by the intended readers. This editing will be successful if the editor systematically analyzes the document and applies the guidelines for editing for organization.

FURTHER READING | T. N. Huckin. 1983. "A Cognitive Approach to Readability." In P. V. Anderson, R. J. Brockmann, and C. R. Miller, eds., *New Essays in Technical and Scientific Communication: Research, Theory, Practice.* Farmingdale, NY: Baywood.

D. E. Rumelhart and A. Ortony. 1977. "The Representation of Knowledge in Memory." In R. C. Anderson, R. J. Spiro, and W. E. Montague, eds., *Schooling and the Acquisition of Knowledge.* Hillsdale, NJ: Lawrence Erlbaum.

DISCUSSION AND APPLICATION |
1. Perform a second editorial pass on the example in figure 12.2. Are the umbrella groupings satisfactory? Should any items be combined? Prepare a list of questions for the writer about items you don't understand to make sure the wording is clear and the grouping accurate. Discuss possibilities for making this list more effective other than by regrouping. For example, should each item have a rationale or explanation, as do items 27, 32, and 42 in figure 12.1? What would be the basis for making such a decision?

2. Determine conventional patterns of organization in your subject field by consulting three periodicals, including at least one research journal. In a class discussion, compare the patterns of organizing research articles in different subjects, such as psychology and chemistry.

3. Compare several user manuals for word processing programs or several manuals in a series for one computer system. Are there any consistent patterns in the manuals? What organizational strategies seem particularly effective? If there are inconsistent patterns, have the document designers had a good rationale for modifying the patterns?

4. The following paragraphs and tables are from the time and cost analysis section of a proposal for landscaping an office park in two phases. Analyze the order of ideas and grouping in the paragraphs and tables, and edit for organization according to the guidelines presented in this chapter.

[1]The estimated cost of this project is based on a cost of $6 per square foot for the patio and $4 per square foot for the sidewalks. [2]The first phase includes the upper patio, lower walks, planters, and stairway. [3]The cost for the patio is higher because it is made of bricks. [4]There are 80 linear feet of planters at $10 per square foot and 4,600 square feet of lower sidewalk at $4 per square foot. (See Table 1.)

[5]The estimated time of completion of phase one is four to six weeks depending on the weather.

Table 1. Phase One Cost Analysis

	Sq. Feet	Cost
Upper level	6,400	$38,000
Planters	80	$800
Lower walk	4,600	$18,400
Stairway	300	$3,000
Total	11,380	$60,200

[6]The second phase of construction will consist of the installation of six concrete sidewalks and the reconstruction of a blacktop sidewalk into concrete.

[7]The estimated time of completion of phase two is two to three weeks depending on the weather.

Table 2. Phase Two Cost Analysis

	Sq. Feet	Cost
Sidewalk 1	1,926	$7,680
Sidewalk 2	2,400	$9,600
Sidewalk 3	1,280	$5,120
Sidewalk 4	1,280	$5,120
Sidewalk 5	1,760	$7,040
Sidewalk 6	640	$2,560
Sidewalk 7	2,000	$20,000
Total	11,286	$57,120

[8]The total minimum cost for the proposed changes in $117,720.

5. A six-page guide for users of a major city library is organized alphabetically. Topics are listed below. Each topic is followed by one to four sentences explaining location or use. Discuss the merits and limitations of alphabetical organization for this document if the readers are first-time users of the library. How well will the alphabetical organization work if the readers are experienced users? What other patterns of organization might work for this document? Arrange the topics in another order based on the needs and interests of first-time users. Does the reorganization suggest any revisions in content? That is, should any topics be added or deleted? For your information, the comment for the "personal property" topic advises patrons not to leave their property unattended.

acquisitions
arrangement of the
    library
bindery
book returns
borrowing books
call numbers
card catalog
cataloging
change machine
circulation

computer assisted
    search services
copy center
current periodicals
director's office
elevators
fines
food and drink
gifts/exchange
government documents

hours of the main
   library
information
interlibrary loan
library cards
loan periods
lost and found
lounge areas
magazines (see
   periodicals)
materials processing
meeting rooms
microforms
newspapers
online computer search
   (see computer
   assisted search)
oversize books

periodicals
periodicals list
personal property
personnel office
rare books
reserve materials
restrooms
smoking
sorting areas
stacks
stairs
study areas
technical processing
telephone directories
telephones
typing rooms
water fountains

13 FORMAT

Format refers to the general appearance of the page and of the document as a whole. Its root word, *form*, reveals that format is a physical concept. Format options for any given document cover a range of possibilities: presentation through prose paragraphs, graphic devices, or lists; headings; the placement of document components on the page, such as the heading of a letter at the top of the letter; margins and number of columns; features of type, such as double or single spacing, paragraph indentation, and type style (e.g., bold, italic, roman); and document size, shape, and binding.

The definition of format is confusing because format relates so closely to other document features, including organization, document type, graphic design, and document design. It is important to use terms correctly so that you know what you are editing for and so that you can communicate your editorial decisions accurately.

Format is closely related to, but is not a synonym for, organization. *Organization* relates to the sequence of information in a document and the overall plan for arrangement of information, whether chronological, spatial, general to specific, or some other plan. Format is the primary *visual signal* about how a document is organized. Signals such as headings, paragraph indentation, and enumeration reveal the document's organization. The format signals must be consistent with the organization.

Format is also closely associated with types, or genres, of documents —

format can be a visual identifier of document genre. For example, a "letter format" will help a reader recognize that the document is a letter, and multiple narrow columns visually signal that the document is a newspaper, magazine, or other periodical. However, many genres do not have a single format that identifies them. The terms *report format, proposal format,* and *manual format,* for example, are misleading because reports, proposals, and manuals may use different formats, such as single spacing or double spacing and long or wide page orientation. Furthermore, a report or proposal may be presented in another format, the letter format. Thus, although format may identify document genre, it is not the same as document genre.

Format is also closely related to layout and to graphic design in that all three reflect decisions about the appearance of a document. Although decisions about format and about layout and graphic design overlap, *format* is more of a writing and editing term, while *layout* is a design term. **Layout** is the graphic designer's plan for the document and includes specifications for type and spacing. It determines some format decisions, such as one or two columns, and it also shows the exact placement on the page of headings and illustrations. In the process of layout, the designer will move text and illustrations around on the page to achieve the desired look of the page within the overall plan; formatting is more concerned with the look of the document overall. The layout may include a grid to show line length, placement of headings and visuals, and justification. The grid includes a sample for any format choices, such as an offset list (as opposed to a list run into prose paragraphs), that the writer or editor has made. Figure 13.1 shows a designer's grid for the layout of a page in a newsletter.

Both format and graphic design are concerned with function and aesthetics, but the emphasis in format is on function while decisions about **graphic design** may be more aesthetically oriented. In addition, the graphic designer will be more concerned with the details of the choices than the editor making format choices. The editor may specify paragraph indentation, for example, but the graphic designer will specify whether it is 1-em or 2-em indentation. The editor may specify boldface or italics for

Figure 13.1
Designer's Grid
for This Book

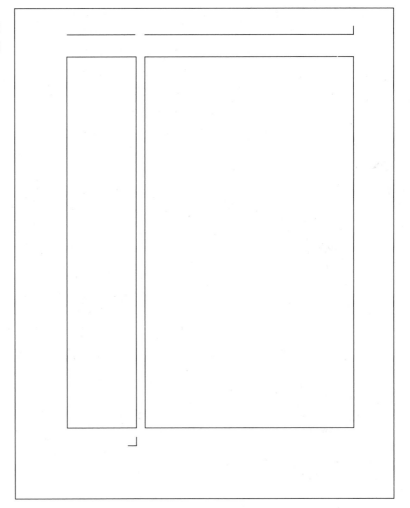

terms used as terms and may even request a serif style typeface, but the graphic designer will select the typeface from the serif category. (Serifs are short lines perpendicular to the ends of individual letters.) The specific responsibilities of the editor and the graphic designer will be established in each publishing organization.

Document design is a more comprehensive term than *format.* Format decisions will be part of the document design, but **document design** refers to all the choices about a document that enable the document to work in the intended way. Design decisions include content, organization, and style as well as format and graphic design.

This chapter first identifies format options in order to define the concept in more detail. It then discusses bases for making the choices and outlines the functions of format. It includes a section on headings that pertains to several functions of format. The chapter concludes by identifying guidelines for making editorial choices about format. This chapter presumes that format is more functional than aesthetic. It also presumes that the editor has broad responsibilities for format and that the distinctions between format and graphic design are blurred.

FORMAT OPTIONS

Writers and editors have some choices about format, just as they have choices about writing style. Depending on the complexity of the reading material, the characteristics of readers, and the methods of production, an editor may choose a minimally formatted text (prose paragraphs) or various other options. The following list also introduces some of the bases for choosing among the various options, all of which are discussed in more detail later in the chapter, and indicates some of the ways in which the intended use of a document affects format choices.

- **Prose or visual representations.** Prose paragraphs are best for explanation and narrative. When the information is highly complex, or when the reading is selective, a more graphic format may aid in comprehension and selection. For example, flowcharts visually show the sequence of steps, and outlines show the hierarchy of ideas. Tables are appropriate when the readers must locate specific items of information.

- **Number and length of paragraphs.** Short paragraphs are quicker to read, but longer paragraphs permit the development of complex thoughts and reveal the relationships between ideas.

- **Indentation.** Indentation is the conventional signal for a new paragraph in a double-spaced typescript as well as for a block quotation set off from the rest of the text. Because of most readers' familiarity with outline form, indentation also signals subordination. Thus, an item indented under another should be subordinate to the first. Offset lists often use a **hanging indent,** where a major heading protrudes farther into the left margin than does a minor heading. (Alternatively, list headings may be set in different type sizes or styles to indicate level of importance.)

- **Listing.** Especially when there are parallel ideas or a clear sequence of items, a list will reveal the structure more quickly than will embedding the items within prose paragraphs.

- **Headings.** Headings identify key points, serve as transitions, show the overall structure of the document, and permit access to specific sections for selective reading.

- **Line length and number of columns.** Lines that are too long or too short slow down reading. Generally, a maximum of 2½ alphabets is the maximum line length for easy reading. This means that 65 characters per line across the page is the limit, whatever your type size. If you are working with small type on a large page, you may choose to use large margins or multiple columns.

- **Page orientation.** Most books for "armchair" reading use **portrait orientation;** that is, they are taller than they are wide. Because these books fit on most bookshelves, they are easy to store. Sometimes, however, the wide or **landscape orientation** better suits the text or its storage requirements; for example, many user manuals use landscape orientation. Pages with the landscape orientation have multiple columns or margins as wide as columns so that the lines will not be too long for easy reading. Shifts in orientation (e.g., text printed portrait, tables printed landscape) distract from the primary reading or performance task because they require readers to flip the document around.

- **Numbers, letters, bullets.** Numbers, letters, and bullets distinguish items in a list and may provide other information as well. Numbers and letters may be used in lists embedded in paragraphs or in offset lists. **Bullets** (dark or open circles or squares preceding an item) are used with lists that are offset. Numbers can show different levels in the structure, as in the decimal system of numbering where "2.3.3" would mean that the part is the third item within main part 2, subpart 3. They also indicate sequence and quantity. Numbers and letters are both useful for cross-reference, as when a step in instructions refers the reader back to "step 2." If itemization alone is the goal, bullets are sufficient and probably less likely to suggest meaning they don't have.

- **Variation in type style.** Any change in type invites attention. These changes can be a shift to italic when the body is set in roman, a shift from lowercase to capital letters, a shift from the primary typeface to boldface, and so on.

- **Underlining.** Like changes in type, underlining emphasizes the material. This device is primarily useful for typewritten documents for which other type style options are not available. The computer's options of boldface, italics, and variations in type size are preferable to underlining because underlining makes words harder to read, as well as being visually distracting. The line itself interferes with perception of the **descenders** on letters (the tails below the line), information a reader uses in identifying the word. Computers permit desktop publishers to follow the same conventions as typesetters, who set underlined words in typescripts in italics unless instructed otherwise.

- **Boxes, white space, shading, pointers, symbols.** These visual devices also call attention to a part of the text. A box around a warning, white space surrounding type, and shading all draw the reader's eye to the text thus emphasized. Pointers are arrows or hands with pointed fingers that direct a reader's attention to a certain place. Certain symbols, such as a skull and crossbones, have developed universal meanings as signals of danger and can be useful in calling attention to warnings or substituting for verbal warnings.

- **Binding, folding, size.** Documents may be bound or not and folded or not—the decision depends on use, storage, and economics. For example, a spiral binding lets a manual rest open on a desk while it is used, but it is less durable than a hard cover with a library binding, and it does not permit a printed title on the spine. **Perfect binding,** the attachment of paper covers with adhesive, allows easy armchair reading, but such bindings do not hold up for repeated use and photocopying. A brochure that will be mailed may need to fit into an envelope.

BASES FOR FORMAT CHOICES

Format choices should respect conventions, but conventions only guide them up to a point. The choices should relate to the complexity of the content and its demands on the reader. The choices also relate to the means of production and its cost. Sometimes the bases for decision making conflict with one another. For example, the need to make a document inviting to read will suggest a liberal use of white space, but cost considerations may require the editor to conserve space.

Reading Complexity   Complexity of format is proportionate to content complexity or to the reading demands. Texts whose method of development is narrative or expository, such as journals and essays, require minimal formatting. The use of prose paragraphs, which are identified by indentation or space between the paragraphs, presumes that readers will be reading to acquire information or even to be entertained rather than to concentrate on complex information, perform a task, or locate specific facts. The use of prose paragraphs without additional format, such as headings, further presumes that reading will proceed in a linear way, from beginning to end. Most novels are printed in paragraph format with a minimum of other format signals except for chapter titles. The readers of the novel are probably motivated to read and will read from beginning to end. The minimal formatting is also an economic decision. In paperback novels especially, pages are crammed with text set in small print and characterized by narrow margins. These decisions do not benefit the reader, but they do lower the cost of printing for the publisher.

When a text demands that readers understand complex or unfamiliar information or when readers will read selectively, the writer and editor will use other format devices to assist the reader. A text might be described as demanding if the readers are expected to comprehend complex technical information, to perform a task while reading simultaneously, or to read material that they are not motivated to read. A helpful formatting device in such documents may be headings for major parts and subparts. The headings aid in comprehension by identifying main topics and the overall structure of the document. They also aid in selective reading. Short paragraphs help readers absorb difficult ideas in manageable "chunks." Graphic displays of text, such as flowcharts or outlines, show the structure of the information and also help with selective reading. Numbers are another format device to indicate the sequence of steps in a task and to help readers relocate themselves on the page after they have looked up to perform a task. Increasing the white space on the page will also make the text more inviting. Finally, when readers must locate specific facts, especially quantitative facts or names of products or places, a tabular format rather than prose paragraphs will facilitate reader reference.

Production Methods   The methods of production determine which formatting options are available. Full-service typesetting allows a wide range of typefaces, styles, and sizes as well as page sizes and column options. Desktop publishing allows many of the same options. A typewriter allows fewer.

Formatting needs and economics partly determine which production method is chosen. For example, an in-house report informing managers about the status of a project will be produced with in-house equipment—a typewriter or word processor—and its format is likely to be double-spaced prose paragraphs. However, an instruction manual that is written for a complex machine or procedure, that is aimed at a large number of readers, and that has a substantial budget, may justify typesetting and its far greater options.

Computers and desktop publishing increase formatting options available to editors—and also the editors' responsibilities for effective format decisions. People playing at their machines with typefaces, sizes, and styles and page makeup programs can produce visual monstrosities whose format interferes with other document functions. Editors must resist the chance to use formatting a document as an excuse for learning the capacities of a machine. More is not necessarily better, and simpler is usually safer. Overformatting calls attention to the format itself and distracts attention from the content. Good formatting is subtle; it enters the reader's subconscious but not his or her conscious mind. Conversely, an editor may suspend judgment when reviewing a document tastefully formatted with desktop publishing. It is easy to say "*Looks* good!" and to neglect evaluation of whether it *is* good.

FUNCTIONS OF FORMAT

An editor cares about format because format is functional. Format influences how well a reader uses and understands a document. The five main functions of format establish some principles for editing for format. These functions are to meet reader expectations, to motivate readers, to provide access to selected parts of the document, to aid the readers in comprehension, and to facilitate its continued use.

Meeting Reader Expectations

Convention controls some format decisions. Any deviance from the convention will call attention to itself and thus distract readers from the meaning. Unconventional format in a serious document is also likely to invite contempt for the writer and distrust of the contents. For example, a letter of application that lacks a return address and that scrunches the text to the top of the page signals that the writer does not know the conventions of business letters. By extension, the writer's competence and judgment may be questioned. Format deviation, being visual, is easy to recognize and makes a powerful first statement to the reader.

Conventions may be established by wide practice. For example, a business letter always includes the return address and date in the heading at the top of the letter. Writers do have the option of aligning all the parts of the letter on the left margin (full-block format) or aligning the heading, closing, and signature on a second margin just right of center (semi-block format). But both options are consistent in the placement of the major parts. That is, the heading will always be at the top, and the signature will always be at the bottom. When this convention is violated, readers are forced to hunt for the information. Although this search may take only a few seconds, it risks irritating the reader. Business letters are single spaced by convention.

Newspapers and magazines conventionally use multiple narrow columns to facilitate quick reading: readers can read chunks of text down the page rather than line by line across the page. In a book, convention requires that a long quotation be blocked and indented rather than run into a paragraph. The blocking and indentation visually signal that the text is a quotation, just as quotation marks signal a shorter quotation run into a prose paragraph rather than set off from the body of the text.

Conventions may also be established within an organization and be pertinent only there. For example, all in-house reports may be typed in the Courier typeface and single spaced. Title pages may include identifying information right justified at the bottom of the page. In another organization, reports will be double spaced, and identifying information will be centered on the title page. Readers will have developed expectations for format from reading previous reports and will be disoriented and perhaps irritated by substantial shifts, particularly if the shifts make it difficult to find information they need. Likewise, different disciplines have their own conventions about formatting details, such as the placement of titles on visuals (e.g., top or bottom). At the very least, adherence to the format conventions helps to establish that the writer belongs to the discourse community.

Conventions may also be established by a document set. For example, all the manuals for one piece of equipment, including the installation manual, the tutorial, and the reference manual, may be wire bound and of the same size and shape. Warnings may always be boxed with red. From using one manual, readers come to expect format consistency in the other manuals as well. They will be surprised and disoriented by changes. Likewise, a periodical publication will establish a format and follow it consistently throughout each issue. The consistency saves time for the editors and publishers because it relieves them of the responsibility of making new format decisions for each issue. It is also reassuring for readers because it is predictable.

The format of such a document set is not bound by law, of course, and should be changed if it is inadequate for any reason. Sometimes format changes are legitimate just to freshen the look of the document. However, to change the format randomly and constantly is expensive in terms of decision time and possible retyping of format templates. Frequent changes also place the visual identity of the document at risk, as well as disorienting readers. In a technical document whose purpose is serious, it is rarely appropriate to change a format simply for variety.

Conventions may also be established by logic. Figure 13.2 depicts a 4¾ × 11-inch flier intended for people to tape to their medicine chests or enclose in a car first-aid box. A larger version (13 × 24) appears as a poster in restaurants. The purpose of these documents is to provide ready first-aid information to be used in case of emergency. The format is inconsistent, however: the verbal instructions sometimes appear to the left of the illustrations and sometimes to the right. On the poster version, instructions in Spanish alternate right and left with the English instructions. Thus, readers who have completed one step will have to hunt for the instructions for the second step; the format forces their eyes to scan the page rather than guiding them back to a fixed point. Perhaps that arrangement lent the flier and poster a kind of aesthetic balance, but the inconsistency will slow the reader in an emergency, and critical time may be lost.

A more functional format for the two-language version would establish all the instructions in one language to the left of the illustrations and all the instructions in the second language to the right. In the single-language version, the most efficient format would place the pictures consistently to the left. Placed there, they would give the reader an almost instantaneous concept of the step to be performed before he or she read the text. The text would verify the concept and provide details. After reading the first example, the reader would expect the illustrations to fall on the left and to identify the beginning of a new step. Because of the format consistency, a reader looking up from the task to review the next step in the process would return to the right place on the poster without searching. Even when function overrides aesthetics, the document may still be attractive.

One successful format device on the flier is the use of space between steps and numbers to identify where one step ends and another begins. The reader may look away from the flier when he or she encounters a space and will look for that space again when he or she is ready for new information. The white space and short lines also facilitate reading.

Matching a document's format to reader expectations is, in part, a copyediting task. The editor checks for conventions that are established by wide practice, by the organization, or by the document set. Beyond these matching tasks, editing for format becomes substantive editing based on awareness of the way the reader will use the document.

Figure 13.2
Inconsistent Relationship
of Visuals and Text

First Aid For Choking

1

- **ASK: Are you choking?**

- If victim cannot breathe,
  cough, or speak . . .

2

- **Give the Heimlich Maneuver.**

- Stand behind the victim.

- Wrap your arms around the victims waist.

- Make a fist with one hand. PLACE your FIST (thumbside) against the victim's stomach in the midline just ABOVE THE NAVEL AND WELL BELOW THE RIB MARGIN

- Grasp your fist with your other hand

- PRESS INTO STOMACH WITH A QUICK UPWARD THRUST.

3

- Repeat thrust if necessary.

- **If a victim has become unconscious:**

- Sweep the mouth

4

5

- Attempt rescue breathing.

6

- Give 6-10 abdominal thrusts.

- Repeat Steps 4, 5, 6 as necessary.

American Red Cross

**LOCAL EMERGENCY
TELEPHONE NUMBER: EMS 743-9911**

Everyone should learn how to perform the steps
above for choking and how to give rescue
breathing and CPR. Call your local American Red
Cross chapter for information on these and other
first aid techniques.
Caution. The Heimlich Maneuver (abdominal
thrust) may cause injury.
Do not *practice* on people.

Courtesy of the American Red Cross.

Motivating Readers   Because format is visual, it creates the first impression a reader has of the document. Thus, it helps to determine, along with the reputation of the document or publisher and the reader's inherent motivation, whether a reader will read. An attractive document with some white space on the page is more inviting than a crowded page with solid lines of text running from margin to margin. But what is motivating in format depends on readers. Formatting decisions to meet the criterion of motivation are based on an assessment of the motivation that the readers will bring to the text.

Some readers are highly motivated and will read no matter what the format (assuming that the content meets their expectations). Thus, professional journals use limited formatting because the readers have an inherent motivation to read in order to keep up with developments in their profession. (These journals also have small budgets because advertising revenues and circulation are limited.) The pages in a professional journal are likely to be filled with small print. Popular magazines, by contrast, compete with other magazines for a reader's discretionary time. Their elaborate and colorful formats attract attention and interest. Popular magazines also have a larger readership, greater advertising income, and bigger budgets than do professional journals. But even if the journals had larger budgets, they would not be likely to adopt the format of popular magazines. The professional nature of the journal is identified by its austere format, and a flashier format would tend to repel rather than attract readers who are professionals in the field.

If readers are discouraged by a document's format, they may not read at all. Users of equipment who can't find the information they need may abandon the manual and simply experiment with their machines or procedures. Managers may skim introductions and conclusions without reading the whole report. In many circumstances, such experimentation is satisfactory and even desirable; an editor should not feel a moral obligation to make readers absorb every word. However, one risk of ignoring the issue of motivation is that unmotivated readers may overlook necessary information. For example, users may discover just a small part of a machine's capacity or may fail at some procedure. And if they fail or get stuck, they may not be future customers. Managers may not read the warning in the report and may ignore a recommendation for a modification in equipment. Format can direct a reader's attention to vital information about health and safety. Highlighting with boldface type or boxes or space should encourage readers to read at least those sections.

Readers without motivation need the encouragement of an attractive document. Budgets permitting, two colors of ink, graphics, large margins, illustrations, and the liberal use of formats other than merely prose paragraphs will encourage reluctant readers.

Facilitating Ongoing Use

This function of format relates mostly to size, shape, material, and binding of the document. Especially if the document will be used more than once, the size, shape, material, and binding must permit easy storage and continued use. The document may need to fit into an envelope, a file drawer, or even a pocket. Or it may need to be attached to a piece of equipment, as with a safety warning on a portable electric tool.

Other possible document uses that will dictate format include its hanging on a wall, staying open on a desk, or standing on a bookshelf. If the document will be used outside or carried around, lamination may be necessary to protect it from weather and from torn edges. If it will be used in low light, the type size may have to be large and white space abundant to compensate for the low visibility. If it will stay open on a desk, spiral binding will be a good choice, but if it will need to be identified on a bookshelf by a title on its spine, spiral binding will be unsatisfactory. Good editorial decisions for format, as for all document features, require the editor to imagine the document in use once it leaves production.

Providing Access to Information

A fourth function of format is to provide readers with easy access to specific information within the document. As noted in Chapter 2, readers are likely to read technical documents selectively rather than from the first word straight through to the last. Readers therefore need a way of quickly finding the information they need. The primary format devices serving the function of access to a document as a whole are the table of contents and headings within the text. In addition, a document may contain **running heads** (section or chapter titles—sometimes abbreviated—at the top or bottom of each page), page numbers, and chapter numbers as well as titles; also, important terms or sections may be highlighted by boldface or italic type or by shading. Access devices other than format devices include indexes and outlines at the beginning of sections or prose introductions describing the document's structure.

Editors should be aware of several ways to make headings functional as access devices. These concern the wording of the headings, the type style and placement to indicate levels of headings, and the frequency of headings. Because headings relate to comprehension as well as to access, they are discussed in the next section.

To ensure reader access to selected parts of the document, you should check the accuracy and frequency of the headings, the wording in the table of contents against the headings in the text, and the adequacy of various access devices according to the probable methods a reader will use to search a text.

Aiding Comprehension

As you learned in Chapter 12, comprehension depends in part on awareness of the structure of the information. An organized document is easier to understand than a disorganized one, and the structure of the document must match the structure of the information. Format aids in comprehension because it reveals visually the structure of the document and, in turn, of the information.

To illustrate, consider the document reproduced in various formats in figures 13.3–13.7. The document was part of a program plan for research on the use of radar systems on aircraft or missiles to identify stationary military targets. Such a radar system has to distinguish targets from "background clutter," that is, everything else in the scene (e.g., trees, grass, buildings).

Target identification might begin with a "detection algorithm," a mathematical procedure (in the form of a computer program) that searches the radar image for bright objects. Then a "classification algorithm" (the subject of this example) might examine each detected bright object and classify it as a tank, a truck, or neither. The classification algorithm would work by looking at such things as an object's size and characteristic features (e.g., trucks have wheels whereas tanks have treads and gun barrels).

An algorithm is "robust" if it works well under a variety of conditions (e.g., wet, dry, snowy). Development of classification algorithms involves devising different approaches, testing how well they work, and then using the test results to plan improvements. A "seeker" is a missile programmed to search for a particular type of target. "MMW" means millimeter-wave, a particular band of radar wavelengths. "SAR" stands for synthetic aperture radar, a type of radar that produces detailed imagery. A "standoff sensor" is a radar or other system on an aircraft designed to view a battlefield from a long, relatively safe distance.

The purpose of the program plan resembled that of a proposal: to persuade a manager that the research was well conceived and would lead to the development of effective algorithms. The manager was expected to have a good technical background but to want to read quickly.

The five versions of the document in figures 13.3–13.7 illustrate how different format choices may influence both the speed of reading and the accuracy of comprehension. Figure 13.3, the original version, uses minimal formatting. It is one long prose paragraph, with indentation to identify it as a paragraph, plus a heading and numeric label. The sentences in the original were not numbered, but numbers are included here for reference. Figures 13.3–13.5 show the information with increasing levels of formatting. Figures 13.5–13.7 use the same list format, but because the format changes the emphasis, readers are likely to interpret the different versions in different ways.

The writer used several verbal indicators of the document structure. In

Figure 13.3   Original Version of a Section from a Program Plan

4.3 CLASSIFICATION ALGORITHM PERFORMANCE AND UNDERSTANDING

[1]This section of the program plan describes the goals and objectives of the stationary target classification effort and outlines the proposed utilization of radar data to achieve these goals and objectives. [2]The most fundamental goal of the target classification effort is to develop and understand target classifiers which work reliably in a highly variable background clutter environment. [3]Different levels of algorithm complexity would be based upon various target classification scenarios. [4]For example, one simple scenario is the MMW seeker searching a small acquisition region in search of a priority (e.g., tank) target. [5]Another scenario of intermediate complexity might be the MMW seeker having the ability to gather multiple looks at the target or even a reduced resolution SAR. [6]A third, more complex scenario is the standoff sensor application which would have the capability of utilizing high range and cross-range SAR data with a 2-D classification algorithm. [7]Algorithms for these three typical applications might be considerably different in complexity and performance, but the goal is to develop algorithms, understand the underlying signal processing, and to characterize their robustness in highly variable clutter environments. [8]Finally, the promise of new algorithms to be developed in the future, both by universities and industry, will be evaluated as part of the effort in search of a promising solution to this difficult problem.

sentence 4, the transition "for example" signals the reader that what follows will illustrate the concept just stated. The phrase invites the reader to look for examples of scenarios. In sentence 5, the transition "another scenario" signals that the list of scenarios continues. The words "intermediate complexity" recall "simple" in the previous sentence, thus signaling that the structure of the list is from simple to more complex. ("Simple" would have made more sense when readers first encountered it if a forecasting statement had been included to establish the order from simple to complex.) Sentence 6 affirms the structure of both the list and the order from simple to complex: "third" signals that this is the third example, and "more complex" defines this scenario in relation to the first two examples. These verbal signals increase the chances that the reader will leave the reading of this paragraph sharing the writer's concept of the scenarios, in terms of both number and complexity.

In the final sentence, the word "finally" is somewhat misleading. Because of the strong verbal signals about the three scenarios, a reader might first assume that the word signals the fourth item on the list. However, because the sentence does not describe a fourth scenario, the reader can conclude either that "finally" merely signals the end of the paragraph (which we can see visually) or that it identifies the final goal or task in the research project. The misdirection of the signal may require readers to reread at least the final sentence, if not others, to determine how the sentence relates to preceding ones.

Figure 13.4 maintains the paragraph format but breaks the one paragraph into three. The three paragraphs are the introduction, the elaboration of the primary goal (to develop target classifiers), and the statement of other, less elaborate goals. Note that in this version, the list items are numbered to help identify them. The numbers are not necessarily superior to verbal signals, but they are more readily apparent on quick reading.

In figure 13.5, the three scenarios are set off, or blocked out, from the prose paragraph. Thus, the visual signal predominates over the verbal signals. Paragraphs are double spaced; the space between them indicates when a new paragraph begins, making indentation redundant.

Figure 13.6 differs from figure 13.5 only in the use of subheadings in the list to indicate levels of complexity. A reader who is skimming will almost instantly see, because of the underlining, that the concept of complexity is important. The subheads thus elevate the concept of complexity to a higher level in the document structure and make readers more aware of this concept. The justification for such a change would be that the concept is important enough to warrant the changes—a matter of judgment.

The version of the document in figure 13.7 tries to solve the problem of the troublesome "finally" in the last sentence. It uses a list format, but the two levels of lists show a hierarchy of ideas. Subheadings and underlining are omitted from the "scenarios" list because the page would look cluttered with so much underlining. Verbal information added to the list introduction establishes the simple-to-complex organization.

This format elevates the project objectives above the three scenarios in terms of importance. This version of the document will produce a different concept by the reader than the versions in 13.5 and 13.6 even though all three use lists and all contain the same information. The visual format signals are easier to process than are verbal signals (though both are important). They give readers an initial concept of the information; that

Figure 13.4   Paragraph Format with Numeric Indicators

4.3 CLASSIFICATION ALGORITHM PERFORMANCE AND UNDERSTANDING

This section of the program plan describes the goals and objectives of the stationary target classification effort and outlines the proposed utilization of radar data to achieve these goals and objectives.

The most fundamental goal of the target classification effort is to develop and understand target classifiers which work reliably in a highly variable background clutter environment. Different levels of algorithm complexity would be based upon target classification scenarios. (1) One simple scenario is the MMW seeker searching a small acquisition region in search of a priority (e.g., tank) target. (2) Another scenario of intermediate complexity might be the MMW seeker having the ability to gather multiple looks at the target or even a reduced resolution SAR. (3) A third, more complex scenario is the standoff sensor application which would have the capability of utilizing high range and cross-range SAR data with a 2-D classification algorithm.

Algorithms for these three typical applications might be considerably different in complexity and performance, but the goal is to develop algorithms, understand the underlying signal processing, and to characterize their robustness in highly variable clutter environments. Finally, the promise of new algorithms to be developed in the future, both by universities and industry, will be evaluated as part of the effort in search of a promising solution to this difficult problem.

is, they help readers form a schema for the data into which the verbal details will fit. If this emphasis is wrong—if the main structure is the three scenarios rather than the three goals—the format will mislead readers. Changing their concept later will be difficult because the concept outlined by the format will be fixed in memory. The paragraph version would be preferable to a highly formatted version if the formatting would mislead. Readers of the paragraphs might still comprehend incorrectly, but the format would not contribute to their misunderstanding.

Figure 13.5   Paragraph Reformatted to Display the List.

4.3 CLASSIFICATION ALGORITHM PERFORMANCE AND UNDERSTANDING

This section of the program plan describes the goals and objectives of the stationary target classification effort and outlines the proposed utilization of radar data to achieve these goals and objectives.

The most fundamental goal of the target classification effort is to develop and understand target classifiers which work reliably in a highly variable background clutter environment. Different levels of algorithm complexity would be based upon target classification scenarios:

1. One simple scenario is the MMW seeker searching a small acquisition region in search of a priority (e.g., tank) target.

2. Another scenario of intermediate complexity might be the MMW seeker having the ability to gather multiple looks at the target or even a reduced resolution SAR.

3. A third, more complex scenario is the standoff sensor application which would have the capability of utilizing high range and cross-range SAR data with a 2-D classification algorithm.

Algorithms for these three typical applications might be considerably different in complexity and performance, but the goal is to develop algorithms, understand the underlying signal processing, and to characterize their robustness in highly variable clutter environments. Finally, the promise of new algorithms to be developed in the future, both by universities and industry, will be evaluated as part of the effort in search of a promising solution to this difficult problem.

Figure 13.6   List Format with Subheadings

4.3 CLASSIFICATION ALGORITHM PERFORMANCE AND UNDERSTANDING

This section of the program plan describes the goals and objectives of the stationary target classification effort and outlines the proposed utilization of radar data to achieve these goals and objectives.

The most fundamental goal of the target classification effort is to develop and understand target classifiers which work reliably in a highly variable background clutter environment. Different levels of algorithm complexity would be based upon three target classification scenarios:

1. <u>Simple</u>. The MMW seeker searches a small acquisition region in search of a priority (e.g., tank) target.

2. <u>Intermediate complexity</u>. The MMW seeker has the ability to gather multiple looks at the target or even a reduced resolution SAR.

3. <u>Most complex</u>. The standoff sensor application would have the capability of utilizing high range and cross-range SAR data with a 2-D classification algorithm.

Algorithms for these three typical applications might be considerably different in complexity and performance, but the goal is to develop algorithms, understand the underlying signal processing, and to characterize their robustness in highly variable clutter environments. Finally, the promise of new algorithms to be developed in the future, both by universities and industry, will be evaluated as part of the effort in search of a promising solution to this difficult problem.

Figure 13.7   List Format with Two Levels; Emphasis on the Goals Rather Than on the Scenarios

4.3 CLASSIFICATION ALGORITHM PERFORMANCE AND UNDERSTANDING

This section of the program plan describes the goals and objectives of the stationary target classification effort and outlines the proposed utilization of radar data to achieve these goals and objectives. There are three main goals:

1. To develop target classifiers which work reliably in a highly variable background clutter environment. This is the most fundamental goal of the target classification effort. Different levels of algorithm complexity would be based upon three target classification scenarios of increasing complexity:

   a. The MMW seeker searches a small acquisition region in search of a priority (e.g., tank) target.

   b. The MMW seeker has the ability to gather multiple looks at the target or even a reduced resolution SAR.

   c. The standoff sensor application would have the capability of utilizing high range and cross-range SAR data with a 2-D classification algorithm.

2. To develop and understand algorithms based on target classifications. Algorithms for these three typical applications might be considerably different in complexity and performance. Subgoals for the understanding of algorithms will be:

   a. To understand the underlying signal processing.

   b. To characterize their robustness in highly variable clutter environments.

3. To evaluate the promise of new algorithms. These new algorithms would be developed in the future, both by universities and industry, as part of the effort in search of a promising solution to this difficult problem.

Is it more important for readers of the radar document to understand the three scenarios or to understand the three goals? The answer will tell you whether the version in figure 13.7 is preferable to the versions in figures 13.5 and 13.6. The section of the document you have before you is too small a part of the whole for you to answer the question with complete confidence, though the introductory statement suggests that the section is about goals, and the "finally" in the last sentence suggests that the dominant structure is the goals. On the other hand, there is so little elaboration of the goals after the first one that an editor may rightly assume that the three scenarios are dominant or that there is one goal with subgoals. Reading closely, however, is the first task of the editor. Your editing will not improve the document if it distorts the meaning through powerful format signals.

In addition to close reading, you have the option of consulting other, similar documents. Is the pattern of comparable sections in other program plans to list goals and objectives? Such a pattern would reinforce the decision to list goals. Even more important, you can query the writer about the appropriate emphasis, perhaps illustrating two or more possibilities to clarify your query.

Which format—paragraph, internal numbering, listing—is best? There is no easy answer. List format is not always preferable to paragraph format or vice versa, nor is the two-level list necessarily preferable to the single-level list. Formats are not good or bad in any absolute sense. In terms of comprehension, they are good if they enable readers to comprehend the text accurately, and they are bad if they distract or mislead. Speed of reading is also a factor because readers become impatient when forced to reread. Thus, format must enable readers to comprehend both accurately and quickly. A list format may help with complex material because it reveals the structure of the information. But it would become tiresome and counterproductive if used to the exclusion of paragraphs in a long book meant to be read with concentration.

Often, your efforts at increasing comprehensibility through reformatting will reveal gaps in the information. In the sample passage, the writer may wish to add details to some of the goals. Alternatively, he or she may collapse two or more goals into one—maybe there aren't really three goals after all. Some questions about word choice also emerge from the close reading that reformatting requires. For example, in the last sentence of figures 13.3–13.6, is it accurate to say that the "promise" of new algorithms will be evaluated? Is the title of the section clear enough?

In figure 13.8, the document has been edited for style, organization, and completeness of information as well as for format. Some of the substantive changes were based on inquiries to the researcher who wrote the original paragraph.

Figure 13.8   Paragraph Edited for Format and for Style, Organization,
and Completeness of Information

4.3 CLASSIFICATION ALGORITHM DEVELOPMENT

Introduction This section describes classification algorithm
development as well as the proposed utilization of radar data in this
development effort.

The basic purpose of the radar target classification effort is to
develop target classification algorithms that work reliably in highly
variable clutter environments, and to understand how they work.
Different levels of algorithm complexity will be based on different
target classification scenarios:

A. One relatively simple scenario would be a MMW seeker searching a
   small acquisition region for a priority target (e.g., a tank).

B. A scenario of intermediate complexity would involve a MMW seeker
   that could gather multiple looks at the target and then process
   them by (1) noncoherently integrating them to reduce radar
   scintillation or (2) coherently processing them to construct a
   reduced-cross-range-resolution SAR image.

C. A relatively complex scenario would involve a standoff sensor
   capable of utilizing high-resolution range and cross-range SAR
   data in a 2-D classification algorithm.

Algorithms for these three typical applications might be
considerably different in complexity and performance; in each case,
however, the goal would be to develop the algorithm, understand the
underlying signal processing, and characterize the algorithm's
robustness in highly variable clutter environments. An additional part
of classification algorithm development will be evaluation of new
algorithms that will be developed in the future by both universities
and industry.

One point should be clear: if you as editor have questions about the structure of the information—about the number of items or about their relative importance—the reader probably will, too. The reader is less likely than you are to probe for the correct meaning and may "learn" the information incorrectly—unless you help by inserting the correct signals into the document, whether they be format or verbal signals.

HEADINGS

Headings are important in technical documents for purposes of access and comprehension. Both comprehension and access are reasons to pay attention to the wording of headings and to the accurate representation in the levels of headings of the hierarchy and relationship of ideas. As editor, you can make headings functional by checking the wording, levels, and frequency of the headings.

Wording

Informative headings provide more information than do structural headings. For example, the headings "Equipment Costs," "Installation Costs," and "Purchase Costs" tell more than do "Part 1," "Part 2," and "Part 3." Exceptions are "introduction" and "conclusion," which indicate both content and structure. One-word headings generally tell less than do headings containing several words; for example, "Costs" tells less than "Installation Costs," and "Discussion" tells less than "Data Analysis and Interpretation."

Some research results indicate that headings phrased as questions work better than do headings phrased as statements because questions invite readers to examine what they are reading. Readers also remember more when the headings are worded as questions rather than statements. The heading "How Do I Apply?" may appeal to readers more than does "Application Procedures." For the purpose of access, however, either heading works because both contain the two key concepts, "application" and "procedures." Questions would be less functional in a scholarly article than in a brochure because of conventions established for each document type and because of reader expectations.

Parallel structure in headings provides consistency. Groups of headings within a section should consistently all be phrases, or questions, or complete sentences. Steps in a task should be identified consistently in descriptive terms or as commands but not as a mixture of the two.

Levels of Headings

Different levels of headings reveal structural levels of document parts— main parts and subordinate parts. A short document, such as a brochure, will probably have only one heading level, but a longer, more complex document, such as this textbook, may have as many as four levels. Theoretically, it could have even more levels, but readers probably would have trouble following such a complex structure. By contrast, a report of four to eight pages is not structurally complex enough to support more than one or two levels.

If the headings are to reveal the structure, readers must distinguish first-level (main) headings from second- and third-level headings. First-level headings must be more powerful visually than other levels. "Power" can be achieved by centering, by spacing before and after the heading, by setting in boldface type, by increasing the type size, and by capitalizing. That is, a centered heading is more powerful than a left-justified heading; space before and after the heading indicates a higher level of heading than a heading run into the text; boldface is more powerful than regular type; and so forth. Italics are less visually powerful than roman type and therefore not useful for main headings. They can be useful for minor headings, such as paragraph headings. In typewritten documents, main headings are often centered and capitalized while subordinate headings are left justified and perhaps underlined. Paragraph headings run into a paragraph rather than using a separate line.

Typesetting and desktop publishing offer more and better options for distinguishing headings. Boldface type is more readable than either capitalized or underlined type and thus is the preferred treatment. Variations in type size can show differences in levels of headings, but readers probably won't recognize a difference of less than four points. (A **point** is a printer's measure; 72 points equal approximately one inch.) For example, if the second-level heading is set in 10-point type, the main heading will have to be at least 14-point type unless (or even if) there are other distinguishing features such as spacing.

Graphic designers advise left-justified headings rather than centered ones because of the left-to-right reading pattern. The left margin is a common point of orientation for readers whether the text is display copy (i.e., headings and titles) or body copy. Furthermore, designers advise that at least two lines of text follow a heading on a page. It is preferable to leave an unusually large bottom margin than to allow a heading to appear alone at the bottom of the page.

The rules for outlining generally apply to headings: just as a roman numeral "I" implies that at least a "II" will follow and an "A" implies at least a "B," one heading at any level implies at least a second heading at the same level. Two headings of different levels will be separated by text.

An editor verifies that the headings accurately reflect the structure of the document and that the different levels, if any, can be distinguished. An editor may also advise on the style and placement of headings.

Frequency of Headings If headings are good, are more headings better? Not necessarily. Headings, like other format devices, are signals. They should not replace the text, nor should they interfere with the continuity of reading. Too many headings can distract from the content.

There are no rules for the amount of text per heading. Some types of documents, such as brochures, have proportionately more headings than do textbooks or reports. Each chunk of information may be identified by a heading in a brochure. If each paragraph of a textbook had a heading, however, it would be difficult to read long sections—the book would seem to "hiccup."

As editor, you will have to use judgment about the frequency of headings, thinking about reading patterns and the structural complexity of the document at hand. For a brochure, with small chunks of information meant to be absorbed quickly, headings will predominate on the page. Longer, more complex documents, such as long reports and textbooks, need longer prose sections in order to develop complex ideas.

GUIDELINES FOR
EDITING FOR FORMAT

Formatting, like writing, is an inexact task, especially as an editor moves beyond conventions and uses format to aid comprehension and access. Your formatting judgments will be sound if you understand the function of each choice you make and if you can imagine the document in use, not just as type on a page. Some specific suggestions for editing for format follow.

1. **Know the conventions of formatting.** You can find universal conventions, such as letter format, in textbooks and in style manuals such as *The Chicago Manual of Style.* Your own publishing organization may have a style manual with a section on formatting. Even if it does not, you can check previously published copies of documents of the type you are editing. Style manuals for disciplines (see Chapter 3) also provide information on formatting conventions within the disciplines. If the document is a response to a request for manuscripts, such as a proposal in response to an RFP or a journal article in response to a call for papers, consult the instructions for preparing manuscripts. At the least, as editor, you must ensure that the document conforms to the conventions.

2. **Make format decisions early in document planning.** If the writer knows the format specifications and options from the start, he or she can prepare the first draft of the document according to these decisions. That means less work for you as

editor, less chance for conflict if you make significant changes, and a greater chance that the writer will make sound formatting decisions.

3. **Read for meaning before emending format.** Format is such a powerful signal to content because it almost instantly identifies the structure of the information. If you give the wrong visual signal, it will be difficult, if not impossible, for the words to correct that impression. Be absolutely sure that your visual signals accurately reflect the structure of the information.

4. **Ensure that format enhances content rather than distracting from it.** Format should be subtle. If it calls attention to itself and away from the meaning, then the document suffers. Readers are distracted by anything unconventional. Writers and editors can use that knowledge to the document's advantage, as when they increase the type size and use boldface for warnings. But extensive shifts at best annoy and at worst interfere with comprehension.

   If the reader first sees a visual hodgepodge rather than a document, the format needs to be simplified. Note, for example, that in figure 13.9, the type shifts at least 22 times, and some of the typefaces are difficult to read. The right justification in the column on the right gives readers no common starting point as they move from line to line. The busy look is inconsistent with the image of classical music that the flier seeks to promote.

   Generally, the best format is the simplest format that will achieve the goals of meeting reader expectations, motivating the reading process, facilitating ongoing use, providing access, and aiding comprehension. One good check against overformatting is to force yourself to articulate the reason for any format emendation. When doing so, use the same terms that this chapter uses. For example, you might insert a heading saying to yourself, "The reader needs to know here that the discussion is complete and the conclusion begins." If you have reformatted merely because "it looks good" or "just for variety," your reasons are fuzzy and your priorities in editing are skewed.

5. **Match the level of formatting to the demands of the text.** For short and simple documents and documents that will likely be read straight through or at least in large sections, the simple format of prose paragraphs is probably best. Most textbooks consist primarily of prose paragraphs because the books are meant to be read in sections and their content is tailored for their readers.

Figure 13.9
Distracting Formatting

RADIOTHON

1990

June 7-9 1990
7:00 AM - 12:00 midnight

Classical Radio
87.9 KZZZ

LIVE PERFORMANCES!

GUEST HOSTS!

All your favorite classics!

All at once!

Prizes! Challenges! Fun!
Art! Community Support!
Great Music! E x t e n d e d
Broadcast Hours! More Fun
than Humans Should Be Al-
lowed to Have! All at 87.9 FM,
the All- New *Classical* Option for
the Tri-State Area.

Here's your opportunity to join in on one of the best things to happen to the Tri-State area in a long time: KZZZ-FM, Classical Radio. As a listener-supported station, KZZZ relies entirely on support from its listeners and the community at large to meet operational expenses. RADIOTHON '90 is the time for our listeners to show how much they value and appreciate the musical alternative that we provide. Tune in during the RADIOTHON to hear some of the area's finest musicians in performance, as well as joining guest hosts from the community to suport the newest FM choice, Classical 87.9 KZZZ

Imagine trying to read a text of several hundred pages that was formatted as extensively as the document in figure 13.7. You would tire quickly because the formatting would place excessive demands on you.

For documents longer than one or two pages or documents that readers may read selectively, headings can be useful for purposes of both access and comprehension. Documents with complex technical information may benefit from more elaborate formatting, such as creating lists and numbering to indicate sections. Documents that are meant to be read quickly and selectively, such as résumés, are also highly formatted.

Instructions require particular attention to format because the reader moves from the text to the task and back. Steps in the task need to be clearly differentiated, perhaps separated by white space or lines. Not only can numbering of steps help readers find the right place on the page when they move back to the text, it can be useful in cross-reference, as when you need to refer to a previous step.

6. **Check headings.** Make sure the levels of headings match the information—that is, that level-one headings indicate the main points. Check for parallel structure. Evaluate their frequency: Are there enough that readers can identify main points? Are there so many that they interrupt reading?

SUMMARY

Format is a powerful device that motivates reading, facilitates access and ongoing use, and aids comprehension. Format is always subordinate to meaning and use; that is, editors do not use formatting options to decorate a page but to enable a reader to understand and use the document. Editors must make judgments about format based on their knowledge of the document as it will be used.

FURTHER READING

Thomas M. Duffy and Robert Waller, eds. 1985. *Designing Usable Texts*. Orlando: Academic Press.

Daniel B. Felker et al. 1981. *Guidelines for Document Designers*. Washington, DC: American Institutes for Research.

James Hartley. 1985. *Designing Instructional Text*. 2nd ed. London: Kogan Page Ltd.

DISCUSSION AND APPLICATION

1. In the library, locate a professional journal and a trade journal, preferably on the same subject. For example, consult the *Journal of Clinical Psychology* and *Psychology Today* or *Mechanical Engineering* and *Popular Mechanics* or *Journal of Finance* and *Money*. Identify the format features of both journals, including the document as a whole (size, shape, binding, and paper) and page format (number of columns and line length, use of headings, white space, illustrations, and color). Using the evidence of content, format, and journal preface (if any), describe the readers for the two journals, considering their interest in the subject, probable reading habits, and back-

grounds. Then explain how the format decisions relate to the assumptions about readers. Compare and contrast the two journals, and evaluate the format for both on the criteria of access, comprehension, and motivation. If you were editor of either journal, would you recommend changes? If so, what would be your reasons?

2. Continue the analysis and evaluation of the document in figure 13.2. What format options do you identify? What other format choices might have been better ones?

3. The subject of the following two paragraphs is radar. Both paragraphs, like the document in figure 13.3, have embedded lists. Format the two paragraphs to display the lists. Edit for punctuation, spelling, and completeness of information as well as for format. Then, with other class members or in writing, discuss the bases for making a decision about whether the original paragraph format, the list format, or perhaps a third alternative is the best choice for these paragraphs. If you have questions about meaning, formulate queries for the writer.

Example 1

```
Test planning--Mission planning defines the
number and type of missions together with the
actual flight plans for the mission to
efficiently gather the data. The needed data
includes distributed clutter, discretes, and
targets in clutter under varying conditions such
as: clutter types: meadows, trees, tree lines,
desert; target types: both civilian and military,
in these clutter environments and in various
target configurations; and environmental
conditions: wet, dry, snow. The mission planning
will reflect inputs solicited from the MMW
government and industry communities to make the
data base widely useful.
```

Example 2

```
Three difficulties exist with 2-D images from a
data analysis point of view. 2-D images are
```

```
typically processed over a narrow angle of
rotation (1° is typical). 2-D images in radar
coordinates are also difficult to compare at
different aspect angles because the target
orientation is different in each image. The third
difficulty is the elevation ambiguity inherent in
2-D radar imagery.
```

4. In your own words, explain how format affects comprehension. Give some specific examples of how an editor can use format to influence what a reader learns from a document.

5. Find three different documents, such as a letter, announcement, and textbook. Identify the different formatting options used for each. Explain what formatting functions each of the options fulfills. Identify any formatting options that seem superfluous or that seem to interfere with the document purpose. As editor, suggest alternatives and explain why they might be preferable.

6. Compare the documents in figures 13.3 and 13.8. Identify the editorial changes in content, organization, and style. Evaluate the editing: What is better about the version in 13.8? What information is new? Imagine the editorial procedure: How did the editor begin? What questions did he or she ask the writer?

7. Find a document with at least two levels of headings. Identify the type of wording: Informative or structural? One word or several? Phrases or questions? Identify the ways in which the levels are distinguished visually. Do the headings provide the information a reader needs? Do they enable selective reading? Can a reader distinguish the levels visually? Do they distract?

14 VISUALS

When technical communication emerged as a career specialization during World War II, the typical technical document was mostly words. Furthermore, the page was packed with words: narrow margins, scant interlinear spacing, and the lack of headings let the words crowd the page. Technical documents have changed dramatically since then as writers have discovered the power of graphics and format. Writers use format to enhance comprehension and access, and documents without visuals are rare. Some documents are wholly visual with illustrations substituting for text. The term *visuals* is comprehensive: it refers to tables, graphs, flowcharts, diagrams, line drawings, and photographs. Line drawings and photographs are also called *illustrations* and *pictorials.* The term *graphics* is sometimes used as a comprehensive term to mean visuals, especially in identifying a type of computer program.

A parallel move from words to visuals is evident in online instructions for using computers. When computers became available to general users, commands changed from programming codes to words such as "delete" and "move." Now instructions increasingly rely on **icons,** or visual representations of procedures, rather than on words. Users and readers, too, have discovered the power of visuals.

Visuals, just like text, require the full range of editing: copyediting and substantive editing. Copyeditors check accuracy, correctness, consistency, and completeness. Substantive editors confirm the match of form and content, the logical arrangement of elements within the illustration, and the integration of visuals with the text.

The same principles of good communication that editors apply to text also apply to visuals. Knowing those principles prepares editors for working with visuals. Just as with text, readers seek information in visuals and ease of access to the information. Just as with text, visual information must be organized in a way that shows the overall concept as well as the relationship of parts to the whole. The presentation must be free of the distraction of messiness or undue clutter.

This chapter summarizes reasons to use visuals, reviews types of visuals, and discusses the checks an editor performs in substantive editing. It also examines the process of preparing visuals for print and the use of computers in editing visuals. Chapter 3 covers copyediting of visuals, and Chapter 8 discusses tables.

REASONS TO USE VISUALS

In technical communication, the reasons to use visuals parallel the reasons for making any other choice about a document. These reasons derive from what we know about readers of technical documents (see Chapter 2). Readers seek information, read selectively, and expect the document to follow conventions. They often read in order to act. They create meaning based on previous learning. They learn organized information more readily than random or chaotic information. Visuals help readers comprehend information and provide easy access to it. They support the text and enable action. Thus, visuals in technical documents are primarily functional rather than decorative. Editors evaluate how well visuals achieve their function. Aesthetic issues are secondary.

These reasons for using visuals form a firmer basis for evaluating visuals than does taste. All the visuals in a document should achieve one or more of these objectives. You need to have a better reason than your like or dislike of a visual to modify it.

Conveying Information

Visuals in technical documents may convey information more readily than text would convey the same information. A line drawing or photograph shows readers the whole object as well as the shapes, proportions, and relationship of parts more readily than could words. Some instructions are mostly or even wholly visual because users will work with objects. Visuals help users relate the information in the document to the object in their hands. Visuals also to some extent bypass words in instructions. Whereas verbal instructions must be translated for international users, visual instructions may save the costs of translation and printings in multiple languages. And they may enable less competent readers to complete a task.

Visuals also represent quantitative and structural data efficiently. For example, lists of numbers get buried in sentences, but they are accessible in tables or in graphs. A flowchart readily reveals the structure of an organization or process, whereas sentences that attempted to present the same information would be tedious.

Facts, however, do not tell much in isolation—they need to be interpreted. The fact that a company's earnings in the third quarter of the fiscal year were $2.3 million means less than a comparison of those earnings to the same period of the previous year or to the earnings of a rival company. Not only do visuals aid interpretation, they make the facts accessible by showing relationships and enabling comparisons. A line graph, for example, shows instantly a trend over time or some other independent variable, and a bar graph provides a quick comparison. These visuals facilitate the formation of schemata or concepts in the reader's mind. Sometimes the broad concept will suffice, as in an oral presentation. Sometimes the reader will study the visual for more details, and the text will elaborate on the visual schema.

Visuals also provide a structure for organizing information. Assuming the structure works for the content, the structure will increase the comprehensibility of the information.

Supporting the Text   Occasionally visuals stand alone in instructions for less competent readers or international users. More frequently, however, they support text. They reinforce the meaning in the text by presenting it in a different mode. Some people learn better by seeing rather than by reading, and most people learn better if they can check the verbal information with the visual, and vice versa. The two sources of information complement each other.

Sometimes visuals support the text by motivating readers. For example, including a cartoon in serious material can relax readers and invite them into the text. An illustration can provide relief from the steady columns of print. A photograph can rouse sympathies. These purposes are valid, but as editor you need to apply good judgment when seeking to motivate readers through the inclusion of visuals—the visual must be there for a valid reason. Unless a visual is clearly a cartoon, readers will expect information from the visuals. Merely decorative illustrations (those without information) distract from the text rather than enhancing it. Instructions for hanging wallpaper may be enhanced by a line drawing of a person pressing a strip of paper against the wall, but a drawing of a person engaged in no particular action would simply distract. Efforts to be cute—for example, adding hands and a face to a piece of electronic equipment—may insult readers. As with all editing, you must know your readers, and your choices about visuals must relate to the overall purpose of and design for the document.

In order to support the text, visuals must be integrated with it. Integration means, in part, that readers can tell when visuals and text are connected. Placement of the visual near the text that discusses it helps readers connect related parts of the document. Other devices of integration include verbal references to the visual and consistent use of terms in the visual and the text. Integration of text and visuals also means that both forms communicate the same message. The message would be mixed if the text gave instructions on a serious safety procedure while the visual illustrated a smiling employee in a casual pose.

Enabling Action   "Action" for a user of visuals may consist simply of finding a number in a table. The table itself makes the numbers more accessible than would sentences. In complex tables, devices such as shading and spacing increase the ease with which a user can find the right number. Shading blocks of data and inserting extra space between groups of lines propel the eye across the page and help readers stay on the right line.

Readers also depend on visuals in learning to perform a task. While writers and editors often assume readers will use both the text and visuals, in fact, readers may try to take shortcuts and read only the visuals. Illustrations that enable them to perform the task quickly, without extensive reading, will accomplish the goals of the document (completion of a task) and please the readers as well. Good editors evaluate visuals as though readers will pay attention only to the visuals.

The purpose of enabling action dictates a consistent placement of visuals and corresponding text on the page, particularly when the two are side by side. Readers want to find the text and visuals in the same place each time they look up from the task rather than finding visuals sometimes to the right of the text, sometimes to the left, sometimes on top, sometimes beneath.

TYPES OF VISUALS   Different types of visuals serve different functions and convey different information. For example, a table provides access to specific data while graphs provide a concept of how pieces of quantitative data relate to one another. Table 14.1 summarizes types of visuals and their uses. As editor, you will need to know what visuals achieve what purposes in order to edit

TABLE 14.1 TYPES OF VISUALS

Tabular

table

Defiant (%)	Obedient (%)	All (%)
40.0	47.8	43.5
43.8	35.7	40.2
15.3	14.8	15.1

Displays information, quantitative or verbal, in rows and columns. Tables enable location of exact quantities or items.

Graphic

bar graph

Compares quantitative information in horizontal bars. Bars are preferable to columns (vertical) when the information is linear, as when the comparison is of distance. Identifying labels are easy to read on bars because they are horizontal. Columns better show trends over time.

column graph

multiple bar/column graph

Compares groups of items on a single point. Emphasizes the value of the individual items.

segmented bar/column

Compares groups of items on a single point. Emphasizes the whole formed by the individual items.

pictograph

Forms bars or columns from images of the object being compared.

line graph

Plots change over time, temperature, or other independent variable.

multiple line graph

Plots multiple changes over time, temperature, or other independent variable.

pie or circle graph

Shows the relationship of parts to the whole.

TABLE 14.1 (continued)

Structural

schematic diagram

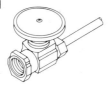

Shows the structure of an object but not in a representational way. Used frequently in wiring diagrams and science.

flowchart

Identifies steps in a process or the hierarchy of an organization.

Representational

line drawing

Outlines an object without shading, background, and other realistic details.

exploded drawing

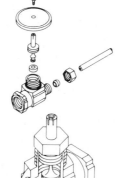

Separates the parts of an object to show how they are connected.

cutaway drawing

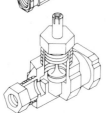

Shows the object as though its front had been peeled away lengthwise. Reveals the internal structure.

cross-section

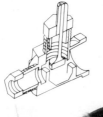

Shows the object as though it had been cut in half crosswise. Reveals the internal structure.

photograph

Represents objects realistically; the least abstract of visuals. Background clutter may distract from a part to be emphasized.

for form, organization, and content. One of your tasks will be to check the match of form and content. You also need to use the correct terms in referring to types of visuals. A correct technical vocabulary enables accurate communication and helps to establish your mastery of your subject matter.

Visuals may be classified according to four broad categories: tabular, graphic, structural, and representational. Tables place verbal or quantitative items in rows and columns for easy access to particular pieces of information and for comparison. Graphs display quantitative information for purposes of comparison. Structural visuals—flowcharts and schematic diagrams—emphasize the structure of the data rather than comparisons or representation. Representational visuals—drawings and photographs—depict two- and three-dimensional items. Some examples of these categories of visuals are displayed in table 14.1.

SUBSTANTIVE EDITING OF VISUALS

Substantive editing of visuals means evaluating their content, organization, form, and style in terms of overall document purpose and readers' needs. The visual must make sense. The parts must cohere, and readers must be able to identify and interpret what they see. Sometimes substantive editing results in restructuring of the visuals or in additions or deletions. Visuals may be rescaled or resized depending on the desired emphasis. Guidelines can aid in these decisions, but judgments about readers' interpretation and use of the visuals will also be required.

Appropriateness and Number

A fundamental substantive evaluation determines whether the visuals are appropriate for the document. Preferably, some policies about visuals will be established before a draft is prepared. For example, a writer should find out before having 30 photographs made that only three line drawings will be acceptable. Editors should be consulted in the making of these policies.

Decisions about whether to include visuals and how many to include may be based on economics—visuals cost money. They may also relate to the document set. If other manuals in a series are illustrated in one way, the set has established conventions that must be followed in subsequent manuals.

Beyond these practical matters, you should consider whether visual or verbal presentation will better convey information and enable action and how visuals may support the text.

Match of Form, Content, and Purpose

The form of the visual (e.g., line graph, table, photograph) should reinforce the content. It should also enable readers to use the information in it. This principle relates to the selection of types of visuals.

A graph shows almost instantly the shape of the data, so a reader's ini-

Figure 14.1
Mismatch of
Form and Purpose

This line graph misrepresents the data by suggesting some progression from point A to point C. All three scores are one-time scores by different people. A column graph would better compare absolute values.

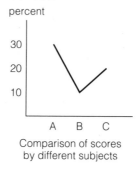

Comparison of scores
by different subjects

tial interpretation is very fast. The graph thus helps in concept formation. Consider, however, the graph in figure 14.1. The message of the content is a comparison of three people's scores on a test. However, the line graph does not help a reader conceptualize the information. Its form conveys the message of movement over time rather than a comparison of values. It also suggests visually that subject A progresses toward subjects B and C.

If the purpose were to compare one person's score at three different periods, the line graph would work fine to show the change. A column graph would work better than a bar graph if the intent were to compare the three scores of three separate subjects. Measuring scores implies "high" and "low" scores. The vertical presentation would suggest that vertical concept.

Arrangement:
Sequential and Spatial

Visuals must make sense in relationship to one another and to the text. The arrangement of parts within a visual shows their relationship spatially.

In a sequence of visuals, the whole should come before the part—a general-to-specific arrangement. Readers need to comprehend the whole before the parts make sense. Readers might not recognize a part of a mechanism if they have not seen the context in which the part exists.

The ordering of details within the visual can show the relationship of parts and help readers form concepts. Some standard arrangements are more important to less important, larger to smaller, and first to last. Thus, the bars in a bar graph might be ordered from largest to smallest unless some other communication purpose (e.g., chronological order) dictates a different arrangement.

Visuals linked with text in instructions should generally appear on the left with the text to their right. This arrangement corresponds to the left-to-right reading pattern. Readers form the concept of the step from the visual and then consult the text for the details. If for some reason (e.g., space considerations) a two-column pattern is technically impossible, the arrangement can be vertical, with the visual at the top and the text below. The visual should be introduced by a step number or heading to show that it belongs with the text that follows rather than the text that precedes.

If the visual illustrates component parts, the parts should maintain essentially the same positions as they would in use. A computer's mouse, for example, would be inappropriately displayed above the monitor. Instead, it should appear to the right of the monitor where it is used by right-handed people. This functional arrangement overrides aesthetic considerations, such as balance.

Should graphs and tables be placed in the text or in an appendix? The answer depends on whether most readers need the visuals at the point where they are mentioned or whether the visuals present supplementary information that only some readers may check. If they are supplementary and would interfere with the comprehension of the text, place them in an appendix. If they provide important concepts that all readers must know, place them in the text.

Emphasis and Detail

When visuals combine with text, the visuals inherently emphasize what they display. Readers tend to pay more attention to the visuals than to the text, so the inclusion of a visual announces that this information is important. Emphasis helps readers interpret information by showing the hierarchical structure.

Within a visual, readers pay attention to details that are emphasized. Details may be highlighted in these ways:

Size: large attracts more attention than does small.

Color or shading: bright colors and dark shading attract the most attention.

Labels: important parts are labeled, others are not.

Foregrounding: important parts appear in the front.

White space: details surrounded by space generally attract more attention than do details crowded by others.

Shape: in a matrix of circles, one notices the lone triangle; in a segmented circle, one notices the segment separated from the others.

Sequence: first and last seem more important than middle.

Typographic cues: boxes and arrows focus attention.

Consider the following illustration,* which aims to help readers complete the task of inserting a stylus for a tonearm on a turntable into a cartridge.

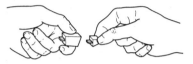

Note, however, that the drawing emphasizes hands rather than the task. Not only are the hands larger, the stylus and cartridge are so small as to be unidentifiable, even in the context of the instructions. It is impossible to tell from the visual whether to pull the two components apart or to insert the stylus into the cartridge. Faulty emphasis results here from the actual size of hands in proportion to the objects; the message that results from faulty emphasis is "place the objects in your hands" rather than "assemble the objects." The hands might just as well have been omitted.

The readers' needs determine which details should be emphasized. Readers must be able to identify in the visual any details they will use, such as parts they need to assemble or numbers they need to interpret. Details must be accurate and complete. By contrast, details unrelated to the concept or task diminish the power of visuals. The form can be buried in the clutter, so that readers spend as much time plowing through excessive details as they would reading the information in paragraph form. Thus, as editor, you should simplify or use multiple visuals if the clutter hides the important information. Remember from Chapter 12 that seven items is generally the maximum memory load. Because the visual power of a circle graph or a multiple line graph diminishes once the number of segments or lines exceeds seven, a graph may not be the right form for such data. Likewise, the detail of a photograph may make it difficult for readers to locate specific parts they need to connect, in which case several photographs, or perhaps a different type of visual, should be used.

In evaluating the level of details, ask what readers need to know and do from the visual. If the visual presents more than necessary, delete what is unnecessary. If readers need to know all the information but the details intimidate or inhibit quick reading, consider using more than one visual for the same data.

Perspective, Size, and Scale   Perspective, size, and scale give readers useful information and influence the interpretation of the information. Perspective shows depth: the place

---

* Courtesy of Stanton Magnetics

Figure 14.2
Scale and Line Graph

Expansion of the vertical scale in the graph on the right exaggerates the incline.

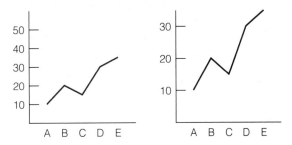

of an object in a three-dimensional field from the front of the visual to the back. Whether an object is standing on end or on a horizontal plane is a matter of perspective. Because objects appear smaller in proportion to their distance from the viewer, proportionately small objects seem farther away.

Size is a factor in identification. Visuals should be big enough that they can be read, but rarely so large that they dominate the text and never so large that they "scream" on the page. Size can also indicate importance. Visuals should be sized proportionately within a document so that shifts in size indicate shifts in importance. Assuming comparable complexity and importance, one line graph will have essentially the same size boundaries as another line graph, but if one line graph is more important or complex than another, it should be larger. Parts of objects may be drawn proportionately larger than the whole to show detail.

The scale of graphs should reflect numeric values. Distortion results from expansion or condensation of the x or y axis or both or from improper measurement. Editors determine whether the visual conveys its information accurately. If the graph gives the wrong first impression, it will be difficult to correct it later with words or other details because the schema will already be formed in short-term memory.

Bar and column graphs and pie graphs can be scaled quantitatively. Assuming that the bar or column begins at zero, each bar can be measured so that its length equates to its numeric value. The segments on a pie graph can be calculated with a protractor. By contrast, scale on line graphs is more difficult to establish because two dimensions can be manipulated. The "right" scale is a matter of judgment rather than measurement. Note that the two line graphs in figure 14.2 present the same data. However, the graph on the right gives the impression of a much greater incline than the graph on the left. The expansion of the x axis creates a steeper incline; contraction of the y axis can also steepen an incline.

Psychological factors and convention will contribute to the judgment about whether a scale is right. For example, if a 20 percent increase in sales is an astonishing gain for a company, a fairly steep incline will be appropriate. But if a company gains 20 percent every year, the increase will be correctly represented in a flatter line. The line graph that appears in the business section of the newspaper each week exaggerates the movement of the Dow Jones average of stock prices, but convention has established the scale, and readers interpret accurately on the basis of prior experience.

In technical documents, even persuasive ones, the goal is always to provide accurate information. Purposeful distortion of data may be accepted in sales documents, whose readers expect to be sold, but it is not acceptable in technical documents, whose readers expect to be informed.

Relationship of Text and Visuals

Visuals convey information, help readers form concepts, and enable action. Usually, though, text is needed for explanations and interpretation of significance. Thus, visuals support text rather than substituting for it. Even in documents that are mostly visual, text is the glue that unifies the document and creates coherence. Editors must consider whether the visual and verbal information together convey the whole message. Often the visual, whether tabular, graphic, structural, or representational, provides the initial concept, and the text elaborates.

Problems with interpretation may occur when the creators of documents try to bypass words altogether in order to reach an international audience. Emergency instructions in airplanes, for example, are frequently visual only, using no words. Some office equipment includes only visual instructions for installation and use. The measure of effectiveness for such documents is the same as the measure for verbal documents: Can readers interpret and use the information? Because visual information has limitations (as does verbal), sometimes the visuals alone do not provide enough information.

Some concepts and procedures are easier to represent visually than others. The goal of nonverbal instructions may not be possible for some topics. Consider the following illustration: The dial on the left appeared in the instructions for a machine that makes ditto masters and transparencies to be used with overhead projectors. It is recognizable as a dial in context, but the visual by itself does not convey the entire instruction; a user has to determine, by trial and error, the best setting of the dial for a given purpose and mark the illustration so that subsequent users will know where to set the dial. Because this illustration is the first of four in a sequence, users might interpret that the first step is to set the dial, but then they will be frustrated trying to determine how and where. It is unlikely that they will use the illustration to mark the setting unless they have a verbal prompt. If an arrow is added to the illustration to indicate

Figure 14.3
Visual and
Verbal Information

The visual information in the dial on the left is insufficient to tell readers to mark the appropriate setting on the instruction sheet. The arrow in the dial on the right substitutes for a verb phrase: "turn the dial clockwise."

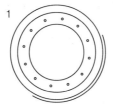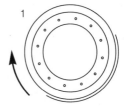

visually a direction to move or place something, readers will know immediately that they are to perform some action. The illustration in figure 14.3 does more than identify a thing (a knob or dial)—it tells the user to turn it clockwise. Words will still be necessary to recommend marking the dial on the instruction sheet to indicate the optimal setting.

In editing visuals, use words as necessary for identifying and explanatory information. If your company cannot afford translators and printings in different languages, take the chance that at least some users will speak English. Remember, too, that the visual information must complement the verbal information. The text and visual should use the same terms. For example, if the text refers to a piece of data or a part of a mechanism, that information should be labeled on the visual. Likewise, if the visual names a part, the text will probably discuss it. Placement of the visuals in relation to the text can also reinforce the parallels between text and visual.

Discriminatory
Language and
Good Taste

The guidelines for avoiding discriminatory language and maintaining good taste in prose (see Chapter 11) apply equally to visuals. Visuals can discriminate whether they use words or not. For example, a document illustrating white males in professional positions and females in menial positions shows bias whether the accompanying text is biased or not. Representations of people in line drawings and pictographs should suggest racial and sexual equality.

Good taste involves respect for adult readers and the seriousness of document purpose. For example, comic visuals can motivate and reinforce ideas, but lewdness insults. Corny cartoon characters are risky because they can equate readers with children or with incompetent or subliterate adults. The formality of visuals should match the formality of the prose and format to maintain a consistent persona and tone. Thus, cartoons may work for casual brochures, but they would be detrimental to a bank's annual report printed on heavy, cream-colored paper.

Figure 14.4 shows a portion of the owner's manual for a cassette player. The manual as a whole is an 8½ × 11-inch booklet, with pages stapled down the center. These particular instructions tell how to safeguard the cassette against accidental erasing. Editing follows the familiar procedure of analyzing the readers and communication situation, evaluating the illustration, and establishing editing goals.

An analysis of the visual and establishment of editing goals may begin with an understanding of readers' use of manuals and the goals of visuals. Readers of these particular illustrations will perform an unfamiliar task using familiar objects, a screwdriver and cassette tape. Representational visuals, in this case line drawings, make sense because readers must recognize the objects and the location of parts on the objects in order to complete the task. On the criteria of appropriateness and match of form, content, and purpose, this type of illustration is acceptable.

Readers look for shortcuts, and if they use the manual at all, they may try first to make sense of it just by looking at the pictures. An editor can be confident that some readers will do just that. Thus, the visual will have to be self-contained and self-explanatory.

Readers must be able to identify the objects and procedures in order to complete the task. The drawings and the type are large enough to read, and the white space around the separate parts both encourages attention to the visual and establishes the boundaries of the separate details, the way space between words establishes the boundaries of the words. The whole mechanism appears first, establishing the context for the specific parts that the cassette owner will manipulate. The cassette and screwdriver are easy to identify. Perspective is clear—the cassette does not stand on its end but rather lies on a horizontal plane, much the way a reader will hold it in order to complete the task. The device of circling indicates parts of the whole. Circling also clarifies that the scale for the illustration of the part is bigger than the scale for the whole. The callouts clearly attach to the part or process they identify.

Chances are your first impression is positive, especially if you compare this illustration mentally with cheaply produced and confusing instructions. However, the positive features of the illustration— appropriateness of the concept, easy recognition of items, use of space, overall attractiveness—may actually interfere with a more substantive evaluation of whether the readers will get accurate, usable information. The substantive evaluation will need to consider other features, such as the relationship of text and visuals, the arrangement of information, and the emphasis and details.

Figure 14.4
Part of an Owner's Manual
for Using a Cassette Player

The form suits the content and purpose. Objects are easily identified, sequence clarifies the part-whole relationship, and circling identifies parts and a shift in scale. Editorial analysis reveals some problems, however.

Safeguard Against Accidental Erasing

Every time a recording is made, the sound previously recorded is erased. The cassette and the recorder are equipped with a special device to safeguard valuable recordings from being erased accidentally. On the back of the cassette on either side are two lugs. If you want to be sure that a recording cannot be accidentally erased, break out these lugs with a knife. If only one track is to be protected, break out the lug to the left when the tape is in position for using that track. When the lug is broken out, the RECORD switch cannot be depressed.

To record on a cartridge in which the lug has been broken, place a piece of tape over that area and proceed as in the instructions for Recorder.

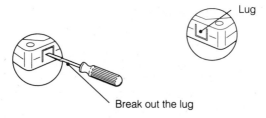

Lug for side 2

Lug for side 1

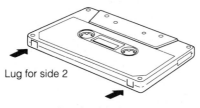

Lug

Break out the lug

Cover with tape

- **Relationship of text and visuals.** Because of the relationship of text and visuals, they cannot be edited in isolation. As editor, you must check on the verbal and spatial correspondence between the two. That is, you will make sure the text and the visual convey the same message, that they use the same terms, and that location on the page indicates the relationship of text and visual.

  Note, for example, that the text and illustration do not correspond in some terminology. The text directs the owner to use a knife to break out the lugs, but the visual illustrates a screwdriver. The text refers to protecting "tracks," but the illustration refers to "sides." The device is called both a "cassette" and a "cartridge." The reference to "Recorder" in the last line may misdirect readers. You cannot tell from the selection illustrated here, but the heading that follows the illustration is "Cassette Tape Player/Recorder." Thus, readers may assume that the next section provides the instructions for recording. In fact, the instructions appear three columns back, identified by a buried (indented) heading "Recorder." The potential for confusion could be eliminated by retitling the appropriate section "How to Record."

  The terms in the visual must also parallel terms in the "unwritten text," the terms readers use in referring to the items in the visual. "Lug" may not be the best choice of words. It may be technically correct, but more readers will recognize *tab*. Similarly, blank tapes typically identify the sides by letters rather than by numbers. Readers, relating the visual to the objects in their hands, may more readily recognize sides A and B than sides 1 and 2. Terms should be edited to match in the text and the visual.

- **Arrangement.** The structure of the illustration is to move from definition of parts to steps for completing the process. The two instructions "Break out the lug" and "Cover with tape" suggest a two-part procedure. However, readers who follow the steps literally will defeat their purpose because the tape simply replaces the tab. Additional words are necessary in the callouts or as headings to indicate that the second step reverses the first rather than completing it.

  To prevent erasure
  Break out the tab

  To record after the tab has been removed
  Cover the opening with tape

Another possibility to show the relationships of steps would be to place the paragraph about recording on a cartridge in which the lug has been broken between the "break out" and "cover" steps. Figure 14.5 depicts this arrangement.

Continuing the check for arrangement, we consider the orientation of the illustrations in relationship to the way the objects will be used by readers. A good feature of the illustration is the orientation for the "break out the lug" step. The screwdriver and cassette are positioned in the illustration to emulate the actual position if a right-handed owner performs this step. Thus, the orientation is accurate for about 85 percent of owners. The illustration of the cassette, however, shows the opposite orientation. If readers begin literally or mentally with the orientation they see in the first illustration, they will have to reorient the cassette. Perhaps the orientation shift will not confuse readers for this simple procedure, but readers working with complex objects and unfamiliar procedures, such as assembling complex equipment, may be confused by arbitrary shifts. The cassette should be rotated in the first illustration to emulate a reader holding it in his or her left hand.

- **Emphasis and details.** A check for emphasis and details also reveals some problems. The two procedures receive equal emphasis, yet the first procedure is the more essential one. Separating these steps visually, as suggested previously, will also solve the emphasis problem by clarifying the separate aims, one of which is more important than the other.

The illustration is confusing because owners who wish to safeguard just one side of the tape will have to work to interpret which lug to break out. If side 1 faces up in the illustration, the designation of side 1 and side 2 lugs is correct, but if side 2 faces up, they are backwards. The words in the text help, but they may not be read: "Break out the lug to the left when the tape is in position for using that track." Not all users know when the tape is in position for using the track, especially for machines in which insertion is horizontal rather than vertical. Furthermore, the information about playing position is unnecessary (and therefore gives too much detail).

Marking the cassette in the illustration "side A" will simplify the interpretation of which tab protects which side. The instructions could read: "To protect side A, break out the tab to the left as side A faces you with the label at the top. Break out the opposite tab for side B."

Figure 14.5
Rearrangement of Text
and Illustrations

Separation of the two procedures with text helps to clarify that the procedures are not steps in sequence.

Safeguard Against Accidental Erasing

Every time a recording is made, the sound previously recorded is erased. The cassette and the recorder are equipped with a special device to safeguard valuable recordings from being erased accidentally. On the back of the cassette on either side are two lugs. If you want to be sure that a recording cannot be accidentally erased, break out these lugs with a knife. If only one track is to be protected, break out the lug to the left when the tape is in position for using that track. When the lug is broken out, the RECORD switch cannot be depressed.

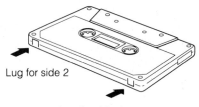

Lug for side 2

Lug for side 1

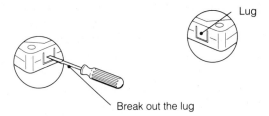

Lug

Break out the lug

To record on a cartridge in which the lug has been broken, place a piece of tape over that area and proceed as in the instructions for Recorder.

Cover with tape

In the illustration, the tabs are inaccurately attached to the cassette. The U shape indicates three open sides. On three major brands of cassette tapes, the tabs are attached on the opposite side from those in the illustration. Top and bottom may matter little in this situation, but they can matter quite a lot in other illustrations. Imagine an illustration showing the "on" and "off" positions for a switch in reverse position.

Figure 14.6 shows the edited illustration and text. The text has been simplified so as to follow principles of good style and to work better with the visual. The reference to the "special device" is deleted because it is unnecessary and prompts readers to locate something that is never referred to again.

The original illustration has a number of positive features, and because it *looks* good, editors may assume that it *is* good. Because of the easy identification of items and the attractiveness, it would be difficult to anticipate, on first observation, that problems would arise. The discovery of the problems is a chainlike process that begins with imagining a reader using the illustration. When some obvious problems emerge, an editor looks further, guided by principles of good communication, such as accuracy, consistency, and patterning instructions according to patterns of learning and use, as well as by the specific checks in the substantive editing of visuals. The check of the mechanism itself results from the confusion over which tab to break out for a given side of the cassette.

Does the editing really matter? Owners can probably determine by trial and error which tab to break to protect a given side, and common sense may tell them that taping a hole just created is counterproductive. However, good instructions should prevent the need for trials by ensuring that owners do the job right on the first attempt. Otherwise, we'd just leave owners to their own devices to begin with and skip the manual. A few editorial emendations can save interpretation time and prevent errors. The gains from emendations such as those made here would be proportionately greater with a more complex procedure. In more complex procedures, a reader does not so readily correct a simple misstep or make the adjustments in orientation required to do the job correctly.

PREPARING VISUALS FOR PRINT

The task of editing visuals may include selecting photographs and noting instructions for printing as well as deciding about form and content. The instructions relate to reductions and enlargements, cropping, redrawing, and halftones for photographs.

You may recommend reductions and enlargements to fit the visual in the available space, to indicate emphasis, and to ensure readability. Some-

Figure 14.6
Edited Instructions

Text and illustrations are parallel. The cassette is rotated to correspond to the mechanism in use and to subsequent illustrations. Words clarify which side of the cassette faces up so that the owner can select the correct tab. Headings identify the two procedures as separate steps.

Safeguard Against Accidental Erasing

A recording erases the sound previously recorded. To prevent accidental erasure by a new recording, you can break out the tabs on the back of the cassette with a screwdriver. To protect the recording on only one side of the tape, break out the tab to the left when the label for that side faces you and the label is at the top. When the tab is broken out, the RECORD switch cannot be depressed. To record on a cassette after the tab has been broken, place a piece of tape over that area and proceed as in the instructions in the section "How To Record."

Protective tabs

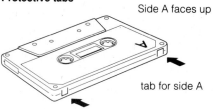

Side A faces up

tab for side A

tab for side B

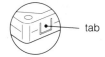

tab

To prevent erasure

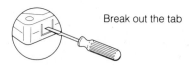

Break out the tab

To record after the tab has been removed

Cover the opening with tape

times reduction will improve the quality of photographs and line drawings by de-emphasizing irregular or broken details in the original. Be sure, however, to consider the legibility of the type as well as of the illustration itself. The amount of reduction or enlargement may be expressed as a percentage, but it is easier to communicate the desired dimensions by specifying one of the measurements, for example, "reduce to 18 picas wide." The reduction in height will be proportionate. (A **pica** is a printer's measure, equivalent to about one-sixth of an inch.)

Cropping means cutting off a portion of an illustration. The effect will be a reduction, but instead of an overall reduction, part of the length or width or both is removed. A cropped illustration can subsequently be enlarged or reduced. Cropping serves both to center and to emphasize the focal point of the illustration. Cropping removes extraneous borders or details so that the visual focuses on the important information. Figure 14.7 illustrates reduction and cropping. Both procedures reduce the size, but they do so in different ways and with different objectives.

Some visuals will be submitted in rough sketch form and will need to be drawn by an artist or computer specialist. These visuals will require marking for copy clarification (e.g., labels and callouts) and for size and type of drawing.

Photographs and shaded drawings, unlike drawings made with black lines, must be converted to **halftones** before printing. That is because ink prints in one color rather than in shades. A halftone, made by photographing the original through a screen, converts the shadings into dots of various sizes and density. Large dots densely grouped create the image of a dark shade while small dots well spaced create a light shade. The dots are printed, but most viewers will not recognize the dot composition.

Visuals are handled in printing separately from text. Thus, they should be separated from the typescript and marked with the instructions. Because some visuals require special treatment, unless they are submitted in camera ready form, they should be handled early in the production process so that they will not hold up the text.

EDITING VISUALS WITH COMPUTERS

Computers and graphics programs have enabled writers and editors to prepare high-quality visuals that previously would have been drawn by an artist. Three types of programs are especially useful. One is a graphics package that allows a user to draw. Some of these packages allow you to draw freehand; others are more oriented to geometric shapes. Some permit rotating and shading objects. The ability to expand, shrink, and crop graphics is a valuable one for editors.

A second useful program is an electronic clip art, or *click art,* pro-

Figure 14.7
Reducing and
Cropping Visuals

Top, the original; lower right, reduced; lower left, cropped and enlarged.

gram. It includes ready-made illustrations of a variety of subjects that can be pasted electronically into your document. These programs vary in quality as well as in subject matter, so check the examples before you choose one.

If you prepare a lot of graphs, you will appreciate a program that automatically converts numeric data to the type of graph you specify. You can feed numbers into the program and instruct it to create, say, a circle graph. Some of these programs are combined with spreadsheets and databases so that you can use numbers already entered in a file to create the graph.

Hardware should include a high-quality printer, preferably a laser printer. A scanner may also be useful, because it will allow you to create a halftonelike print of a photograph. You could also use a scanner to convert a line drawing to an electronic file and then modify the file with a graphics program.

A word processing program in which graphics can be inserted easily or a page layout program will help you integrate text and graphics.

SUMMARY

Visuals communicate according to the same principles by which prose communicates. In technical documents, visuals convey information, support the text, and enable action. The appropriateness of the type of visual depends on the content and the purpose of the visual. Editors also consider the arrangement of visuals in the text and of details within the visual; emphasis and details; perspective, size, and scale; and relationship to the text. Editors can evaluate visuals and suggest improvements even if they are not trained artists.

FURTHER READING

Judith Butcher. 1981. *Copy-Editing: The Cambridge Handbook,* 2nd ed. Cambridge: Cambridge University Press. See especially Chapter 4, "Illustrations."

Sam Dragga and Gwendolyn Gong. 1989. *Editing: The Design of Rhetoric.* Farmingdale, NY: Baywood.

A. J. MacGregor. 1979. *Graphics Simplified: How to Plan and Prepare Effective Charts, Graphs, Illustrations, and Other Visual Aids.* Toronto: University of Toronto Press.

Frank R. Smith. 1973. "Editing Technical Illustrations." *Journal of Technical Writing and Communication* 3: 177–204.

Edward R. Tufte. 1983. *The Visual Display of Quantitative Information.* Cheshire, CN: Graphics Press.

DISCUSSION AND APPLICATION

1. The tax table on page 334 comes from the IRS manual for completing an income tax return. After a person determines taxable income, he or she locates the tax due according to filing status. Identify ways in which the table conveys information, supports the text (the instructions in the manual), and enables action.

1989 Tax Table—Continued

23,000 – 25,000

At least	But less than	Single	Married filing jointly *	Married filing separately	Head of a household
23,000					
23,000	23,050	4,036	3,454	4,435	3,454
23,050	23,100	4,050	3,461	4,449	3,461
23,100	23,150	4,064	3,469	4,463	3,469
23,150	23,200	4,078	3,476	4,477	3,476
23,200	23,250	4,092	3,484	4,491	3,484
23,250	23,300	4,106	3,491	4,505	3,491
23,300	23,350	4,120	3,499	4,519	3,499
23,350	23,400	4,134	3,506	4,533	3,506
23,400	23,450	4,148	3,514	4,547	3,514
23,450	23,500	4,162	3,521	4,561	3,521
23,500	23,550	4,176	3,529	4,575	3,529
23,550	23,600	4,190	3,536	4,589	3,536
23,600	23,650	4,204	3,544	4,603	3,544
23,650	23,700	4,218	3,551	4,617	3,551
23,700	23,750	4,232	3,559	4,631	3,559
23,750	23,800	4,246	3,566	4,645	3,566
23,800	23,850	4,260	3,574	4,659	3,574
23,850	23,900	4,274	3,581	4,673	3,581
23,900	23,950	4,288	3,589	4,687	3,589
23,950	24,000	4,302	3,596	4,701	3,596
24,000					
24,000	24,050	4,316	3,604	4,715	3,604
24,050	24,100	4,330	3,611	4,729	3,611
24,100	24,150	4,344	3,619	4,743	3,619
24,150	24,200	4,358	3,626	4,757	3,626
24,200	24,250	4,372	3,634	4,771	3,634
24,250	24,300	4,386	3,641	4,785	3,641
24,300	24,350	4,400	3,649	4,799	3,649
24,350	24,400	4,414	3,656	4,813	3,656
24,400	24,450	4,428	3,664	4,827	3,664
24,450	24,500	4,442	3,671	4,841	3,671
24,500	24,550	4,456	3,679	4,855	3,679
24,550	24,600	4,470	3,686	4,869	3,686
24,600	24,650	4,484	3,694	4,883	3,694
24,650	24,700	4,498	3,701	4,897	3,701
24,700	24,750	4,512	3,709	4,911	3,709
24,750	24,800	4,526	3,716	4,925	3,716
24,800	24,850	4,540	3,724	4,939	3,724
24,850	24,900	4,554	3,731	4,953	3,735
24,900	24,950	4,568	3,739	4,967	3,749
24,950	25,000	4,582	3,746	4,981	3,763
25,000					
25,000	25,050	4,596	3,754	4,995	3,777
25,050	25,100	4,610	3,761	5,009	3,791
25,100	25,150	4,624	3,769	5,023	3,805
25,150	25,200	4,638	3,776	5,037	3,819
25,200	25,250	4,652	3,784	5,051	3,833
25,250	25,300	4,666	3,791	5,065	3,847
25,300	25,350	4,680	3,799	5,079	3,861
25,350	25,400	4,694	3,806	5,093	3,875
25,400	25,450	4,708	3,814	5,107	3,889
25,450	25,500	4,722	3,821	5,121	3,903
25,500	25,550	4,736	3,829	5,135	3,917
25,550	25,600	4,750	3,836	5,149	3,931
25,600	25,650	4,764	3,844	5,163	3,945
25,650	25,700	4,778	3,851	5,177	3,959
25,700	25,750	4,792	3,859	5,191	3,973
25,750	25,800	4,806	3,866	5,205	3,987
25,800	25,850	4,820	3,874	5,219	4,001
25,850	25,900	4,834	3,881	5,233	4,015
25,900	25,950	4,848	3,889	5,247	4,029
25,950	26,000	4,862	3,896	5,261	4,043

26,000 – 28,000

At least	But less than	Single	Married filing jointly *	Married filing separately	Head of a household
26,000					
26,000	26,050	4,876	3,904	5,275	4,057
26,050	26,100	4,890	3,911	5,289	4,071
26,100	26,150	4,904	3,919	5,303	4,085
26,150	26,200	4,918	3,926	5,317	4,099
26,200	26,250	4,932	3,934	5,331	4,113
26,250	26,300	4,946	3,941	5,345	4,127
26,300	26,350	4,960	3,949	5,359	4,141
26,350	26,400	4,974	3,956	5,373	4,155
26,400	26,450	4,988	3,964	5,387	4,169
26,450	26,500	5,002	3,971	5,401	4,183
26,500	26,550	5,016	3,979	5,415	4,197
26,550	26,600	5,030	3,986	5,429	4,211
26,600	26,650	5,044	3,994	5,443	4,225
26,650	26,700	5,058	4,001	5,457	4,239
26,700	26,750	5,072	4,009	5,471	4,253
26,750	26,800	5,086	4,016	5,485	4,267
26,800	26,850	5,100	4,024	5,499	4,281
26,850	26,900	5,114	4,031	5,513	4,295
26,900	26,950	5,128	4,039	5,527	4,309
26,950	27,000	5,142	4,046	5,541	4,323
27,000					
27,000	27,050	5,156	4,054	5,555	4,337
27,050	27,100	5,170	4,061	5,569	4,351
27,100	27,150	5,184	4,069	5,583	4,365
27,150	27,200	5,198	4,076	5,597	4,379
27,200	27,250	5,212	4,084	5,611	4,393
27,250	27,300	5,226	4,091	5,625	4,407
27,300	27,350	5,240	4,099	5,639	4,421
27,350	27,400	5,254	4,106	5,653	4,435
27,400	27,450	5,268	4,114	5,667	4,449
27,450	27,500	5,282	4,121	5,681	4,463
27,500	27,550	5,296	4,129	5,695	4,477
27,550	27,600	5,310	4,136	5,709	4,491
27,600	27,650	5,324	4,144	5,723	4,505
27,650	27,700	5,338	4,151	5,737	4,519
27,700	27,750	5,352	4,159	5,751	4,533
27,750	27,800	5,366	4,166	5,765	4,547
27,800	27,850	5,380	4,174	5,779	4,561
27,850	27,900	5,394	4,181	5,793	4,575
27,900	27,950	5,408	4,189	5,807	4,589
27,950	28,000	5,422	4,196	5,821	4,603
28,000					
28,000	28,050	5,436	4,204	5,835	4,617
28,050	28,100	5,450	4,211	5,849	4,631
28,100	28,150	5,464	4,219	5,863	4,645
28,150	28,200	5,478	4,226	5,877	4,659
28,200	28,250	5,492	4,234	5,891	4,673
28,250	28,300	5,506	4,241	5,905	4,687
28,300	28,350	5,520	4,249	5,919	4,701
28,350	28,400	5,534	4,256	5,933	4,715
28,400	28,450	5,548	4,264	5,947	4,729
28,450	28,500	5,562	4,271	5,961	4,743
28,500	28,550	5,576	4,279	5,975	4,757
28,550	28,600	5,590	4,286	5,989	4,771
28,600	28,650	5,604	4,294	6,003	4,785
28,650	28,700	5,618	4,301	6,017	4,799
28,700	28,750	5,632	4,309	6,031	4,813
28,750	28,800	5,646	4,316	6,045	4,827
28,800	28,850	5,660	4,324	6,059	4,841
28,850	28,900	5,674	4,331	6,073	4,855
28,900	28,950	5,688	4,339	6,087	4,869
28,950	29,000	5,702	4,346	6,101	4,883

29,000 – 31,000

At least	But less than	Single	Married filing jointly *	Married filing separately	Head of a household
29,000					
29,000	29,050	5,716	4,354	6,115	4,897
29,050	29,100	5,730	4,361	6,129	4,911
29,100	29,150	5,744	4,369	6,143	4,925
29,150	29,200	5,758	4,376	6,157	4,939
29,200	29,250	5,772	4,384	6,171	4,953
29,250	29,300	5,786	4,391	6,185	4,967
29,300	29,350	5,800	4,399	6,199	4,981
29,350	29,400	5,814	4,406	6,213	4,995
29,400	29,450	5,828	4,414	6,227	5,009
29,450	29,500	5,842	4,421	6,241	5,023
29,500	29,550	5,856	4,429	6,255	5,037
29,550	29,600	5,870	4,436	6,269	5,051
29,600	29,650	5,884	4,444	6,283	5,065
29,650	29,700	5,898	4,451	6,297	5,079
29,700	29,750	5,912	4,459	6,311	5,093
29,750	29,800	5,926	4,466	6,325	5,107
29,800	29,850	5,940	4,474	6,339	5,121
29,850	29,900	5,954	4,481	6,353	5,135
29,900	29,950	5,968	4,489	6,367	5,149
29,950	30,000	5,982	4,496	6,381	5,163
30,000					
30,000	30,050	5,996	4,504	6,395	5,177
30,050	30,100	6,010	4,511	6,409	5,191
30,100	30,150	6,024	4,519	6,423	5,205
30,150	30,200	6,038	4,526	6,437	5,219
30,200	30,250	6,052	4,534	6,451	5,233
30,250	30,300	6,066	4,541	6,465	5,247
30,300	30,350	6,080	4,549	6,479	5,261
30,350	30,400	6,094	4,556	6,493	5,275
30,400	30,450	6,108	4,564	6,507	5,289
30,450	30,500	6,122	4,571	6,521	5,303
30,500	30,550	6,136	4,579	6,535	5,317
30,550	30,600	6,150	4,586	6,549	5,331
30,600	30,650	6,164	4,594	6,563	5,345
30,650	30,700	6,178	4,601	6,577	5,359
30,700	30,750	6,192	4,609	6,591	5,373
30,750	30,800	6,206	4,616	6,605	5,387
30,800	30,850	6,220	4,624	6,619	5,401
30,850	30,900	6,234	4,631	6,633	5,415
30,900	30,950	6,248	4,639	6,647	5,429
30,950	31,000	6,262	4,650	6,661	5,443
31,000					
31,000	31,050	6,276	4,664	6,675	5,457
31,050	31,100	6,290	4,678	6,689	5,471
31,100	31,150	6,304	4,692	6,703	5,485
31,150	31,200	6,318	4,706	6,717	5,499
31,200	31,250	6,332	4,720	6,731	5,513
31,250	31,300	6,346	4,734	6,745	5,527
31,300	31,350	6,360	4,748	6,759	5,541
31,350	31,400	6,374	4,762	6,773	5,555
31,400	31,450	6,388	4,776	6,787	5,569
31,450	31,500	6,402	4,790	6,801	5,583
31,500	31,550	6,416	4,804	6,815	5,597
31,550	31,600	6,430	4,818	6,829	5,611
31,600	31,650	6,444	4,832	6,843	5,625
31,650	31,700	6,458	4,846	6,857	5,639
31,700	31,750	6,472	4,860	6,871	5,653
31,750	31,800	6,486	4,874	6,885	5,667
31,800	31,850	6,500	4,888	6,899	5,681
31,850	31,900	6,514	4,902	6,913	5,695
31,900	31,950	6,528	4,916	6,927	5,709
31,950	32,000	6,542	4,930	6,941	5,723

* This column must also be used by a qualifying widow(er).

Continued on next page

2. The line drawing below* illustrates the cleaning of a stylus on a tonearm. The verbal instructions give more details. Discuss this visual in terms of the following:

The information conveyed

The appropriateness of the visual information

Match of form, content, and purpose

Emphasis and detail—are the important facts illustrated?

Perspective of the two circles

Relationship of text and visuals

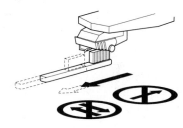

STABILIZER AND STYLUS CLEANING
To clean the Stabilizer, **use no fluids.** Use the brush supplied with the cartridge.
To clean the stylus, use the brush supplied with the cartridge with alcohol or an alcohol-distilled water solution.
Brush only from back to front as shown. Commercial cleaning solutions may cause stylus damage.

3. The following two columns of information are part of a brochure for members of a professional society.† It is a simple kind of annual report. Evaluate the text and graphs. Begin by analyzing the purpose of the information: What should readers know, and what should their attitude toward the organization be after reading this information? Evaluate the graphs according to the criteria identified in this chapter. Also consider the guidelines for copyediting visuals in Chapter 3. Suggest editing goals.

---

* Text and illustration courtesy of Shure Brothers Incorporated.

† Reprinted by permission of the Society for Technical Communication.

OPERATIONS

The Society promotes a wide variety of activities under the auspices of some 67 committees. The work of these committees ranges from developing professional standards and Society goals to planning for future directions of the Society, conference planning, membership analysis and needs, and publications. Each of these activities requires financial support, some of which is donated by individual members or corporate sponsors. The bulk of the costs, however, is supported by the Society. The chart below shows how our funds are spent. Other expenses—particularly dues, rebates to chapters, and office operations—account for the balance. Note that our costs exceed the income received from membership dues; dues received pay for 87.4 percent of our expenses.

EXPENSES

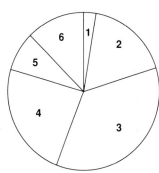

1	Miscellaneous	2.6 %
2	Member Dues Refund to Chapters	17.6 %
3	Office	35.7 %
4	Publications	23.6 %
5	Committees	8 %
6	Awards & Grants	12.5 %
	Total	100 %

Income to the Society comes primarily from four sources: dues, conferences, sale of publications and interest from investments. Income varies somewhat from year to year depending on the number of members, the success of the publications sales program, and the financial success of our annual conference. The Society has been fortunate to have had two well-managed and financially successful conferences back to back—Pittsburgh and Boston. The success of these conferences has significantly improved the net worth of the Society.

INCOME

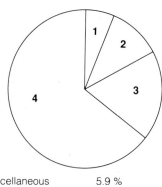

1	Miscellaneous	5.9 %
2	Publications	11 %
3	Conferences	18.4 %
4	Dues	64.7 %
	Total	100 %

A widely-accepted standard within the professional society community calls for reserves (net worth) of about three years operating expenses. During the past five years our net worth has improved from $163,600 to $399,071, an increase of $235,471. Since 1980, the increase has been $183,171. The last two conferences, with other factors, have significantly contributed to our present position of 1.3 years of reserve for our more than $300,000 annual budget. We cannot rely on the continual financial success of the conferences. Therefore, the Board has taken under consideration several options to improve our financial base. Increased membership is one of these options as is an increased technical exhibit at the conference. We have made significant strides and are taking the necessary actions to assure our continued financial stability.

PART IV MANAGEMENT AND PRODUCTION

15 COLLABORATING WITH WRITERS

A review of the literature on technical editing revealed that the most frequently discussed topic is establishing a productive working relationship between editor and writer. The journal articles and book chapters point to a pervasive conflict between editor and writer and seek ways to solve that problem. The proposed solutions usually relate to interpersonal skills.

The frequency with which this topic is discussed in the literature is surprising in a sense; one would think that the procedures of editing would be the more common topic. Perhaps the issue of the editor-writer relationship would not be so pervasive if the literature included more about editing effectively. The conflicts would diminish if the editing were always excellent. But in another sense, the frequency with which this issue is raised is not surprising. Editing requires contact with other people, and good work relationships are based on competence and professionalism. In addition, when people collaborate, they must place the demands of the task above their personal whims and their egos.

Effective editing requires the editor to win the trust and cooperation of the writer. This chapter gives some suggestions for how to do just that. It begins with a description of the relationship between editors and writers to explain why these relationships work or fail. It then identifies strategies of editing, management, and interpersonal skills to make the relationships work. It also offers suggestions for how and when to phrase queries to writers, how to conduct editor-writer conferences, and how to compose letters of transmittal to writers.

THE EDITOR-WRITER RELATIONSHIP

Like other interpersonal relationships, the relationship between editor and writer may be positive and marked by cooperation, or it may be negative and marked by conflict and stress. Why should editors and writers cooperate? They both have something to gain from such a relationship. They may gain personally from having a positive work experience. But they also gain professionally: working as partners—collaborating—they can produce a better document than either could alone. Both editor and writer work on behalf of readers.

Sometimes writers can be described most accurately as researchers or subject matter specialists. They may have no special training in language or document design. Editors provide that expertise. Even when writers are expert writers, editors provide a different, perhaps more objective point of view about a document. Editors benefit from the writer's subject matter expertise and from the writer's research to generate the text. The collaborative ideal results from the realities of different specializations.

Relationships fail for three reasons: poor editing, poor management, and oversized egos. Writers have no reason to respect incompetent editors, and they justifiably resent unnecessary or incorrect intervention in a text. Stress in editor-writer relationships will be caused by unnecessary delays in work by either writer or editor or by poor communication among all the members of the production team. Writers and editors may place their egos above the more important goal of making the document work for readers. A writer may regard every editorial comment as personal criticism and become defensive or even reject the editing. An editor may regard the writer as an inferior and develop a contemptuous attitude that only encourages defensiveness.

Ernest Mazzatenta, former president of the Society for Technical Communication, has collected statements from writer-researchers about what they like and dislike about editors. They are representative of statements offered by hundreds of scientists and engineers who have participated in his technical writing courses. These statements are paraphrased in the following lists.

What Writers Like Most About Editors

- Restructures the report so that the train of thought is smooth and logical.
- Points out ideas and explanations in the report that are not clear to the reader and then rewrites them.

- Catches misspelled words.
- Generally improves readability.
- Usually returns the paper within five working days.
- Approaches the writer considerately concerning any changes.
- Edits fairly promptly. Does it without malice.
- Shows patience.

What Writers Dislike Most About Editors

- Asks the writer to rewrite a section without giving any indication of what's wrong with it or any direction to take.
- Makes changes only to incorporate the editor's style of writing.
- Is somewhat conservative in that the editor suggests qualifiers and disclaimers to analyses that, in the writer's professional judgment, are excessive.
- Uses words that are not acceptable to the writer or others and won't change them.
- Replaces words with synonyms.
- Requires too many iterations (e.g., 10).
- Makes comments that are inconsistent with the department head's comments.

Relationships between editor and writer are potentially good—and potentially stressful. They can be characterized by collaboration or by competition. Editors and writers have choices about what type of relationship they will have, and editors especially can do much to create a productive working relationship.

STRATEGIES FOR WORKING WITH WRITERS

One place to begin in developing strategies for working with writers is to analyze the statements in likes/dislikes list. Note that most of the likes and dislikes concern editing per se (the editor's work with organization, spelling, and style). Others concern good management (promptness, coordination with a department head or other reviewer). A few imply personal qualities, such as consideration or stubbornness. The strategies discussed here parallel this classification of likes and dislikes.

Editing Effectively

Editing effectively is the most important thing you can do to make your relationship with a writer productive and cooperative. Part of effective editing involves collaborating with the writer to design the document for readers even before the first drafts are written. When the draft is written, you approach editing as a process of collaboration with the writer to make the document work for readers. If you focus on readers rather than on errors, writers will appreciate your rescuing them from writing clumsy or incoherent or inaccurate documents.

As this textbook has emphasized throughout, effective editing also requires you to be correct, objective, and sensitive to the needs of readers. You must base your emendations on known principles of effective communication rather than on your taste. You must restrict your changes to those that will make the document more comprehensible and usable. You must resist making changes simply to satisfy your own style unless you can articulate reasons why those changes will make the document better for readers. And when you do make changes, you must be sure you are right, and not make changes out of ignorance.

Writers are justifiably impatient, and even angry, when editors change their meaning. They are frustrated when editors simply change things to no apparent benefit. For example, one editor who edited instructions on Basic Life Support was disconcerted by the faulty parallelism in the ABCs of cardiopulmonary resuscitation (CPR). The list read: "Airway clear of obstructions, Breathing or ventilation, and Circulation by cardiac compression." So she changed the phrasing and gained parallelism—but lost the ABCs. The problem is that ABC is a mnemonic device taught in CPR classes nationwide. The instructions had to be re-edited (or unedited), and the editor had to rebuild her relationship with that writer. An effective editor knows the subject matter well enough to avoid introducing errors and knows the resources to check when content questions arise. These resources include subject matter dictionaries and handbooks as well as the writer.

Managing Efficiently
Efficient management saves time because the job gets done right the first time and does not have to be redone. Efficient management also respects production schedules and other people's deadlines. As editor, you can take a number of steps to ensure that the job is managed efficiently.

1. **Participate early.** If you can participate in the planning stage of the project, you and the writer and the team manager can agree on overall project goals from the start. This strategy helps to eliminate the conflict that arises when the editor enters the project at the end and has different ideas about the way it should have developed. Editing is conceptual and therefore part of the early stages of project development. The idea that editors are only fixers of errors at the end of development invites conflict.

2. **Clarify your expectations.** Guidelines should be available to writers before they write that cover usage, punctuation, and

spelling conventions (e.g., spelling of technical terms), documentation style, and format (e.g., headings, margins, spacing). These guidelines won't be as complete as the style sheet you prepare while editing because you won't be able to anticipate all the possible variations in style until you edit, but they can cover general ground. Guidelines save editing time because writers prepare the documents correctly. Figure 15.1 shows the guidelines for authors published in the front of every issue of *Technical Communication*. This page establishes standards for punctuation, style, manuscript preparation, and documentation. If your organization has a house style guide (see Chapter 3), make sure writers know about it and use it.

You should also reach an agreement with writers in advance on the assumptions about readers and purpose, illustrations (e.g., size, number, whether rough or ready for printing), and length. Write down these assumptions if necessary.

You can sometimes clarify expectations for content. If you know that a document will have to cover certain topics in a certain order, provide the outline. If some parts of the document will be **boiler plate,** that is, repetitions of existing text, include those sections with the outline. These aids can also prompt a writer to get started. The project may look manageable because something is already written.

A schedule is also necessary from the start, whether it is prepared by the editor or team leader or collaboratively. If you will need a document by a certain date in order for production to proceed on schedule, clarify that from the start. You may be justifiably irritated if you receive documents so late that you cannot do your job well, but you can also help to prevent that situation by establishing when you will need the various drafts. Estimate your time realistically, but be aware that people who are not editors underestimate how long it will take to edit. You have to educate them or they may abuse you innocently. (Scheduling and estimation of time are discussed in more detail in Chapter 18.)

3. **Work with the writer throughout development.** Ongoing collaboration follows from advance planning. If plans need to be adjusted for any reason, it's better to do so midway than to wait until the end. The initial plan for document development should establish some points of review after sections are complete but before the whole is finished. This plan keeps the writer on

Figure 15.1   Guidelines for Authors Submitting Articles to *Technical Communication.* Reprinted by permission of the Society for Technical Communication.

GUIDELINES FOR AUTHORS

CONTENT

Technical Communication publishes articles of professional interest to technical communicators—including writers, editors, artists, teachers, managers, consultants, and others involved in preparing technical documents. Before writing an article, look over several recent issues of the journal to make sure your topic and approach are appropriate for our readers.

Also, please look over the literature in the field and cite any relevant publications, so that your article builds on and extends previous work, if there is any. For example, see previous issues of the journal, the *Proceedings* of the annual International Technical Communication Conference, the IEEE's *Transactions on Professional Communication,* the *Journal of Technical Writing and Communication,* and appropriate textbooks.

STYLE

The purpose of *Technical Communication* is to inform, not impress. You should therefore write in a clear, informal style, avoiding jargon and acronyms. All decisions on style and usage should be guided by common sense: what is the most common, most clearly understandable way to present the information? Our authority on spelling and usage is *The American Heritage Dictionary;* on punctuation and format, the *Chicago Manual of Style.*

Avoid language that might be construed as sexist. The most common problem is use of gender pronouns in a way that implies sexual stereotyping, such as, "A writer delivers *his* completed sections to a secretary so *she* can type it." Easy ways to avoid this problem include using plurals ("Writers take their completed sections to secretaries for typing"), using second person if appropriate ("Take your completed section to the secretary for typing"), and recasting the sentence ("A secretary types each section as soon as the writer completes it").

MANUSCRIPT PREPARATION

Articles should usually not exceed 4000 words (about 16 double-spaced pages). They should be typed, either double- or triple-spaced, on one side only of good-quality paper. Please indent all paragraphs, and underline any words you want italicized. Number the pages, put your name *only on a cover sheet* to permit copies to be sent anonymously to referees, and submit three complete copies.

Journal format allows three levels of headings for paragraphs or sections of your article:

MAJOR HEADING	(all caps, on a line by itself)
Minor Headings	(initial caps, on a line by itself)
Sub-headings.	(initial caps only, in italics, as part of the first line of the paragraph)

Illustrations should be camera ready (just the way you want to see them in the journal). Submit one reproducible, plus two photocopies if the art is not reproduced in the text. Please keep in mind the limited space we have—most illustrations will be printed 14, 21, or 29.5 picas wide (approximately 2⁵⁄₁₆, 3½, or 4⅞ inches), although the full page width of 45 picas (7⅜ inches) is used on occasion. If your art is prepared oversize, allow for reduction in choosing type size and line widths.

Number figures and tables in separate sequences, using Arabic numerals. *List figure captions on a separate page.* In the text, be sure to refer to all figures and tables by number, and discuss the important features or summarize the message of each. (But don't, for example, simply repeat the numbers from a table.)

Also include a biographical sketch (approximately 100 words) of yourself and similar sketches of any co-authors. If your article is selected for publication, we will request an ASCII version of the text or a diskette prepared with any standard word processor if you can supply it. We will also ask for a glossy black-and-white photo of you and any co-authors.

Before submitting your manuscript, *please proofread it carefully.*

REFERENCES, NOTES, AND BIBLIOGRAPHY

References and notes are identified in the text by sequential bracketed numerals, except that the original numeral is used when the same source is cited again. In such cases the brackets should include the page number of the cited material: [2,156]. All references and notes are then listed in numerical order at the end of the article in *Chicago Manual of Style* format:

1. Bergan Evans and Cornelia Evans, *A Dictionary of Contemporary American Usage* (New York: Random House, 1957), 387-88.	*Book*
2. Don Bush, "The Passive Voice Should be Avoided—Sometimes," *Technical Communication* 28, no. 1 (First Quarter 1981): 19-20.	*Article in a professional or scholarly journal*
3. "Hurtling Through the Void," *Time,* 20 June 1983, 68.	*Article in a popular magazine or newspaper*
4. Paul M. Postal, "On So-called Pronouns in English," in *Readings in English Transformational Grammar,* ed. Roderick A. Jacobs and Peter S. Rosenbaum (Waltham, Mass.: Ginn and Company, 1970), 57.	*Article in an anthology or conference proceedings*

Sources listed as references do not need to be repeated in a bibliography. If, however, you wish to include a bibliography of other related sources, arrange the entries in alphabetical order, again using *Chicago Manual of Style* format:

Fowler, H.W. *A Dictionary of Modern English Usage.* 2nd ed. Revised and edited by Sir Ernest Gowers. New York and Oxford: Oxford University Press, 1965.	*Book*
Held, Julie Stusrud. "Teaching Writers How to Write: What Works?" *Technical Communication* 30, no. 2 (Second Quarter 1983): 17-19.	*Article in a professional or scholarly journal*
Lu, Cary. "Second-generation Microcomputer Report." *High Technology,* June 1983, 28-30.	*Article in a popular magazine or newspaper*
Creager, Cynthia. "Format Design: Help Your Readers Use Your Manuals." In *Proceedings* of the 30th International Technical Communication Conference, pp. W & E 147-150. Washington, D.C.: Society for Technical Communication, 1983.	*Article in an anthology or conference proceedings*

Note: Some regular columns—such as Book Reviews and Recent and Relevant—use other formats that are better suited to their purposes. Contact the column editor for guidelines.

COPYRIGHTS

The Society for Technical Communication holds the copyright on all material published in *Technical Communication.* (The Society grants republication rights to authors on request.) If your article has been previously published or presented elsewhere, please tell us when you submit your manuscript.

ADDRESS FOR SUBMITTING ARTICLES

All manuscripts and correspondence should be sent to
Dr. Frank R. Smith, Editor
Technical Communication
910 Milldale Drive
St. Louis County, MO 63011

schedule, but it also allows rethinking of the plan before too much writing is complete.

4. **Don't surprise.** Share your plans for editing with the writer. If it is understood that you will edit only for spelling, consistency, grammar, and punctuation, don't surprise the writer with elaborate revisions of style and format. And, if you change your mind about your editing plans, have good reasons for doing so, and discuss your thinking with the writer before you show him or her a document smeared with red pencil marks.

   If you plan extensive revision, it is a good idea to discuss the plans before you do revise or ask the writer to revise. You can also prepare a writer for bad news. In a phone call you might say, "I had to reorganize extensively." Then, when the document arrives, the writer expects reorganization, which may not look so ominous as he or she feared. Give the writer a chance to review the editing early enough in production to make changes. It's not fair or efficient to edit heavily and then show the writer the edited version only after it has been set in page proofs and cannot be changed.

5. **Be prompt.** Keep your expectations for yourself as high as for others. Get your work done on time. To avoid misunderstanding, let others know in advance when you will complete the work, and keep them informed about necessary schedule revisions.

Developing an Attitude
of Professionalism

Even if the writer is not good at writing, you can respect the person and his or her expertise in other areas. You can focus on the task rather than on the person. Assume that your goals and the writer's are mutual: to make the document work for its readers and purpose. Assume that you are players on the same team, not that you are an expert correcting an incompetent.

You can encourage professionalism in writers by setting an example. Complete your work on time and be prompt for meetings. Even language, dress, and posture can communicate your attitude toward your job and to your colleagues. Flexibility and good humor can help as well. If the writer's choices are as good as yours, or if they are relatively unimportant, you can yield. That doesn't mean you have to compromise on principles of good writing, but you can recognize that to risk a relationship or an entire project for a comma or variant spelling is to misorder your priorities.

Sometimes you will be wrong. You will misinterpret information or emphasis, and you will miss some errors. The review of edited copy by the writer acknowledges the possibility of editorial error. (In fact, the review should be seen in that light rather than as a time to show the writer all the failings in the document.) The way you respond to someone who discovers imperfect editing will model the way you want writers to respond to you. If you are defensive and aggressive or try to blame someone else, you will encourage writers to respond in the same way to edited copy. You can be gracious. You can thank the writer for rescuing you from mistakes. You can say, "Now I understand," rather than accusing the writer of being unclear to begin with.

Clear, neat, and accurate marks show respect for the writer as reader of your marks and indicate your professional commitment to your task. You may even gain some psychological advantage by using a black or green pencil rather than a red one. Red reminds some writers of critical schoolteachers and blood. Be cautious, however, about choosing blue if you will need to photocopy the edited typescript as blue does not photocopy well.

THE EDITOR-WRITER CONFERENCE

A good working relationship requires frequent face-to-face meetings or, in the case of long-distance editing, contact by phone or letter. The way you manage yourself in these meetings will set the tone for your relationship. Conferences may occur for planning, progress reports, and review. The review conference, in which the edited document is examined or plans for further editing are made, is the most sensitive because of the potential for implied or real criticism.

Sometimes documents may be passed back and forth between writer and editor without a conference, and it saves time to do so. However, if the editing will be extensive, it may be better to plan a conference to talk about the changes than to surprise a writer with a heavily marked document.

Even if a meeting has the potential to generate tension, it is preferable to exchanging heavily edited documents without discussion. It allows for give and take—the opportunity to question and clarify and to make nonverbal gestures of accommodation, such as nodding your head and smiling. You can make these conferences go well by organizing your comments, by using tactful and goal-oriented language, and even by arranging the furniture in a certain way.

Conference Purpose

As you plan for the conference and its organization, think of the overall goals. The purpose of the conference is to clarify the next steps in document development. All conferences should result in some agreement and understanding among collaborators, arrived at through information sharing and negotiation. Planning and review conferences should end with understanding and clarification of goals, tasks, responsibilities, and schedule.

Some editors use the review conference as instruction time. That purpose distracts from the main conference purpose and from the focus on the document at hand. Instruction also demotes the writer to the role of student rather than colleague and collaborator. Save instruction for another setting, or limit it to responding to questions the writer asks. If you repeatedly edit one writer for persistent, correctable problems, it's quite reasonable to suggest a time for instruction. But don't mix instruction with the development and production of a specific document.

Conference Organization
A conference is a form of communication, just as a printed or graphic document is. Thus, the conference should adhere to principles for effective communication, such as organization. Before you meet with the writer, you should have a plan in mind of what you want to address and the order in which you will cover it. Notes of topics you want to cover and pages to which they apply will help the conference proceed efficiently and with a minimum of fumbling. An organized conference should increase the writer's confidence in you as editor and manager. It will reflect your comprehension of the whole project as well as your respect for the writer's time.

An overview statement, like the introduction to a document, identifies the topic and goals of the conference and the order in which you will proceed. After the overview statement has been made, the conference should proceed in a coherent way. You may wish to organize by topic, perhaps asking questions about content and then offering comments about style. In a review conference, you may wish to proceed through the document from beginning to end, chronologically. The conference could reasonably end with suggestions for revision and a schedule.

Review of the
Edited Typescript
In a review conference, do not feel that you have to call attention to every emendation in the document. You do not have to initiate a conversation about all the punctuation changes, for example, but you should be prepared to explain them if the writer should ask. Your goals are to verify that your editing is correct and consistent with the overall document goals and, working with the writer, to establish the next steps in project development, whether revision or approval for continuing production. It is inefficient to plan a line-by-line review of the document in conference. A writer who is determined to consider each emendation may appreciate a copy of the edited document before the conference. He or she can then do a line-by-line review on his or her own time.

A heavily marked typescript may intimidate or alienate a writer and create defensiveness that can spoil the conference. Thus, you may prefer to retype heavily edited sections so that the writer sees a clean copy without marks. Especially if you are editing electronically, it is easy to prepare clean copy that makes the editing invisible. Policies in your organization may provide the answer to how much freedom you have to edit silently, that is, without marking the changes. Some organizations want all the editorial "tracks" to be evident so that a writer can check on each change to make sure the editor has not inadvertently introduced errors.

If policy and the writer's trust permit you to share clean rather than marked copy, three positive results can be achieved. First, a clean copy is less threatening than a marked one, so the egos of the writer and editor are less likely to interfere with the work of producing an effective document. Second, it will be easier to spot additional editing needs in a clean copy than in one in which the marks distract from reading. Finally, a clean copy will show the results of editing and demonstrate its value.

A compromise is to prepare sample clean pages to show substantive changes such as reorganization and reformatting. Keep a record of the original pages, though, so that you will be able to point to specific changes and, if necessary, to restore the original version.

The Language of Good Relationships

The words you choose, your nonverbal expressions, and the way you listen all affect how well a writer receives your messages. Your language can communicate a sense of collaboration, or it can communicate power and arrogance.

Active listening. One purpose of a review conference is information gathering. Thus, an important method of communication is listening. *Active* listening means drawing out the writer and working to understand his or her point of view. It contrasts with the pretense of listening while mentally formulating your own statements. If writer and editor listen to each other only superficially, the chances of real communication taking place are not good.

One strategy of active listening is to repeat or paraphrase something a writer says.

```
Are you saying, then, that...?
```

The echo of the writer's statement guards against misinterpretation. If your paraphrase is inaccurate, the writer can correct you. This strategy also forces you to listen carefully enough to repeat. An active listener also probes for more information when a writer expresses ideas incompletely. Encouraging and probing statements force the writer to elaborate.

```
Please go on.

What do you mean by...?
```

```
How will readers use this information?

How does this point relate to...?

Please explain how...
```

These are not statements to challenge the writer's competence, but ones that seek the information you need to complete the editing.

With active listening, you also encourage the writer to share and cooperate. You can show your interest with nonverbal signals (e.g., nodding your head, smiling, leaning forward) and with verbal signals (e.g., "I see," "uh-huh").

Positive language. The words you choose in the conference can encourage partnership or they can provoke defensiveness. Goal-oriented language will produce better results than will criticism. Consider a writer's probable response to different ways in which an editor may say the same thing.

Critical	*Goal-oriented*
wordy	Condensing the text will increase the chance that a person in an emergency will find the necessary information quickly.
poorly organized	The tasks are rearranged chronologically so that the crew will know when to do each one.

The goals (e.g., finding information in an emergency, knowing when to do the tasks) are explanations that show the editing to be purposeful rather than arbitrary. By contrast, critical language may derive from modeling inappropriately after composition teachers. An editor, like a teacher, must evaluate, but the evaluation is not an end in itself. It should suggest goals for revision based on reader needs.

Another way to emphasize document goals rather than resort to criticism is to use "I" statements when you may seem critical, but "you" statements when you are praising. "I" statements do not announce that you are stupid but rather that you are assuming the role of readers who may not have enough information.

`I don't understand how this example explains the`

`thesis.`
(not "You haven't been clear here.")

`I can't tell whether I should turn off the hard`

`drive or the monitor first.`
(not "Your instructions are incomplete.")

`You did a good job of interpreting the table.`
(good news)

Try to focus on neutral subjects—the document and the reader—rather than on the writer and editor.

One final caution: avoid words that suggest inappropriate editorial intervention, especially *change*. No writer wants to hear that you have "changed" his or her text. In fact, writers fear that editors will change the meaning. While polysyllabic euphemisms are generally undesirable stylistically, it may be better when dealing with a sensitive writer to substitute *emendation* for *change*.

Confidence. Your own confidence in your editing will encourage the writer's confidence. Wishy-washy comments can turn off writers as much as aggressive comments can. You should not apologize for your good suggestions and honest explorations, nor should you avoid making recommendations for fear of alienating a writer. Keep in mind that you and the writer are partners working on behalf of the readers.

Furniture Arrangement

Psychologists talk about nonverbal communication, such as the information we give by our posture and facial expressions. Similarly, arrangement of furniture in a room suggests the relationship between the people in the room. In figure 15.2, the "executive" arrangement, with an executive protected behind an imposing desk, suggests a relationship of superior to inferior. Such a relationship is inconsistent with the partnership of editor with writer, as well as being inefficient when writer and editor look at a document together. In this arrangement, editor and writer look at each other, perhaps confrontationally.

The "collaborators" arrangements, by contrast, place editor and writer in more equal positions, as partners. These arrangements allow editor and writer to look together at a document and therefore encourage the focus of the conversation on the document rather than on personalities. (See Rosemarie Arbur, cited in Further Reading.)

A conference room may be a better place to meet than the office of writer or editor. In the words of psychologists, it is more neutral territory.

Figure 15.2   Chair Arrangement for the Editor-Writer Conference

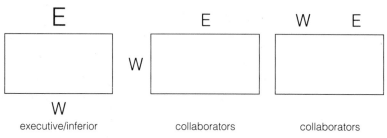

executive/inferior   collaborators   collaborators

Likewise, a table may be more appropriate than a desk that belongs to either the writer or the editor.

CORRESPONDENCE WITH WRITERS

Some of your comments to writers will be on paper or online rather than face to face. Especially when the editing requires no major changes but rather simple revisions and clarification of points of information, you can pass the edited document back to the writer without having to schedule a conference. Correspondence takes the form of queries written on or in the document and letters or memos of transmittal.

Queries

Whether you are working long distance with the writer or face to face, you will probably write queries to the writer on the document itself, in the margin if you are editing on hard copy or possibly in the text if you are editing electronically. Queries may be questions about content (e.g., "What is CLHM?"), they may ask for more information or for verification that an emendation is correct, or they may explain a substantive emendation, such as reorganization. It makes sense to place the queries right where the questions arise rather than just keeping a separate list. Even if you use the queries only in the review conference, they are helpful reminders of points you wish to discuss with the writer. (See Chapter 4 for a discussion of the mechanics of using query slips.)

The same principles of positive language that apply to conferences apply to queries. Evaluative comments, especially negative evaluations, are inappropriate because they do not direct the writers in revision. An occasional positive evaluation (e.g., "interesting" or "good") may be encouraging, but such comments—whether positive or negative—may imply that your goal has been evaluation of the writer's work rather than preparation of the document for publication.

You will be able to answer for yourself some questions that arise on first reading—by careful reading of the text or by checking other sources.

Don't query every little change or go running to writers when the answers are fairly obvious. You not only interrupt the writer's work with constant queries, you convey lack of confidence. Save the queries for points of information that you cannot determine on your own.

Letters of Transmittal

A letter or memo of transmittal with an edited draft, like any letter of transmittal, tells what the document is, what the writer should do with it, and when he or she should return it to the editor. A secondary purpose may be to motivate. The letter of transmittal is used for long-distance editing or for in-house editing when the writer will study the emendations before meeting with you.

The letter or memo may be transmitted on paper or online. The tone of the letter should be formal (though some situations may allow some informality), and the language should be in standard, high-quality English. Use the conventional letter or memo format, as the situation requires, and be sure to edit your own writing. You gain credibility as editor if your own writing meets the same standards you expect from other writers.

Like all letters, this one has a three-part structure paralleling the three purposes. The introduction is a statement of transmittal. The body of the letter explains the goal of editing and the goal of revision. The conclusion asks for a response. Figure 15.3 illustrates how a letter of transmittal might read.

Figure 15.3	Letter of Transmittal to a Writer

statement of transmittal

Here is the edited version of the first draft of your proposal for the pulse welding research project.

explanation of editing and request for revision

I have checked for accuracy of information and correctness of usage and punctuation. I have also verified that the format conforms to the RFP. Please check the editing, especially the rewording on pages 2 and 3. The numbers in the table on page 3 don't add up to the total shown, so please check to see whether the costs for each item are accurate or whether the addition is incorrect.

request for response

I will need the revised copy for final proofreading by July 2 if the proposal is to be mailed to meet the deadline. Call at extension 292 if you have questions.

Note the businesslike focus on the task at hand, not on evaluation. The statement of transmittal quickly orients the writer to this project, and the letter clarifies what he or she is to do. The emendations are explained in terms of purposes that the writer and editor share. The letter does not rehash every change the editor has made but calls attention to specific key points the writer must consider.

Writers should always have final review privileges. That is, you will not send an edited copy directly to production without inviting the writer to check for content and accuracy. By all means, you should call the writer's attention to editing where you had questions or revised substantially.

Make sure you know the expectations in your organization about leaving a record of editorial emendations before you edit away the original on a computer. Always keep a copy of the unedited original draft so that you can check it later if necessary.

SUMMARY

Good relationships with writers follow from good editing and good management as well as from good interpersonal skills. Good editing makes a document better, not just different and certainly not wrong. Good management means establishing expectations early, communication among all people involved with the project, and then promptness in completing work. Interpersonal skills and tactful communication encourage cooperation. The focus should be on the document, the task, and the reader rather than on the personalities of the writer or editor. If editor and writer collaborate, they create more effective documents than either could alone.

FURTHER READING

Rosemarie Arbur. 1977. "Student-Teacher Conference," *College Composition and Communication* 28:338–342.

Ernest Mazzatenta. 1975. "GM Research Improves Chemistry Between Science Writers, Editors." *Proceedings, 22nd International Technical Communication Conference.* Washington, DC: Society for Technical Communication.

Lola M. Zook, ed. 1975. *Technical Editing: Principles and Practices.* Washington, DC: Society for Technical Communication. See the chapters by Nelson A. Briggs, "Editing by Dialogue," and Eva P. Dukes, "The Art of Editing."

DISCUSSION AND APPLICATION

1. Consider the following case studies as topics for class discussion or journal entries.

   a. You are editing an anthology of 10 articles written by various subject matter experts. Part of your punctuation style is to use a comma before the final item in a series. When you return the edited copy to one writer who has omitted commas before the final item, he protests aggressively, challenges your knowledge, and threatens to withdraw the article from the collection unless you remove the commas you have inserted. What is your response? Before you decide finally how you will respond, think about your goals for the anthology.

b. You are a recent college graduate editing a research proposal for a senior staff member with a Ph.D. The proposal is full of academic jargon that you think may invite the proposal reviewers to smirk at the researcher rather than to respect her. You simplify some of the sentences and vocabulary. You return the proposal to the writer, who, in turn, delivers it to the typist. Later you learn from the typist that the writer has written on the copy, "Ignore the editorial comments. Type as originally written." You're furious at the put-down and the waste of your time; furthermore, you are convinced that the pretentious style will jeopardize funding. What do you do?

c. The writer whose work you are editing is a very nice person, but his writing is terrible. You can't understand many of the sentences, not because the subject matter is unfamiliar but because the construction is so bad. Frankly, you're appalled at the lack of writing skill, and you know your attitude is getting in the way of your work. What can you do?

d. For cases a, b, and c, identify specific ways in which efficient management might prevent the conflict.

2. Conduct editor-writer conferences in class and then answer the accompanying questions. Each student should bring a document he or she has written to a classmate for editing. The document should be in a technical rather than a creative genre. In a brief planning session, the writer explains to the editor the purpose and readers of the document and any particular editing needs that he or she has identified. The editor, in turn, may query the writer. If the document is substantial, the editing will take place out of class. After editing is complete, each student editor meets the writer for a review conference. After the conference, the writer evaluates the editing and the editing conference and makes suggestions for future conferences. These questions can be used for evaluation:

a. Consider the editing. Was it complete? Accurate? Objective? Did the editor overlook any editing needs? Was the editor too aggressive on some issues? Comment.

b. Consider the conference. Was it well organized? Did the editor clarify his or her plan for the conference at the beginning? Was the language goal oriented? Was the editor confident? How did you feel about being edited by this editor? Comment.

The exchange may work best if the writer is not also the editor of that writer's work.

3. Describe a specific example of each of the three strategies discussed here for productive working relationships: good editing, good management, interpersonal skills.

4. If you have had experience—good or bad—working as an editor with a writer or as a writer with an editor, analyze where the relationships succeeded or failed by considering editing skill and procedures, management, and interpersonal skills.

5. Think of ways to express these critical statements in a way to encourage productive revision. You will have to invent specific details.
   a. These sentences are awkward.
   b. The whole section of the report is unclear.
   c. The brochure is poorly organized.
   d. It's impossible to tell why the project you propose is important.

16 COMPUTERS AS EDITORIAL ASSISTANTS

Computers have enabled a revolution in both the procedures of editing and the scope of the editing job. Whereas documents were formerly written and edited on paper, computers enable electronic manipulation and transmission of the document. Whereas documents were formerly retyped at various stages of production (frequently with new errors introduced at each stage), the initial keyboarding by the writer may now suffice—with corrections—through printing. Whereas editors were mainly word experts who turned over typescripts to graphic designers and professional printers once the text was established, desktop publishing has given editors responsibilities for page design and document layout.

The changes are welcome because they relieve editors of some of the tedious aspects of editing, such as corrections of typos, and some of the time-consuming, expensive aspects of production, such as rekeyboarding. Graphics programs enable graphic artists to produce visuals in less time than they could on paper and even enable people with limited artistic training to produce some visuals. Desktop publishing enables small-budget publications to produce documents close to the quality previously reserved for professionally typeset publications. Computers are also a management tool, facilitating the tracking of documents.

The capacity of computers, however, has not automatically produced competence in users. Computers can be used to produce poor design as well as good design and confusing graphics as well as informative ones. An editor who does not understand principles of organization will do no better with substantive editing on the computer than on paper. Computers can hide editorial intervention, making it difficult for writers to guard against the introduction of errors by editors. Few programs are designed particularly for editors, and editors therefore must adapt programs to their own use. As with any new tool, enthusiasm must be tempered by a willingness to investigate the tool and to seek the training that the new technology and responsibilities may require.

This chapter reviews the types of editorial procedures for which the computer is a helpful assistant, including copyediting and substantive editing, graphics, design and production, and management. It reviews types of programs and hardware rather than specific programs. Editors who wish to purchase programs and hardware are advised first to define the functions they want to fulfill, then to consult sales representatives, other users, and printed reviews to identify possible programs and hardware, and finally to test the programs by trying each of the functions on the list of wants. To facilitate selection according to this procedure, the chapter is organized by editing functions rather than by types of programs.

COPYEDITING

Word processing programs enable electronic corrections. A writer using a word processing program can easily submit clean copy to begin with rather than copy marred by typos or by clumsy white-out and handwritten corrections. Even if you then edit on hard copy, you will not be distracted by superficial errors.

One prerequisite for using the computer in copyediting is that the document be available electronically. Ideally, the writer and editor work with the same word processing program and machine. If you edit in-house writers, you will probably work with the same brands of hardware and software. If writers submit work long distance, variations are more likely. In such a case, you may request that writers use a particular program and machine and that they submit a floppy disk along with the hard copy. Alternatively, you should have the capacity to convert the writer's file into one for your own software and hardware. Transmission of a document by way of a modem and phone line relies on standard characters that are not program specific. Thus, a document prepared with one program may be edited with another program. Conversion programs are also available to change a file prepared with one machine and program for use with others. For example, a document prepared on an IBM machine using 5¼-inch floppy disks may be converted for use on a Macintosh using 3½-inch disks.

You may be willing to accept hard copy only from the writer and to rekeyboard for copyediting, especially if you are using desktop publishing. Because the document will be keyboarded at the production stage anyway, it may be keyboarded early for use in copyediting.

Verbal Text Once copy is available electronically, you can copyedit using the delete and insert and the cut and paste functions of the word processor to correct the document. All word processing programs permit these procedures. If you are purchasing a word processing program to be used for editing as well as writing, consider the ease by which a user can delete, insert, cut, and paste copy.

Other types of programs are useful for copyediting, particularly spelling checkers and proofreading programs. Proofreading programs check, in addition to spelling, whether quote marks and parentheses have been closed and whether new sentences begin with a capital letter. Some word processing programs include spelling checkers. Programs dedicated to spelling checks are also available; a good electronic dictionary includes at least 80,000 words. A spelling checker useful for technical editors should allow users to add their own terms because the basic dictionary will omit many technical terms.

The checker should also require the user to approve any suggested changes. The newsletter *Simply Stated,* from the Document Design Center, reported in March 1989 the amusing results of a spelling change implemented by a computer. The Barclay Banks in England used a spelling checker on a document prepared for depositors. When the checker did not recognize "Barclay," it substituted "Broccoli." Depositors were confused — and amused — when they received correspondence from the Broccoli Bank!

All of these programs work by comparing data stored in the computer's memory with data in a user's active file. For example, when a spelling program encounters a string of letters enclosed by spaces, it searches its memory for a match. If the string of letters does not match any string in memory, it marks the word as misspelled. A proofreading program looks for a pair of parentheses or quote marks; if it finds only one, it prompts a user to insert the second part of the pair. If a program identifies a period and space (the signal that a new sentence begins), it checks to see if the next word is capitalized.

Programs can recognize signals of possible grammar problems, but they cannot identify for certain errors such as lack of subject-verb agreement or dangling modifiers. That is because sentence structures are so complex that huge amounts of computer memory would be required to store all the possible versions of typical grammar errors to be available for matching with the document in the computer's active file. For example, a *to be* verb followed shortly by a past participle might signal a dangling modifier; on the other hand, the construction might be grammatically correct. Thus, the programs that promise to find grammar errors need informed users to decide whether the errors are in fact present and how they should be corrected. If you are considering purchasing a program that promises to check grammar, test it out using text with typical grammar errors to judge how much it can really do.

Some programs provide online reference help such as a thesaurus or handbook. These programs do not automatically check your text as the spelling checker and proofreader do, but they are available for you to consult as you edit.

Quantitative and Technical Material

Quantitative and technical material requires detailed copyediting because of the spacing requirements and other special treatment of formulas and unusual symbols. When computers are not available, formulas and special symbols are often drawn by hand after the typing is complete. This task is time consuming, particularly when the document requires several revisions and the formulas must be drawn several times. Fortunately, a number of programs have been developed for preparing formulas and other technical material. (See Chapter 8.)

Indexes and Other Front and Back Matter

Computers can automatize the preparation of a table of contents, an index, and footnotes or endnotes. Some word processing programs will produce an index of key words and their page numbers and save substantially on the time it takes to produce an index manually. Automatic indexing is more reliable for name indexes than for subject indexes because the subjects may be broader than key terms suggest. Thus, automatic indexing is best supplemented by some human intervention, but it can provide a starting point.

Some programs will create a table of contents by printing out the headings in the document. Some will create a list of endnotes based on data you insert throughout the text. The alphabetizing capability of the sort function facilitates the preparation of any lists that need to be alphabetized, such as a glossary or list of references.

Risks and Responsibilities of Electronic Copyediting

One risk of electronic copyediting is that it may be wrong. An editor could substitute a term for one perceived as wrong, not knowing that an apparently misspelled word was just an unfamiliar one. The computer lets an editor make such changes without leaving tracks of the change. Proofreading and technical review may or may not catch such errors. Material may also inadvertently be cut and lost forever. To minimize such errors and losses, always keep dated hard copies of the original and edited versions. If a question arises about the wording on the original text, you can refer to it. Also, you should save the original and the edited versions in separate electronic files with backup copies—the original can be recalled if questions arise.

Some companies will require that you mark electronically or manually anything that you change rather than simply making the corrections. The copyedited electronic copy would thus look much like a copyedited hard copy. (Editorial trespass and keeping a record of editing changes are discussed in more detail later in the chapter.)

A second risk of electronic copyediting is that editors and writers may depend too completely on the computer's work. It is tempting to assume that the spelling check has found all spelling errors, but as you learned in Chapter 5, some words that the checker might approve as correct are wrong in their context. The capacity of computers to assist with copyediting does not yet eliminate the human editor's responsibility for reviewing the document although it can increase the accuracy and speed of that review.

SUBSTANTIVE EDITING

The computer can assist with editing for style, organization, and format as well as with copyediting. However, most editors use hard copy at least for the initial work of substantive editing. The computer screen encourages line-by-line editing or editing of small sections while substantive editing requires awareness of the whole document. It is easier to get a sense of the whole with hard copy because it is easier to see the whole when flipping through actual pages than when scrolling online.

As with any editing, you must be careful not to change the writer's meaning when you edit online. You have to take special care to preserve the meaning even if you edit for style, organization, and format. An online text is fragile because it can so easily be destroyed or lost. Before you plunge into changing an electronic file, learn the devices your computer provides for trying out changes and preserving multiple versions. For example, the split screen function will let you compare passages side by side. You can read closely to be sure your version improves the original without changing the meaning. (The issues of preserving the original and recording editorial intervention are discussed more fully in the section on editorial trespass.)

Style   Of the various types of substantive editing, style editing is probably the easiest to accomplish online because the work occurs at the sentence level. You will likely establish goals for editing the document for style by reading hard copy. Then you can use the insert, delete, and cut and paste functions of word processors to edit sentences to achieve such goals as using active voice and avoiding sexist terminology.

You can also use the change or the search and replace functions of word processing programs for some editorial changes. For example, you could tell the computer to change "he" to "he or she"; the computer would then locate each instance of "he." If you knew you wanted to change all instances (rather than, say, changing some to "they"), you could tell the computer to change all. Use the global change function cautiously, however. With some programs, you must be sure, for example, to indicate spaces around complete words or the "change all" direction could result in changes *within* words. The letters *he* appear within other words, such as "they." Unless you have specified spaces around "he," the computer will not discriminate between the letters as a whole word and the letters within other words. A change thus could result in "the or shey." Some programs allow you to indicate that a change affects whole words only.

Style analysis programs can identify such characteristics of style as passive voice, *to be* verbs, and wordy phrases. Like the spelling checker and proofreader programs, they work by matching words and phrases in the active file of the document with words and phrases stored in memory. They can also count number of words per sentence and calculate an average sentence length as well as count the average number of syllables per word. Their values are based on quantitative measures of "readability" as defined by such scales as Gunning's Fog Index. This index, and other readability scales like it, attempt to define the level of education required to read a given document according to values such as average sentence length. A style is "foggy" if it is too complex for the intended audience as defined by sentence and word length and other features such as passive voice.

Questions have been raised about the validity of readability scales for determining how well readers will comprehend. Janice Redish and Jack Selzer have nicely summarized the limits of readability formulas. (See the "Further Reading" section for further information on their analysis.) The quantitative measures overlook some other text features such as content, context, organization, and layout that powerfully influence whether a document can be understood. Furthermore, the scales have not been developed for, nor have they been tested on, technical documents. The measures that apply to textbooks for children may not apply to technical documents for adults. Finally, and perhaps most important, some of the underlying premises may be wrong. For example, the sentence "The elephant rode on the elevator" would be measured as more difficult than "There was a run on the bank" because of the multisyllabic words; yet a child could understand the first sentence more readily than the second one with its metaphoric use of "run."

Because the computerized style analysis programs are based on the principles of readability formulas, editors should be wary of trusting them too completely. They may be more useful to writers learning their own styles because they can identify habitual use of the passive voice and other potentially ineffective or erroneous stylistic devices.

Organization   The size of the computer screen may interfere with editing for organization online when the document is more than a few pages long. Major organizational changes (unlike paragraph changes) require awareness of the total document.

A good way to evaluate the organization of a document is to review its headings. Some word processing programs automatically generate an expanded table of contents by selecting the level-one and level-two headings. Even if your table of contents will include only chapter or section titles, you can use the table of contents function to generate an outline that will show how the document develops.

Once you have planned the details of reorganization, the computer is an excellent tool for manipulating the text with the cut and paste functions. With hard copy, an editor either makes marginal notes about where to move sections or literally cuts text to paste or tape where it is to be moved. However, these procedures create sloppy copy, as well as taking time. Furthermore, the reorganization is difficult to evaluate if reading requires flipping back and forth among pages. By contrast, electronic cut and paste yields a clean copy in which sections appear where they are intended to.

Format   Options for format available on the computer can increase both comprehension and ease of use. Editors can use variations in type style, such as italics and boldface, and variations in type size and typeface for emphasis and display copy. Assuming these choices are made judiciously (unlike those for the radio ad in figure 13.9), the document should be more readable than documents in which display copy is identified by underlining or capital letters.

Centering and right justification (i.e., aligning the right margin) are easy with computers. Some word processing programs permit multiple columns, footnotes at the bottom of the page, automatic page numbering, running heads, boxing of sections, and a mixture of graphics with the words. All of these devices may increase both the usefulness of the document and the attractiveness of the page.

If the editor sends documents on hard copy to a typesetter, he or she marks these format choices on the typescript. If the copy is transmitted electronically, the editor may enter the format choices into the file. That is, instead of marking a word to be set in italics, the editor may electronically convert the word to italic type.

The design specifications should be established before you begin to enter the format choices. You need to know, for example, whether second-level headings are set in 10-point or 12-point type and whether all the words or just the initial word is capitalized. A graphic designer may establish the design, but in small companies in which a graphic designer is not available, an editor may assume design responsibilities. That means editors must know something about effective formatting.

To format consistently, you keep the specifications at hand on a piece of paper or in an electronic file. You may also store electronic templates of basic pages, including margin setting and typeface, as well as standard headings, such as "Problem Statement" and "Recommendations." You then pull the template to use whenever you begin a new document or chapter.

Even better than these options for achieving format consistency is the **electronic style sheet,** a feature of powerful word processing programs. A style sheet in the context of word processing refers to format. (As discussed in Chapter 3 in reference to copyediting for consistency, a style sheet is the page a copyeditor creates to record choices in mechanical style for a document.) A *style* in word processing defines the appearance of text.

To define a style, you specify a font, type style (e.g., boldface, italics), margins, spacing, indentations, and position (e.g., centered, left justified). You can define different styles for different types of text. That is, you can define styles for level-one headings, level-two headings, bulleted lists, body copy, and any other type of text in the document. Once you have defined styles, you can select them for individual parts of the text. For example, you select the level-one heading style for the words in the level-one headings, and the format of that heading will automatically conform to the defined style.

Electronic style sheets help you achieve the goal of format consistency. Your task is to identify the different features of text, such as a level-one heading, not to remember the specifics of indentation, type size, spacing, and so on. In addition, the style sheets minimize the number of key strokes required for using the formatting features of a computer. Once you have defined the style, the computer applies it automatically.

GRAPHICS

The division of responsibilities between editors and graphic artists is closing as graphics programs let people without specific artistic training produce professional-looking graphics. Thus, instead of sending a sketch of a graph or even a line drawing to an artist to be rendered and returned, an editor may simply create the graphic on the computer.

Different types of programs are available for different types of graphics. If you are choosing a program, you need to determine first what types of graphics you will need to produce: tables, graphs, or line drawings. Some programs are best for quantitative data and will, for example, automatically convert numeric data to pie charts. Some permit freehand drawing while others are best suited for straight lines and geometric shapes.

Some graphics programs include **clip art** or click art, or predrawn illustrations of common objects such as cars, flags, and faces. Dedicated clip art packages are intended for use with another graphics package or with word processing. Most graphics packages also allow expansion or contraction of graphics. Some sophisticated packages allow rotation of objects, creation of mirror images, and shading. Some even create digitized versions of freehand drawings, done with a wand.

Scanners may be useful if you reproduce photographs. With an inexpensive scanner, you can insert a photograph or other drawing into an ordinary dot matrix printer and create a digitized version of the illustration that can then be modified with the graphics program or printed from a laser printer.

These features will not produce great artwork unless the person using the program is skilled. If you can't draw a horse on paper, chances are you won't draw it any better using the computer. Conversely, being able to produce great visuals with the computer doesn't mean that a person will use visuals effectively in a document to support learning and application. You use the computer as a tool for creating graphics, not as a producer of miracles.

DESKTOP PUBLISHING

In traditional publishing, an edited hard copy typescript is sent for typesetting and page layout to a company that specializes in providing these services. Typesetting equipment and output devices are expensive and therefore available only to companies that use them all the time. The development of computers and programs to emulate typesetting has given writers and editors the capacity to produce at their desks documents with a typeset appearance. **Desktop publishing** refers to the use of office computers and page layout programs to perform some of the tasks of publishing. It bypasses typesetting and layout at another site. Desktop publishing requires a word processing program with the capacity to produce fonts like those used in typesetting (e.g., Times and Helvetica) and a laser printer. In addition, a page layout program can facilitate the placement of text and graphics on the

Figure 16.1
The Desktop Publishing
Process

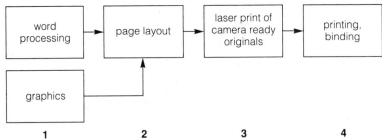

page and increase the options for page layout. Camera ready copy produced with these programs and equipment is then taken to a printer for reproduction in quantity, either by offset printing (for quantities above 500) or by high-quality photocopying. The copy is called "camera ready" because the printing process requires photography or photocopying.

Four major steps are typical in desktop publishing. Companies that own a computer, software, and a laser printer can complete the first three steps in house. Because printing equipment and facilities require a larger investment, many companies must contract for printing and binding of multiple copies. Figure 16.1 summarizes the desktop publishing process; the following list discusses the four steps in detail.

- **Step 1:** a *word processing* program is used to create and minimally format the document. If a document consists of several parts, such as a newsletter, separate files are created for each part. Formatting includes the selection of typeface and type size. A *graphics* program is used to create graphics. Each graphic is stored in a separate file.

- **Step 2:** a *page layout* program is used to design the pages, including such features as number and width of columns and the amount of space between them, size of margins, and pagination. Text and graphics files are placed into the page layout file and adjusted to fit. Text may be edited, but the page layout program is slower for word processing than is a word processing program. Graphics may be enlarged or reduced. A word processing program may offer adequate formatting options for simple documents and the ability to size and place graphics, making the page layout program unnecessary.

- **Step 3:** a *laser printer* is used to print *camera ready originals* of each of the pages.

- **Step 4:** the originals are delivered to a printing company for *printing* in quantity and for *binding*.

Desktop publishing appeals to companies as a way of upgrading documents, such as newsletters and annual reports, previously produced with typewriters or dot matrix printers. It makes the typeset look available without the expense of typesetting. However, the quality of copy that is professionally typeset may be superior to the copy produced by desktop publishing, depending on the output device and on page layout. Quality is measured in part by **resolution,** or the number of dots of ink per inch (dpi) for the letters on the printed page. A typical laser printer produces a resolution of 300 dpi, while typesetting produces a resolution of 2,400 dpi. The characters produced on a laser printer are thus relatively coarse, and ragged edges on large characters may be apparent even without magnification. The alphabets below illustrate 36-point type produced on a laser printer and by professional typesetting. Note that the rounded and sloped lines of characters produced on the laser printer have bumpy edges.

ABCDE

36-point type: laser printer

ABCDE

36-point type: typesetting

Quality is also measured by such page layout features as how well the top margins of facing pages align and whether "rivers" of white space run through the type. Typesetting and manual layout offer more control over these features than does desktop publishing. Furthermore, in traditional publishing, a trained graphic designer is likely to design the document and lay out the pages. Amateur designers may use the type and formatting features of desktop publishing equipment less effectively than would professionals. Thus, while desktop publishing can upgrade the quality of documents formerly produced with typewriters, it has not replaced traditional publishing for documents that require the highest quality.

However, desktop publishing and traditional publishing are merging, and the quality gap is narrowing. The electronic files of documents generated on personal computers can now be printed on the same high-quality output devices formerly reserved for professional typesetters. Thus, the print quality of documents keyboarded at the desktop can match that of professional typesetting.

The method of preparing files for these output devices depends on the type of desktop publishing system. Some systems are "wysiwyg" systems ("what you see is what you get"). If italic type is desired, the keyboard operator selects the italic style. The type looks on the screen the way it will look on the printed page. Other systems require coding characters in the typescript along with the text. For example, `<p>` may signal that a paragraph begins while `</p>` signals that a paragraph ends. The angle brackets are delimiters that indicate instructions rather than text, so neither the brackets nor the codes within them are printed in the final output. The text file needs to be prepared with a minimum of formatting. This is because the formatting directions in the word processing program differ from those in the typesetting program and cannot be automatically converted. Thus, the keyboard operator will not type italic type where it is desired but will type roman type plus codes to direct italic output.

Figure 16.2 illustrates the typescript page of an article for the journal *The Technical Writing Teacher*. The characters enclosed in angle brackets give instructions about the typeface, type style, and type size. The file represented by this typescript is converted electronically, without rekeyboarding, to the typeset page you see in figure 16.3. You would need to consult with a typesetter to determine what programs and codes would work for such a conversion in your own situation. Writers who submit electronic copy for conversion need clear directions about what codes to use before they prepare their documents.

Traditional and desktop publishing also merge when companies accept keyboarding and layout responsibilities but also insist on professional graphic design. A trained designer establishes the design specifications for the document, and the writer and editor, working on the document at computers, format according to the specifications. All transmission of the text is electronic. Professional design and high-quality output devices result in a final product of the same high quality as that produced when all the typesetting and layout take place at a shop that specializes in these services.

Because editors are the link between writing and printing, they are the obvious choices for preparing camera ready copy. Many editors welcome these responsibilities because they can use the power of the typeset page to achieve other goals of editing, including readable type, appropriate emphasis, and attractive graphic design. Desktop publishing also gives editors more control over the printed document because fewer people work on the document through production. Instead of telling others what to do, editors can just do it. Furthermore, desktop publishing can save production time because documents do not need to be physically transported between publisher and printer for the various stages of proofreading and correction.

These advantages need to be weighed against the increased responsi-

Figure 16.2   Typescript Coded for Conversion to Typesetting

NOTE: FONTS 5,6,9,12,13,15. MAX LINE LENGTH 25.6, INSERT TWT VOLUME NUMBER AND
DATE ON TOP AND COPYRIGHT ON BOTTOM OF 1ST PAGE OF EACH ARTICLE, INSERT TWT
TITLE (INSIDE) AND PAGE NUMBER (OUTSIDE) ON TOP OF EACH PAGE...END NOTE.

<PS14<LS14<F9<LL25.6<AL<HYX>Reading to Learn to Do
<ALD15<PS12<LS12<FT6>Janice C. Redish
<PS10<FT5>American Institutes for Research
<ALD10<RULE>
<ALD6<PS9<LS10<FT13> Classroom reading primarily involves reading to learn or
reading that centers on topics, whereas workplace reading primarily involves
reading to do or reading that specifies actions. Redish discusses her
development of "reading to learn to do" materials or tutorials that help users
both to use a program and to learn. Her comparison to the research of Carroll
and colleagues and her guidelines for developing effective tutorials provide
help for the technical communicator's design of tutorials and implications for
the educator's design of assignments.
<ALD6<RULE>
<ALD10<PS10<LS11<FT12> In the late 1970's, Tom Sticht and his colleagues,
studying literacy problems in the Army and Navy, found it useful to
distinguish two types of reading tasks, which they called reading to do and
reading to learn (Sticht et al. 1977; Sticht and Welty-Zapf 1976). When
reading to do, the reader's primary goal is to extract information for
immediate action. As Sticht says "once located and applied, the information
can be forgotten. Because the information is stored in the book, it does not
have to be 'stored in the head'; it can simply be looked up if needed again"
(Sticht 1985, 317). Reading to do materials include: instructions for
installing, operating, and maintaining equipment, decision memos, employee
benefits handbooks and insurance policies, and forms to be filled out.
    By contrast, when reading to learn, the reader's primary goal is to absorb
information for future recall. As Sticht says, in a reading to learn task,
readers employ various study strategies to extract and retain information "in
the head." Reading to learn materials include textbooks, journal articles, and
essays.!1
    Sticht and his colleagues found that students in school spend most of their
time reading to learn while workers on the job spend most of their time
reading to do. Other research in industrial settings has confirmed both the
value of distinguishing between reading to learn and reading to do and the
fact that most workers, most of the time, read to do. Mikulecky's (1981)
research in schools and in industrial settings strongly supports Sticht.
Sticht's and Mikulecky's conclusions are that only 15% of what students read
in school is reading to do. On the job, the situation is reversed: only 15% is
reading to learn.

Figure 16.3   Typeset Version of Figure 16.2. From *The Technical Writing Teacher.* Copyright © 1988 Association of Teachers of Technical Writing. Reprinted by permission.

Reading to Learn to Do

Janice C. Redish
American Institutes for Research

Classroom reading primarily involves reading to learn or reading that centers on topics, whereas workplace reading primarily involves reading to do or reading that specifies actions. Redish discusses her development of "reading to learn to do" materials or tutorials that help users both to use a program and to learn. Her comparison to the research of Carroll and colleagues and her guidelines for developing effective tutorials provide help for the technical communicator's design of tutorials and implications for the educator's design of assignments.

In the late 1970's, Tom Sticht and his colleagues, studying literacy problems in the Army and Navy, found it useful to distinguish two types of reading tasks, which they called reading to do and reading to learn (Sticht et al. 1977; Sticht and Welty-Zapf 1976). When reading to do, the reader's primary goal is to extract information for immediate action. As Sticht says, "once located and applied, the information can be forgotten. Because the information is stored in the book, it does not have to be 'stored in the head'; it can simply be looked up if needed again" (Sticht 1985, 317). Reading to do materials include: instructions for installing, operating, and maintaining equipment, decision memos, employee benefits handbooks and insurance policies, and forms to be filled out.

By contrast, when reading to learn, the reader's primary goal is to absorb information for future recall. As Sticht says, in a reading to learn task, readers employ various study strategies to extract and retain information "in the head." Reading to learn materials include textbooks, journal articles, and essays.[1]

Sticht and his colleagues found that students in school spend most of their time reading to learn while workers on the job spend most of their time reading to do. Other research in industrial settings has confirmed both the value of distinguishing between reading to learn and reading to do and the fact that most workers, most of the time, read to do. Mikulecky's (1981) research in schools and in industrial settings strongly supports Sticht. Sticht's and Mikulecky's conclusions are that only 15% of what students read in school is reading to do. On the job, the situation is reversed: only 15% is reading to learn.

bilities. Instead of depending on graphic designers to make decisions about type and layout, editors may have to learn to design in a professional way. Instead of depending on professional printers to adjust misaligned columns or missized graphics, editors make the adjustments themselves. If your company is considering desktop publishing and assuming you will do the work of page layout, make sure they will provide the necessary support in terms of training and time allotted for projects.

Computers, software, and laser printers have put powerful typesetting and page layout options and responsibilities on the editor's desk. Much editing and publishing are still completed in traditional ways, but one thing is certain: a number of publishing tasks formerly completed in type-setting and printing shops are now completed by an editor working at a computer.

MANAGEMENT

Scheduling and document tracking are necessary parts of the production of any substantial document. The computer may be useful for creating the forms and letters that are used during development and production. Project management software may be adapted for editing projects. This software can help an editor to create a flowchart of tasks and due dates at the outset of project development and then to keep on the set schedule.

If the editor and writer are linked by electronic mail or by a network, they can correspond and send documents back and forth electronically. Electronic transmission cuts down substantially on the amount of time required for exchanges, as well as eliminating photocopying and postage costs.

Spreadsheets are useful for keeping financial records, such as bids on printing and paper, and any other quantitative data, such as inventories. Databases can be useful for keeping lists of contributing writers and their addresses, files of documents and their revision dates, and product specifications.

EDITORIAL TRESPASS: MARKING ELECTRONIC CHANGES

With good reason, writers have reservations about editors "changing" their texts. They may welcome "improvement" but do not want to be held accountable for having said in print things they didn't write in the type-script. They do not want editors to change their meaning. Although some companies may give editors the final say, all writers should be given the opportunity to review and approve editorial changes.

Editing on hard copy provides a record of every editorial mark. By contrast, electronic editing may leave no tracks, raising the question of editorial trespass—editors may inadvertently introduce errors or edit for style too aggressively. The problem, and the goal, then, is to mark the text electronically or manually to alert writers to editorial emendations. A counterproblem, however, is that constant marking diminishes the efficiency of online editing because it is time consuming both to insert the marks and to remove them when the changes have been approved. The marks may create problems psychologically as well because they call attention to errors rather than to strengths. Even editors working on hard copy do not necessarily show writers the marked copy; rather, they prefer a clean copy with changes incorporated and a general description of the changes.

The hidden text function of powerful word processing programs solves some of these problems. With this feature, you can edit a passage in the document and then "hide" the original text. It is not lost, but it does not appear on the screen. A writer can review your editing without the distraction of a heavily marked page, but he or she can also call up the hidden text to compare the original passages to the hidden ones. And the hidden originals can be reinserted into the document.

The notepad feature of word processing programs will let you try out a revision without making changes in the original. If the revision does not work, you simply do not save it. If it does work, you can cut and paste from the notepad into the original, hiding the text for which the notepad version substitutes.

The type style options in word processing programs can be used to mark insertions, deletions, and moves. For example, all insertions might be underlined. If they are ultimately approved, the underlining can be deleted easily while the inserted words remain. Other markers, such as asterisks, slash marks, or double brackets, could signal insertions, moves, or deletions. These markers can ultimately be removed from the document with the search and replace function of the word processing program.

Some programs have been designed to permit the introduction of editorial comments into the text while keeping the comments separate from the text. The program may remove the editorial marks automatically once the editing is completed and approved. Alternatively, a program may use windows to separate reviewers' or editors' comments from the original text. Some programs work by comparing original and edited versions of a document, highlighting the differences.

If marking and removing marks seems to take too much time or if the available software does not enable such electronic marking, the same goal can be achieved manually. That is, the editor can note on the edited hard copy where changes have been made. The marks would not even be in the computer file, so no deletion would be required.

SUMMARY

The computer can be a useful editorial assistant in the whole range of editing tasks, from copyediting to page layout and production. The key program for editing is the word processing program. Other programs reduce the time required for proofreading. Desktop publishing requires a computer connected to a laser printer or access to a typesetting-quality printer. All of these programs and capabilities require skilled and knowledgeable users.

FURTHER READING

Shirley S. Ackerman and William W. Turechek. 1988. "The Risks and Rewards of Online Editing." *IEEE Transactions on Professional Communication* 31(3): 122–123. Discusses editorial trespass and a system for marking electronically.

Chicago Guide to Preparing Electronic Manuscripts. 1987. Chicago: University of Chicago Press. A thorough guide for authors and publishers on coding computer-generated manuscripts for conversion to typesetting.

David K. Farkas. 1987. "Online Editing and Document Review." *Technical Communication* 34(3): 180–183. Reviews benefits and limits of online editing and types of programs useful for online editing.

Janice Redish and Jack Selzer. 1985. "The Place of Readability Formulas in Technical Communication." *Technical Communication* 32(4): 46–52. Analyzes the limits of readability formulas.

DISCUSSION AND
APPLICATION

1. The conclusions from a loan analyst's report on the evaluation of an application for a loan was checked by the style analysis program. The results appear here. The phrases that the style analysis program questioned are underlined, and the specific comments appear in the list following the document.

Analyze the writer's style on the basis of the guidelines presented in Chapter 11, and develop goals for editing the writing style of this document. Then analyze the style analysis provided by the program. What style characteristics did it identify well? What needs for style editing, if any, did it overlook? How good would the editing be if the editor depended on this style analysis program? How might the program improve your own editing? How might it help a writer before a document was submitted for editing? Could it interfere with good writing and editing?

Some explanations: "A Lumber Company" substitutes for the company's real name. The lumber company proposes expansion. "Kraft" is a heavy paper made from wood pulp, and chips are wood products. Kraft Pulp (capitalized) is the name of the company in which A Lumber Company wishes to invest. Sentence 5 means that because the company does not have the cash for the expansion, it will borrow money. The "M" in $3,300.0M means "thousands." "Highly leveraged position" in sentence 15 means that the company has a relatively small amount of its own capital invested.

CONCLUSION*

[1]Admittedly, the averages used to project an appropriate profit level for 1977 contain a number of impurities, but they are accurate enough to indicate that the company will need to monitor its present condition. [2]The company will find it difficult enough to maintain present operations without considering a posture of further expansion.

[3]In consideration of the fact that the company is approaching default on the total debt and the worth/debt terms of our loan agreement as amended on January 14, 1987, it seems apparent that modifications in the loan agreement are again imminent. [4]The cash flow problems of the company are evident in its failure to meet the balance requirements of our loan agreements. [5]The company does not have the cash available to proceed with the Kraft Pulp project and proposed, among other means, to fund its contribution of $3,300.0M in part with seasonal lines of credit, which is not a proper source of funds for a long-term capital investment.

[6]It would appear that it would be in the bank's best interest to hold A Lumber Company to

a commitment to consolidate its position <u>further</u>
before agreeing to any further expansion. [7]While
the lumber industry appears strong in the long
run, it may be subject to some financial
pressures in the short run. [8]Because A Lumber
Company has just gone through a major expansion
phase, it <u>is in a position to</u> benefit greatly
from the expected upturn in the industry, but it
may suffer severely if allowed to commit to any
further expansion funded by debt. [9]If the economy
does not remain strong enough to provide
substantial profits, the company may be forced to
deplete its own timber resources to provide the
cash needed for the debt service. [10]Rapid
depletion of timber resources will be felt in an
increase in the cost of goods sold in subsequent
years, adding more pressure to profits by
decreasing profit margins and by increasing the
need to replace depleted timber resources.

[11]With regard specifically to the Kraft Pulp
project, the file does not contain sufficient
information to evaluate it. [12]The benefit to A
Lumber Company appears to be as a source of
additional income through the sale of a mill by-
product. [13]<u>There is</u> no indication whether <u>this</u>
income will provide an appropriate offset for the
company's capital expenditure to gain "chips" to
other Kraft processors, it may be better to
continue <u>this</u> until the company is in a better
capital position to fund the project.

[14]With continued strong, active management,
<u>this</u> company is positioned to benefit by an
upturn in the lumber industry, and to benefit to

an even greater extent by the growth expected in
the Southeast. [15]There are, however, <u>too many</u>
<u>indications that</u> the cash flow pressures on its
highly leveraged position could cause a serious
financial crisis. [16]<u>It is this analyst's opinion</u>
<u>that</u> the bank should exercise its control in
<u>this</u> situation by advising the company to
restructure its debt and its operations <u>to be in</u>
<u>a position to</u> handle its cash flows from
operations, <u>rather</u> than from increases in long-
term debt, before any <u>further</u> expansion is
contemplated.

Analysis   Note: numbers refer to sentences. The evaluation refers to the word or
phrase underlined in the sentence.

1. wordy phrase
   suggestion: several, many, some

2. commonly misused word
   suggestion: farther; further = time, degree, quantity

3. wordy phrase
   suggestion: revise phrase

3. redundant phrase
   suggestion: seems, is apparent

3. commonly misused word
   suggestion: eminent, immanent; imminent = about to happen

5. wordy phrase
   suggestion: omit if followed by verb or adjective

6. commonly misused word
   suggestion: farther; further = time, degree, quantity

8. wordy phrase
   suggestion: can

13. wordy phrase
    suggestion: this phrase often indicates wordiness

13. error—unspecified
    suggestion: vague pronoun: specify referent, as in "this x"

15. wordy phrase
    suggestion: this phrase often indicates wordiness

16. wordy phrase
    suggestion: this phrase often indicates wordiness

16. error – unspecified
    suggestion: vague pronoun: specify referent, as in "this x"

16. wordy phrase
    suggestion: can

16. vague adverb

16. commonly misused word
    suggestion: farther; further = time, degree, quantity

Percent of sentences using the "to be" verb: 82
Average number of words per sentence: 30.5

2. If you have not already developed some skill in using a computer for word processing, use campus computer facilities or other facilities to master these functions: create a file, save, insert, delete, cut and paste, and search and replace.

17 TYPE AND PRODUCTION

As the link between the development and the publication of documents, editors have always had to know something about type and production. *Type* refers to the shape and size of the letters on the page. *Production* refers to the creation of camera ready originals, printing, and binding. Sometimes editorial tasks are divided among different editors; a production editor may supervise the design, printing, and binding after development editors and copyeditors have prepared the text. However, all editors should know what happens to the document once the text is established, because choices about production influence early editorial decisions.

Knowledge of type facilitates good decisions about graphic design, whether editors work with graphic designers or do the work themselves. Some negotiation between editor and graphic designer is desirable. Although graphic designers are expected to know principles of typography and layout, they do not necessarily know the content, purpose, and readers of a given document—information that will affect design decisions. Editors generally want the chance to approve design decisions for their suitability to the document content, purpose, and readers, but they need to understand design principles in order to make informed decisions.

Knowledge of the steps in production also facilitates good management. An editor in charge of production schedules editing tasks with the production schedule in mind. All scheduling is ultimately controlled by the intended document distribution date. Thus, editors will need estimates from printers about the time required for typesetting. Editors also negotiate bids for printing and binding but first must know the options for publication.

Desktop publishing increases the responsibilities of editors to know about type and production. Editors are less likely with desktop publishing to send the document to outside experts in type and production to prepare the document for publication. They assume more responsibilities for themselves.

This chapter provides an overview of type and production in order to familiarize editors with concepts and terms. Its purpose is to enable you, as editor, to communicate with graphic designers and printers, not to teach you how to prepare expert designs. A good book on graphic design will provide more complete information.

TYPE FUNDAMENTALS

Letters within the English alphabet can be recognized in a variety of shapes and sizes. The space between letters, between words, and between lines of type can also vary. Professional typesetting provides more options for type and spacing than does typewriting or computer-generated type, though laser printers with computer systems emulate typesetting nicely.

Typography matters for practical as well as for aesthetic reasons. Typefaces and spacing affect the ease with which readers can read. Typefaces also express different qualities of character, such as avant garde, elegant, quiet, or masculine, that shape the way readers respond to a document. Using type well is an art, but the principles underlying the uses of type are also based on scientific research.

Typefaces

The shapes of characters identify particular designs of types. Of the hundreds of existing designs or faces, all may be classified according to whether they are serif style or sans serif. **Serifs** are cross strokes at the ends of the main strokes of letters. You can see examples in both the lower-case and capital letters in the words "Times Roman" below. Both vertical and horizontal cross strokes appear in the capital letters. A **sans serif** style omits the cross strokes. Note how the strokes for the capital letter H in "Helvetica" simply end.

Times Roman Helvetica
TIMES ROMAN HELVETICA

The serif styles are traditional while sans serif styles are more recent designs. Some designers favor sans serif styles for their clean, modern look, and the style has been particularly popular in science and technology publications and in advertising. However, research shows that the serif styles may be easier to read. One theory is that the horizontal lines of the serifs propel the eye across lines of type. Another theory is that the serif styles are more familiar to many readers. Many designers prefer a serif style for long blocks of text in magazines and books.

The examples below show a few of the many typefaces available, with serif styles on the left and sans serif on the right.

Bookman   Eras

Fenice   **Futura Black**

Schoolbook   Optima

You can see how Futura Black could be difficult to read in paragraphs, but it can be attractive for display type such as headings and titles. Unless you are an expert in design, it is smart to stick with the proven favorites, such as Times Roman, Baskerville, Bookman, Palatino, Garamond, New Century Schoolbook, and Helvetica. It is also best for amateur designers not to mix typefaces in a document because the mixture can create a cluttered look.

Your choice of typeface will also depend on the faces available from the typesetter or on the laser printer. Professional typesetters can show you a type specimen book illustrating the available faces and sizes. A complete set of characters in a typeface in one size is called a **font.** A printer may have available the 10-point Times Roman font but lack the 24-point font in the same typeface. You need to check the availability of the typeface in all fonts you will need.

Type Size   Printers use the **pica** as a standard measure. The replication of a **pica stick** in the left-hand margin of this page compares picas and inches. You will note that 6 picas equal approximately an inch. Type is measured in **points,** with a point equal to one-twelfth of a pica. Thus, 12-point type will fill slightly less than a pica of vertical space, and six lines of 12-point type will fit in approximately an inch of space.

The measures are not exact, however, and 12-point type in one typeface will be larger than 12-point type in another typeface. You can see in the examples below how the different typefaces in the same size will fill different amounts of vertical and horizontal space.

This line is set in 12-point Times Roman.

This line is set in 12-point Avant Garde.

This line is set in 12-point Helvetica.

This line is set in 12-point Palatino.

This line is set in 12-point New Century Schoolbook.

This line is set in 12-point Bookman.

Note, too, the proportionate size of the parts of the letters. Helvetica and Avant Garde letters have a proportionately large **x-height,** the part of the letter equivalent in height to the lowercase *x*. Thus, the **ascenders** (the projections above the body of the letter, as on the *b* and *h*) and the **descenders** (the projections below the body of the letter, as on the *p* and *y*) are proportionately shorter than in Palatino and Schoolbook. The capital letter *M* is shown below in various sizes in the typeface Times Roman.

6 8 9 10 12 14 18 24 30 36 48 60 72

Type size affects readability, but it also affects document length. The choice of typeface and type size can make a difference of a number of pages in a long document such as a manual or book. It can determine whether a story fits into one column in a newsletter or spills into a second column. (The section on copyfitting later in the chapter has more to say about this.)

Most blocks of text—the body copy as opposed to the headings or display copy—are set in 10-point or 12-point type. Type smaller than 9-point type is difficult to read and is reserved for footnotes, indexes, and other material that readers will read selectively and in small quantities. Type 14 points or larger is reserved for children's books, large-print books for visually impaired readers, and display copy.

Headings may be set in the same size as the body copy if they are set in boldface. Boldface alone will let readers distinguish visually the headings from the body. For headings of different levels, you may distinguish the levels with space alone. For example, a level-one heading could be centered but in the same size as a level-two heading set on the left margin.

If size is the only variable in the headings, you will have to skip at least one size between levels if readers are to recognize the levels. Thus, if a level-one heading is left justified in 14-point type, a level-two heading can be set in 10-point type.

Leading, Letterspacing, Wordspacing, and Line Length

Various options for the treatment of individual letters and words and lines of type—including leading, word- and letterspacing, and line length—are available.

Leading. Type would not be readable if the descenders in one line smashed into the ascenders of the line below. Thus, good typesetting includes **leading** (pronounced *ledding*) between the lines. The term derives from the days when type was set from metal molds. Strips of metal were placed between the lines of characters. Even if the type is set *solid* (without leading), there will be a tiny bit of space between the lines. Most type is set with 1 or 2 points of extra leading. Thus, 10-point type may be set on a 12-point line. The expression "set 10 on 12" and the marginal notation "10/12" both direct the typesetter to use 10-point type on a 12-point line.

The following examples show type set with the right amount of leading, with too little leading (solid), and with too much leading. The leading affects the ease of reading. The first paragraph is set in 10-point Helvetica on a 12-point line. The extra 2 points of leading are especially important for sans serif type in order to help readers distinguish lines and read comfortably.

Right Amount of Leading

Leading, the space between lines of type, helps the eye move horizontally. Too little leading increases reading difficulty because the type seems crowded and the letters cannot be distinguished. Too much leading makes the text look childish. The right amount of leading is comfortable to read and helps the eye find the correct line when it moves from the right back to the left margin.

The next paragraph is set in 10-point Helvetica on a 10-point line (no leading). The crowding increases reading difficulty and the chance that readers will skip lines when they look for the next line at the left margin.

Too Little Leading

Leading, the space between lines of type, helps the eye move horizontally. Too little leading increases reading difficulty because the type seems crowded and the letters cannot be distinguished. Too much leading makes the text look childish. The right amount of leading is comfortable to read and helps the eye find the correct line when it moves from the right back to the left margin.

The final paragraph is set in 10-point Helvetica on a 24-point line. The extra space, besides being wasteful and looking unprofessional, could interfere with comprehension in a long document especially by spatially separating related ideas.

Too Much Leading

Leading, the space between lines of type, helps the eye move

horizontally. Too little leading increases reading difficulty

because the type seems crowded and the letters cannot be

distinguished. Too much leading makes the text look childish.

The right amount of leading is comfortable to read and helps the

eye find the correct line when it moves from the right back to the

left margin.

One or 2 points of leading are typical for body copy, assuming 10- or 12-point type. The longer the line, the more leading is needed (to help the eye move horizontally). Sans serif type generally requires more leading than serif type, and larger type sizes require more leading than smaller type sizes.

Line depth is always measured baseline to baseline. The **baseline** is formed by the bottom of the letters excluding descenders. The T-square feature of a pica stick makes accurate measurement easy.

Letterspacing and Wordspacing. The horizontal spacing as well as the vertical spacing affects readability. Typesetting uses proportional spacing, meaning that each letter receives space proportionate to its width. By contrast, most typewriters and many computer printers give each letter the same width so that an *i* takes as much space as an *m*. Proportional spacing makes type easier to read.

Letterspacing refers to how close together the letters are set; **word-**

spacing refers to the amount of space between words. As with leading, too much or too little letter- (or word-) spacing interferes with reading. The following examples show letterspacing that is just right, too tight, and too open. All three paragraphs are set in the same size (10/12-point) and face (Times Roman) of type.

Correct Letterspacing

Correct letterspacing helps readers recognize words because they can easily identify the shapes of the words. It also affects the number of times the eye stops in its move across a line of type. Too much letterspacing requires the eyes to make more stops than desirable. The eye has to make a wider sweep for fewer words. The crowding of condensed type also increases reading difficulty.

Too Tight Letterspacing

Correct letterspacing helps readers recognize words because they can easily identify the shapes of the words. It also affects the number of times the eye stops in its move across a line of type. Too much letterspacing requires the eyes to make more stops than desirable. The eye has to make a wider sweep for fewer words. The crowding of condensed type also increases reading difficulty.

Too Open Letterspacing

Correct letterspacing helps readers recognize words because they can easily identify the shapes of the words. It also affects the number of times the eye stops in its move across a line of type. Too much letterspacing requires the eyes to make more stops than desirable. The eye has to make a wider sweep for fewer words. The crowding of condensed type also increases reading difficulty.

You can trust a reputable typesetter to letterspace correctly. You can also ask to see samples of the typesetter's work before you contract for your job. If you are using desktop publishing to emulate typesetting, use conventional spacing rather than playing with the computer's capacity for expanding or condensing type.

Line Length. The amount of space between words and, to some extent, between letters is partly determined by line length and justification of margins. The left margin is almost always straight in body copy; that is, the beginning letters of each line align horizontally, so the text is *left justified*. If the lines of type align on the right margin, the text is *right justified*. If the lines align on the left but not on the right, the text is set **ragged right.**

Left-Justified Text

The dogmas of the quiet past are inadequate to the stormy present. The occasion is piled high with difficulty, and we must rise with the occasion.

Right-Justified Text

The dogmas of the quiet past are inadequate to the stormy present. The occasion is piled high with difficulty, and we must rise with the occasion.

Centered Text

The dogmas of the quiet past are inadequate to the stormy present. The occasion is piled high with difficulty, and we must rise with the occasion.

Left- and Right-Justified Text

The dogmas of the quiet past are inadequate to the stormy present. The occasion is piled high with difficulty, and we must rise with the occasion.

To achieve both left and right justification, extra space must be inserted between words and letters. High-quality typesetting equipment can achieve the spacing in such a way that the eye often won't recognize the extra space, but even with good equipment, the wordspacing may be obviously exaggerated. This calls a reader's attention to the type rather than to the content and thus interferes with reading. The likelihood of exaggerated spacing is greater with short lines, such as newspaper columns. Many designers, therefore, prefer ragged right text. Perhaps the page as a whole looks a little less tidy (or, from another point of view, less rigid). The choice of ragged right, however, acknowledges the goal of readable type; in this case, the reader's ease in moving across lines of type supercedes the desire for a straight right margin.

Optimal line length is relative to type size. As a rule of thumb, lines include 1½ to 2½ alphabets, or 39 to 65 characters. The line for 12-point type will thus be longer than the line for 10-point type. Lines produced with this guideline will include 9 to 10 words. If the line length is short and words are long, end-of-line hyphenation may be necessary to prevent excessively short lines.

Copyfitting
Copyfitting, sometimes called **casting off,** is a calculation of the amount of printed space a typescript will require when typeset. An estimate of characters in a typescript can be used to calculate how many picas, inches, or pages will be required for the document assuming a certain typeface and type size, column length, and page depth. Copyfitting lets an editor see, prior to typesetting, whether the material planned for a document will fit in the intended space. Knowing the space requirements, editors can plan content to fill the space. They can also condense material that does not fit before they have paid to have the material typeset. Copyfitting helps

with the page layout on tightly formatted pages, such as those in newsletters and brochures. It also provides an estimate of a document's length, information that is necessary for a cost estimate.

In order to calculate the space your typescript will fill, you need an approximate character count. You also need to know the typeface and type size, line length, and page depth. To get the character count, estimate the number of characters per line and the number of lines per page in the typescript. If the typescript uses a 60-character line and has 25 lines per page, each page of typescript includes about 1,500 characters. A typescript of 5½ pages would include about 8,250 characters (5.5 × 1,500). The computer simplifies this process. Some word processing programs provide character counts for the files.

The typesetter will be able to provide you with facts on the number of characters per pica that can be set with a given typeface and type size. For example, 10-point Times Roman type will print 2.6 characters per pica, while 10-point Helvetica will print 2.4 characters per pica. If the line length is 20 picas, each line will hold about 520 characters of Times Roman (20 × 2.4) and 480 characters of Helvetica (20 × 2.6).

The total number of lines required can be found by dividing the total number of characters by the number of characters per line. Setting in Times Roman would yield 15.6 lines (8,250/520), while setting in Helvetica would yield 17.4 lines (8,250/480). A couple of lines could be added to each estimate to account for partially filled lines at the end of each paragraph.

If the 10-point type were set with an extra 2 points of leading (i.e., 10 on 12), the column depth would be the same number of picas as the number of lines. Thus, the 5½ page typescript would fit into a column 17 picas deep (for Times Roman) or 19 picas deep (for Helvetica).

To summarize, the steps in calculations are as follows:

1. Estimate the total number of characters in the typescript: multiply the number of characters per line by number of lines per page; multiply this figure by the number of pages.

2. Determine the typeface, type size, line length, and page depth of the printed document.

3. Determine the number of characters per pica that the typeface will print in the chosen size. Consult a typesetter or a type specimen book for this information.

4. Determine the number of characters that each line will hold: multiply the number of characters per pica (step 3) by the number of picas per line (step 2).

5. Determine the number of lines required: divide the total number of characters in the typescript (step 1) by the number of characters per line (step 4).

6. Determine the depth in picas that the number of lines will fill: multiply the number of lines (step 5) by the depth of a single line (type size plus leading); divide the result (the number of points) by 12 (the number of points per pica). For example, 10 lines of 12-point type set on a 14-point line will require 140 points of space, the equivalent of 11.7 picas (140/12).

If you are using a "wysiwyg" computer system to prepare the document for print, you set margins and choose the typeface and type size according to the design specifications for the printed document. Then you can see on the screen whether the document will fit in the available space and how long it will be. The calculations of casting off will not be necessary.

PAPER

Paper, like typeface and layout, affects readability. Paper may be too transparent and allow shadows of the print from the reverse side to show. Paper may not accept ink well and the type may smudge, or it may be too absorbent and the type may bleed. It may have a shiny coating that glares. If you are responsible for selecting paper, you will consider size, weight, opacity, and finish as well as color.

Except for quick print jobs in small quantities (i.e., photocopying), most printing is done on large sheets of paper that are later trimmed to the proper size or on large rolls of paper. The standard size of "book" paper in the United States is 25 × 38 inches. (Sizes vary slightly in countries using the metric system.) As the diagram in figure 17.1 shows, a sheet of paper this size will yield eight 8½ × 11 **folios** (a page that can be printed front and back) or sixteen 6 × 9 folios. The broken lines show additional cuts for the 16 folios. Extra space is available for trimming.

The standard size for "bond" paper is 17 × 22 inches. This paper yields four 8½ × 11 folios. "Cover" paper measures 20 × 26 inches.

Standard paper sizes determine standard page sizes. It is possible to print a book in a size other than 6 × 9 or 8½ × 11, but the per page cost will increase because of the waste of paper. Standard paper sizes also determine desirable book length, generally a multiple of 16 pages. Each group of pages printed and bound together is called a **signature.** The most common signature size is 8-page or 16-page. Thus, a book of 97 pages rather than 96 will require a whole extra sheet of book paper for one page of text. Editing to condense slightly will be cost effective.

Figure 17.1
Book Paper,
25 × 38 Inches,
Showing Cuts for Pages

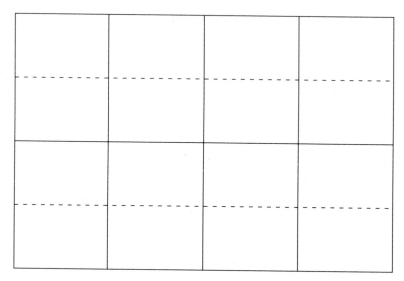

The **basis weight** of the paper is derived from the weight of a ream of the paper in its uncut size. Thus, a ream of book paper may weigh 60 pounds while a ream of the same weight bond paper weighs 24 pounds. The following table shows equivalent weights of different kinds of paper.

Book Paper	Cover Paper	Bond Paper
basis: 25″ × 38″	basis: 20″ × 26″	basis: 17″ × 22″
45 pounds	25 pounds	18 pounds
50	27	20
60	35	24
70	40	28
80	45	32

Fifty- or 60-pound book paper is generally satisfactory for books and text-books. Classier publications may use 70- or 80-pound book paper.

Opacity and finish, as well as weight, affect the character of the document, success of the printing, and the extent to which the paper supports or interferes with the document's use. *Opacity* refers to how easy it is to see the ink through the page. Shadows from the reverse of the page distract readers. Paper weight is just one factor in opacity. *Finish*, or treatment to the surface of the paper, affects how well the paper accepts ink and whether the paper seems elegant or businesslike. Finishes, arranged in order of increasing smoothness, are antique, eggshell, vellum, and machine finish. Coating makes the paper smoother. Coated paper also reproduces photographs and colored inks better than does uncoated paper. The raised patterns seen on some fine stationeries are created by embossing. The choice of paper should depend on opacity and finish as well as on size and weight.

THE PRODUCTION PROCESS

Traditional publishing, as opposed to desktop publishing with commercial printing, requires a number of procedures and handwork. The text is typeset, made up into pages, and proofread. Illustrations may need special treatment. If the document is a book, the pages are grouped into signatures (8 or 16 pages) for printing on book paper or rolls of paper. Metal plates are made from the signatures and then affixed to the printing press. Once the sheets are printed, they are folded, trimmed, and bound. During this process, the editor will be in contact with the printer to ensure that the job is proceeding on schedule and that the typescript is being printed correctly. More detailed information on this process follows.

Typesetting and Page Makeup

Typesetting refers to the process of using professional-quality equipment for forming the characters. If the text has been transmitted on hard copy, a typesetter keys in the characters, much like typing, but also inserts codes that direct the equipment in establishing line length, justification, letter spacing, and type style. If the text has been transmitted electronically, it should not need to be rekeyboarded.

For long or complicated documents, the text may be typeset first into **galleys**, long sheets of text in the chosen typeface, type size, and line length. The galleys are proofread and corrected before they are broken into pages. Corrections could change the amount of type on a given page, and the pages would have to be redefined. Galleys may be skipped if the document is uncomplicated or if pages have already been formed with desktop publishing equipment.

Once the galleys have been corrected, pages are made up, either electronically or manually, with room left for illustrations. The page proofs are then checked against the proofread galleys to ensure that no copy was omitted and to confirm the accurate correction of galleys, the correct sequence of pages, the proper placement of illustrations, meaningful page breaks, and so on.

Illustrations

Line drawings may be printed from camera ready originals just as type may be. The originals may be produced by the computer and laser printer or drawn in ink by a skilled graphic artist. Preparation of these visuals

Figure 17.2   Halftone and Magnified Section

for printing, besides their creation in camera ready form, may include enlargement or reduction.

Photographs, or continuous tone art, include shades of gray as well as black and white and require special treatment before printing. A printing press cannot print shades of a given ink color—if the ink is black, only black can be printed on the page. Thus, a photograph must first be converted to a **halftone.** The photograph is reproduced through a **screen,** which converts the grays to dots of various sizes. These dots will be printed in black. Large dots densely grouped will appear dark gray when printed, while small dots widely spaced will look like light gray. A coarse screen will produce dots that the eye can recognize, but the dots produced by a fine screen will show only if magnified. A coarse screen is used when the paper quality is poor, like newsprint. Figure 17.2 illustrates a magnified halftone to show the dot composition as well as a print of an object with a 133-line screen. This is regarded as a fine screen.

The creation of a halftone adds some expense to the printing, and the halftone has to be inserted into the proofs by hand. The cost is reasonable, but when you are getting bids for your document, you will need to specify the number of photographs to be included in order to get an accurate bid.

Scanners are available for desktop publishing systems to create a halftonelike version of a photograph, but the quality of halftones prepared professionally is better.

Imposition, Stripping, and Platemaking

When the page proofs have been proofread and corrected and illustrations approved, proofs called *reproduction proofs* or **repros** are created. The proofs and illustrations are then arranged into signatures of 8 or 16 pages. The pages must be arranged so that they will be in sequence when the sig-

Figure 17.3
Arrangement of Pages
After Imposition

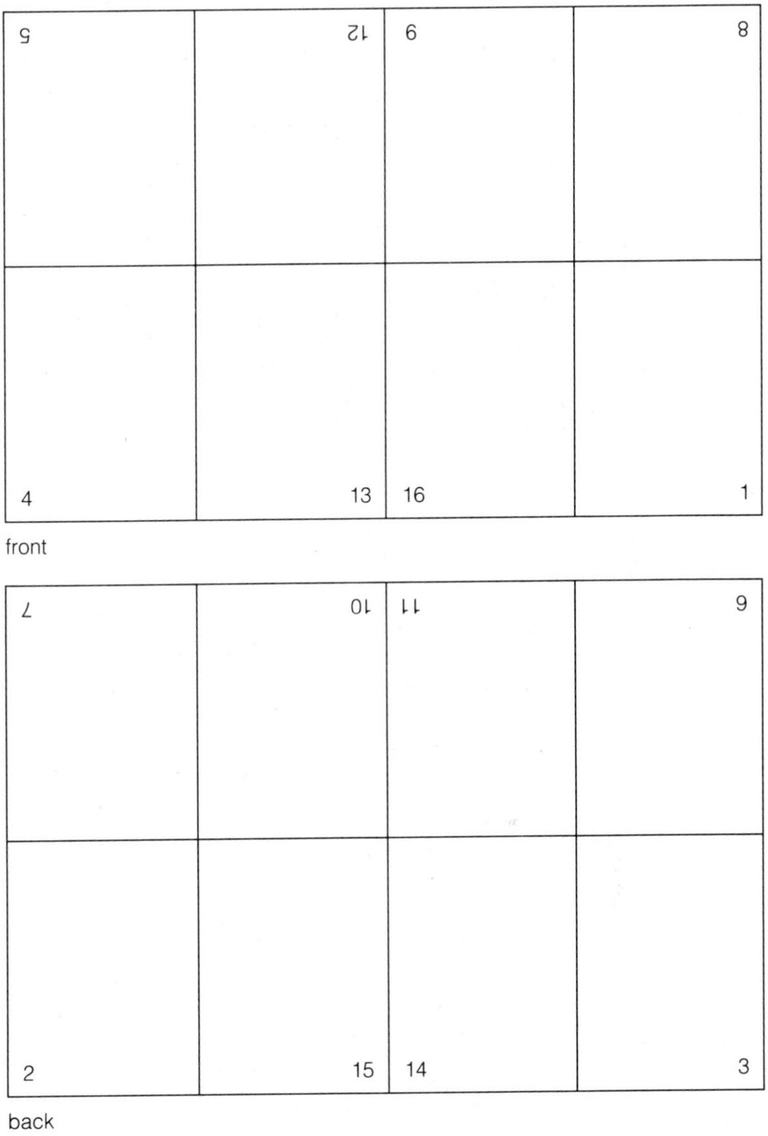

5	12	6	8
4	13	16	1

front

7	10	11	9
2	15	14	3

back

nature is folded and trimmed. They must be aligned so that top and bottom margins of pages in the book or other document will be the same. Figure 17.3 shows one sequence of pages for a book. Note that the pages across the top are upsidedown. The page will be folded in half lengthwise after printing so that all the pages in the bound book will face up. The process of arrangement and alignment is called **imposition.**

A photograph is made of the signature. The negatives are arranged in a form called a **flat,** and negatives of illustrations are taped in. This process is called **stripping.** A thin metal **plate** is exposed to the negatives in a processor, and the image is transferred to the plate. A proof copy may be made of the document at this point showing not just the separate pages (as in page proofs) but their sequence and alignment as well once the signature is folded. These proofs are called **blueprints** or **bluelines** because they are printed with a pale blue ink. This is the final chance to check the document before printing.

Printing: Offset Lithography

Different types of printing presses make their impressions on paper in different ways, but most large-scale commercial printing is done by a process called **offset lithography.** "Offset" refers to the fact that the image is transferred from a metal plate onto a rubber blanket and then onto the paper. "Lithography" means writing on stone. In art, it is a way of reproducing illustrations from plates formed by greasy crayon on stone.

A basic principle of chemistry explains printing by lithography: oil and water do not mix. The ink used in printing is oil based. The metal printing plates are treated chemically so that the plate will accept water while the type image repels water. The plates are dampened with water. Then, when the ink is applied, it adheres to the type but not to the space behind and around the characters.

The metal plate is fixed to a cylinder on the printing press. It rotates while a second cylinder, covered with a rubber blanket, rotates against it in the opposite direction. A third cylinder, the impression cylinder, presses the paper against the blanket cylinder. The inked image is transferred from the metal plate onto the blanket and from the blanket onto the paper. Because the blanket is flexible, it conforms to rough surfaces on the paper. Figure 17.4 illustrates how this process works.

When the printing is complete, the sheets are folded to create the signatures. Then, because the edges of the paper will be folded or uneven, the folded signatures are trimmed.

The production process is represented by the flowchart in figure 17.5.

Figure 17.4
Offset Lithography:
Schematic

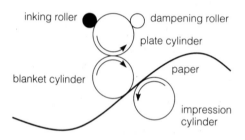

inking roller

dampening roller

plate cylinder

blanket cylinder

paper

impression cylinder

Figure 17.5
The Production Process

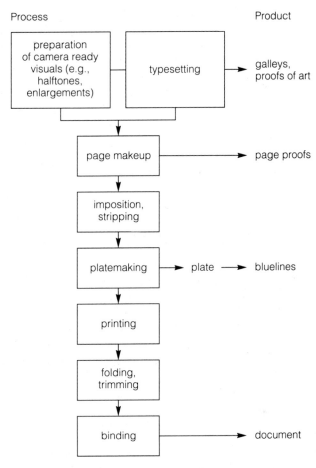

The editor's responsibility during this process is proofreading — at the galley, page proof, and blueprint stages. The editor also monitors the production schedule so that the printing will be completed on time.

Color Printing   The least expensive printed documents use only one ink color. When a second color is added, the expense nearly doubles, because the paper may have to run through the press separately for each ink color. The press will have to be cleaned and set up for each new ink color, adding to the labor cost. Some presses can print more than one color at one time, but because they are more elaborate than the single-color presses, they cost more to operate than do single-color presses.

The **four-color process** produces the optical illusion of all the colors that the eye can see with just four colors of ink. The four-color process works on the principle that any color can be created from the primary colors. The four colors of ink are magenta (bluish red), cyan (greenish blue), yellow, and black.

The hues of the original color photograph or painting must first be separated into the primary colors plus black. This process, called **color separation,** may be done by a laser scanner, or it may be done photographically. A filter on the camera lens filters out all but one hue; for example, a blue filter produces the yellow separation. A halftone image is created for each of the four ink colors.

The document is printed first with yellow ink; then it is run through the press again with magenta, cyan, and black. The black is used to correct for deficiencies in ink pigments that muddy the basic colors and to increase the overall image contrast. The press operator must be careful to align the printing images for all the colors to achieve **registration,** or the precise superimposition of one over the other. Otherwise, the final print will have streaks of yellow, magenta, and cyan rather than the desired rainbow of hues.

The extra procedures, time, and skill required for color printing explain its cost.

Binding   Decisions about binding need to be made before pages are laid out. Binding requires extra space on the page, and different types of binding require different-sized margins. Bindings also vary in durability, and they determine how easily a book will stay open or stand on a shelf.

Manuals are typically bound in a three-ring binder or with wire spirals or plastic combs. These bindings require $\frac{5}{16}$ inches of space along the binding edge. When you plan the page, you should allow the $\frac{5}{16}$ inches plus the margin of space around the words.

Other types of binding are saddle stitching, side stitching, perfect binding, and library binding. **Saddle stitching** is appropriate for booklets. The pages are laid open, and staples are forced through the middle. A saddle-stitched booklet stays open easily. **Side stitching** is similar to saddle stitching, but the pages are closed before staples are placed near the edge of the fold (see figure 17.6). Side stitching is used when the bulk is too great for saddle stitching. It requires about $\frac{3}{8}$ inches of space for binding.

Perfect binding is used for paperback books. The signatures are collected, and the spine is roughened. The cover is then affixed with an adhesive. If the adhesive dries out too much, it cracks when stressed.

The most durable binding is a **library binding,** a type of hardcover binding. The durability results partly from the sewing together of the sig-

Figure 17.6
Common Methods
of Binding

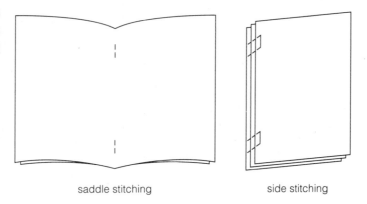

saddle stitching   side stitching

natures and from reinforcements on the spine. The rounded back allows the cover to open and close properly.

SUMMARY

Knowing the specialized vocabulary of graphic designers and printers enables you to communicate with them and make informed decisions about type and printing. When you are in doubt about type or have to design your own documents, choose 10- to 12-point type, in the Times Roman or Helvetica face, and set it on a line length of 2½ alphabets or about 27 picas wide. For a book, use 50- or 60-pound paper. Schedule enough time for printing to allow for all the steps of preparation, printing, proofreading, and finishing.

FURTHER READING

James Craig and William Bevington. 1989. *Working with Graphic Designers.* New York: Watson-Guptill.

Judy E. Pickens. 1985. *The Copy-to-Press Handbook.* New York: Wiley.

Jan V. White. 1988. *Graphic Design for the Electronic Age: The Manual for Traditional and Desktop Publishing.* New York: Watson-Guptill.

DISCUSSION AND APPLICATION

1. Find examples of typography that encourage reading or discourage reading. Evaluate the typography in the context of the document. Do the bad examples seem to be accidental or intentional? What could be done to improve the typography? What are the positive features of the good examples?

2. If you have access to a computer with different typefaces such as Times Roman and Helvetica, type in a paragraph and then reformat it in at least two typefaces. Compare the amount of space each one takes. Characterize the type: Is it inviting? Quiet? Sophisticated? Masculine? Elegant?

3. Copyfit a typescript to determine how much space it will require when typeset, assuming line length and page depth in picas that your instructor provides. Or use the report in the "Discussion and Application" section in Chapter 16 for this task. Assume that the typescript will be set in 12-point Helvetica type with an extra 2 points of leading on a 30-pica line. The number of characters per pica for 12-point Helvetica type is 2.0.

4. To illustrate how the paper is folded on the signature, create a miniature sheet of book paper by using notebook paper. Divide it into sections, and number the sections according to the plan on page 395. Then fold the paper in half so that the two shorter sides touch and the front is outside. Fold in half again, with this fold at right angles to the first. Fold a third time at right angles to the second fold. Your pages should be numbered in sequence from 1 to 16.

5. Examine your textbook and other bound documents you possess. Identify the type of binding used.

5		12	6		8
4		13	16		1

front

7		10	11		9
2		15	14		3

back

18 MANAGEMENT

Editors at all levels, beginning with the copyeditor, are managers. Document production requires work over a period of time and cannot be assigned on an hourly or daily basis. Thus, all editors manage their time and organize activities to maintain efficiency throughout the day and to complete their tasks according to the document production schedule. As editing responsibilities increase, so do management responsibilities. Copyeditors progress in their careers to become project editors and then managers of production departments. Responsibilities increase accordingly from the management of time to management of long-term document development projects and supervision of employees. In addition, editors make policy decisions, ranging from style and format considerations to types of documentation for a project to procedures for document review and quality control. Editors also ensure that documents fulfill legal and ethical requirements.

Good documents require good management. With good management, editors gain the time, resources, and support to complete their tasks at a high level of quality. Without good management, editors must cut corners and compromise. Good working relationships require good management. With good management, editors gain the support of writers, production staff, and upper-level managers. Without good management, editors will conflict with others in the company and establish defensive positions for themselves.

This chapter introduces managerial issues for editors, including estimating time, scheduling document production and tracking progress, soliciting bids, and setting policy. The chapter also reviews the legal aspects of editing.

ESTIMATING TIME

Writing and editing always take longer than originally thought, not only longer than writers and editors anticipate, but almost certainly longer than engineers or managers without communication backgrounds predict. Unless editors can estimate the time required for assigned tasks accurately and credibly, they are likely to be squeezed up against impossible deadlines and to either compromise the quality of their work or work overtime to complete tasks. Time estimates help to control the expectations of superiors and train them to calculate editing time in their own product development schedules. Estimates also suggest the editor's professionalism and mastery of his or her own activities.

Estimates for document development require agreement on the type and level of editing required. Estimates also require the document specifications and records from past projects. If the document is already in typescript form, you can combine records from similar projects with samples of the existing pages.

Classification of Editorial Responsibilities

Good management begins with a clear sense of editorial responsibilities. Editing is so complex a process that it does not have a single meaning. To some people, editing means proofreading. A person with that understanding may assume that an editor can "edit" a 200-page document in a day. Yet, if the editor understands editing to mean substantive editing and if the document is complex or difficult to follow, he or she may be able to complete only 2 pages in an hour or 16 pages in a day. Scheduling, supervising, and contracting for printing take time beyond the editor's work with the text and are often invisible processes to people contracting for editing services. Unless you consider all the editorial tasks involved in an editing job and communicate the time required for each, you may be allotted too little time to complete a job. Furthermore, you may edit more aggressively than the writer or project supervisor desire and create hard feelings, as well as wasting time.

A good manager communicates with the writer or supervisor about expectations for editing, plans to accomplish specific tasks, and estimates

TABLE 18.1 EDITORIAL TASKS AND RESPONSIBILITIES

Task	Responsibility (Purpose)
Copyediting	
spelling, grammar, punctuation	correctness
consistency: verbal, visual, mechanical, content	consistency
match of cross-references, callouts, TOC, etc.	consistency
completeness of parts: sections, visuals, front matter, back matter, headings, etc.	completeness
accuracy of terms, numbers, quotations, etc.	accuracy
visuals	correctness, consistency, completeness, accuracy
copymarking for graphic design	correct typesetting
Substantive Editing	
document planning	suitability for readers, purpose, budget
style: persona, diction, sentence structure	suitability for readers, purpose; comprehension
organization	reader comprehension
format	reader comprehension, access
visuals	reader comprehension
Coordination, Management	
document tracing, transmission	keep production on schedule
correspondence	inform collaborators of responsibilities
scheduling editors, proofreaders, field tests	keep production on schedule; allow time for quality
getting permissions	meet legal requirements
applying for copyrights	protect the writer or company's rights

time for the job on the basis of the tasks that have been agreed upon for the document. The classification of tasks and responsibilities in table 18.1 will help you define the tasks you are expected to complete and the desired outcome for the document and for the readers. It is the basis for the contract for editorial services in figure 18.1

When an editing job is assigned, you can use the classification in table 18.1 to clarify the editing tasks that you are expected to complete, and you can estimate the required time and cost for your services on the basis of those

TABLE 18.1 (continued)

Task	Responsibility (Purpose)
Production	
negotiating with typesetter, graphic designer, printer: bids, schedule	quality, economy; meet deadlines
graphic design	reader use, comprehension; document attractiveness
Desktop Publishing	
keyboarding text, corrections	camera ready copy
page layout	camera ready copy
preparation of visuals	camera ready copy
Indexing	
preparation of an index	index
Product Testing	
running program, using product	usability, readability, completeness, safety
organizing field tests	usability, readability, completeness
Instruction	
writing	writer competency
program/product use	user competency

expectations. Clients should understand just what they will receive and understand time requirements in terms of the editing tasks that they request.

The copyediting and substantive editing tasks are typical for editors responsible for the text and visuals. The coordination, production, and desktop publishing tasks may be performed by a production editor, but in some small companies, editors assume the full range of responsibilities. Preparation of an index, product testing, and instruction are responsibilities beyond the usual expectations for editors, but these tasks are often assigned to editors. Be sure to ask for clarification of such responsibilities and include them, if applicable, in your estimate.

An estimate sheet, such as the one in figure 18.1, can prompt you to consider all the tasks that will be involved in the editing job and to clarify expectations with the person who requests editing. Many projects may be estimated informally, but it may be policy within your organization to have such an estimate signed by both the editor and the person requesting editing so that each individual will understand the expectations from the start and agree to meet them.

_____ Figure 18.1   Editing Agreement

Client _____   Phone number _____

Document: title _____   Type _____

Date submitted _____   Date due _____

Length in typescript pages _____   Form submitted: hard copy _____   disk _____

Visuals: total number____   photos ____   tables ____   graphs ____   other_____

Other nonprose material _____

Editing required

_____ spelling, grammar, punctuation   _____ copymarking for graphic design

_____ consistency   _____ style: persona, diction, sentence structure

_____ match of cross-references etc.   _____ organization

_____ completeness of parts   _____ format: headings, type, etc.

_____ accuracy of terms, numbers, etc.   _____ preparation of camera ready pages

_____ visuals   _____ preparation of camera ready visuals

Other related tasks (reference check, product testing, permissions requests, etc.)

_____

_____

Online editing acceptable? ____ yes   ____ no

Estimates of time: ____ hours   ____ working days

Date promised: _____

The estimate is based on document specifications and editing tasks as
shown here. It is binding only so long as the specifications and editing
tasks remain constant and the document is available for editing on the
date cited. Any changes will require a new estimate.

_____   _____
editor   date   writer   date

Record Keeping   Estimates for documents already developed can be based on records from past projects. If you know, for example, that you can proofread 50 inches of galleytype for nontechnical text in an hour, you use that figure for estimating the proofreading of an entire job. Likewise, substantive editing may require an hour for each two pages of typescript. Good estimating begins with good record keeping. For each job you do, you should record the job type and completion time. Soon you will have averages on which to base future estimates. Your records could be organized according to categories such as these:

Date	Job	Scope	Time
Jan. 2	proof newsletter	4 camera ready pages	30 minutes
Jan. 2–6	copyedit proceedings	200 typescript pages	25 hours
Jan. 9–13	copyedit technical manual	100 typescript pages	23 hours
Feb. 4–5	edit proposal: substantive	32 typescript pages	9 hours

You can begin record keeping even as a student. When you are assigned an editing project, estimate the time it will take. Then keep records and compare the estimate with the reality. For long projects, estimating separate tasks may be useful. For example, you may estimate substantive editing, copyediting, and preparation of camera ready pages for a single project. These records will give you rough bases for future estimates. You should also see some increase in productivity over time. For example, if substantive editing requires an hour per page on your first project, it may require, by the end of the term, only a half hour per comparable page.

Your records can also be useful for demonstrating productivity over time. Your department may be required to assess your achievements periodically, perhaps in quantitative form. To many outsiders, the work of editing is invisible, and to quantify in terms of pages or documents distributed shows productivity in a form that makes sense to other managers. Collectively, the records of individuals within a document production group form the basis of estimates for large projects. For example, you may learn that the documentation for a particular project will take 800 hours, including 250 hours of editing. This information helps project managers estimate the entire project, including documentation, rather than expecting the documents simply to appear. The collective records may also justify the hiring of new employees.

Sampling

Averages imperfectly predict the time required for a future job because of variations in writers' levels of skill, in subject matter, and in the condition of the typescript or proof. Thus, for long projects, averages should be accompanied by reviews of sample pages. Sampling is especially important if you are working with a new writer or project. To estimate based on sampling, first skim the entire document to determine the number of pages of text and the number and type of illustrations, the amount of technical material, the extent of reference material, and any other features that will help you assess the scope of the editing task. Editing technical material and tables will probably take longer than editing straight prose. Then edit sample pages, perhaps the first few prose pages of two chapters and pages with technical information from two parts of the document. On the basis of the time it takes you to do this work, estimate the entire editing job.

If the document has just been scheduled for development, you should request from the project manager specifications for the document and estimate on the basis of the projections. These projections should be in writing in case the expectations develop to include, say, a reference manual as well as a tutorial without a proportionate increase in time.

If you estimate costs as well as time, as in freelancing and contracting as compared with editing for a salary, you will still base the estimate on a prediction of time. You may communicate your estimate to the client in terms of cost per hour, per page, or per job. However, clients deserve to know the total estimate. If they assume you can edit a 200-page typescript in three hours, your hourly fee will not accurately predict the total cost for a job that actually requires 18 hours.

Setting Priorities

In spite of all these efforts to predict and control time, editors invariably have too little time. What do you do when you estimate 100 hours for a task but only 40 hours are available? There's no easy answer to this question. Part of the solution is to establish clear priorities. The manual that accompanies the $600 software package on which your company stakes its reputation deserves more of your time than the in-house employee newsletter. So if you must cut corners, you cut them on the lower-priority documents.

It has been said that writers and editors never finish their work; they simply abandon it. Sometimes you will have to let go of documents knowing you have not yet done your best work on them just so that you will not sacrifice more important tasks. No document is ever perfect, and in that sense writing and editing are never complete.

DOCUMENT SCHEDULING
AND TRACKING

Document development is usually a long-term project controlled by a specific distribution date. Projects are typically measured in terms of weeks, months, or even years rather than in hours or days. Furthermore, document development is typically collaborative, with the achievements of one collaborator determining how quickly and well another collaborator can finish his or her tasks. Editors are particularly vulnerable to inadequate scheduling or delays because the bulk of their work usually comes at the end of the development cycle. They may be expected to make up for the delays of others so that the document can be distributed according to the original schedule. A thorough and realistic schedule established at the beginning of the development cycle, with periodic due dates rather than a single due date at the end, distributes the responsibility for keeping a project on schedule on all collaborators rather than disproportionately on editors. Efficient development requires a detailed management plan at the beginning of the development cycle and periodic tracking.

Management Plans

A management plan at the beginning of the project establishes the tasks and dates for completing each task. Some projects are simply document development projects. These may include newsletters, proposals, and annual reports. Other projects, particularly documentation for products, depend on the development of the product itself as well as on the document. The management plan should be formed at the beginning of the project. For example, if the project is to develop a personal computer, the plan should make allowances for the development of both the equipment and the documentation. Editors need to participate early in the scheduling in order to ensure sufficient time for editing.

A management plan begins with identification of the full range of tasks. For document development, these may include conceptualization of the document with consideration of readers and purpose, research and generation of a draft, technical review, substantive editing, copyediting, and production. Each of these broad steps includes substeps. If document development is part of a larger project, the management plan includes product development tasks and due dates as well. For the most efficient management, editors will participate at the outset of project development so that their work can be scheduled in advance and also so that they can begin their work simultaneously with project development.

To establish due dates, managers frequently work backwards from the necessary or desired distribution date. For example, 100 copies of an annual report may be due in Washington, DC, on September 2. The document consists of 25 individual research reports to be prepared by eight staff members. Its estimated length is 300 pages of single-spaced, 8½ × 11 camera ready pages prepared by secretaries. The researchers prepare drafts of the reports on the computer. Because the reports follow a standard format, an electronic template setting margins, typeface, and headings is available for the researchers. This template results in relatively uniform reports that need minimal formatting by secretaries. The report will be printed and bound by a quick-copy shop.

Some dates must be established by phone calls to contractors, especially, in this case, the printer. Other dates may be negotiated by consulting with the contributors. The following production schedule is based on the assumption that the typist will spend no more than six hours per day on this task and the copyeditor no more than four hours per day because of other concurrent assignments.

Task	*Completion Time*	*Beginning Date*
Mail date		August 23
Printing and binding	2 days	August 20
Typing, proofreading	@ 2 hours × 25 50 hours	July 18
Copyediting	@ 4 hours × 25 100 hours	July 16

Copyediting must begin at least 25 workdays before the report is delivered for printing and binding. If concurrent projects place other demands on the copyeditor, the beginning date may be pushed backwards. To maintain a regular production pace, a copyeditor might request one report draft each day beginning five weeks before the report is scheduled to be delivered for printing and binding. However, document tracking will be easier with fewer deadlines; thus, the reports may be collected in groups of five each week.

The schedule of assignments needs to be distributed far enough in advance of the first deadline to make it possible for researchers to complete their first reports on their due dates. They will work on subsequent reports while the first reports are being edited and proofread. Researchers should be consulted for their preferences about due dates. If research projects are already completed, the reports may be due early in the schedule. The later dates should be reserved for projects that are still being actively pursued. Some researchers may wish to have all their reports due at one time to facilitate their own time management.

The schedule could be as simple as the following one, letting each researcher see at a glance when reports are due. Researchers are identified here, for simplicity, by letter, and report topics by number.

REPORT DUE DATE

Researcher	July 16	July 23	July 30	Aug. 6	Aug. 13
A	1		2	3	
B	4	5		6	7
C	8		9	10	
D	11		12	13	14
E		15	16		17
F				18	19
G	20		21		22
H		23, 24, 25			

Without such planning, researchers are likely to wait until the last minute to write their reports, and the editor and secretaries will face a 150-hour task to be completed in just a few days. The job is not likely to be finished on time, its quality is certain to suffer, tempers will be strained—and the organization may lose funding from Washington.

More complex projects, especially those requiring substantive editing and technical review, those with illustrations or complex page layouts, and those being commercially typeset and printed, will require more complex scheduling.

Tracking When there are multiple documents or sections of a document, or when the production is complex, involving typesetting and illustrations as well as editing, some systematic way to track the document through the production sequence will aid in management. You need to know both how the whole project is developing and how each individual project is progressing. You will probably maintain a file on each project, including correspondence, if any, and notes of meetings establishing due dates plus the versions of the document as it moves through editing and production.

You may also wish to attach a tracking sheet to the document itself so that, when the document lands on your desk, you can tell at a glance exactly what needs to be done next. In the following example, the sheet will identify the report and the steps completed in production. As each step is completed, it is dated and initialed by the person who does the task.

report #   researcher _____

	date	initials
received		
copyedited		
writer proof		
editor's check		
final typing		

In addition, you will maintain a file on the whole project, indicating its progress by showing how the individual projects are progressing. The simple form below assumes that the procedure is for the copyeditor to edit electronically. After she enters her corrections and notes queries, the report goes back to the writer for proofreading and emendations that the queries initiated. It is then returned to the copyeditor for another check. Finally, it goes to the secretary, who prepares the camera ready form.

report	received final	copyedit	writer prf	check	final
1	7/16	7/16	7/18	7/20	7/23
2					
3					
etc.					

The form records each action on the project and each time it changes hands. The form helps the editor to keep production moving and to locate any missing documents. A more elaborate project, with acquisition, graphics, and typesetting stages, would require a more elaborate tracking form.

SOLICITING BIDS

If you contract for services, such as printing, you will look for both economy and quality. To request bids, you will need to describe the intended document accurately and comprehensively. The specifications allow a fair comparison of bids. They also become the basis of a legal contract for services.

To request bids for typesetting and printing, you should provide the following information. If you will prepare camera ready copy, you can delete the data about typeface and fonts.

Quantity to be printed

Page size

Estimated number of pages

Composition: typeface, type style, fonts required

Halftones

Paper stock: cover, body

Ink colors

Binding

Cover (whether it requires artwork or typesetting)

Proofs required: galleys, page proofs, bluelines

Delivery site

Submission date

Delivery date (finished product)

Payment

In addition, the bid sheet may include policy statements about overruns (whether you will be responsible for buying them), author's alterations (whether they will be charged per line or otherwise), and subletting (whether the bidder may sublet work to another printer).

SETTING POLICY Editorial policies may govern documents, collectively and individually, and editorial procedures. In editing the text, editors will establish mechanical style. Specific documents will require other, more comprehensive policy decisions. For example, the editor of the proceedings of a conference will need to decide whether to publish printed papers or transcripts of the oral presentations.

Editors may also need to establish policies about the scope and quality of publication, including the use of illustrations in documents (e.g., whether to include illustrations, whether to allow photographs as well as line drawings, whether to make writers responsible for camera ready copy), the means of creating camera ready copy (e.g., typewriter, computer, typesetting), the use of color in printing, and paper and binding. The policies may differ for different types of documents, such as those for in-house distribution and those for mass public distribution. Policies can always be revised as new situations arise so they can be helpful without being rigid.

Policies may also establish editing procedures. For example, each publishing organization should have a policy about marking in online editing, clarifying what changes may be made directly and what ones need prior approval. In electronic publishing when computer files are con-

verted for typesetting, editors determine whether to have writers or someone in house code the material. Quality control may require a policy of
two proofreadings by someone other than writer and editor at the page
proof stage.

Just as style sheets increase editing efficiency, so can established publication policies increase efficiency by minimizing the amount of time
required for decisions.

LEGAL ASPECTS OF EDITING

Although writers are primarily responsible for upholding laws that pertain
to documents, editors also assume responsibility for protecting documents
legally and for ensuring that they do not violate copyright or libel laws.
Editors must also ensure that permissions to reprint portions of other
people's publications are obtained and work to ensure that potentially
dangerous products contain adequate warnings.

Copyright

The United States Copyright Act of 1978 protects authors of "original
works of authorship," whether or not the works are published. The Copyright Act gives the owner of a **copyright** the right to reproduce and distribute the work and to prepare derivative works based on the copyrighted
work. No one else has these rights, and reproducing work copyrighted by
someone else violates the copyright law. Because of treaties signed by the
United States and certain other countries, the law protects some works
published in other countries and your work in some countries. As editor,
you must be alert to requirements for using copyrighted material and take
steps to protect documents published by your company.

Ownership. Copyrights belong to the author who created the work unless
the author wrote the work to meet responsibilities of employment. In the
case of work for hire, the employer owns the copyright. Some publishers
require authors to surrender the copyright to them. Works by the U.S. government are not eligible for copyright protection; they are in the "public
domain." Collections with contributions by multiple authors are generally
protected by a single copyright, but the sections may also be copyrighted
individually. The copyright extends 50 years beyond the copyright owner's
death. Works written for hire are protected 75 years beyond publication.
When the copyright expires, works are in the public domain and may be
reproduced and distributed by others.

Notice of copyright. For the best protection, a published work should
include a notice of copyright. In a book, the notice usually appears on the
verso page of the spread that contains the title page and is sometimes

called the copyright page. The notice includes the symbol ©, abbreviation "Copr.," or the word "Copyright"; the year of publication; and the owner's name. Here is an example: © 1991 Wadsworth Publishing Company.

Registration and deposit. Works are protected by the Copyright Act whether or not they are registered with the Copyright Office. Copyright is automatic as soon as the work exists in fixed form. However, registration gives maximum legal protection in the case of a lawsuit. Registration requires sending an application form (Form TX for most technical documents), a fee ($10 in 1990), and two copies of the document to the Register of Copyrights in the Copyright Office.

You can get more detailed information on copyrights from the Copyright Office, Publications Section, LM-455, Library of Congress, Washington, DC 20559. Particularly useful publications are Circular 1, "Copyright Basics," and Circular 3, "Copyright Notice."

Permissions   Because work is protected by copyright, permission must be obtained to reprint sections of someone else's work. Usually the writer requests permission from the copyright holder, but editors must be sure the permissions have been acquired before the document goes to print. The permission ought to exist in writing, whether in a letter or on a form. The correspondence will establish exactly what will be reprinted and where. If permission is denied, the material cannot be used.

A request for permission to reprint copyrighted material should include the following information:

Title, author, and edition of the materials to be reprinted

Exact material to be used: include page numbers and/or a photocopy

How it will be used: nature of the document in which it will be reprinted, author, intended audience, publisher, where the material will appear (e.g., quoted in a chapter, cited in a footnote)

Permission to use copyrighted material in one publication does not give one the right to use it elsewhere. Permission must be acquired for each use. Sometimes the copyright owner will charge a fee for use of the material.

Libel   Libel is a defamatory statement that shames or lowers the public reputation of an identifiable person. People who can prove libel may win damages from a publisher. The possibility of being sued for libel worries editors of fiction and periodicals more than it does technical editors because people are more likely to be discussed, referred to, or otherwise cited in works of fiction and in periodicals than in technical documents. Nevertheless, all editors should read alertly for facts to verify the accuracy of any negative statements that may be made about individuals.

Product Safety   Some people who have been injured by products have claimed in their suits that the printed warnings were inadequate or that instructions failed to anticipate particular types of misuse. Writers, who know the product and its use better than editors, are more responsible than editors for completeness and clarity of safety information. However, editors can assist in anticipating what information readers will need and how readers will interpret the words they encounter. Read with a critical eye any instructions about product use, and make sure warnings are prominently displayed. Ask questions of product developers if you have any doubts.

COMPUTERS AS MANAGERIAL ASSISTANTS

In the course of corresponding with writers and production people, editors will depend on their word processors for form letters and individual letters and memos. Editors may also use their computers to create forms for document scheduling and tracking. Many of the files that used to be stored in cabinets can now be stored electronically.

Project management software may be useful in planning and tracking document development and production. Spreadsheets ease the task of maintaining financial records and calculating costs. Databases may maintain files of contributing writers, staff, and contract editors as well as files on printers and on different types of documents. Combined with graphics and word processing programs, spreadsheets and databases may yield reports for upper-level managers on department productivity, goals, and needs.

Much business software has been developed to aid managers. It is as applicable to the management of document production as to any other type of management.

SUMMARY

Good management means communicating clearly with others in establishing expectations for editing, scheduling adequate editing time, and keeping projects on schedule. As managers, editors also set policy and may negotiate the business of production. They guard the legal and ethical integrity of documents. All substantial editing projects require good management.

FURTHER READING

CBE Journal Procedures and Practices Committee. 1987. *Editorial Forms: A Guide to Journal Management.* Bethesda, MD: Council of Biology Editors.

Robert Van Buren and Mary Fran Buehler. 1980. *The Levels of Edit,* 2nd ed. Pasadena, CA: Jet Propulsion Laboratory, publication 80-1. Also available from the Government Printing Office, stock #033-000-07585-0.

DISCUSSION AND APPLICATION

1. You are the editor of an anthology of articles by different writers in different locations on the subject of computer documentation. The anthology will be published by a small commercial press. The press will print and bind the anthology from camera ready copy you provide. Make policy decisions on the following issues with the goal of creating a useful, high-quality anthology that also can be produced economically and efficiently. Identify the bases for decision making.

   a. How will the articles be acquired? How can you get quality articles and a broad coverage of topics? Will there be a general solicitation in journals that potential contributors read? Will some people be invited to contribute, and if so, will acceptance of their articles be offered in advance or will their articles be subject to peer review? Will only original articles be accepted, or will reprints also be accepted?

   b. How will camera ready copies be obtained? Will writers submit camera ready pages according to your specifications? Will they submit disks? Will they submit hard copy that will be rekeyboarded?

   c. Printing economy dictates 8½ × 11-inch pages. Will pages be laid out in two columns or in one column with wide margins? Two columns would probably be more readable and would allow more words per page, but they would be harder to produce because of controlling for column breaks as well as page breaks and because multiple writers may be doing the initial keyboarding.

   d. How consistent must the individual chapters be? If one includes a list of references for further reading, must all of them?

   e. How and where will contributor biographies be printed: at the beginning of the anthology or with each chapter?

   f. What kinds of illustrations and how many per chapter will be allowed? What will be the responsibilities of authors for providing camera ready copy?

2. For the same situation, make management decisions on the following issues with the goal of getting the anthology ready for production by the date the press has specified.

   a. When will chapters be due? Will they be due on the same date, or will you establish variable dates? If the dates vary, which ones should come first?

   b. In what order will you edit the chapters? Will you edit them in sequence, from 1 to 12, or might there be reasons to proceed in a different order? What factors will determine the order?

   c. On the basis of policies you have established for the book, what information will you have to communicate to the contributing writers about preparation of typescripts? Consider, for example, documentation style and length. Make a list of points to cover in document specifications.

   d. Suppose one contributing writer has a due date of the first of the month, and two weeks later you still have not received the chapter. What can you do?

   e. Suppose one contributing writer has submitted an improperly coded electronic file. It cannot be converted to your word processing system without extensive intervention in the text. Should you ask one of your own secretaries to do the work (which means removing that secretary from another important project and also increasing the costs of producing the anthology), or should you ask the writer to revise and resubmit the file? Your answer may not be the same for all writers involved. What will determine your choice?

   f. Outline a form for tracking the progress of the anthology overall, including acquisition, acknowledgment of the manuscript, acceptance or rejection, and other production stages.

GLOSSARY

abstract Summary or description of document contents; part of the body of a report or book.

acknowledgments Credits to persons who have helped with the development of a publication; usually the concluding part of a preface.

adjective Part of speech whose function is to modify a noun.

adverb Part of speech whose function is to modify a verb, adjective, or other adverb.

appositive Noun or noun phrase placed with another as equivalents; e.g., "Joe, *the new writer, . . .*"

ascender Part of the letter that rises above the x-height, such as the top part of the letters *b, d,* and *h.*

back matter Parts of a book following the body, including the appendix, glossary, and index.

baseline Imaginary horizontal line at the base of capital letters of type. Used in measuring space between lines.

basis weight Weight of a ream of paper in its uncut size; e.g., a ream of 20-pound bond paper weighs 20 pounds in its uncut size of 17 × 22 inches.

blueline or **blueprint** In offset lithography, a proof following the making of metal printing plates that shows page sequence and folding, not just the individual pages. Typically printed with blue ink.

body type Type for the text of a document as opposed to its headings and titles.

boiler plate Text that is standard for various documents and can be inserted, with minimal or no revision, in a new document.

bullet Heavy dot (•) used to mark items in a list. Sometimes set as a square or unfilled circle.

call for manuscripts Printed request for articles to be published in a periodical or anthology. May be printed in a periodical or on a flier.

callout Words placed outside an illustration but referring to a part of the illustration.

camera ready Document that may be photographed for printing without a change in type or format or special processes such as screens.

caption Brief explanation or description of a visual.

case Form of a noun or pronoun that shows its relationship to other words in the sentence, whether subjective, objective, or possessive.

casting off Process of calculating the document length according to the number of characters in a typescript and the specifications for typeface and type size, line length, and page depth of the final document. The calculation requires a character count and the number of characters per inch in a given typeface and type size.

clause Group of words that contains a subject and verb.

> **dependent/subordinate** Group of words with a subject and verb plus a subordinating conjunction or a relative pronoun. Cannot be punctuated alone as a sentence.

> **independent/main** Group of words with a subject and verb but not a subordinating conjunction or relative pronoun to make it dependent; may be punctuated as a complete sentence.

> **nonrestrictive** Modifying clause beginning with a relative pronoun (e.g., *who, which*) that gives additional information about the subject but that is not necessary to identify what the subject is. A comma separates this clause from the subject; e.g., "Nita Perez, *who is president this year of the users' group, . . .* "

restrictive Modifying clause beginning with a relative pronoun (e.g., *who, that*) that restricts the meaning of the subject (gives necessary identifying information); no punctuation separates the modifier from the subject it modifies; e.g., "The officer *who sat at the end of the head table . . .* "

clip art Predrawn pictures of common objects that can be pasted into documents. Available on paper and disk.

color separation Photographic process of creating the four primary printing colors from a full-color original.

complement Words used to complete the sense of the verb. A subject complement completes a linking or intransitive verb, while an **object** completes a transitive verb.

complex sentence Sentence structured with a dependent as well as an independent clause.

compositor Person who uses typesetting equipment to key in text for a typeset document; a typesetter. Person who assembles type and illustrations into pages.

compound sentence Sentence composed of at least two independent clauses.

compound-complex sentence Sentence consisting of two independent clauses, one of which contains a dependent clause.

conjunction Word that joins words (nouns, verbs, modifiers) or clauses in a series.

> **coordinating** Joins items of equal value, including two independent clauses; e.g., *and, but, or, for, yet, nor, so.*

> **subordinating** Joins items of unequal value, especially a dependent to an

independent clause. Makes a clause dependent; e.g., *although, because, since, while.*

copy   Typescript or graphics used in preparing a document for publication.

copyediting   Emendation of a document to ensure its correctness, consistency, accuracy, and completeness.

copyfitting   Process of fitting copy into a prescribed space. May be done mathematically, before typesetting, with the character count and document specifications from casting off, or electronically, with a page layout program.

copymarking   Placing notations on a typescript to inform the keyboard operator of corrections and directions for spacing, typeface, and type style.

copyright   Protection provided by the laws of the United States to authors of literary, dramatic, musical, artistic, and certain other intellectual works, both published and unpublished. The law gives the owner of copyright the exclusive right to reproduce, distribute, perform, or display the copyrighted work and to prepare derivative works.

copyright holder   Person or organization that owns the rights to the copyrighted work.

copyright page   Page in a document identifying the copyright; usually the back of the title page.

cropping   Cutting one or more edges from an illustration to remove irrelevant material and to center and emphasize the essential material.

dead copy   Version of a document during production that has been superceded by a later version. The typescript becomes dead copy once typesetting has produced a galley.

descender   The part of a letter that descends below the baseline, such as the tail on the letters *g* and *y.*

design, document   The plan for a document and all its features (content, organization, format, style, typography, paper, binding) to make it useful and readable.

design, graphic   The plan for the visual features of the document, including typeface, size, and style, page size, line length and depth, paper, and binding.

desktop publishing   The preparation of final (camera ready) copy using office equipment and thus bypassing the professional typesetter; usually done with a computer, laser printer, and graphics and page layout programs that emulate the quality of typesetting. The printing and binding might then be done professionally.

discourse community   A group of readers and writers with similar expectations for documents, similar patterns of thinking, common vocabulary and style, and similar background. May be defined by a profession or discipline (e.g., research chemists), by an organization (e.g., IBM), or by the document (e.g., readers of a particular magazine or computer manual).

discovery   The process of choosing and creating content for a document; in editing, the process of analyzing document purpose and context and establishing editing goals.

display type   The titles and headings of a document as opposed to the body copy.

document set   A group of related documents, such as all the manuals for a piece of equipment or all the manuals published by a particular organization.

dummy   A graphic designer's sketch of pages as they are to be printed, showing line length, margins, and placement of headings and illustrations.

edited American English   The practices that educated, careful users of the language take to be correct; standard American English.

editing, substantive   Evaluation of a document's substance — including content, organization, format, and style — in context of intended readers and purpose, and recommendations for revision.

em   Linear measure about equal to the width of a capital letter *M* in any given typeface and size; the square of a typesize; the normal paragraph indent in typeset copy.

en   Half an em.

field test   Trial of the document in use by representative readers.

figure   Illustration that is not tabular; e.g., line drawing, photograph, bar graph, line graph.

flat   Form in which the pages of the signature are arranged before platemaking.

folio   (a) Page number. (b) Leaf of a manuscript, including front and back sides.

font   Collection of characters for a typeface in one size, including roman and italic characters, capital and lowercase characters, and sometimes small caps. Any one typeface may be available in different fonts, such as Times 10 and Times 12.

footnote   Explanatory information or publication data at the bottom of an illustration or page of text.

foreword   Part of the front matter of a book; introductory remarks written by someone other than the writer or editor.

format   Placement of text and graphics on a page. Relates to the arrangement of information, to the number and width of columns, to the size of margins, to the amount of spacing, and to the dimensions of the type; also relates to whether the text is in prose paragraphs or some other form.

four-color printing   Printing of full-color reproductions from four ink colors, the three primary colors plus black.

front matter   Parts of a document that precede the body; e.g., title page, table of contents, preface.

galley proof   Copy of text after typesetting but before page breaks have been established. Printed on long shiny paper. Used to check accuracy of typesetting.

gerund   Noun substitute formed from a verb plus the suffix *-ing*. See **verbal**.

glossary   Short dictionary, with definitions, of key terms used in the document.

grammar   System of rules governing the relationships of words in sentences.

graphics   (a) Text with a strong visual component consisting of more than words arranged in paragraphs; e.g., tables, line drawings, graphs. (b) Visuals with mathematical content (as would be drawn on graph paper); e.g., graphs, architectural drawings.

gutter   Inner margin of a book, next to the binding.

half title   Page at the beginning of a book or division that names only the main title, not the subtitle or other identifying information.

halftone Picture with shading (different tones of light and dark) created by dots of different density. Produced by photographing the subject through a screen.

hanging indent Paragraph or list form in which the first line protrudes farther into the left margin than subsequent lines.

hard copy Typescript printed on paper as opposed to the electronic version.

house style Mechanical style choices preferred by a publishing organization. Derives from the designation of any publishing organization as a *house*.

icon Visual representation of a process or concept; a visual symbol.

imperative mood See **mood.**

imposition The arrangement of page proofs in a form before platemaking so that they will appear in correct order when the printed sheet is folded.

index List at the end of a book or manual of key terms used in the document and the page number(s) where they are used.

indicative mood See **mood.**

infinitive Verbal consisting of the word *to* plus the verb; e.g., "to edit." Used primarily as a noun.

inflection Change in the form of a word to show a specific meaning or a grammatical relationship to another word. The verb *edit* would be inflected as follows: *edit, edits, edited.* The adjective *good* inflected is *good, better, best.*

in house Adverb or adjective indicating that work is completed or applies within the organization rather than without; e.g., an in-house style manual designates style choices preferred by that organization but not necessarily by other organizations.

interjection Part of speech expressing an exclamation; e.g., "Oh!"

intransitive verb Verb that does not have an object to complete its meaning. It is followed by a subject complement or adverb.

introduction Substantive beginning section for a document; in a book, generally the first chapter rather than part of the front matter.

italics Style of printing type with the letters slanted to the right.

iteration Version of the typescript as it moves through various editorial passes. A new iteration incorporates some editorial emendations.

justification Adjustment of lines of text to align margins.

keyboard operator Person whose job is to type copy for a new version of a document. This person may be a typist, word processing specialist, or typesetter (compositor), depending on the equipment he or she uses.

landscape orientation Position of lines of type on pages parallel with the long side of the page to create pages wider than they are tall. See **portrait orientation.**

layout (a) Spread and juxtaposition of printed matter. (b) Dummy or sketch for matter to be printed.

leading (pronounced *ledding*) Space between lines of type.

legend Explanation of symbols, shading, or type styles used in a graph.

legibility The ease with which type or illustrations can be read. Legibility refers to recognition, while readability refers to comprehension.

letterspacing   Amount of space between the characters in a word. Terms describing letterspacing include *condensed, narrow,* and *expanded.*

library binding   Hardcover book binding that is durable because the signatures are sewn and the binding is reinforced.

line drawing   Drawing created with black lines, without shading. It may be photographed for printing without a halftone.

linking verb   Verb that connects a subject with a predicate adjective or predicate nominative rather than with a direct object. The *to be* verbs are linking verbs.

list of references   List of works cited in a document, with publication data.

manuscript   Unpublished version of a document. Because the term literally suggests handwriting, it is often replaced by *typescript.*

markup   Process of marking a typescript for typesetting or typing in final form.

mood   Verb form indicating the writer's attitude toward the factuality of action or condition expressed.

imperative   Verb form used to express commands; e.g., "Turn on the computer."

indicative   Verb form used for factual statements; e.g., "The computer is turned on."

subjunctive   Verb form used to indicate doubt; e.g., "If the computer were left on every night, the heat would damage some of the inner components."

noise   Distracting material in a document, such as errors, excess words, or an inappropriate voice, that interferes with the reader's attention to the content.

nominalization   Noun formed from a verb root, usually by the addition of a suffix; e.g., *consideration, agreement.*

nonfinite verb   See **verbal.**

noun   Part of speech representing a person, place, thing, or idea.

object   Noun or noun substitute that is governed by a transitive active verb, a nonfinite verb, or a preposition. A direct object tells what or who. An indirect object tells to whom or what or for whom or what.

offset lithography   Common printing method. The design or print is photographically reproduced on a plate, which is placed on a revolving cylinder of the printing press; the print is transferred to, or *offset* on, the paper by means of a rubber blanket that runs over another cylinder.

online   Connected by cable or phone line to a mainframe computer or workstation at a remote site. Also used informally to refer to data in electronic rather than print form, as in *online* documentation.

page proof   Copy of typeset text that follows correction of the galley proofs and page breaks. Used to check the accuracy of corrections and the logic of page breaks.

parallel structure; parallelism   Use of the same form (e.g., noun, participle) to express related ideas in a series.

participle   Modifier formed from a verb with the addition of the suffix *-ing* or *-ed* (e.g., *dripping* pipe, *misplaced* cap).

perfect binding   Binding for paperback books in which the cover is attached to the pages with adhesive.

persona Character or personality of the writer as projected in a document by his or her style.

phrase Group of related words that function as a grammatical unit; does not contain both a subject and verb.

infinitive phrase Includes the infinitive form of a verb plus modifiers.

noun phrase Consists of a noun and its modifiers; e.g., "stainless steel."

participial phrase Includes a participle plus modifiers; e.g., "diffusing quickly."

prepositional phrase Begins with a preposition; e.g., "above the switch."

pica Unit of linear measure used by graphic designers and printers; roughly one-sixth of an inch. Used to describe both vertical and horizontal measures.

pica stick, pica ruler Measuring device marked with increments of both picas and inches.

plate Light-sensitive sheet of metal upon which a photographic image can be recorded. When inked, will produce printed matter in offset lithography.

point Unit of linear measure used by graphic designers and printers especially in describing type size; one-twelfth of a pica.

portrait orientation Position of lines of type on pages parallel with the short side of the page to create pages taller than they are wide. See **landscape orientation**.

predicate Division of a sentence that tells what is said about the subject. It always includes a verb; may also include a complement of the verb and modifiers.

preface Part of the front matter of a document stating the purposes, readers, scope, and assumptions about the document. Often includes acknowledgments as well.

preposition Part of speech that links a noun with another part of the sentence.

printer Person who reproduces or who supervises the reproduction in multiple copies of a document.

production Process of developing a document from manuscript to distribution. Requires scheduling and coordination of services such as editing, graphic design, typesetting, printing, and binding.

pronoun Part of speech that takes the position and function of a noun. May be personal (*I, we, you, they*), relative (*who, whose, which, that*), indefinite (*each, someone, all*), intensive/reflexive (*myself*), demonstrative (*this, that, these*), or interrogative (*who?*).

prose Words in sentence form, as opposed to verse.

publisher Person or organization that funds the publication and owns rights to its distribution. Usually separate from the printer.

query Question to the writer posed by the editor requesting information that is necessary for completing the editing correctly.

query slip Piece of paper on which a query is written; attached to the edge of the typescript.

ragged right Irregular right margin. Characters are not spaced to create lines of equal length.

readability As applied with *formula*, a quantifiable measure of the ease with which a text can be read. Based on counts of sentence and word features such as number of syllables and number of words per sentence. More broadly, the ease with which a reader can read and understand a document, based on content, level of technicality, organization, style, and format.

ream   500 sheets of paper.

recto   In a book, the righthand page, numbered with an odd number. The *verso* is on the back.

redundant   Duplicate information; unnecessary repetition.

register   Alignment of printing plates one on top of the other to reproduce colored prints accurately.

relative pronoun   Pronoun that introduces a relative clause and has reference to an antecedent; e.g., *who, which, that.*

repro   Reproduction proof; proof copy of the typeset page after corrections have been made. Photographed for platemaking.

resolution   Fineness of reproduction of type, measured by the number of dots of ink per inch (dpi).

RFP   Request for proposals; document that identifies a need for research, a service, or a product and invites competitive proposals to provide it.

river   White space running through a paragraph that forms a distracting diagonal or vertical line.

roman type   Type style characterized by straight vertical lines in characters rather than the slanted lines that characterize italic type.

running head   Title repeated at the top of each page of a book. May be the book title, chapter title, or author's name. May vary on recto and verso pages.

saddle stitching   Binding for a booklet with staples through the fold in the middle.

sans serif   Type style characterized by absence of serifs, or short horizontal or vertical lines at the ends of the strokes in letters. Also called *gothic.* Common sans serif typefaces are Helvetica and Gothic.

schema (plural *schemata*)   Structured representation of a concept in memory.

screen   Glass plate marked with crossing lines through which continuous-tone art must be photographed for halftone reproduction.

semantics   Study of meanings.

serif   Small horizontal or vertical line at the end of a stroke in a letter; also a category of typefaces characterized by the use of serifs, such as Times Roman and Bookman.

side stitching   Binding in which staples are forced through the edge of the book.

signal   Verbal, structural, or visual information about how parts of a sentence, paragraph, or longer text relate; e.g., the word *thus* verbally signals a conclusion.

signature   Group of pages in a book folded from a single sheet of paper. Typically includes 16 pages, but may include 8, 32, or even 64 pages depending on the size of the pages and the number of folds.

simple sentence   Sentence consisting of one independent clause.

solidus   Slanted line (/) used in math to show division and in prose to mean *per* or to indicate breaks in lines of poetry set to fill lines on a page.

standard American English   Widely accepted practice in North America in spelling, grammar, and pronunciation; the speech and writing patterns of educated persons in America; edited American English.

stripping In printing, the arrangement and taping of negatives from text and illustrations in a flat before platemaking; also the cutting and pasting of corrections on proof.

style Choices about diction and sentence structure that affect comprehension and emphasis, as well as projecting a voice or persona.

style, mechanical Choices about capitalization, spelling, punctuation, abbreviations, etc. when more than one option exists.

style manual Collection identifying preferred choices on matters of mechanical style including capitalization, abbreviations, and documentation.

style sheet Record, on hard copy or electronic file, of the copyeditor's choices for a specific document in capitalization, spelling, numbers, abbreviations, and other mechanics. Used to achieve mechanical consistency.

style sheet, electronic Feature of word processing programs used for defining capitalization, type style, margins, and spacing of different types of text, such as headings, block quotations, and body copy. Used to achieve format consistency.

subjunctive mood See **mood.**

syllable Unit of a word spoken as a single uninterrupted sound. Includes a vowel or a syllabic consonant.

syntax Structure of phrases, clauses, and sentences.

table Text or numbers arranged in rows and columns.

table of contents List in the front matter of a document of the major divisions, such as chapters, and the page numbers on which the divisions begin.

tense Form of the verb that indicates time of the action as well as continuance or completion. Indicated by inflection.

past tense Inflection of the verb that indicates time in the past. With regular verbs, formed with the addition of the suffix *-ed.*

present tense Verb form that indicates current time.

future tense Verb form that indicates action that will occur in the future. Usually formed with a helping verb, *shall* or *will.*

title page Page in the front matter of a document identifying the title. May include other information, such as the name of the writer or editor, date of publication, and publisher.

tone Sound that the voice of the writer projects — serious, angry, flippant, concerned, silly, etc.

type size Height (and proportionate width) of a letter, expressed in points. For example, 12-point type will almost fill a 12-point (1-pica) line and is good for body copy, while 72-point type will almost fill a 6-pica line and is so large that its use would be restricted to banners, announcements, and book titles.

type style Shape of letters as determined by the slant and thickness of the lines and the presence or absence of serifs. *Roman* style uses vertical lines while *italic* style uses slanted ones; *serif* style uses serifs while *gothic* or *sans serif* style does not. *Bold* or regular weight and *condensed* or *expanded* may also define type styles. Also denotes classes of type as *body type*, or the body of the text, as compared with *display type*, or titles and headings.

typeface   Type design produced as a complete font and named; e.g., Times Roman, Helvetica.

typescript   Typed copy of a document, before it is typed in final form or typeset; the copy on which an editor works; the parallel of *manuscript,* when documents were written first in longhand.

typeset   Adjective describing text that has been prepared by photoelectronic typesetting equipment rather than by a typewriter or desktop publishing equipment. Typeset copy is of higher quality than copy produced by a typewriter or desktop publishing because the letters are more finely shaped and the options for spacing and type style are greater.

typesetter   Person whose job is to prepare typeset copy. May refer to the owner of a typesetting business or to the compositor, the person who keyboards the documents.

typesetting   Process of keying text into photoelectronic typesetting equipment in order to produce typeset galleys. Formerly done manually or mechanically, with lead characters.

usability   Ease with which a document, such as a manual, can be used.

usage   Accepted practice in the use of words and phrases.

verb   Part of speech that denotes action, occurrence, or existence. Characterized by tense, mood, and voice.

intransitive   Verb that does not require a direct object to complete its meaning.

transitive   Verb that requires a direct object to complete its meaning.

verbal   Verb used as a noun, adjective, or adverb. Verbals may be *participles* (modifiers formed from a verb plus the suffix *-ing* or *-ed*), *gerunds* (noun substitutes formed from a verb plus the suffix *-ing*), and *infinitives* (verbs plus *to,* used chiefly as nouns). Also called *nonfinite* verbs.

verso   In a book, the page on the left side as the book lies open, numbered with an even number; the back side of a recto page.

voice   Form of the verb that indicates the relation between the subject and the action expressed by the verb.

active voice   Verb form indicating that the subject performs the action expressed by the verb.

passive voice   Verb form indicating that the subject of the sentence receives the action expressed by the verb; always identified by a *to be* verb plus a past participle.

white space   Graphic design concept: blank space on the page that functions to draw attention to certain parts of the page, to provide eye relief, to signal a new section, or to provide aesthetic balance.

wordspacing   Amount of space between words. Manipulated in order to achieve right justification and to eliminate rivers.

x-height   Size of a letter without its descender or ascender, or the equivalent to the *x* in the alphabet.

INDEX